CASES AND MATERIALS ON

THE LEGAL PROFESSION
Second Edition

By

Robert F. Cochran, Jr.
Louis D. Brandeis Professor of Law
Pepperdine University

Teresa S. Collett
Professor of Law
South Texas College of Law

AMERICAN CASEBOOK SERIES®

Mat #40094971

American Casebook Series and West Group are
registered trademarks used herein under license.

ISBN 0–314–14391–2

TEXT IS PRINTED ON 10% POST
CONSUMER RECYCLED PAPER

To my law professors at the University of Virginia who encouraged me to pursue a career in law teaching, especially Tom Bergin, Walter Wadlington, and Cal Woodard.

Robert F. Cochran, Jr.

To my dad, Jim Payne; my husband, Bob Collett; and my senior partner in law practice, Allen Evans, who taught me to live a life of integrity.

Teresa S. Collett

PREFACE

The focus of this casebook is on the rules of the legal profession. We focus on the rules of the profession because they are important. The rules establish minimum standards for lawyers. They establish a framework within which lawyers operate. Their importance to lawyers and law students is obvious: violations of the rules may subject lawyers to professional disapproval, discipline, fines, procedural sanctions, and, in some cases, liability.

But there are aspects of the legal profession other than the rules that are also important. We made this book short, so that professors and students will have time to explore these other aspects of the profession. One of the many subjects that merit discussion in a legal profession class is the relationship between morality and the practice of law.[1] Professional rules outline what a lawyer must do (unless she exercises civil disobedience); morals determine what a lawyer should do. A second issue worthy of exploration is that of the relationship between the legal profession and society.[2] The public's opinion of the legal profession has reached new lows in recent years.[3] Is this a function of changes that have occurred our society or in the legal profession, or merely poor public relations?

We do not include material in this book on each of the rules of the legal profession. Instead, we highlight the rules that will most often apply to the day-to-day practice of law. For exposure to the specific rules of the profession, we refer students in each section of this book to read the professional rules concerning the topic of that section. The cases and materials contained in this book focus on particular problems within each subject area that we think are of importance and which develop the underlying issues of that subject area.

It is our hope that this book will enable students to evaluate the legal profession critically and yet avoid the cynicism that so often dominates discussions of professional norms. We want to encourage an appreciation of the value of our profession and a recognition of the difficult struggle that it continues to engage in out of our collective desire to realize its highest aspirations.

---

[1] Recent books on morality and the lawyer include Monroe H. Freedman and Abbe Smith, *Understanding Lawyers' Ethics* (2002); Deborah L. Rhode, *In the Interests of Justice* (2000); William H. Simon, *The Practice of Justice* (1998), Thomas L. Shaffer and Robert F. Cochran, Jr., *Lawyers, Clients, and Moral Responsibility* (1994); and David Luban, *Lawyers and Justice* (1988).

[2] Recent books on lawyers and society include Richard A. Posner, *Overcoming Law* (1995); Mary Ann Glendon, *A Nation Under Lawyers: How the Crisis in the Legal Profession is Transforming American Society* (1994); Anthony T. Kronman, *The Lost Lawyer: Failing Ideals of the Legal Profession* (1993); and Richard L. Abel, *American Lawyers* (1989).

[3] For a summary of the disturbing results of a recent ABA survey on public perceptions of the legal profession, *see infra* page 6.

ACKNOWLEDGMENTS

We thank Dean Richard Lynn, Dean Frank Read, Robert Rodes, and Thomas Shaffer for their support and encouragement in this project. We thank Bob Destro and Sandra DeGraw for giving us their invaluable suggestions. We thank Julie McGoldrick, Tammie Carpenter, David Merrill, Tim Heverin, Kathryn Elias, and Bob Muise for their assistance in research and Candace Warren and Sheila McDonald for their assistance in manuscript preparation.

We are indebted as well to the following authors and publishers who gave us permission to reprint portions of their work:

American Bar Association/The Bureau of National Affairs, Inc., *Lawyers' Manual on Professional Conduct*. Reproduced with permission from *ABA/BNA's Lawyers' Manual on Professional Conduct*, Ethics Opinion 86-1518, p. 901:305-06 (December 10, 1986) Copyright 1986 by the American Bar Association/The Bureau of National Affairs, Inc. (800-372-1033), and Formal Ethics Opinion 94-389, pp. 1001:248-58 (Feb. 22, 1995). Copyright 1995 by The Bureau of National Affairs, Inc. (800-372-1033).

Brill, Steven, "When A Lawyer Lies," *Esquire* (Dec. 19, 1978). Reprinted with permission of the author.

Committee to Improve the Availability of Legal Services, "Final Report to the Chief Judge of the State of New York," 19 HOFSTRA L. REV. 755 (1990). Reprinted with permission of the *Hofstra Law Review*.

Cramton, Roger C., "Delivery of Legal Services to Ordinary Americans," 44 *Case W. Res. L. Rev.* 531 (1994). Reprinted with permission of the author and *Case Western Reserve Law Review*.

Margolick, David, "The Action of a Lawyer in Occupied France Raises the Question: Is Nit-Picking Collaboration?," *N.Y. Times*, May 17, 1991. Reprinted with permission of the *New York Times*.

Pollock, Ellen Joan, "Limited Partners: Lawyers for Enron Faulted Its Deals, Didn't Force Issue—Vinson & Elkins Rejects Idea Firm Should Have Taken Doubts to Client's Board—Face to Face with Fastow," *Wall Street Journal*, May 22, 2002, at A1. Reprinted by permission of *Wall Street Journal*, Copyright © (2002) Dow Jones & Company, Inc. All Rights Reserved Worldwide, License number 597330702033.

Rotunda, Ronald D., "The Notice of Withdrawal and the New Model Rules of Professional Conduct: Blowing the Whistle and Waving the Red Flag," 63 *Ore. L. Rev.* 455 (1984). Reprinted with Permission. Copyright © 1984 by University of Oregon.

Helen Thompson, "Freedom Fighter: Galveston Lawyer Anthony Griffin Is Committed To Protecting the First Amendment Even If It Means Defending the Ku Klux Klan," *Texas Monthly*, March 1, 1995. Reprinted with Permission of *Texas Monthly*.

Tigar, Michael E., "Setting the Record Straight On the Defense of John Demjanjuk," *Legal Times*, September 6, 1993, at 22. Reprinted with permission of *Legal Times*. Copyright 1993.

Wasserstrom, Richard, "Lawyers As Professionals: Some Moral Issues," 5 *Human Rights* 1 (1975). Copyright © 1977 American Bar Association. Reprinted by permission of the American Bar Association and the author.

Wishman, Seymour, From *Confessions of a Criminal Lawyer* by Seymour Wishman. Copyright © 1981 by Seymour Wishman. Reprinted by permission of Random House, Inc.

Zacharias, Fred C., "Rethinking Confidentiality," 74 *Iowa L. Rev.* 351 (1989). Reprinted with permission of the author and the *University of Iowa Law Review*.

SUMMARY OF CONTENTS

TABLE OF CONTENTS

TABLE OF CONTENTS

TABLE OF RULES, STATUTES, AND ABA OPINIONS

TABLE OF RULES, STATUTES, AND ABA OPINIONS

ABA Canons of Professional Ethics

California Rules and Statutes

ABA Model Code of Judicial Conduct

Federal Rules of Civil Procedure

Federal Rules of Evidence

Restatement (Second) of the Law of Agency

Restatement (Third) of the Law Governing Lawyers

ABA Standards for Criminal Justice

TABLE OF RULES, STATUTES, AND ABA OPINIONS

TABLE OF ARTICLES AND BOOKS

Articles and books in bold print are excerpted herein.

TABLE OF ARTICLES AND BOOKS

TABLE OF ARTICLES AND BOOKS

TABLE OF CASES

xxv

TABLE OF CASES

TABLE OF CASES

CASES AND MATERIALS ON

THE RULES OF
THE LEGAL PROFESSION

Chapter One

INTRODUCTION TO THE LEGAL PROFESSION

A. Law as a Profession

Lawyers, along with doctors and the clergy, have traditionally been referred to as "professionals." Throughout this book, we will explore the attributes of a professional. Generally, professionals have a substantial amount of education and training, certification by others in the profession, a commitment to public service, high social prestige, and high income. Professionals provide a service that is vitally needed. They are generally self-regulatory, setting the standards, and controlling admission and discipline of those within the profession.[1]

It may be that we have lost something of the meaning of the term, "professional." Ninth Circuit Judge John Noonan has suggested that originally, being a professional meant that one professed something.

> What are lawyers professing? At a minimum, a belief in the ability of human beings to communicate with each other by means of rational argument. At a slightly deeper level, a belief that human beings can arrange their affairs fairly. At a still deeper level, a belief in the value of purposeful process.[2]

Law can be a high calling, but there are risks and temptations that accompany professionalism. As noted, professions generally regulate themselves. This is due, at least in part, to the difficulty nonlawyers have in accurately assessing an attorney's performance. Just as a patient's death does not necessarily indicate incompetent medial care, a client's loss does not necessarily indicate incompetent legal care. But self-regulation can become self-protection. At times, talk of professionalism has been used to keep blacks, immigrants, women, Catholics, and Jews out of the legal profession.[3] Arguably, lawyers

---

[1]   For a fuller development of the attributes of a professional, *see* Charles W. Wolfram, *Modern Legal Ethics* 14-17 (1986) and sources cited therein.

[2]   John T. Noonan, Jr., "Choice of a Profession," 21 *Pepp. L. Rev.* 381, 383 (1994).

[3]   *See* Richard Abel, *American Lawyers* 85-108 (1989).

have regulated prices, and prohibited advertising, solicitation,[4] and unauthorized practice in order to limit competition. As you study the rules of our profession, consider whether some of the rules merely protect lawyer interests.

A second risk that accompanies professionalism is that emphasis on the *special* knowledge and skills of professionals can lead to a belief, by both professionals and clients, in the *general* superiority of professionals. This sense of the superiority of professionals is reinforced by the secretaries that protect professionals from clients, the large desks that professionals sit behind (in chairs that are higher than those of clients), the certificates with which professionals fill their walls, and the power ties and suits that professionals wear. This sense of superiority can lead to professional paternalism. Some professionals tend to control decisions in clients' lives that have little to do with professional expertise.[5]

A final risk that accompanies professionalism is that professionals will draw a sharp line between what they do in their professional roles and what they do in the rest of their lives. Some professionals exercise different moralities in their professional lives and in their personal lives. Some lawyers use their role as a professional to excuse doing things that they believe to be wrong.[6] As you study the rules of the legal profession, you might ask whether they call on you to do things that you believe to be wrong. In some cases, reflection may lead you to accept the justifications for what some lawyers do; in some cases it may not.

---

[4]   The United States Supreme Court has outlawed minimum fee schedules, Goldfarb v. Virginia State Bar, 421 U.S. 773, 95 S. Ct. 2004, 44 L. Ed. 2d 572 (1975), and most limitations on advertising, Bates v. State Bar of Arizona, 433 U.S. 350, 97 S. Ct. 2691, 53 L. Ed. 2d 810 (1977). For consideration of the current rules on advertising and solicitation, *see infra* Chapter Seven.

[5]   Richard Wasserstrom explores lawyer paternalism in his classic article, "Lawyers as Professionals: Some Moral Issues," 5 *Human Rights* 1 (1975). Portions of Wasserstrom's article dealing with paternalism along with other materials on paternalism appear *infra* in Chapter Two, Part C.

[6]   For a discussion of the dangers of professional role morality, *see* Wasserstrom, *id.* Portions of that article dealing with role morality are reprinted *infra* in Chapter Five, Part A.

B. The History of Legal Ethics: A Few Highlights

A complete history of the legal profession would fill many volumes. We identify only a few highlights of that history that provide background for the rules of the profession and for some of the more troublesome problems that the profession confronts today. We highlight aspects of that history related to the ethics of lawyers, regulation of the profession, and diversity (and lack of diversity) in the profession.

In the early days of the United States lawyers learned their trade, not in law schools, but in law offices, while serving as apprentices to practicing lawyers.[7] Control of lawyers came from judges and clients. Judges controlled what went on in their courts and clients decided who was worthy of hire. There were no formal codes of professional conduct, but expectations of lawyers were established by lawyers as a matter of practice and habit.

The first written statement of lawyer norms in the United States was David Hoffman's "Observations on Professional Deportment," in his *A Course of Legal Study*, published in 1817.[8] Hoffman's resolutions were rules of morality and professional courtesy, rather than rules of law. His resolutions placed significant limits on what we have come to know as the adversary ethic. For example, Hoffman advised that lawyers refuse to plead the statute of limitations for a client who owed a just debt: "[The client] shall never make me a partner in his knavery."[9] Hoffman advised lawyers not to advocate an unwise rule of law. "[S]hould the principle also be wholly at variance with sound law, it would be dishonorable folly in me to endeavor to incorporate it into the jurisprudence of the country."[10]

---

[7]   Four states (California, Vermont, Virginia, and Washington) still allow an individual to sit for the bar exam based on study of the law in a law office. Bradley A. Smith, "The Limits of Compulsory Professionalism: How the Unified Bar Harms the Legal Profession," 22 *Fla. St. U. L. Rev.* 35, 67 n.164 (1994).

[8]   Substantial portions of the second edition of Hoffman's *A Course of Legal Study* (2nd ed. 1836) are included in Thomas L. Shaffer, *American Legal Ethics: Text, Readings, and Discussion Topics* 59-68, 94-96, 114-15, 132-34, and 146-49 (1985).

[9]   *Id.* at 64.

[10]   *Id.*

Some speak of the criticism of the legal profession that has occurred since Watergate as if lawyer criticism is a new thing in the United States. But the public esteem of lawyers has gone through ebbs and flows. The industrial revolution brought a revolution, not only for industry, but for lawyers' ethics as well. Its effect on many in the legal profession can be illustrated in the life of one man: David Dudley Field. In the mid-1800s, Field was a law reformer and drafter of New York's predecessor to the modern rules of civil procedure in the mid-1800s.[11] In 1855, in a speech to the Albany Law School, Field noted that lawyers have not only a duty to the client, but a "duty to the Court, that it shall be assisted by the advocate" and "a duty to truth and right, whose allegiance no human being can renounce."[12] But in the 1860s and early 1870s, Field represented James Fisk, Jay Gould, Daniel Drew, and the Erie Railroad in some of the most infamous lawyer shenanigans this country has seen. Commodore Vanderbilt began to buy stock in the Erie Railroad and Field's clients "began printing unauthorized shares of Erie stock on a private press as fast as Vanderbilt could buy up the genuine stock."[13] When Vanderbilt obtained an injunction against them, Field, well aware of the weaknesses of the Code which he had drafted, obtained a counter-injunction from another judge. Within a month, five judges had issued seven inconsistent injunctions. The Erie directors sought additional help from the legislature at a price of $5000 a vote. Vanderbilt settled. In another legal battle involving the Erie railroad, the son of the owner of the Albany and Sesquehanna Railroad was authorized to serve a writ of contempt on Fisk and Gould. The son's body was found floating in the Hudson River. An exchange of 20 letters between Field and Samuel Bowles, editor of the *Springfield Republican*, followed in which Bowles asserted, and Field denied, that lawyers are publicly and morally responsible for their actions as lawyers.[14]

---

[11]   This history of David Field is drawn from Michael Schudson, "Public, Private, and Professional Lives: The Correspondence of David Dudley Field and Samuel Bowles," 21 *Am. J. of Legal History* 191 (1977).

[12]   *Id.* at 207.

[13]   *Id.* at 194.

[14]   This argument continues today as illustrated by the exchange of Professors Monroe Freedman and Michael Tigar, *infra* at Chapter Two, Part A..

In the face of a mountain of criticism of the legal profession, some lawyers in 1870 organized the Association of the Bar of the City of New York, with the avowed purpose "to maintain the honor and dignity of the profession of the law, to cultivate social intercourse among its members and to increase its usefulness in promoting the due administration of justice."[15] In speeches before the Association, Field was subject to much criticism for his use of illegal tactics.[16] He was investigated by the Association, but never formally censured.[17]

The first state code for lawyers was adopted by the Alabama legislature in 1887.[18] On the national level, the American Bar Association had been founded in 1878, but it was not until 1908 that it adopted a set of rules for lawyers, the Canons of Professional Ethics. The Canons largely copied the Alabama Code. The Canons were widely adopted by the states, in some states through legislation, in some as court rules, and in some as rules of the state bar association.[19]

In 1969, the American Bar Association adopted the Model Code of Professional Responsibility, the first new set of lawyer rules since the ABA Canons of 1908. The Model Code contained both Disciplinary Rules (DRs), the violation of which would subject lawyers to discipline, and Ethical Considerations (ECs), which set aspirational standards for lawyers. But the Watergate break-in and cover-up in the early 1970s brought calls for increased lawyer regulation. The organized bar responded to public criticism in several ways. The ABA initiated and, in 1983, adopted another set of rules for lawyers, the ABA Model Rules of Professional Conduct. In 1997, the ABA established the Ethics 2000 Commission. It proposed numerous changes to the Model Rules, most of which were adopted by the ABA in 2002. Model Rules do not set aspirations for lawyers; they are

---

[15]   *See* Schudson, *supra* note 11 at 202, *quoting* Article II of the Constitution of the Association of the Bar of the City of New York.

[16]   *Id.* at 202-03.

[17]   *Id.* at 204.

[18]   Alabama Code of Ethics, 118 Ala. xxiii (1899).

[19]   *See* Wolfram, *supra* note 1 at 55-56 and sources cited therein. The following section discusses the Canons and other sources of law for lawyers.

almost exclusively rules that subject lawyers to discipline.[20]   In addition, state bar associations required that lawyers pass a special professional responsibility examination before admission to practice law; and law schools required that students take a professional responsibility class while in law school.

In spite of (some suggest because of)[21] the greater attention by lawyers to rules, the profession seems to have gone through a continual crisis (or series of crises) since Watergate. Lawyers played leading roles in the corporate takeover scandals and Enron and the savings and loan scandals of the 1980s. The Whitewater investigations discovered serious ethical failings by lawyers. A survey, commissioned by the ABA, found that only 22 percent of the public describe lawyers as "honest and ethical," while 40 percent say that lawyers are not "honest and ethical."[22] The results are even more troubling than might initially appear; those who regularly have contact with lawyers "tend to have the most negative perceptions of the profession."[23] Lawyers charge clients increasingly higher fees, associates feel increasing pressure to bill more hours, legal tactics are marked by increasing incivility, most poor and middle class people lack legal representation, and court dockets are backed up for years. You are entering a troubled profession, a profession that needs the innovation, energy, and integrity that you can bring to it. As you study the legal profession, consider the ways in which it might need to be changed.

---

[20]   The following section contains a discussion of the ABA Canons, Model Code, and Model Rules, as well as the other sources of law that regulate lawyers.

[21]   Reed Elizabeth Loder, "Tighter Rules of Professional Conduct: Saltwater for Thirst?" 1 *Georgetown J. of Legal Ethics* 311 (1987).

[22]   Gary A. Hengstler, "Vox Populi: The Public Perception of Lawyers: ABA Poll," 79 *ABA Journal* 60, 63 (September 1993).

[23]   *Id.* at 61.

C. Sources of Law Governing Lawyers

Read the Preamble, Scope, and Rule 1.0 of the Model Rules[24]

Throughout this book, you will see courts drawing on various sources of law that govern lawyers. The major sources are:

1. Professional Responsibility Codes—All states have a set of rules that governs lawyers. Typically, these rules have been proposed by the state bar association and approved by the state supreme court. The major professional responsibility codes for lawyers in this country are:

a. ABA Model Rules of Professional Conduct (Model Rules)—adopted by the ABA in 1983. Contains almost exclusively mandatory rules and commentary. Approximately 45 jurisdictions have adopted some form of the Model Rules, but almost all of these states have amended significant portions of the Rules. In 2002, the ABA adopted the first pervasive set of changes to the Model Rules–the Ethics 2000 Commission proposals. The focus of this book will be on the Model Rules. At the beginning of each section, we will suggest that you read the Model Rules that deal with the topic of that section. In the cases and articles that cite a rule other than the Model Rules, we cite the comparable Model Rule in brackets.

b. ABA Model Code of Professional Responsibility— adopted by the ABA in 1969; the predecessor to the Model Rules. It is composed of Ethical Considerations (ECs), which suggest aspirations for lawyers, and Disciplinary Rules (DRs), which are mandatory rules. Shortly after its adoption by the ABA in 1969, almost all jurisdictions adopted the Model Code without amendment. Today, approximately five jurisdictions continue to apply the Model Code; the largest is New York.[25]

---

[24]   *Cf.* MODEL RULES OF PROFESSIONAL CONDUCT Preamble and Scope (2002); MODEL CODE OF PROFESSIONAL RESPONSIBILITY Preamble and Preliminary Statement (1993); CALIFORNIA RULES OF PROFESSIONAL CONDUCT Rule 1-100 (1992). The Model Code contains Ethical Considerations (hereinafter "EC") and Disciplinary Rules (hereinafter "DR"). The California Rules of Professional Conduct are hereinafter referred to as "Cal Rules."

[25]   Throughout this book, when we suggest that you read a Model Rule provision, we cite the comparable Model Code provision in an accompanying footnote. *See, e.g., infra* n.32.

c. California Rules of Professional Conduct—adopted by the California Supreme Court in 1988. California has a history of going its own way in many respects and its lawyer rules are no different. Some of the California Rules include language from Model Rule provisions; some include language from Model Code provisions; most have their own language.[26]

d. ABA Canons of Professional Ethics—adopted by the ABA in 1908; the predecessor to the Model Code. Consisted initially of 32 (eventually 47) Canons that are largely hortatory in nature. Whether through legislation, supreme court rule, or bar association rule, the Canons became the source of lawyer rule and discipline in almost every state.

2. Legislation—Legislatures generally have left regulation of lawyers to the legal profession and the state's supreme court, but several legislatures regulate lawyers in some areas. In California a substantial number of the rules governing lawyers are in the state code.[27] Rules 11 and 26(g) of the United States Code of Civil Procedure and comparable state provisions permit penalties for lawyer abuse of legal procedure.[28] A number of provisions limit the attorney's fees that lawyers can charge for types of legal work.[29]

3. Ethics Opinions—The ABA, as well as state and local bar associations, issue ethics opinions in response to questions from lawyers. These opinions do not have the effect of law, but occasionally are cited by bar associations or courts that are considering discipline of a lawyer.

4. Restatement (Third) of the Law Governing Lawyers—In 2000, the American Law Institute published the Restatement of the Law Governing Lawyers. It is the first restatement of the law of lawyers, but the ALI is working on its third series of restatements,

---

[26]   Throughout this book, when we suggest that you read a Model Rule provision, we cite the comparable California Rule in an accompanying footnote. *See, e.g., infra* n.32.

[27]   *See California Business and Professions Code*, Articles 4, 6, 7, 8.5, 9, 13, & 14.

[28]   *See, e.g.*, Washington State Physicians Ins. Exch. & Ass'n v. Fisons Corp., 122 Wash. 2d 299, 858 P. 2d 1054 (1993).

[29]   *See, e.g.*, 28 U.S.C.A. § 2678 (1994) (setting maximum contingent fee under the Federal Torts Claims Act at 25% of the judgment); and Supreme Court of New Jersey Rule 1:21-7 (setting maximum contingent fee schedule).

and named the restatement concerning lawyers to conform to the other third restatements.

5. Tort Law—Lawyers are subject to professional malpractice liability for failure to exercise reasonable care on behalf of clients. The law of attorney malpractice is primarily common law, law that has evolved over years of judicial decision-making.[30] A later section of this chapter discusses the malpractice liability of lawyers.

6. Agency Law—Lawyers act as agents of their clients, and much of agency law applies to lawyers. Many sections of the Restatement of Agency Law provide illustrations applying agency principles to conduct of lawyers.

D. Admission to the Practice of Law

Read Model Rule 8.1[31]

One must be admitted to the bar in order to practice law. State supreme courts typically control admission to the practice of law. Requirements vary from state-to-state, but typically one must have both undergraduate and law school degrees, be twenty-one years of age or older, take an oath, pay a fee, and pass a bar examination and a character review.

Application of William W. Gahan
for Admission to the Bar of Minnesota
279 N.W.2d 826 (Minn. 1979)

TODD, Justice.

William Gahan seeks admission to the bar of the State of Minnesota. * * *

* * *

The facts in this matter are not in dispute. Gahan received his law degree from the University of San Francisco, California. He was admitted to practice law in California in 1976 and subsequently was admitted to practice law in Wisconsin. Gahan is single, has never

---

[30]   *See* Ronald E. Mallen and Jeffrey M. Smith, *Legal Malpractice* (3d ed. 1989).

[31]   *Cf.* DR 1-101; EC 1-1 to -3; Cal. Rules 1-200.

been married, and has no dependents. During the time of his education, at both the undergraduate and graduate level, Gahan required financial assistance to obtain his law degree. To achieve this goal, he obtained a series of student loans under a federally funded guaranty program. At the time of his graduation from law school, the total amount of these loans was approximately $14,000. At the time he received the loans, Gahan agreed to repay and understood that he would be expected to repay the loans upon or shortly after graduation.

* * *

[Gahan filed for bankruptcy in 1977. "During the period prior to bankruptcy, he was employed for most of the time at an annual salary of $15,000 and then $18,000."] Immediately prior to filing his petition for bankruptcy, Gahan mortgaged his 1959 Jaguar automobile to a friend for a loan of $2,500. He deposited $1,000 of the loan funds in an exempt account at a savings and loan institution and deposited the remaining $1,500 in an exempt account at a co-op credit union. Under California law, these deposits were the maximum amounts which could be claimed as exempt from creditors. ["Gahan's bankruptcy petition showed total liabilities of $19,717.40 and $4,007 worth of assets, $4,000 of which was exempt."]

* * *

There is nothing connected with Gahan's bankruptcy to suggest that there was any fraud, deceit, or conduct which could be considered to involve moral turpitude. However, based on this evidence, the Board of Law Examiners found in part:

"XXIII.

"Procuring discharge of this indebtedness (and no other) with so little effort to repay or extend the same and with only temporary loss of employment, no exceptional financial or health problems and no major misfortunes, while neither illegal nor constituting action evincing moral turpitude, nonetheless is conduct which would cause a reasonable man to have substantial doubt concerning applicant's honesty, fairness, and respect for the rights of others and for the laws of this state and nation amounting thereby to a lack of good moral character having a rational connection with applicant's fitness or capacity to practice law.

"XXIV.

"Applicant continues to have and maintain a lack of recognition and appreciation of the underlying moral obligation and social (as opposed to legal) responsibility which arose when he was entrusted with the student loan funds in question."

As a result of these findings, the Board found Gahan was not a person of good moral character within the contemplation of our Rules of Admission and recommended that he not be admitted to practice law in Minnesota. Gahan petitioned this court for review of this recommendation.

* * *

Rule II of the Rules for Admission to the bar of the State of Minnesota states in part:

"No person shall be admitted to practice law who has not established to the satisfaction of the State Board of Law Examiners [that he is a person of good moral character;"]

* * *

"*Character traits that are relevant to a determination of good moral character must have a rational connection with the applicant's present fitness or capacity to practice law, and accordingly must relate to the State's legitimate interest in protecting prospective clients and the system of justice."

* * *

The Florida court is apparently the only court to specifically consider whether a bar applicant's failure to repay his student loans demonstrates lack of good moral character so as to justify denial of admission. The Florida court has considered the issue twice, and the contrast in the cases is instructive. In the case of *Florida Bd. of Bar Examiners re G.W.L.*, 364 So.2d 454 (Fla. 1978), the applicant, G.W.L., had approximately $10,000 in student loans upon graduation from law school. As of several months before graduation, he had not obtained law-related employment. Three days before graduation, he executed a voluntary petition for bankruptcy. Approximately 7 months later, the applicant was adjudicated bankrupt and released from his debts. At approximately the same time, the applicant obtained a job as law clerk at $70 per week. He applied for admission to the Florida bar, and the Board recommended that applicant not be admitted. The Florida Supreme Court agreed with the Board, stating (364 So.2d 459):

"* * * We find that the Board had ample record evidence from which it could conclude that the principal motive of the petitioner in filing his petition for bankruptcy was to defeat creditors who had substantially funded seven years of educational training. Whether that motive was present as the debts were incurred or was formed toward the end of his law school training, the Board could fairly conclude from the petitioner's own testimony and prior behavior that he exercised his legal right to be freed of debt by bankruptcy well before the first installments on his debt became due, with absolutely no regard for his moral responsibility to his creditors.* * *"

In the second Florida case, *Florida Bd. of Bar Examiners re Groot*, 365 So.2d 164 (Fla. 1978), the court held that an applicant who had discharged his student loans in bankruptcy should nevertheless be admitted because the circumstances surrounding his default were justified. In distinguishing the case from *Florida Bd. of Bar Examiners re G.W.L.*, *supra*, the court said (365 So.2d 168):

"Unlike G.W.L., Groot was the father and legal custodian of two children born of his recently-terminated marriage. His expenses included not only his own living costs and those of his dependents, but to some degree those of his former wife. When his personal resources became exhausted, he was forced to prevail upon family members to loan him the money, to meet current living expenses while he was without a job. Thus, unlike G.W.L., Groot had suffered unusual misfortune at the time he finally secured employment, and he had a valid present need to devote his entire employment income to his current, not past, financial responsibilities. His circumstances warranted his turning to the remedy provided by federal law for persons in just such situations, and we hold that Groot's conduct under these circumstances is not morally reprehensible or indicative of a present unfitness for admission to the bar."

* * *

We hold that applicants who flagrantly disregard the rights of others and default on serious financial obligations, such as student loans, are lacking in good moral character if the default is neglectful, irresponsible, and cannot be excused by a compelling hardship that is reasonably beyond the control of the applicant. Such hardships might include an unusual misfortune, a catastrophe, an overriding financial obligation, or unavoidable unemployment.

* * *

A student loan is entrusted to a person, and is to be repaid to creditors upon graduation when and if financially able. Moreover, repayment provides stability to the student loan program and guarantees the continuance of the program for future student needs. A flagrant disregard of this repayment responsibility by the loan recipient indicates to us a lack of moral commitment to the rights of other students and particularly the rights of creditors. Such flagrant financial irresponsibility reflects adversely on an applicant's ability to manage financial matters and reflects adversely on his commitment to the rights of others, thereby reflecting adversely on his fitness for the practice of law. It is appropriate to prevent problems from such irresponsibility by denying admission, rather than seek to remedy the problem after it occurs and victimizes a client.

Applying the above principles to this case, we conclude that Gahan's failure to satisfy his obligations on the student loans cannot be excused for some compelling hardship reasonably beyond his control. * * *

* * *

Notes

1.   To what standards should bar applicants be held? If Gahan did not break the law, should he be denied the opportunity to practice law? Did Gahan's bankruptcy have anything to do with his ability to practice law?

2.   Should applicants be denied admission if they have broken the law? What if Gahan previously had been convicted of possession of marijuana?

3.   Should an applicant be denied admission if he abuses his wife? If she abuses her child?

4.   *Admission pro hac vice*—Most courts will allow a lawyer who is licensed in another state to be admitted to handle a single case before the court. Generally, the lawyer must associate a local attorney. This is referred to as admission *pro hac vice* (for this turn only). In Leis v. Flynt, 439 U.S. 438, 99 S. Ct. 698, 58 L. Ed. 2d 717 (1979), Larry Flynt and *Hustler* magazine had been indicted for violations of Ohio's pornography laws. The Ohio trial court, without a hearing, denied Flynt's lawyers' request for admission *pro hac vice*. The United States Supreme Court held that the due process clause does not entitle a lawyer to be admitted *pro hac vice* nor to a hearing

on the issue. These matters are left entirely to the trial judge's discretion. The Court did not address, nor did the lawyers raise, the issue of whether such a denial would violate the client's constitutional rights.

5. *Admission to Practice in Federal Courts*—Lawyers must be admitted into each federal court before which they practice. Typically, one only has to be admitted to practice in the state in which a United States district court sits to be admitted to practice in the district court.

6. *Reciprocity Admission*—The vast majority of states will admit a lawyer to practice if that lawyer has practiced law for a period of years (typically five) in another state that extends the same privilege to lawyers of the admitting state.

7. *Unauthorized practice*—If a lawyer practices law in a state in which he is not authorized to practice, the lawyer is subject to criminal sanction in the state in which he engages in the unauthorized practice, and to discipline in the state in which she is admitted, *see* MR 5.5. The 2002 Amendments to MR 5.5 identified several situations in which practice in a state in which one is not admitted is appropriate. For further discussion of this matter, see Chapter Seven, Part B.

E. Sanctions for Lawyer Misconduct

Read Model Rules 8.2 to 8.5[32]

Lawyer Discipline

Attorneys who engage in professional misconduct (*see* MR 8.4) are subject to discipline, which typically is conducted by the state bar and supreme court. In addition, federal courts have their own disciplinary procedures. The following is a description of disciplinary procedures in a typical state. The details of the procedures vary from state-to-state.

Discipline is initiated by a complaint filed with the state bar. Most often complaints are filed by an attorney's client or opposing counsel, but they can also be initiated by a judge or prosecutor. The state bar then conducts an investigation. In some states, volunteer attorneys

---

[32] *Cf.* DR 1-103, 1-102, 9-101(c); EC 1-4; Cal. Bus. & Prof. Code §§ 6101-6106.9 (West 1995), *as amended by* 1995 Cal. Legis. Serv. Ch. 730 (A.B. 1466) (West).

conduct the investigation, but increasingly the investigation is conducted by bar counsel--full time attorneys hired by the bar for this purpose. A bar counsel acts very much like a prosecutor. She determines whether there is probable cause to proceed with a hearing. Where there is a very minor violation, bar counsel may reach some form of accommodation between the attorney and the complainant. In some states, bar counsel can engage in plea bargaining with the attorney.

If the allegations are sufficiently serious and there is sufficient evidence to support them, bar counsel files formal charges and the matter is brought before a bar disciplinary committee for a hearing. In some jurisdictions, the disciplinary committee will include non-lawyers. The attorney is entitled to notice of the hearing, legal counsel of his choice, the opportunity to confront witnesses, and the right to put on his own evidence. Under an exception to the confidentiality rule, a "lawyer may reveal information relating to the representation of a client to the extent the lawyer reasonably believes necessary . . . to respond to allegations in any proceeding concerning the lawyer's representation of the client. . ." MR 1.6(b)(4). The committee does not follow strict rules of evidence. Typically, bar counsel must prove the attorney's guilt by clear and convincing evidence. Following the presentation of evidence by both sides, the bar committee renders a decision, either dismissing the charges or finding a violation and recommending punishment.

The state supreme court retains ultimate control over attorney discipline. In some states, the decision of the bar committee automatically goes to the supreme court; in other states, the state bar counsel or the disciplined attorney may appeal to the supreme court. The supreme court does not hear additional evidence, but typically conducts a *de novo* review of the decision of the bar committee.

When an attorney is found to have committed a violation, the severity of the discipline is likely to be based on:

> (1) the extent to which the lawyer's misconduct caused injury to others; (2) the blameworthiness of the lawyer under the circumstances; (3) the lawyer's general character; (4) the lawyer's prior disciplinary history or other indications of whether the conduct was isolated or part of a pattern of repeated behavior; (5) the lawyer's demeanor during, and reaction to, the disciplinary process; (6) the likely need to deter lawyers generally or the offending lawyer in particular from similar conduct in the future;

(7) the desirability of parity among similar cases; and (8) the justness of the sanction for other reasons.[33]

The state bar and supreme court have four possible sanctions. The mildest form of discipline is a private reprimand--an unpublished communication with the lawyer. For somewhat more serious violations, a lawyer may receive a public reprimand, typically a published report of his violation in the state bar journal. More serious violations may result in suspension of the lawyer from law practice for a time which can range from several days to several years. The attorney may be required to meet conditions before returning to practice, for example the completion of a drug treatment program. For the most serious violations, an attorney is subject to disbarment–the suspension of the lawyer's license to practice. In some jurisdictions, an attorney may apply for readmission to the bar after a period of time. A lawyer who petitions for readmission bears the burden of showing that he has reformed. The state supreme court may require a lawyer w ho h as petitioned for readmission to meet certain standards, including one that you may face in a few months–passing the Multi-state Professional Responsibility Exam. If the disbarred lawyer's original violation was sufficiently serious, the court is unlikely to allow readmission.

Traditionally, the bar disciplinary procedure was confidential until there was a final resolution of the complaint. The argument for confidentiality is that the reputation of an innocent attorney should not be tainted by a report that is ultimately unsubstantiated. Increasingly, however, bar discipline is open to public view. The Oregon Supreme Court has held that the Oregon public record's statute applies to bar disciplinary proceedings from the time of the filing of the original complaint.[34] In many jurisdictions, complaints are made public at the time that bar counsel files formal charges against the lawyer.

---

[33]   Charles W. Wolfram, *Modern Legal Ethics* § 3.5.2 (1986). For a more thorough discussion of disciplinary procedures and sanctions, *see id.* at §§ 3.4-3.5.

[34]   Sadler v. Oregon State Bar, 275 Or. 279, 550 P.2d 1218 (1976).

Notes

1.   Charges against defendants in criminal cases are a matter of public record.   Should complaints against attorneys be treated differently? If so, why?

2.   Should non-lawyers sit on bar disciplinary committees? Should a majority of the disciplinary committee be non-lawyers? What arguments support inclusion of non-lawyers? What arguments support exclusion?

3.   In *Gahan, supra*, Gahan was denied admission to practice law in Minnesota because he declared bankruptcy to avoid repayment of student loans. If Gahan had declared bankruptcy after he became a lawyer, would he have been subject to discipline under MR 8.4? As we saw in the *Gahan* case, in evaluating admission to practice law, bar associations consider the morality of a lawyer's actions, whether or not they are illegal. Gahan was denied admission to the Minnesota bar. He was already a member of the California and Wisconsin bars at the time that he declared bankruptcy, and there is no indication that the bankruptcy got him into trouble in those jurisdictions. Should we hold lawyers to lower standards than bar applicants? To higher standards?

In re **Himmel**
125 Ill. 2d 531, 533 N.E.2d 790, 127 Ill. Dec. 708 (1988)

* * *

In October 1978, Tammy Forsberg was injured in a motorcycle accident. In June 1980, she retained John R. Casey to represent her in any personal injury or property damage claim resulting from the accident.   Sometime in 1981, Casey negotiated a settlement of $35,000 on Forsberg's behalf. Pursuant to an agreement between Forsberg and Casey, one-third of any monies received would be paid to Casey as his attorney fee.

In March 1981, Casey received the $35,000 settlement check, endorsed it, and deposited the check into his client trust fund account. Subsequently, Casey converted the funds.

Between 1981 and 1983, Forsberg unsuccessfully attempted to collect her $23,233.34 share of the settlement proceeds. In March 1983, Forsberg retained respondent to collect her money and agreed to pay him one-third of any funds recovered above $23,233.34.

Respondent investigated the matter and discovered that Casey had misappropriated the settlement funds. In April 1983, respondent drafted an agreement in which Casey would pay Forsberg $75,000 in settlement of any claim she might have against him for the misappropriated funds. By the terms of the agreement, Forsberg agreed not to initiate any criminal, civil, or attorney disciplinary action against Casey. This agreement was executed on April 11, 1983. Respondent stood to gain $17,000 or more if Casey honored the agreement. [Forsberg ultimately recovered a total of $23,233.34, the amount that Casey initially owed her. Respondent received no fee.]

* * *

In April 1985, the Administrator filed a petition to have Casey suspended from practicing law because of his conversion of client funds and his conduct involving moral turpitude in matters unrelated to Forsberg's claim. Casey was subsequently disbarred on consent on November 5, 1985.

* * *

The Hearing Board found that respondent received unprivileged information that Casey converted Forsberg's funds, and that respondent failed to relate the information to the Commission in violation of Rule 1-103(a) of the Code [*Cf.* MR 8.3]. The Hearing Board noted, however, that respondent had been practicing law for 11 years, had no prior record of any complaints, obtained as good a result as could be expected in the case, and requested no fee for recovering the $23,233.34. Accordingly, the Hearing Board recommended a private reprimand.

* * *

Our analysis of this issue begins with a reading of the applicable disciplinary rules. Rule 1-103(a) of the Code states:

"(a) A lawyer possessing unprivileged knowledge [that a lawyer has engaged in `illegal conduct involving moral turpitude' or `conduct involving dishonesty, fraud, deceit, or misrepresentation'] shall report such knowledge to a tribunal or other authority empowered to investigate or act upon such violation." [C] [*Cf.* MR 8.3(a)]

* * *

Though we agree with the Hearing Board's assessment that respondent violated Rule 1-103 of the Code, we do not agree that the facts warrant only a private reprimand. As previously stated, the evidence proved that respondent possessed unprivileged knowledge of Casey's conversion of client funds, yet respondent did not report Casey's misconduct.

This failure to report resulted in interference with the Commission's investigation of Casey, and thus with the administration of justice. Perhaps some members of the public would have been spared from Casey's misconduct had respondent reported the information as soon as he knew of Casey's conversions of client funds. We are particularly disturbed by the fact that respondent chose to draft a settlement agreement with Casey rather than report his misconduct. As the Administrator has stated, by this conduct, both respondent and his client ran afoul of the Criminal Code's prohibition against compounding a crime, which states in section 32-1:

> "(a) A person compounds a crime when he receives or offers to another any consideration for a promise not to prosecute or aid in the prosecution of an offender.
>
> (b) Sentence. Compounding a crime is a petty offense." [C].

Both respondent and his client stood to gain financially by agreeing not to prosecute or report Casey for conversion.

* * *

Accordingly, it is ordered that respondent be suspended from the practice of law for one year.

Respondent suspended.

Notes

1.   Is requiring lawyers to turn one another in the way to police lawyers? What pressures might discourage lawyers from disclosing incompetence on the part of an attorney that opposes them?

2.   DR 1-103(A) of the Model Code, required lawyers to report any violation of the professional rules. MR 8.3(a) requires lawyers to report a violation of the rules "that raises a substantial question as to that lawyer's honesty, trustworthiness or fitness as a lawyer in other respects." California does not require lawyers to report lawyer misconduct. Which is the better rule? Why?

3.   Is failure to report a fellow lawyer's misconduct less or more serious than failure to report a fellow student's cheating? Does your answer change depending upon whether the school has an honor code?

Is failure to report a lawyer less or more serious than failure to report a burglary that you observe in your neighborhood?

Malpractice Liability

In addition to the risk of disciplinary actions by governing professional bodies, lawyers who engage in misconduct are subject to the risks of malpractice actions[35] and procedural sanctions by courts or government agencies.

Negligence claims constitute the most common form of legal malpractice action.[36] In order to prevail the client must show (1) that the attorney had a duty to the client, (2) that the duty was breached through the attorney's negligence, and (3) that the breach proximately caused (4) injuries to the client.

The existence of a duty is usually established by showing an attorney-client relationship. Whether an attorney-client relationship existed is determined by asking whether it was reasonable for the person asserting client status to believe that an attorney-client relationship existed.[37] If so, the attorney has a duty to take reasonable steps to fulfill the client's purposes in hiring a lawyer. One of the increasingly contested points in legal malpractice actions is whether the complained of action or inaction fell within the client's purposes when hiring the lawyer. The focus of these disputes is whether an attorney agrees to protect all interests of the client, or only those interests that are directly

---

[35] Successful malpractice claims are relatively new. "Between 1979 and 1986, not only did the number of legal malpractice cases double, but the average settlement nationally soared from $3,000 to $45,000." Manuel R. Ramos, "Legal Malpractice: The Profession's Dirty Little Secret," 47 *Vand. L. Rev.* 1657, 1678 (1994) (citing Mary Ann Galante, "Insurance Costs Soar; Is There Any Way Out?; Firms Seek Creative Solutions," *Nat'l L. J.* 1 (March 10, 1986)).

[36] Mallen & Smith, *supra*, note 30 at § 8.10.

[37] Section 14 of the Restatement (Third) of The Law Governing Lawyers says: "A relationship of client and lawyer arises when: (1) a person manifests to a lawyer the person's intent that the lawyer provide legal services for the person; and (either)(a) the lawyer manifests to the person consent to do so; or (b) the lawyer fails to manifest lack of consent to do so, and the lawyer knows or reasonably should know that the person reasonably relies on the lawyer to provide the services; or (c) a tribunal with power to do so appoints the lawyer to provide the services."
Restatement (Third) of The Law Governing Lawyers § 14 (1998).

The question of when an attorney-client relationship is established is explored in greater depth in Chapter Two, Part A.

at issue in the representation?[38] This question is usually cast as an issue about the "scope of representation."[39]

Independent of the duty and scope of representation questions, is the standard of care an attorney must exercise in performing the duties owed to clients. "[T]he attorney should exercise the skill and knowledge ordinarily possessed by attorneys under similar circumstances."[40] Similar circumstances include considerations of custom, locality, and specialization.[41] For example, a plaintiff seeking to recover under a malpractice claim for failure to provide contractual protections beyond those afforded by patent law would be more likely to prevail against a Washington, D.C. lawyer holding herself out as a specialist in patent law than against a general practitioner in Lawrence, Kansas.

In establishing a standard of care, plaintiffs often seek to introduce evidence that the lawyer violated a rule of professional conduct. Courts are split over the relevance of such evidence. The majority of courts recognize that violation of the rules of professional conduct may provide evidence of breach of duty,[42] but only a few courts go so far as to accept the rules of professional conduct as the standard of care. This reluctance to accept the rules of ethics as the standard of care stems both from the language in the preamble to the rules which discourages such use, and the argument that disciplinary actions and malpractice claims seek to vindicate different interests.[43]

The third element of a legal malpractice claim based upon negligence is that the negligence proximately caused injuries to the client. As in all negligence cases, the plaintiff must show both actual and legal causation.

In order to show actual cause, a plaintiff must show that "but for" the negligence of their attorneys, the initial case would have had a different result; plaintiff may be required to win a "trial within a trial." This can be particularly difficult where the attorney's negligence precluded the client from ever bringing suit. For example, the plaintiff

---

[38]   *See* Birchfield v. Harrod, 640 P.2d 1003 (Okla. App. 1982).

[39]   *See* MR 1.2.

[40]   Mallen & Smith, *supra* note 30 at § 15.2.

[41]   *Id.*

[42]   *See, e.g.,* Woodruff v. Tomlin, 616 F.2d 924, 936 (6th Cir. 1980); and Kirsch v. Duryea, 21 Cal. 3d 303, 578 P.2d 935, 146 Cal. Rptr. 218 (1978).

[43]   *See* Mallen & Smith, *supra* note 30 § 15.7.

complaining that an attorney allowed the statute of limitations to run on a claim must show, not only that the attorney failed to file suit within the statutory period, but also that if the attorney had filed suit, the client would have been successful. A showing of legally recoverable damages is the final element of a negligence claim against a lawyer. The client must show that any judgement or settlement would have been collectible from the original defendant or her insurance company.

In addition to negligence, attorneys can be liable to clients under theories of breach of fiduciary duty, fraud or deceit, breach of contract, and violation of consumer protection laws.

Non-clients can also sue lawyers for injuries suffered due to intentional torts and violation of contractual duties. However, as agents of the client, attorneys generally are not liable for legal actions taken pursuant to the representation. Only when the lawyer exceeds the authority granted by the client or fails to disclose his or her representative status, are lawyers usually subjected to personal liability.

Liability to non-clients for negligence is rare, although increasing. In a majority of states, plaintiffs must show that they were in privity of contract with the lawyer. The harshness of this rule is illustrated by those cases that refuse to recognize a claim by intended beneficiaries attempting to sue an attorney after the decedent's death for failure to draft the will in accord with a decedent's wishes. Some states allow suit where the plaintiffs can show that they were the intended beneficiaries of the legal services obtained by the client.[44]

California has replaced the privity of contract requirement with a six-factor test that considers: 1) the extent to which the transaction was intended to affect the plaintiff; 2) the foreseeability of the harm to the plaintiff; 3) the degree of certainty that the plaintiff suffered injury; 4) the closeness of the connection between the defendant's conduct and the injury; 5) the policy of preventing future harm; and 6) whether recognition of liability under the circumstances would impose an undue burden on the profession.[45]

Courts' reluctance to allow claims by non-clients can best be explained by considering the consequences that potential liability would create. Courts fear that lawyers would compromise clients' interests in

---

[44] See, e.g., Stowe v. Smith, 184 Conn. 194, 441 A.2d 81 (1981); Needham v. Hamilton, 459 A.2d 1060 (D.C. 1983).

[45] Lucas v. Hamm, 56 Cal. 2d 583, 364 P.2d 685, 15 Cal. Rptr. 821 (1961).

order to avoid potential liability to adversaries or others. Conflicting demands of clients and non-clients would result in lawyers balancing the interests of each and second guessing client decisions in a way that is inconsistent with the traditional understanding of the lawyer as zealous advocate.

The Scope section at the beginning of the Model Rules states, "Violation of a [Model] Rule should not itself give rise to a cause of action against a lawyer nor should it create any presumption in such a case that a legal duty has been breached. ...Nevertheless, since the Rules do establish standards of conduct by lawyers, a lawyers violation of a Rule may be evidence of breach of the applicable standard of conduct." Yet, the general rule of tort law is that violation of a statute can give rise to negligence per se–not merely evidence of negligence, but negligence as a matter of law. Why not treat the Model Rules in the same way? Legislation is adopted by the legislature, but the legal profession's rules are adopted by the state supreme court. In a torts suit, should not rules of the state supreme court have the same standing as legislation?

Sanctions by Courts and Regulatory Bodies

The courts and administrative agencies before which a lawyer practices may also punish lawyer misconduct. Rules 11, 26, and 37 of the Federal Rules of Civil Procedure, and their state corollaries, acknowledge the power of courts to punish lawyers that engage in misconduct before them. In addition to powers provided in civil procedure codes, courts have contempt powers to ensure the orderly presentation of evidence and argument.

A few agencies of the federal government have established rules of conduct that vary from the state disciplinary rules. For example, assertions of confidentiality will not protect securities lawyers from sanctions by the Securities and Exchange Commission if they have omitted relevant information received during the preparation of a public stock offering. Similarly, several large firms paid millions of dollars to settle claims by the Resolution Trust Corporation ("RTC") that the lawyers and their firms had failed to be candid with regulators of failed savings and loans. Part of the claims by the RTC involved allegations that the lawyers had violated rules of professional conduct.

Loss of Fees

In addition to the other sanctions that might be imposed on a lawyer, a court may deny all or part of the fees of a lawyer who has engaged in a "clear and serious violation" of a duty to the client. Restatement § 37 states:

> "Considerations relevant to the question of forfeiture include the gravity and timing of the violation, its willfulness, its effect on the value of the lawyer's work for the client, any other threatened or actual harm to the client, and the adequacy of other remedies."

Is it appropriate for a court to impose this sanction where, in spite of the lawyer's breach of duty, the lawyer has performed valuable services for the client?

Chapter Two

THE LAWYER-CLIENT RELATIONSHIP

A. Establishing the Lawyer-Client Relationship

Read Model Rules 1.2 (b) and 1.16 (a)[1]

Monroe Freedman, "Must You Be The Devil's Advocate?"
Legal Times 19 (August 23, 1993), *correction appended,* September 6, 1993

Item. A lawyer at New York's Sullivan & Cromwell recently turned down a court appointment to represent Mahmoud Abou-Halima, who is charged with involvement in the car-bombing of the World Trade Center. A Sullivan & Cromwell partner explained to *The Wall Street Journal* that the firm did not want to dedicate its resources to the case, because the bombing was "such a heinous crime" and because the defendant is "so personally objectionable." The partner added that Abou-Halima is "anti-Semitic in the most dangerous way." And the firm was also concerned about adverse reactions from some of its current clients.

Item. Michael Tigar, a professor at Texas Law School, recently argued in a federal appeals court that John Demjanjuk should be allowed to return to the United States when he leaves Israel. The Israeli Supreme Court has reversed Demjanjuk's conviction for participating in the mass murder of Jews in the gas chambers of Treblinka. The court was won over by compelling evidence that Demjanjuk has an alibi. Because he had been engaged in the mass murder of Jews at other Nazi camps, Demjanjuk couldn't possibly have been a guard at Treblinka.

---

[1] MR 1.2(b) has no comparable provision in either the Model Code or the Cal. Rules. For MR 1.16(a), *cf.* DR 2-103(E), 2-109(A), 2-110(B), 2-110(C); EC 2-26, 2-29, 2-30; Cal. Rules 3-700(B)-(C).

Was Sullivan & Cromwell right to refuse to defend Abou-Halima? Was Tigar right to represent Demjanjuk? And what do the rules of ethics say about it?

Before answering those questions, we should recall the ethical obligations that a lawyer assumes by agreeing to represent a client. Under the traditional view, a lawyer is bound to represent a client zealously, using all reasonable means to achieve the client's lawful objectives.* * *

* * *

Thus, a lawyer's decision to represent a client may commit that lawyer to zealously furthering the interests of one whom the lawyer or others in the community believe to be morally repugnant. For that reason, the question of whether to represent a particular client can present the lawyer with an important moral decision—a decision for which the lawyer can properly be held morally accountable, in the sense of being under a burden of public justification.

Free to Choose

That would not be so if each lawyer were ethically bound to represent every client seeking the lawyer's services. If there were no choice, there would be no responsibility. Under both rule and practice, however, lawyers have always been free to choose whether to represent particular clients. Ethical Consideration 2-27 of the ABA Model Code does urge lawyers not to decline representation because a client or a cause is unpopular, but EC 2-26 says flatly that a lawyer has "no obligation" to take on every person who wants to become her client. And the comment to Rule 6.2 of the ABA Model Rules of Professional Conduct says similarly that a lawyer ordinarily is "not obliged to accept a client whose character or cause the lawyer regards as repugnant."

Thus, Sullivan & Cromwell violated no ethical rule in declining to defend Mahmoud Abou-Halima. Indeed, on the facts as reported, the firm would have acted unethically if it had taken the case. Under Disciplinary Rule 5-101 of the ABA Model Code, which is controlling in New York, a lawyer has a conflict of interest if the exercise of her professional judgment on behalf of her client "reasonably may be affected" by her own personal or business interests. [Cf. MR 1.7(b)].

And that is precisely the position of the lawyers at Sullivan & Crowell who find the potential client so personally objectionable that they don't think the partnership should put its resources into the case, who find the crime so heinous that they don't want to be associated with its defense, and who are worried about how other clients and potential clients will view the representation.   Certainly those powerful concerns may reasonably be expected to affect the zeal with which those lawyers would represent that client.

What then about Michael Tigar's representation of John Demjanjuk?

I said earlier that a lawyer's decision to represent a client is a decision for which the lawyer is morally accountable. But I must confess that this has not always been my position. At one time I argued that it is wrong to criticize a lawyer for choosing to represent a particular client or cause. If lawyers were to be vilified for accepting unpopular clients or causes, I said, then those individuals who are most in need of representation might find it impossible to obtain counsel.

But I was mistaken. Lawyers have always been vilified for taking unpopular cases, even by other lawyers and judges, and lawyers have nevertheless been found to represent the most heinous of clients. * * *

Persuasive Debate

What ultimately changed my mind on the issue of moral accountability was a debate I participated in about 25 years ago. It was sparked by the picketing of D.C.'s Wilmer, Cutler, & Pickering by a group of law students led by Ralph Nader. The demonstrators were protesting the firm's representation of General Motors in an air-pollution case. I took the position that the protesters were wrong to criticize a firm for its choice of clients.

My opponent argued that it was entirely proper for the demonstrators to challenge lawyers at the firm to ask themselves: "Is this really the kind of client to which I want to dedicate my training, my knowledge, and my skills as a lawyer? Did I go to law school to help a client that harms other human beings by polluting the atmosphere with poisonous gases?"

Although I didn't realize it for some time, my opponent won the debate in the most decisive way—by converting me to his position. The issue is not whether General Motors should be represented. Of course they should, and there will always be someone who will do it. The real issue for each of us is: Should I be the one to represent this client, and if so, why?

And so I now ask my victorious opponent in that long-ago debate: Mike Tigar, is John Demjanjuk the kind of client to whom you want to dedicate your training, your knowledge, and your extraordinary skills as a lawyer? Did you go to law school to help a client who has committed mass murder of other human beings with poisonous gases? Of course, someone should, and will, represent him. But why you, old friend?

Michael E. Tigar, "Setting The Record Straight On The Defense Of John Demjanjuk"
Legal Times 22 (September 6, 1993)

All of Monroe Freedman's statements about me in this newspaper are wrong, except two: We are—or were—old friends. And I do represent John Demjanjuk.

* * *

Freedman is wrong about what the Israeli Supreme Court did once it found doubt that Demjanjuk was Ivan. That court did not, as Freedman asserts, hold that Demjanjuk was guilty of other crimes. The Israeli court did consider whether Demjanjuk should be convicted as having served at other Nazi death camps, but found that Demjanjuk never had a fair opportunity to rebut evidence of service at other camps.

In 1981, a U.S. district judge found that Demjanjuk should be denaturalized. The judge found that Demjanjuk was Ivan the Terrible, a decision that is now universally conceded to have been wrong. There is powerful evidence that government lawyers suppressed evidence that would have shown that decision to have been wrong when made.

* * *

We must remember the Holocaust, and we should pursue and punish its perpetrators. We dishonor that memory and besmirch the pursuit if we fail to accord those accused of Holocaust crimes the same measure of legality and due process that we would give to anyone accused of wrongdoing. Precisely because a charge of culpable participation in the Holocaust is so damning, the method of judging whether such a charge is true should be above reproach.

Standing Up

So much for the factual difficulties in which Professor Freedman finds himself. Let us turn to his analysis of the ethical issues.

Professor Freedman begins by lauding a major law firm for refusing a court appointment to represent an unpopular indigent defendant. The firm doesn't like the client, doesn't like the fact that he is accused of a "heinous crime," and is afraid that its other clients will object. OK, says Freedman, those are good reasons for the law firm to refuse.

Let us all hurry to the library, and rewrite *To Kill a Mocking-bird*. Atticus Finch is not a hero after all. He should have thought more of maintaining his law practice and refused to represent someone charged with a heinous—and possibly racially motivated crime. * * *

Maybe Sullivan & Cromwell has the right to refuse a court appointment, and maybe it should have that right. I have represented plenty of unpopular folks in my 25 years at the bar and have always stood up to the task of telling my paying clients that they just have to understand a lawyer's responsibility in such matters, or they should take their business elsewhere.

One Man's Conscience

From praise of Sullivan & Cromwell, Professor Freedman then makes a giant leap. He invents a new rule of legal ethics. Based on the supposed right to refuse a court appointment, we are told that every lawyer must bear "a burden of public justification" for representing someone accused of odious crimes. There is no rule of professional responsibility that so provides, and several rules cut directly against his assertions.

If Atticus Finch decides to represent an indigent defendant, Freedman will require him not only to incur the obloquy of his friends and clients, but to undertake a public defense of his ethical right to accept the case.

To put lawyers under such a burden of public justification undermines the right to representation of unpopular defendants. It invites the kind of demagoguery that we are now seeing in the attacks on lawyers for defendants in capital cases. It even invites the kinds of unwarranted attacks on zealous advocacy that have often been directed—and quite unjustly—at Professor Freedman.

I undertook the *pro bono* representation of John Demjanjuk in the 6th Circuit after a thorough review of the facts and law. I can no more be under a duty to make a public accounting of why I took this case than I can be under a duty to open up the files of all my cases to public view.

An Insulting Question

Professor Freedman does not end matters by inventing a pernicious rule. He also claims to remember what he calls a "debate" of 25 years ago. We did, in fact, meet on a stage at the George Washington University law school some 23 years ago. I did not make the statement he attributes to me.

I did say then, and still believe, that lawyers have a responsibility to their own conscience for the kinds of clients they choose to represent and the positions they choose to advance. The lawyers who have upheld that principle, from Sir Thomas More to Lord Brougham to Clarence Darrow, are rightly celebrated.

Having misquoted me, Freedman (who is still at this point in his diatribe calling me his "friend") wonders why I would choose to use my talent for John Demjanjuk, instead of letting some other lawyer do it. I am not sure what alternative scenario he sees being played out here. Maybe he thinks I should represent some of Sullivan & Cromwell's clients instead.

I have answered that question for myself, and it is insulting for Professor Freedman to suggest that I am faithless to my principles. When the most powerful country on earth gangs up on an individual citizen, falsely accuses him of being the most heinous mass murderer of the Holocaust, and systematically withholds evidence that would prove him guiltless of that charge, there is something dramatically wrong. When that man is held in the most degrading conditions in a death cell based on those false accusations, the wrong is intensified. When the government that did wrong denies all accountability, the judicial branch should provide a remedy. I have spent a good many years of my professional life litigating such issues. I am proud to be doing so again.

Monroe Freedman, "The Morality Of Lawyering"
Legal Times (September 20, 1993)

* * *

My question [(Why you?) to Michael] Tigar relates to one of the most fundamental issues of lawyers' ethics and the nature of the lawyer's role. That issue is frequently posed by asking whether one can be a good person and a good lawyer at the same time. Or whether the lawyer forfeits her conscience when she represents a client. Or whether the lawyer is nothing more than a hired gun. * * *

* * *

A Judgment of One's Own

Some of the responses to my column suggest that a lawyer can't "know" that a potential client or cause is morally repugnant until there has been a trial by jury that has determined guilt or innocence. But this confuses a legal adjudication of guilt with the lawyer's personal decision about what is true or false and what is right or wrong based upon the available evidence.

And we make that kind of personal decision all the time. For example, if you have expressed your opinion that either Clarence Thomas or Anita Hill was telling the truth, you have necessarily condemned the other as a perjurer even though that person has not had the benefit of trial by jury.

As to Demjanjuk, there is more than enough basis to convince me, for purposes of a personal decision, that he is guilty of participating in genocide. The Israeli Supreme Court, with honesty and courage, did indeed reverse his conviction on charges that he was "Ivan the Terrible" of Treblinka. But the court's further conclusion cannot be ignored, as Demjanjuk's supporters would have us do. The court also found an accumulation of "clear and unequivocal evidence" that, while Demjanjuk was not Ivan of Treblinka, he was the Ivan who voluntarily participated in genocide at Sobibor and other Nazi death camps.

Specifically, the court concluded that Demjanjuk "volunteered to serve in the S.S." in the *Wachmanner* unit—a unit "devised to establish and operate the Extermination Camps in Sobibor, Lodz and Treblinka" in order to achieve the genocidal Final Solution. * * *

In short, while reversing Demjanjuk's conviction of one loathsome crime, the Israeli Supreme Court condemned him for committing a similar one. Because that was not the specific charge that Demjanjuk had been extradited and tried on, however, the court properly reversed his conviction.

But assurance that Demjanjuk is guilty of a heinous crime does not mean that no lawyer could conscientiously represent him. People who do things that are morally repugnant can have causes that are morally justifiable. That is one significance of the decision of the Israeli Supreme Court. And so it was not merely a rhetorical question when I asked Michael Tigar: Why are you now representing John Demjanjuk, in his effort to re-enter the United States? Why does that cause deserve your extraordinary talents?

* * *

A Moral Defense

It is no surprise that Tigar, in response to my question, has come through with a powerful, persuasive explanation—a moral explanation—of his decision to represent John Demjanjuk. [C]

First, he notes that the memory of the Holocaust should not be dishonored by denying even its perpetrators the fullest measure of legality. One lesson of the Holocaust is that the vast powers of government must constantly be subjected to the most exacting scrutiny in order to guard against their abuse.

Further, Tigar refers to "powerful evidence" that lawyers in the Department of Justice suppressed evidence that would have shown that Demjanjuk should not have been extradited on charges of being Ivan the Terrible. (Note that these government lawyers have not been found guilty after trial by jury, but that Tigar nevertheless—and properly—finds enough evidence of their guilt to justify his personal moral decision.) This kind of corruption of justice is an intolerable threat to American ideals, regardless of one's opinion of the accused.

And Tigar concludes: "When the government that did wrong denies all accountability, the judicial branch should provide a remedy. I have spent a good many years of my professional life litigating such issues. I am proud to be doing so again."

Thus, Tigar's moral response to my question illuminates a crucial issue of enormous public importance about what lawyers do and why they do it. And it illustrates why I am proud to call Mike Tigar my friend.

Notes

1.   In his first article Professor Freedman gives three reasons the lawyers at Sullivan & Cromwell declined representation of Mahmoud Abou-Halima:

> [They] find the potential client so personally objectionable that they don't think the partnership should put its resources into the case, [they] find the crime so heinous that they don't want to be associated with its defense, and [they] are worried about how other clients and potential clients will view the representation.

Are each of these reasons to reject a potential client valid morally? Does it matter whether the person is seeking representation in a criminal or civil matter? Does it matter whether the potential client has access to equally talented lawyers? Would these reasons justify refusing to accept a court appointment? *See* MRs 6.2. and 1.2(b).

2.   Professor Tigar responds that "[Professor Freedman] invents a new rule of legal ethics. Based on the supposed right to refuse a court appointment, we are told that every lawyer must bear a 'burden of public justification' for representing someone accused of odious crimes." Professor Tigar then rightly points out that no such rule exists in any code governing lawyers' conduct. How would such a rule affect the representation? Confidentiality? Client perception of loyalty?

3.   Professor Freedman concludes "that Tigar, in response to my question, has come through with a powerful, persuasive explanation—a moral explanation—of his decision to represent John Demjanjuk." Do you agree? Would members of your family who are not lawyers agree?

4.   Freedman's criticism did not slow Tigar down. He represented Terry Nichols, one of the defendants in the Oklahoma City federal building bombing.

Helen Thompson, "Freedom Fighter:
Galveston Lawyer Anthony Griffin is Committed to
Protecting the First Amendment
Even if it Means Defending the Ku Klux Klan"
Texas Monthly (March 1, 1995)

It is an unreasonably steamy Wednesday in December at Anthony Griffin's Galveston law office, and as usual, lunch is on the house. The catered affair is Griffin's weekly gift to his ten-person staff and any clients or visitors who happen to be around. In an airy room of the two-story, International-style building, amid imposing museum chairs and modern art, they gather at two glass tables set with silverware and china and devour poached salmon and the issues of the day. Griffin, who is forty, sits at one end of a table, but he seldom joins in the camaraderie; instead, he eats alone, using the time to read memos and magazines. Under ordinary circumstances, the lanky, tastefully attired attorney might participate in his colleagues' chitchat. But his life is hardly ordinary these days. His very private disposition reflects the stress of two difficult years in the swirl of a very public controversy.

The facts of the controversy are these: In May 1993 Griffin—who is black—was asked by the Texas affiliate of the American Civil Liberties Union (ACLU) to represent the Ku Klux Klan in a case that originated in Vidor, a predominantly white East Texas town with a decades-old reputation for virulent racism. The Klan had marched near a housing project that had recently been integrated with Vidor's only African Americans, and crosses were burned nearby. Subsequently, the Texas Commission on Human Rights filed suit to force the Klan to release its membership list so its members could be questioned about their involvement in those acts. Griffin, who specializes in constitutional law, immediately recognized the suit as an infringement on the Klan's First Amendment rights and accepted the case. "It took me about twenty seconds to make my decision," he says. There was just one problem: At the time, Griffin was the pro bono general counsel for the Texas chapter of the National Association for the Advancement of Colored People (NAACP).

In the months that followed, as he first lost the case in state court and then won on appeal in the Texas Supreme Court, Griffin's life turned upside down. Outraged officials of the NAACP severed ties to him. Blacks in Texas and across the country labeled him a traitor:

callers to one Chicago radio show suggested that he should be "lynched." White conservative talk-radio hosts cackled at the notion of a black man representing white separatists. The Klan, whose politics were repugnant to Griffin, embraced him as an ally. And he suddenly attracted the attention of more than thirty movie and TV producers, who inquired about the rights to his story— though he was not impressed. "A few months ago, I met with Robert De Niro's screenwriter, a guy with a long ponytail, in New York," he says. "He asked me if I stayed up at night losing sleep over my decision." Griffin bristles at the idea that he might regret sticking to principle. "No one ever has to worry that I lose sleep over making the right decision," he says.

Griffin hasn't yet decided whether to do business with Holly-wood, but for now his attentions are focused elsewhere. He recently finished writing a book that presents his version of the conflict with the NAACP, and he has been lecturing and appearing on radio talk shows almost nonstop since the whole fracas began. Yet his time has been so stretched, he says, that he lost out on nearly $300,000 in billable hours because he had little time to practice law last year. "Only now has my court calendar returned to some kind of nor-malcy," he notes. Of course, normal isn't really normal: One of the cases he is currently working on has him representing the Klan again. It centers on an attempt by the U.S. Department of Justice and the Texas Department of Transportation to block the Klan's "adoption" of the highway next to the Vidor housing project. The Justice Department argues that allowing the adoption would be tantamount to permitting the Klan to threaten black residents of the project—a violation of the Fair Housing Act.

At first glance, little in Anthony Griffin's background or career suggests he would arrive at this paradoxical point. He was born in Dallas in 1954 and spent his childhood in Fort Worth, where his father, Leon, was a waiter and his mother, Georgia, was a seamstress. He and his six siblings were generally happy, but an ominous backdrop to their family life was Leon's dissatisfaction with his work. "My father wanted to go to law school," Griffin says, "but it was the fifties, and opportunities for blacks were limited." One day, Leon quit his job and never went back. "He said he couldn't take it anymore—he became defeated by the system, and he gave up." Anthony remem-bers that his father once said, "I'll never work for a white man again, and a black man can't afford me." Leon withdrew from the family, and when Anthony was seven he and Georgia divorced; two years later she and the children moved to McNair, 25 miles east of Houston.

Anthony finished high school there in three years, raced through the University of Houston in another three years, and in 1978 graduated from the University of Houston Law Center, where he was president of the Black Law Students Association. He won his first case right after he finished law school: He represented his mother in an equal pay for equal work suit against her then-employer, J.C. Penney. Some of the work Griffin has done since has riled Galveston's largely white establishment, such as his 1992 championing of single-member election districts, which increased the likelihood that blacks would win office. But within the legal profession, his spirited defense of the First Amendment and other constitutional protections has received high marks, earning him awards from the ACLU, the Texas Freedom of Information Foundation, and the Thomas Jefferson Center for Protection of Free Expression.

In 1992 Griffin was also awarded the NAACP's Peace and Role Model Award, and soon after, Texas NAACP president Gary Bledsoe asked him to become the state chapter's general counsel. Griffin happily accepted. "It was clear to me that the invitation was one I could not refuse," he says. The NAACP's history of forging gains in this century's civil rights battles appealed to his racial pride and his idealism. And he liked the conviviality of the meetings, which he had attended in the past as a member.

In his new role as general counsel, however, Griffin saw the organization in a different light. At that time, the NAACP was just beginning to grapple with the Klan's activities in Vidor. William Hale, the executive director of the Texas Commission on Human Rights, asked the NAACP to file a friend-of-the-court brief in support of his attempt to get the Klan's membership list. Griffin viewed the commission's list challenge as unconstitutional—and also ironic, because in a 1958 U.S. Supreme Court case the NAACP successfully rebuffed an attempt by the State of Alabama to get its membership list, a landmark civil rights decision that assured a group's right to privacy. Now it was 35 years later, and the proverbial shoe was on the other foot.

Griffin had a sense of foreboding, a feeling that proved correct the following May, when he received a telephone call from Jay

Jacobson, the new executive director of the ACLU's Texas affiliate. Jacobson had just moved to Texas and had never met Griffin—he didn't even know he was black—but ACLU members knew him by reputation. If anyone could defend the Klan's First Amendment rights, they thought, it was Anthony Griffin. When Jacobson phoned to offer the case, Griffin considered the request strictly in legal terms: "I told him it would be an honor."

Gary Bledsoe didn't see it that way. He angrily accused Griffin of a conflict of interest in representing both the NAACP and the Klan. Griffin thought the argument was inherently flawed, not to mention inconsistent: During the same period, he was also defending a murderer on death row who was a member of the Aryan Brotherhood. "No one ever complained about that," he says. Still, the controversy unleashed a raw animosity and anguish that hearkened back to 1977, when the ACLU had defended the American Nazi party's right to march in Skokie, Illinois. Back then, thousands of ACLU members resigned in protest. This time the reaction came from the ACLU's opposition, the NAACP. Black preachers spoke out against Griffin, calling him a disgrace to the organization and to the black community. A petition signed by a North Texas branch of the NAACP called for Griffin's immediate expulsion from the organization. Grover Hankins, a former general counsel for the nationwide NAACP, argued that the constitutional standard set forth in the 1958 Alabama case does not apply to the Klan.

Most members of the KKK, by contrast, did not object to the hiring of a black lawyer. "We talked about it, and we agreed it was in our best interest," says Michael Barnes, the Titan of the Realm of Texas, Knights of the KKK. "There were some who thought it might be a bad idea and then saw it wasn't getting us bad press." The NAACP's repudiation of Griffin inadvertently played into the hands of the "new" Klan, which has subtly shifted away from overt white supremacy under the leadership of Grand Dragon Michael Lowe, whose avowed goal is to make the Texas Knights the nation's largest Klan chapter. "We aren't white supremacists," he says, drawing a fine distinction. "We are segregationists." Ostensibly, federal officials, not blacks, are now the Klan's target. "It's not the color of people's skin that we are talking about," says Barnes. "It's the government forcing the races together that we don't want."

From a public relations standpoint, NAACP officials felt they had no choice but to let Griffin go. And anyway, as Griffin's client, it was their prerogative, insists Wayne Johnson, a Galveston county commissioner who serves on the NAACP state board. Certainly the group's rank and file didn't understand, much less sympathize with, the legal content of Griffin's decision. Indeed, Griffin believes that the organization's leaders caved in because they feared a revolt by the members. "If there had been bold national and state leadership, the members would have stayed," he says. Whatever the case, Griffin was terminated. Bledsoe says that he told Griffin he might have to step down because of the conflict of interest and that he asked the NAACP's national office for further guidance in the matter. (In an odd coincidence, Bledsoe himself would soon be accused of a conflict of interest because he was an assistant state attorney general at the same time he served as president of the NAACP.) The national office recommended that Griffin be removed, and officers of the state chapter made the final decision.

Clearly, the Klan is happy with Griffin's performance thus far and has every reason to be. In fact, the Klan is the only obvious winner in the debacle. The NAACP has indisputably been a loser: Both its image and its legal position have suffered setbacks. Bledsoe grimly admits that the entire matter brought nothing but bad publicity to the NAACP in 1994. The year was, as a result, one of the worst in the state chapter's history; whether it can recover remains to be seen. Meanwhile, it is left without an advocate of Anthony Griffin's caliber, and its biggest opponent, the Ku Klux Klan, now enjoys the services of one of the state's best First Amendment lawyers.

And what of Griffin? He is resuming his busy law practice—slowly. Through it all, he says, he has never had second thoughts about the decision that brought him so much grief. "My experience as a black man growing up in America taught me one thing—I'm always suspect," he says. "I'm the person folks usually try to shut up, so I know how that feels. I'd rather protect my own and everyone else's rights to free speech than worry about a bunch of boys walking around in sheets."

Notes

1. Is the NAACP's response to Anthony Griffin's decision to represent the Ku Klux Klan evidence of an informal rule requiring

lawyers to offer public justification for their acceptance of unpopular cases? What public justification did Anthony Griffin offer for his representation of the Ku Klux Klan? How would Monroe Freedman be likely to react to his justification?

2.   Assuming that a lawyer is qualified, has sufficient time, and that the client can pay, should a lawyer be *required* to represent Mahmoud Abou-Halima? Osama Bin Laden? John Demjanjuk? General Motors? Enron? The Ku Klux Klan? Would you represent such clients?

Read Model Rule 1.1 and 1.8[2]

Togstad v. Vesely, Otto, Miller & Keefe
291 N.W.2d 686 (Minn. 1980)

PER CURIAM.

[John Togstad because paralyzed while in the hospital under the care of Dr. Paul Blake.]

* * *

About 14 months after her husband's hospitalization began, plaintiff Joan Togstad met with attorney Jerre Miller regarding her husband's condition. Neither she nor her husband was personally acquainted with Miller or his law firm prior to that time. John Togstad's former work supervisor, Ted Bucholz, made the appointment and accompanied Mrs. Togstad to Miller's office. Bucholz was present when Mrs. Togstad and Miller discussed the case.

Mrs. Togstad had become suspicious of the circumstances surrounding her husband's tragic condition due to the conduct and statements of the hospital nurses shortly after the paralysis occurred. One nurse told Mrs. Togstad that she had checked Mr. Togstad at 2 a.m. and he was fine; that when she returned at 3 a.m., by mistake, to give him someone else's medication, he was unable to move or speak; and that if she hadn't accidentally entered the room no one would have discovered his condition until morning. Mrs. Togstad also noticed that the other nurses were upset and crying, and that Mr. Togstad's condition was a topic of conversation.

---

[2]   For MR 1.1, *Cf.* DR 6-101(A); EC 6-1 to 6-5; Cal. Rules 3-110. MR 1.18 has no comparable provision in either the Model Code or the Cal. Rules.

Mrs. Togstad testified that she told Miller "everything that happened at the hospital," including the nurses' statements and conduct which had raised a question in her mind. She stated that she "believed" she had told Miller "about the procedure and what was undertaken, what was done, and what happened." She brought no records with her. Miller took notes and asked questions during the meeting, which lasted 45 minutes to an hour. At its conclusion, according to Mrs. Togstad, Miller said that "he did not think we had a legal case, however, he was going to discuss this with his partner." She understood that if Miller changed his mind after talking to his partner, he would call her. Mrs. Togstad "gave it" a few days and, since she did not hear from Miller, decided "that they had come to the conclusion that there wasn't a case." No fee arrangements were discussed, no medical authorizations were requested, nor was Mrs. Togstad billed for the interview.

Mrs. Togstad denied that Miller had told her his firm did not have expertise in the medical malpractice field, urged her to see another attorney, or related to her that the statute of limitations for medical malpractice actions was two years. She did not consult another attorney until one year after she talked to Miller. Mrs. Togstad indicated that she did not confer with another attorney earlier because of her reliance on Miller's "legal advice" that they "did not have a case."

On cross-examination, Mrs. Togstad was asked whether she went to Miller's office "to see if he would take the case of [her] husband. * * *" She replied, "Well, I guess it was to go for legal advice, what to do, where shall we go from here? That is what we went for." Again in response to defense counsel's questions, Mrs. Togstad testified as follows:

Q: And it was clear to you, was it not, that what was taking place was a preliminary discussion between a prospective client and lawyer as to whether or not they wanted to enter into an attorney-client relationship?

A: I am not sure how to answer that. It was for legal advice as to what to do.

Q: And Mr. Miller was discussing with you your problem and indicating whether he, as a lawyer, wished to take the case, isn't that true?

A: Yes.

On re-direct examination, Mrs. Togstad acknowledged that when she left Miller's office she understood that she had been given a "qualified, quality legal opinion that [she and her husband] did not have a malpractice case."

Miller's testimony was different in some respects from that of Mrs. Togstad. Like Mrs. Togstad, Miller testified that Mr. Bucholz arranged and was present at the meeting, which lasted about 45 minutes. According to Miller, Mrs. Togstad described the hospital incident, including the conduct of the nurses. He asked her questions, to which she responded. Miller testified that "[t]he only thing I told her [Mrs. Togstad] after we had pretty much finished the conversation was that there was nothing related in her factual circumstances that told me that she had a case that our firm would be interested in undertaking."

Miller also claimed he related to Mrs. Togstad "that because of the grievous nature of the injuries sustained by her husband, that this was only my opinion and she was encouraged to ask another attorney if she wished for another opinion" and "she ought to do so promptly." He testified that he informed Mrs. Togstad that his firm "was not engaged as experts" in the area of medical malpractice, and that they associated with the Charles Hvass firm in cases of that nature. Miller stated that at the end of the conference he told Mrs. Togstad that he would consult with Charles Hvass and if Hvass's opinion differed from his, Miller would so inform her. Miller recollected that he called Hvass a "couple days" later and discussed the case with him. It was Miller's impression that Hvass thought there was no liability for malpractice in the case. Consequently, Miller did not communicate with Mrs. Togstad further.

* * *

This case was submitted to the jury by way of a special verdict form. The jury found that Dr. Blake and the hospital were negligent and that Dr. Blake's negligence (but not the hospital's) was a direct cause of the injuries sustained by John Togstad; that there was an attorney-client contractual relationship between Mrs. Togstad and Miller; that Miller was negligent in rendering advice regarding the possible claims of Mr. and Mrs. Togstad; that, but for Miller's negligence, plaintiffs would have been successful in the prosecution of a legal action against Dr. Blake; and that neither Mr. nor Mrs. Togstad was negligent in pursuing their claims against Dr. Blake. The jury awarded damages to Mr. Togstad of $610,500 and to Mrs. Togstad of $39,000.

* * *

In a legal malpractice action of the type involved here, four elements must be shown: (1) that an attorney-client relationship existed; (2) that defendant acted negligently or in breach of contract; (3) that such acts were the proximate cause of the plaintiffs' damages; (4) that but for defendant's conduct the plaintiffs would have been successful in the prosecution of their medical malpractice claim. [C].

* * *

We believe it is unnecessary to decide whether a tort or contract theory is preferable for resolving the attorney-client relationship question raised by this appeal. The tort and contract analyses are very similar in a case such as the instant one,[3] and we conclude that under either theory the evidence shows that a lawyer-client relationship is present here. The thrust of Mrs. Togstad's testimony is that she went to Miller for legal advice, was told there wasn't a case, and relied upon this advice in failing to pursue the claim for medical malpractice. In addition, according to Mrs. Togstad, Miller did not qualify his legal opinion by urging her to seek advice from another attorney, nor did Miller inform her that he lacked expertise in the medical malpractice area. Assuming this testimony is true, as this court must do, [C] we believe a jury could properly find that Mrs. Togstad sought and received legal advice from Miller under circumstances which made it reasonably foreseeable to Miller that Mrs. Togstad would be injured if the advice were negligently given. Thus, under either a tort or contract analysis, there is sufficient evidence in the record to support the existence of an attorney-client relationship.

* * *

---

[3]   [Court's note 4] Under a negligence approach it must essentially be shown that defendant rendered legal advice (not necessarily at someone's request) under circumstances which made it reasonably foreseeable to the attorney that if such advice was rendered negligently, the individual receiving the advice might be injured thereby. [C]. Or, stated another way, under a tort theory, "[a]n attorney-client relationship is created whenever an individual seeks and receives legal advice from an attorney in circumstances in which a reasonable person would rely on such advice." [C]. A contract analysis requires the rendering of legal advice pursuant to another's request and the reliance factor, in this case, where the advice was not paid for, need be shown in the form of promissory estoppel. [Cc].

Notes

1.   Should Miller be subject to liability when he charged and was paid nothing for the conference?

2.   Assume that you are a lawyer. At a party, you meet someone and he learns that you are a lawyer. He says, "Oh, so you're a lawyer. The other day, I was . . . Do I have a case?" What is your response? Of course, you have been receiving such questions since your first day in law school. Have you tried to answer them? *See also* MR 5.5 (unauthorized practice of law).

3.   *Togstad* is a legal malpractice case. Note, as suggested in the prior chapter, that plaintiff had to show not only that there was an attorney-client relationship and that the attorney acted negligently, but that the client would have won had the case gone to trial. Togstad had to try (and win) the medical malpractice case within the legal malpractice case.

4.   A lawyer can be disciplined under MR 1.1 for failure to act competently. A lawyer is also subject to malpractice liability for incompetence. Should a lawyer be subject to two sanctions?

B. The Lawyer-Client Relationship

Read Model Rules 1.0(e), 1.2 to 1.4, 1.14, and 2.1[4]

In the following case, the plaintiff is suing her former lawyer on the grounds that without her consent, he pursued arbitration rather than litigation. Arbitration is a private means of dispute resolution. It is generally voluntary. An arbitrator acts much like a judge. There is no jury. Generally, the parties agree that the arbitrator's decision will be binding, though they can agree to non-binding arbitration. The advantages of arbitration are that it is typically quicker, can be arranged at an earlier date, the decision is final, and the parties can choose an arbitrator with expertise in the subject matter that is at issue. The disadvantages are that the parties lose several procedural

---

[4]   There is no counterpart to MR 1.0(e). For MR 1.2, *Cf.* DR 7-102(A)(6)-(7), 2-110(C)(i)(c); EC 7-5, 7-7 to 7-8; Cal. Rule 3-210, 3-510; CAL. BUS. & PROF. CODE § 608 (c). For MR 1.3 *Cf.* DR 6-101(A)(3), 7-101(A)(3); EC 6-4, 7-38; Cal. Rule 3-110(B). For MR 1.4 *Cf.* EC 7-8, 9-2; Cal. Rules 3-500 to -510; Cal. Bus. & Prof. Code § 6068(m). For MR 1.14 *Cf.* EC 7-11 to 7-12; there is no Cal. Rules counterpart. For MR 2.1, *Cf.* EC 7-8; there is no Cal. Rules counterpart. *See also,* DR 5-107(B), Cal. Rule 1-600.

protections, including the rights to a jury trial and the right to an appeal.

Does the arbitration agreement in the following case seem like a reasonable one? Why or why not? Would the attorney have been guilty of malpractice, even if his client had approved of pursuing arbitration?

What decisions should an attorney be able to make for her client? Should the rules require client approval of every decision made during legal representation?

Blanton v. Womancare
38 Cal.3d 396, 696 P.2d 645, 212 Cal.Rptr. 151 (1985)

GRODIN, J.

* * *

On February 17, 1977, plaintiff allegedly suffered a perforated uterus during an abortion performed by a fourth-year medical student at the clinic of defendant Womancare. Plaintiff brought an action for malpractice against the clinic, the student, and the supervising physician. * * *

Wesley Harris was employed by plaintiff as her attorney in the malpractice action * * *. [T]wo days before the case was finally to be tried, Harris requested an agreement from defendants that the case be submitted to arbitration.

An examination of Harris conducted by the trial judge reveals Harris discussed the possibility of arbitration with his client at some point before he approached defendants with his offer to arbitrate. Harris conceded, however, that his client would only consent to arbitration if her right to a trial de novo were preserved. Nevertheless, when on July 28, 1981, Harris obtained a stipulation from defendants that the case be submitted to arbitration, the agreement contained the following provisions:

"1. The captioned case will be taken off the trial calendar and submitted to *binding* arbitration.

"2. Any award rendered to the plaintiff in arbitration shall be limited to a maximum of $15,000.

"3. Daniel S. Belsky, attorney for defendant, Womancare, shall have the right to select the arbitrator pursuant to the following conditions:

"(a) There shall be only one arbitrator.

"(b) The arbitrator shall be an individual reasonably familiar with the law pertaining to medical malpractice.

"(c) Mr. Belsky's right to choose the arbitrator shall be exclusive in the event he chooses an arbitrator whose practice consists primarily of defending medical malpractice actions.

"(d) In the event Mr. Belsky chooses an arbitrator whose practice consists primarily of prosecuting medical malpractice actions, said individual shall also be approved by Mr. Wes Harris." [Emphasis supplied by the Supreme Court].

The stipulation was approved by the court, which issued an order to arbitrate * * *.

Plaintiff did not learn of this stipulation * * * for nearly three months. When apprized that her attorney had submitted her dispute to binding arbitration, she immediately objected, and fired Harris. She then hired new counsel, and through him moved to invalidate the stipulation to binding arbitration executed by Harris * * *.

* * * The trial court, however, affirmed the validity of the agreement for binding arbitration, apparently in the belief the agreement concerned a "procedural" matter within the scope of an attorney's unilateral discretion. After a continuance in the arbitration proceeding was granted to allow new counsel an opportunity to prepare for the hearing, the proceeding was held and the arbitrator ruled for the defense. Plaintiff's new attorney filed a request for trial de novo, but was notified that since the arbitration was binding the request was "not acceptable." Thereafter, the award was entered as a judgment and plaintiff appealed.

* * *

Of course, [a binding arbitration] agreement may often be in the best interests of a client. Here, however, the client did not consent to the agreement; she did nothing beyond retention of the attorney to suggest that he had authority to enter into such an agreement on her behalf; and she repudiated the agreement as soon as she learned of it. The question is whether she is nevertheless bound by her attorney's signature, purportedly on her behalf.

* * *

In our analysis of this question we distinguish at the outset between the rights which a client may have against his attorney for breach of a duty owed the client, and the right which an opposing party or the court may have to rely upon a stipulation or agreement which an attorney has made, purportedly on his client's behalf. The two categories are related, but not necessarily congruent, for a client may be bound by the actions of his attorney and at the same time have a legal claim against him on the ground that those actions were undertaken without or in excess of authority. Here, the question concerns the binding effect of the attorney's agreement.

As a general proposition the attorney-client relationship, insofar as it concerns the authority of the attorney to bind his client by agreement or stipulation, is governed by the principles of agency. [C]. Hence, "the client as principal is bound by the acts of the attorney-agent within the scope of his actual authority (express or implied) or his apparent or ostensible authority; or by unauthorized acts ratified by the client." [Cc].

* * *

An attorney retained to represent a client in litigation is clothed with certain authority by reason of that relationship. "The attorney is authorized by virtue of his employment to bind the client in procedural matters arising during the course of the action.... 'In retaining counsel for the prosecution or defense of a suit, the right to do many acts in respect to the cause is embraced as ancillary, or incidental to the general authority conferred, and among these is included the authority to enter into stipulations and agreements in all matters of procedure during the progress of the trial. Stipulations thus made, so far as they are simply necessary or incidental to the management of the suit, and which affect only the procedure or remedy as distinguished from the cause of action itself, and the essential rights of the client, are binding on the client.'" [Cc].

The authority thus conferred upon an attorney is in part apparent authority--i.e., the authority to do that which attorneys are normally authorized to do in the course of litigation manifested by the client's act of hiring an attorney--and in part actual authority implied in law. Considerations of procedural efficiency require, for example, that in the course of a trial there be but one captain per ship. An attorney must be able to make such tactical decisions as whether to call a particular witness, and the court and opposing counsel must be able to rely upon the decisions he makes, even when the client voices opposition in open court. [C]. In such tactical matters, it may be said that the attorney's authority is implied in law, as a necessary incident to the function he is engaged to perform. [Cc].

An attorney is not authorized, however, merely by virtue of his retention in litigation, to "impair the client's substantial rights or the cause of action itself." [C]. For example, "the law is well settled that an attorney must be specifically authorized to settle and compromise a claim, that merely on the basis of his employment he has no implied or ostensible authority to bind his client to a compromise settlement of pending litigation." [Cc]. Similarly, an attorney may not "stipulate to a matter which would eliminate an essential defense" [citation]. He may not agree to the entry of a default judgment [citation], may not ... stipulate that only nominal damages may be awarded [citation] and he cannot agree to an increase in the amount of the judgment against his client. [Citation.] * * * "Such decisions differ from the routine and tactical decisions which have been called "procedural" both in the degree to which they affect the client's interest, and in the degree to which they involve matters of judgment which extend beyond technical competence so that any client would be expected to share in the making of them.

* * *

It is, of course, accepted practice within the legal profession, and one that is commendable, for attorneys to rely upon representations made by other attorneys with respect to the scope of their authority. As in the case of any other agency, however, apparent authority is created, and its scope defined, by the acts of the principal in placing the agent in such a position that he appears to have the authority which he claims or exercises. If authority is lacking, then nothing the agent does or says can serve to create it. (See Seavey, Agency (1st ed. 1964) Definitions, § 8D, p. 13.)

* * *

[T]he "high plane upon which attorneys customarily place their agreements with each other cannot be allowed to overthrow the well-established principles of the law of agency, where the rights of the clients as between themselves are concerned." [Cc]. * * * [W]hen it comes to such a substantial matter as compromise of an action, "a person dealing with an attorney, as dealing with any agent, must ascertain whether the agent has authority to do the purported act and assumes the risk if in fact the agent has no such authority." [Cc].

* * *

[I]n this case the lack of justifiable reliance is clear.[5] The agreement which plaintiff's attorney entered into, purportedly on his client's behalf, called for binding arbitration which . . . entails a waiver of all but minimal judicial review. It provided for unilateral selection of the arbitrator by the defendant's attorney, from among attorneys whose practice consists primarily in *defending* medical malpractice actions. And, it waived any right to recovery beyond $15,000. By any test, these are consequences which affected substantial rights of the client.

* * *

* * * When a client engages an attorney to litigate in a judicial forum, the client has a right to be consulted, and his consent obtained, before the dispute is shifted to another, and quite different, forum, particularly where the transfer entails the sort of substantial consequences present here.

* * *

The judgment is reversed.

MOSK, KAUS, BROUSSARD, REYNOSO and LUCAS, JJ., concur.

BIRD, Chief Justice, concurring.

* * *

The effective management of litigation requires independent decisions by the attorney regarding not only procedural matters but also certain *substantive* matters--for example, it may include the legal theories or arguments to be advanced. Routine and technical matters, including those ordinary matters which arise in the course of litigation, may be handled independently by the attorney as a necessary aspect of the professional management of the case. On the other

---

[5] [Court's Note 9] One commentator suggests that the traditional subject-matter/procedure test does not adequately explain the cases which address the power of the lawyer to bind his client, and that the cases are better explained on the basis of considerations of prejudice and judicial economy, with the timing of the client's objection being a key consideration. (Spiegel, *Lawyering and Client Decisionmaking: Informed Consent and the Legal Profession,* supra, 128 U.Pa.L.Rev. 41, 54-65). It would appear, indeed, that such equitable considerations have played a role in some of the decisions. (E.g., *Burns v. McCain,* supra, 107 Cal.App. at p. 297, 290 P. 623). In this case, as we observe, *post,* equitable considerations support the plaintiff's position.

hand, decisions which affect "substantial rights," whether they be denominated "procedural" or "substantive," must involve the client.

Rather than define the standard as "substantial rights" versus "procedural matters," the inquiry should seek to differentiate between decisions affecting important, substantial rights and decisions on routine matters. This approach would provide the practitioner with more useful guidance.

* * *

Whatever formulation is used to determine when an attorney has the authority to make decisions on the client's behalf, the decision to waive the fundamental right to a jury trial should rest with the client. By stipulating to binding arbitration, the attorney in this case deprived his client of her right to a jury trial without her knowledge or consent.

* * *

An attorney should explain to the client the strategic considerations that determine whether a jury trial or some other form of dispute resolution should be utilized. The attorney's professional expertise is vital to any decision. However, the ultimate determination to waive a right as fundamental and "substantial" as the right to a jury trial should rest with the client.

Notes

1.   If the court had upheld the arbitration agreement, should the plaintiff's original attorney be subject to malpractice to the plaintiff for failure to allow her to control this choice? If so, what would the damages be? Should plaintiff's attorney be subject to malpractice liability to the plaintiff for other actions that he took in this case? Do you see any problems with the arbitration agreement?

2.   If a deal is set aside as in *Womancare*, because one of the lawyers acts beyond the authority given by his client, should that lawyer be subject to liability to the opposing party? Though a lawyer's duty generally runs only to the client, the Restatement takes the position that this lawyer should be subject to liability to the opposing party. *See* Restatement § 30, citing Restatement (Second), Agency §§ 329, 330.

3.   Much of the current alternative dispute resolution literature suggests that mediation and arbitration generally are cheaper, faster, and less stressful than lawyer negotiation and litigation. Should clients decide whether to pursue arbitration or mediation? Might an attorney who failed to present such an option to a client be subject to liability

under a theory similar to medical malpractice's informed consent theory? *See* Robert F. Cochran, Jr., "Legal Representation and the Next Steps Toward Client Control: Attorney Malpractice for the Failure to Allow the Client to Control Negotiation and Pursue Alternatives to Litigation," 47 *Wash. & Lee L. Rev.* 819 (1990).

4.   Model Rule 1.4 imposes a duty on lawyers to provide clients sufficient information to enable them to "make informed decisions regarding the representation." Does the duty to give information extend to information that may be relevant to the client, but is not of legal significance? *See Baker v. Humphrey*, 101 U.S. 494 at 500 (1879) ("It is the duty of an attorney to advise the client promptly whenever he has any information to give which it is important the client should receive.") Commentary on this issue includes Roger W. Andersen, "Informed Decisionmaking in an Office Practice," 28 *B.C. L. Rev.* 225 (1987) and Susan R. Martyn, "Informed Consent in the Practice of Law," 48 *Geo. Wash. L. Rev.* 307 (1980).

5.   The vast majority of client complaints do not concern the lawyer's knowledge or skills. The vast majority of client complaints are a matter of lawyer procrastination and failure to communicate with clients.

The Holland Case

James Louis Holland, a 47-year-old drifter, was hitch hiking in Utah in 1986. Samuel Frank Patt, age 71, picked Holland up. Holland pulled a gun and ordered Patt to keep driving. Patt tried to grab the gun and Holland shot and killed him. At trial, Holland was convicted of murder and sentenced to death.[6] On appeal, the Utah Supreme Court vacated the death penalty on the grounds that the trial court had not considered the proper criteria and remanded for a new sentencing hearing. According to Holland's attorney, Elliott Levine, Holland wanted the state to impose the death penalty rather than life imprisonment.

> Levine said, Holland believes the prison's ban on smoking would make a life term unbearable.

---

[6]   "Rest Stop Killer's Death Sentence Appealed," *United Press International*, June 7, 1988.

Holland, a heavy smoker, feels "as long as you take that away from him, you might as well take his life away," Levine said.[7]

The Utah Supreme Court described defense attorney Levine's actions on remand as follows:

> At the second penalty hearing, [Levine] introduced no new evidence pertaining to the appropriate punishment. He merely submitted to the trial judge the transcript from the first penalty hearing. He offered no argument either in countering arguable factual propositions urged by the prosecution in support of the death penalty or in arguing that life imprisonment rather than death was the appropriate penalty. The trial judge imposed a death sentence for the second time.[8]

On a second appeal (an automatic appeal from the imposition of the death penalty), the Utah Supreme Court disqualified Levine as Holland's attorney and appointed a new attorney to handle the appeal. On the issue of Holland's desire for the death penalty, the court said:

> We are aware that Holland might prefer the death penalty to a sentence of life imprisonment. Nevertheless, an attorney is not justified in asserting that his client deserves the death penalty, even if his client desires to have that penalty imposed. The statutes governing capital homicide prosecutions provide for a mandatory appeal in all death penalty cases. Those appeals are to assure that all sentences of death are imposed in full and complete compliance with the law. A defendant's wish to be executed does not obviate that requirement and does not constitute a waiver of errors. Concededly, defense counsel is in a difficult position when a defendant wants the death penalty to be imposed. Counsel may then have to inform the court of the client's wish while taking necessary action to ensure compliance with legal requirements. It is simply not permissible for the proceedings on appeal or in the trial court to be *pro forma*.[9]

The court's opinion on this issue prompted the following response from Greg Smith, a Salt Lake City lawyer who represents indigent people:

> Attorneys now face the perplexing question: When should an attorney force her own or the state's will upon a client? Before a lawyer can practice, she must take the lawyers' exam on ethics, known as the

---

[7]   *Id.*

[8]   *State v. Holland*, 876 P.2d 357, 358 (Utah 1994).

[9]   *Id.* at 360-61 n.3. The court also found that Levine violated the duty of loyalty to Holland by arguing for another client in an unrelated case that the other client, unlike Holland, did not deserve to die. *See id.*

Multistate Professional Responsibility Examination. To pass, a lawyer must understand the "duty of loyalty" to clients. Of course, a lawyer cannot break laws for her client, but she must always put the client's interests above her own whenever possible. If she doesn't, she can be sued for malpractice, or be guilty of having a "conflict of interest." Either could lead to disbarment.

* * *

[Remember,] Mr. Holland wanted the death penalty. And his attorney got him exactly what he wanted. Was it Mr. Levine's fault that his client wanted exactly the same sentence that the prosecution also wanted? Where is the rule that an attorney should go along with his client unless the other side wants the same thing as his client? True, a lawyer must provide "competent" counsel for her client. However, for some felons, life in prison is worse than death.

All lawyers have clients whose views differ from their own. According to [Levine's critics], a lawyer's view should trump her client's. [That] implies that clients don't need advocates, they need parents.

* * *

The desires of the client, as long as they are legal, should be of paramount concern to a lawyer. The ultimate decision should invariably rest with the client.[10]

In a concurring opinion in the *Holland* case, Justice Durham was critical of Levine's failure to fight the death penalty at the second penalty hearing. She said:

An effective attorney "must play the role of an active advocate, rather than a mere friend of the court." [C]. Unless an attorney represents the interests of a client with zeal and loyalty, the adversarial system of justice cannot operate.[11]

But for whom should the attorney be "an active advocate"? What are "the interests of the client" and who should identify them? To whom should the attorney show "zeal and loyalty"? When Justice Durham worries that Levine's failure to fight the death penalty will undermine "the adversarial system"—is it Justice Durham who wants the attorney to serve as a "friend of the court"? Is the real justification for the *Holland* decision that there are things that are more important than personal autonomy? What should be the attorney's obligation to the court in such a case? Does society have an interest in insuring that the

---

[10]   Greg Smith, *The Salt Lake Tribune* A5 (January 24, 1994).
[11]   *Holland*, 876 P.2d 357, 362 (Stewart, A.C.J., concurring).

death penalty criteria are met? Does society's interest in limiting the use of the death penalty trump Holland's interest in acquiescing in the death penalty?

———————

Most questions of control of legal representation are not as dramatic as those in the *Holland* case. Assume that you are representing a poor plaintiff in a personal injury action. You estimate that there is a 90 percent chance that she will win a $100,000 verdict. She is afraid of going to trial, both because of the risk that she will lose and because she fears the stress of cross-examination. She has received a $15,000 settlement offer and she is inclined to take it. What do you do? Does it matter whether you are compensated through a contingency fee or an hourly rate?

Consider how the authors of the following two articles would handle the settlement offer problem. How would they handle the *Holland* case?

Richard Wasserstrom, "Lawyers As Professionals: Some Moral Issues"
5 *Human Rights* 1, 15-19, 21 (1975)

[T]he charge that I want to examine here is that the relationship between the lawyer and the client is typically, if not inevitably, a morally defective one in which the client is not treated with the respect and dignity that he or she deserves.

* * *

[To] be a professional is to have been acculturated in a certain way. It is to have satisfactorily passed through a lengthy and allegedly difficult period of study and training. It is to have done something hard. Something that not everyone can do. Almost all professions encourage this way of viewing oneself; as having joined an elect group by virtue of hard work and mastery of the mysteries of the profession. In addition, the society at large treats members of a profession as members of an elite by paying them more than most people for the work they do with their heads rather than their hands, and by according them a substantial amount of social prestige and power by virtue of their membership in a profession. It is hard, I think, if not impossible, for a person to emerge from professional training and participate in a profession without the belief that he or she is a special kind of person, both different from and somewhat better than those nonprofessional members of the social order. It is equally hard for the other members of society not to hold an analogous view of the professionals. And these beliefs surely contribute, too, to the dominant role played by a professional in any professional-client relationship.

* * *

[T]he professional often, if not systematically, interacts with the client in both a manipulative and a paternalistic fashion. The point is not that the professional is merely dominant within the relationship. Rather, it is that from the professional's point of view the client is seen and responded to more like an object than a human being, and more like a child than an adult. The professional does not, in short, treat the client like a person; the professional does not accord the client the respect that he or she deserves. * * *

* * *

[T]he lawyer's conception of self as a person with special competencies in a certain area naturally leads him or her to see the client in a partial way. The lawyer *qua* professional is, of necessity, only centrally interested in that part of the client that lies within his or her special competency. And this leads any professional including the lawyer to respond to the client as an object—as a thing to be altered, corrected, or otherwise assisted by the professional rather than as a person. At best the client is viewed from the perspective of the professional not as a whole person but as a segment or aspect of a person—an interesting kidney problem, a routine marijuana possession case, or another adolescent with an identity crisis.

* * *

Duncan Kennedy, "Distributive and Paternalist Motives in Contract and Tort Law, With Special Reference to Compulsory Terms and Unequal Bargaining Power"
41 *Md. L.Rev.* 563, 638-44, 646 (1982).

* * *

[A]lmost everyone is a principled anti-paternalist, at least by their own account. In this section, I will argue against principled anti-paternalism, and in favor of an ad hoc approach. The basis of such an approach is acceptance of contradictory, or at least unprincipled reactions to particular instances of intervention that overrule people's choices in their own interests. Sometimes these seem not just good interventions, but necessary ones—it would violate a moral duty to neglect them. But sometimes they seem like naked aggression against the human dignity of the supposed beneficiary. To be an ad hoc paternalist is to admit that one has no powerful, overarching test that will allow one anything more than intuitive confidence (either before or after one acts) that one is on the right side of this line. This is not to say that we act at random. Indeed, our first task is to get a sense of what it is like to act paternalistically.

* * *

[T]he actor comes to believe that the other is suffering from some form of false consciousness that will cause him to do something that will hurt him, physically or financially or morally or in some other way. The actor's sense that the other's consciousness is false is an intuition of error—that the clue to what the other is about to do is "having it wrong." The basis of this kind of intuition is one's own experience of being mistaken, and of having other people sense one's mistake.

It is almost never possible to verify the intuition in a positivist sense, and this has great significance. But it is also important that intuitive certainties are real knowledge. To my mind they are more real and more reliable than knowledge of the other built up by formulating and testing hypotheses and models (though that is a form of knowledge, too).

The actor will certainly try hard to persuade the other out of his false consciousness, and sometimes persuasion works. Or it may turn out that it is the other who persuades the actor that the actor was wrong, thereby removing any motive for paternalist action. But sometimes it doesn't happen that way: at the end of the discussion, the actor still feels that the other is mistaken, and is about to do something not in his best interests. Or perhaps there is a limited time or no time at all for persuasion, and the actor has either to act paternalistically right away or not at all.

The actor has to decide whether to act to prevent the injury he sees coming. * * * [However] there are strong reasons for not acting.

The first is that your intuition that they suffer from false consciousness may be wrong. You may be mistaken in just the way you thought they were—it's all backwards, so to speak. This is the relatively "cognitive" version of mistake. The pea was really under the left-hand rather than the right-hand cup, so if you'd let them bet the way they wanted to, we'd all be millionaires now.

Another possibility is that their conduct was based not on the mistake you'd wrongly intuited, but on a larger plan you hadn't understood. They knew all along what you thought they didn't know, but because they had intentions you didn't grasp, their knowledge was perfectly compatible with what they were doing. You thought the developer tricked the condominium buyer into accepting a "sweetheart" contract with a management company. In fact, this contract, which eliminated just about all legal power of the condo owners to meddle in one another's lives, was one of the greatest attractions of this particular development. If you're wrong in one or both of these ways, your intervention will probably make things worse rather than better. If it will make things *much* worse if you're wrong, and only a little better if you're right, maybe intervention is too risky.

There is also the possibility that it would be best for the other to make the mistake and suffer the consequences. It may be a developmentally desirable mistake, with consequences limited enough so the other will survive to do better the next time. It may be more than that—it may be a mistake the other has to make if the other is to survive without the actor's constant paternalistic intervention to bail him out. In every case, the actor has to be aware of the possibility that intervention is breeding more intervention—perpetuating dependence and incompetence just as the apostles of self-reliance are always saying it does. Sometimes the actor must take the chance that the other will destroy himself, in the hopes that if he doesn't he will emerge at a new level of autonomy.

* * * [P]aternalist action, when it works, has a strong positive connotation. Care is something we need; the ability to give care coercively but beneficially is one of the qualities we admire most intensely, whether in parents dealing with young children, in children dealing with aged parents, or in political leaders dealing with the base impulses and misguided beliefs of their constituents. When you feel you have done it right, you will feel fulfillment.

But there is a bad side to it as well, even when it works. The paternalist intervention is aggressive: it involves frustrating the other's project by force (or by fraud, in the case of withholding information in order to control the other's behavior or spare the other pain). Along with frustration, the other is likely to feel rage against unjust treatment. From her point of view, the actor has come along not only with force, but with the self-righteous claim that the force is altruistic so she has no basis for objecting. Paternalist action is inherently risky because it will make someone you are intersubjectively one with furious at you, and they may be right.

* * * While we admire and honor some people in some roles for their successful paternalism, we quite rightly scorn and condemn other people for "playing God," for not minding their own business, for degrading and infantilizing those they are trying to help, and for acting out of selfish motives behind a facade of concern for others.

* * *

* * * The truth of the matter is that what we need when we make decisions affecting the well-being of other people is correct intuition about their needs and an attitude of respect for their autonomy. Nothing else will help. And even intuition and respect may do no good at all. There isn't any guarantee that you'll get it right. * * *

* * *

Notes

1.   Was James Louis Holland "suffering from some form of false consciousness"? Would Professor Kennedy believe that Holland's lawyer would be justified in acting paternalistically and opposing the death penalty? How would Professor Wasserstrom view the actions of Holland's attorney?

2.   Do lawyers come to treat their clients as objects—Karen as the interesting case of vicarious liability, and John as the complex question of bankruptcy homestead? Professor Wasserstrom suggests that lawyers and doctors objectify their clients. Is this inconsistent with the dignity of the individual client? Is it necessary in order to focus on the legal problems of the client?

3.   Professor Kennedy identifies unwarranted paternalism as "naked aggression against the human dignity of the supposed beneficiary." Later he writes "The truth of the matter is that what we need when we make decisions affecting the well-being of other people is correct intuition about their needs and an attitude of respect for their autonomy." Are autonomy and human dignity the same? Is it possible to respect a person's dignity *by* limiting his or her autonomy? Would the following statement by a lawyer be an example of that:

"You are a better person than that, and I will not let you accuse your spouse of child abuse merely to increase your portion of the marital property"?

4.   Model Rule 1.2(a) divides responsibilities between lawyer and client: The client is to control the "objectives" of the representation and the lawyer is to "consult with the client as to the means by which [the objectives] are to be pursued." What result would this yield in *Holland*? In the case of the indigent client that wants to settle for $15,000?

5.   In Jones v. Barnes, 463 U.S. 745, 103 S. Ct. 3308, 77 L. Ed. 2d 987 (1983), the Supreme Court held that the attorney for a criminal defendant can determine what issues to argue on appeal. Obviously, the object of the representation was to reverse the conviction. The tactics were a matter for the attorney to resolve. The court, however, noted that:

> [T]he accused has the ultimate authority to make certain fundamental decisions regarding the case, as to whether to plead guilty, waive a jury, testify in his or her own behalf, or take an appeal, see *Wainwright v. Sykes*, 433 U. S. 72, 93, n. 1 (1977) (BURGER, C. J., concurring); ABA Standards for Criminal Justice 4-5.2, 21-2.2 (2d ed. 1980).

Are these decisions, designated under the Constitution for the criminal defendant, best characterized as "ends" or "means" decisions?

Justices Brennan and Marshall dissented in *Jones*, arguing that, "[t]he role of the defense lawyer should be above all to function as the instrument and defender of the client's autonomy and dignity in all phases of the criminal process." They argued that under the majority's conception of the defense lawyer's role, "[i]n many ways, having a lawyer becomes one of the many indignities visited upon someone who has the ill fortune to run afoul of the criminal justice system." How would Justices Marshall and Brennan be likely to view the attorney's role in *Holland* (the Utah case in which the client wants the death penalty)?

6.   Is the distinction between "objectives" and "means" suggested by Model Rule 1.2(a) and 1.4(a)(2) always clear? David Luban has said:

> [The ends/means rule] assumes a sharp dichotomy between ends and means, according to which a certain result (acquittal, a favorable settlement, *etc.*) is all that the client desires, while the legal tactics and arguments are merely routes to that result. No doubt this is true in many cases, but it need not be: the client may want to win acquittal *by*

asserting a certain right, because it vindicates him in a way that matters to him; or he may wish to obtain a settlement without using a certain tactic, because he disapproves of a tactic. In the end, what the lawyer takes to be mere means are really part of the client's ends.[12]

7.   Are clients likely to get better results if they control the representation or if the lawyer controls the representation? It may be that the questions of competence and client control are closely related. David Rosenthal's study of 59 personal injury cases found that clients who are actively involved in decisions concerning their cases obtain higher recoveries than those that allow their lawyers to unilaterally control the cases. David Rosenthal, *Lawyer And Client: Who's In Charge?* 38-39 (1974). Lawyers may receive more information, work harder, and make fewer mistakes when clients are joint decision-makers.

8.   *Counseling Illegal Conduct*—MR 1.2(d) prohibits a lawyer from assisting a client "in conduct that the lawyer knows is criminal or fraudulent," but permits a lawyer to "discuss the legal consequences of any proposed course of conduct." The difficult question arises when a lawyer is asked a question about the legal consequences of an action, and suspects that the client might use the information in order to violate the law. For a thoughtful discussion of the factors that should be considered when addressing this issue, *see* Stephen L. Pepper, "Counseling at the Limits of the Law: An Exercise in the Jurisprudence and Ethics of Lawyering," 104 *Yale L. J.* 1545 (1995).

9.   In Cogdill v. Commonwealth, 219 Va. 272, 247 S.E.2d 392 (1978), a lawyer violated his state's rule against counseling clients to commit crime:

> On November 16, 1976, Mary Burns, an unmarried 23-year old secretary, approached Cogdill, a 46-year old practicing attorney, for legal advice concerning custody of her illegitimate child. * * * Cogdill . . . began to ask questions about her sex life, "how many guys [she] had ever gone to bed with, how old [she] was the first time", whether she was "liberal with (her) sex", and whether she would "go to bed with a guy for money." He told her that some men gave their women "charge cards to buy what they want" and that "some girls made as much as $300 a night for three or four guys, and [she] could do the same thing." [During the next appointment, Cogdill asked] "how many [men she] could handle in one night," whether she would "do it for . . . drugs, that

---

[12]   David Luban, "Paternalism and the Legal Profession," 1981 *Wis. L. Rev.* 454, 459 n.9.

type of thing"... [Burns] "asked him how people got started" and "[h]e said he would show me around and where to find these people, and he would take care of me." At the end of this conversation, which was recorded with the aid of a transmitter concealed in Burns' purse, it was agreed that Burns would call Cogdill the next day "and he would see what he could set up."

[When Burns called,] Cogdill "said that he thought it would be better if it was just him, to see how I would like it, and get started into it," suggested a fee of $25, and fixed the hour for her to come to his apartment that evening. Burns kept the appointment [and so did the police. They arrested Cogdill.]

Testifying in his own behalf [, Cogdill maintained] that the questions he asked were designed to determine Burns' fitness as a mother. . .

The Supreme Court of Virginia upheld Cogdill's conviction for soliciting prostitution. In a separate action, *Codgill v. First District Committee of the Virginia State Bar*, 221 Va. 376, 269 S.E.2d 391, the Supreme Court upheld Cogdill's disbarment.

Chapter Three

CONFIDENTIALITY AND
THE ATTORNEY-CLIENT PRIVILEGE

Read Model Rule 1.6[1]

At times, the terms "confidentiality" and "the attorney-client privilege" are incorrectly used interchangeably. Though they share the same justifications: encouraging clients to share information with their lawyers and respect for the autonomy of the client, the terms refer to different rules. The duty of confidentiality is a rule of professional responsibility which generally prohibits an attorney from revealing information concerning representation of a client to anyone. The attorney-client privilege is an evidentiary rule under which a client can prevent a lawyer from testifying as to communications of a client. There are significant, somewhat overlapping exceptions to both rules. First, we will explore the duty of confidentiality. We reserve a thorough definition and examination of the attorney-client privilege until the end of this chapter.

Spaulding v. Zimmerman
263 Minn. 346, 116 N.W.2d 704 (1962)

THOMAS GALLAGHER, Justice.

Appeal from an order of the District Court of Douglas County vacating and setting aside a prior order of such court dated May 8, 1957, approving a settlement made on behalf of David Spaulding on March 5, 1957, at which time he was a minor of the age of 20 years.
* * *

The prior action was brought against defendants by Theodore Spaulding, as father and natural guardian of David Spaulding, for injuries sustained by David in an automobile accident, arising out of a collision which occurred August 24, 1956, between an automobile driven by John Zimmerman, in which David was a passenger, and one owned by John Ledermann and driven by Florian Ledermann.

---

[1]   *Cf.* DR 4-101; CAL. BUS. & PROF. CODE § 6068(e) (West 1995).

* * *

* * * [O]n February 22, 1957, at defendant's request, David was examined by Dr. Hewitt Hannah, a neurologist. On February 26, 1957, the latter reported to Messrs. Field, Arveson, & Donoho, attorneys for defendant John Zimmerman, as follows:

> "The one feature of the case which bothers me more than any other part of the case is the fact that this boy of 20 years of age has an aneurysm, which means a dilatation of the aorta and the arch of the aorta. Whether this came out of this accident I cannot say with any degree of certainty and I have discussed it with the Roentgenologist and a couple of Internists. * * * Of course an aneurysm or dilatation of the aorta in a boy of this age is a serious matter as far as his life. This aneurysm may dilate further and it might rupture with further dilatation and this would cause his death.
>
> "It would be interesting also to know whether the X-ray of his lungs, taken immediately following the accident, shows this dilatation or not. If it was not present immediately following the accident and is now present, then we could be sure that it came out of the accident."

* * *

* * * [N]either David nor his father, the nominal plaintiff in the prior action, was then aware that David was suffering the aorta aneurysm but on the contrary believed that he was recovering from the injuries sustained in the accident.

On the following day an agreement for settlement was reached wherein, in consideration of the payment of $6,500, David and his father agreed to settle in full for all claims arising out of the accident.

[The trial court must approve the settlement of the claim of a minor.]

Richard S. Roberts, counsel for David, thereafter presented to the court a petition for approval of the settlement, wherein David's injuries were described as:

> "* * * severe crushing of the chest, with multiple rib fractures, severe cerebral concussion, with petechial hemorrhages of the brain, bilateral fractures of the clavicles."

Attached to the petition were affidavits of David's physicians, Drs. James H. Cain and Paul S. Blake, wherein they set forth the same diagnoses they had made upon completion of their respective examinations of David as above described. At no time was there information disclosed to the court that David was then suffering from an aorta aneurysm which may have been the result of the accident. Based upon the petition for settlement and such affidavits of Drs. Cain and Blake, the court on May 8, 1957, made its order approving the settlement.

Early in 1959, David was required by the army reserve, of which he was a member, to have a physical checkup. For this, he again engaged the services of Dr. Cain. In this checkup, the latter discovered the aorta aneurysm. He then reexamined the X-rays which had been taken shortly after the accident and at this time discovered that they disclosed the beginning of the process which produced the aneurysm. He promptly sent David to Dr. Jerome Grismer for an examination and opinion. The latter confirmed the finding of the aorta aneurysm and recommended immediate surgery therefor. This was performed by him at Mount Sinai Hospital in Minneapolis on March 10, 1959.

Shortly thereafter, David, having attained his majority, instituted the present action for additional damages due to the more serious injuries including the aorta aneurysm which he alleges proximately resulted from the accident. As indicated above, the prior order for settlement was vacated. In a memorandum made a part of the order vacating the settlement, the court stated:

* * *

"The mistake concerning the existence of the aneurysm was not mutual. For reasons which do not appear, plaintiff's doctor failed to ascertain its existence. By reason of the failure of plaintiff's counsel to use available rules of discovery, plaintiff's doctor and all his representatives did not learn that defendants and their agents knew of its existence and possible serious consequences. * * *

"* * *There is no doubt that during the course of the negotiations, when the parties were in an adversary relationship, no rule required or duty rested upon defendants or their representatives to disclose this knowledge. However, once the agreement to settle was reached, it is difficult to characterize the parties' relationship as adverse. At this point all parties were interested in securing Court approval. * * *

* * *

"To hold that the concealment was not of such character as to result in an unconscionable advantage over plaintiff's ignorance or mistake, would be to penalize innocence and incompetence and reward less than full performance of an officer of the Court's duty to make full disclosure to the Court when applying for approval in minor settlement proceedings."

* * *

2.   From the foregoing it is clear that in the instant case the court did not abuse its discretion in setting aside the settlement which it had approved on plaintiff's behalf while he was still a minor. * * *

* * *

Notes

1.   What is the basis of the court's opinion that disclosure was required in this case? Under the court's opinion, would disclosure have been required if plaintiff had been an adult? Only a few years after this opinion, most states lowered the age of majority to 18. Under the new age of majority, plaintiff would have been an adult at the time of this accident and the original settlement would not have been subject to court approval.

2.   The Model Rules as adopted by the ABA House of Delegates in 1983 permitted, but did not require, disclosure of client confidences "to prevent the client from committing a criminal act that the lawyer believes is likely to result in imminent death or substantial bodily harm." MR 1.6(b)(1) (1986). In February 2002, the ABA House of Delegates amended this section to permit, but not require, disclosure of client confidences "to prevent reasonably certain death or substantial bodily harm." MR 1.6(b)(1)(2002). If the 1983 version of MR1.6 had been in effect when the defendant's lawyers received their expert's report, would disclosure have been required? Permitted? Under the 2002 version of MR 1.6, would disclosure be required? Permitted?

3.   Section 66(b) of the Restatement (Third) of the Law Governing Lawyers permits disclosure to prevent reasonably certain death or serious bodily harm, but before such disclosure the lawyer must attempt to persuade the client to not act or to disclose the threat to the victim.

> Before using or disclosing information under this Section, the lawyer must, if feasible, make a good-faith effort to persuade the client not to act. If the client or another person has already acted, the lawyer must, if feasible, advise the client to warn the victim or to take other action to prevent the harm and advise the client of the lawyer's ability to use or disclose information as provided in this Section and the consequences thereof.

What is the purpose of this requirement?

4.   Who do you think made the decision not to reveal the risk to the plaintiff's life? According to surviving members of the Zimmerman family, John Zimmerman was not told of David Spaulding's aneurysm. Why do you think John Zimmerman's lawyer failed to disclose this

information to his client? Does disclosure of a previously unknown injury fall within the client's control of the objectives of representation or the lawyer's control over the means of representation? For a full description of the facts of this case, see Roger C. Cramton & Lori P. Knowles, *Professional Secrecy and Its Exceptions: Spaulding v. Zimmerman Revisited*, 83 *Minn. L. Rev.* 63 (1998).

Should the lawyer for the defendant have discussed the issue with the defendant's insurance company. Should the insurance company have controlled the decision?

> I wonder why we assume that the middle-level manager in the defendant's insurance company—the person probably responsible for settlement decisions–is likely to be more concerned with company profits (or with his career advancement or security) than with the possible death of the plaintiff, or why we think that manager is likely to have less moral sensitivity than the lawyer. If anything can explain the facts underlying this case, it is probably the lawyer and client "playing off" one another: lawyer and corporate client each assuming a "hardball" money-oriented stance, neither pausing to consider a wider context, neither urging such consideration on the other. If either had focused upon and articulated to the other the possibility that they might cause the death of an innocent person, they might have sought a more creative solution to their problem. (One also wonders about the ethics of the physician hired by the defendant who discovered the plaintiff's aneurysm, but did not insist that someone inform the patient.)

Stephen L. Pepper, "Counseling at the Limits of the Law: An Exercise in the Jurisprudence and Ethics of Lawyering," 104 *Yale L.J.* 1545, 1606 (1995).

5. If the client and the professional rules prohibited disclosure would this have been an appropriate case for defendant's counsel to exercise civil disobedience and disclose the risk?

People v. Belge
372 N.Y.S.2d 798, 83 Misc. 2d 186 (Onondaga Co. Ct. 1975)

ORMAND N. GALE, Judge.

In the summer of 1973 Robert F. Garrow, Jr. stood charged in Hamilton County with the crime of MURDER. The Defendant was assigned two attorneys, Frank H. Armani and Francis R. Belge. A defense of insanity had been interposed by counsel for Mr. Garrow. During the course of the discussions between Garrow and his two counsel, three other murders were admitted by Garrow, one being in

Onondaga County.   On or about September of 1973 Mr. Belge conducted his own investigation based upon what his client had told him and with the assistance of a friend the location of the body of Alicia Hauck was found in Oakwood Cemetery in Syracuse. Mr. Belge personally inspected the body and was satisfied, presumably, that this was the Alicia Hauck that his client had told him that he murdered.

This discovery was not disclosed to the authorities, but became public during the trial of Mr. Garrow in June of 1974, when to affirmatively establish the defense of insanity, these three other murders were brought before the jury by the defense in the Hamilton County trial. Public indignation reached the fever pitch; statements were made by the District Attorney of Onondaga County relative to the situation and he caused the Grand Jury of Onondaga County, then sitting, to conduct a thorough investigation. As a result of this investigation Frank Armani was No Billed by the Grand Jury but Indictment No. 75-55 was returned as against Francis R. Belge, Esq., accusing him of having violated § 4200(1) of the Public Health Law, which, in essence, requires that a decent burial be accorded the dead, and § 4143 of the Public Health Law, which, in essence, requires anyone knowing of the death of a person without medical attendance, to report the same to the proper authorities. Defense counsel moves for a dismissal of the Indictment on the grounds that a confidential, privileged communication existed between him and Mr. Garrow, which should excuse the attorney from making full disclosure to the authorities.

The National Association of Criminal Defense Lawyers, as Amicus Curiae, citing *Times Publishing Co. v. Williams*, 222 So.2d 470, 475 (Fla.App.1970) succinctly state the issue in the following language:

> If this indictment stands,
>
> "The attorney-client privilege will be effectively destroyed. No defendant will be able to freely discuss the facts of his case with his attorney. No attorney will be able to listen to those facts without being faced with the Hobson's choice of violating the law or violating his professional code of Ethics."
>
> * * *
>
> "Confidential communications between an attorney and his client are privileged from disclosure. . . as a rule of necessity in the administration of justice."

In the most recent issue of the New York State Bar Journal (June 1975) there is an article by Jack B. Weinstein, entitled "Educating

Ethical Lawyers". In a sub-caption to this article is the following language which is pertinent:

> "The most difficult ethical dilemmas result from the frequent conflicts between the obligation to one's client and those to the legal system and to society. It is in this area that legal education has its greatest responsibility, and can have its greatest effects."

In the course of his article Mr. Weinstein states that there are three major types of pressure facing a practicing lawyer. He uses the following language to describe these:

> "First, there are those that originate in the attorney's search for his own well-being. Second, pressures arise from the attorney's obligation to his client. Third, the lawyer has certain obligations to the courts, the legal system, and society in general."

Our system of criminal justice is an adversary system and the interests of the state are not absolute, or even paramount.

> "The dignity of the individual is respected to the point that even when the citizen is known by the state to have committed a heinous offense, the individual is nevertheless accorded such rights as counsel, trial by jury, due process, and the privilege against self incrimination."

A trial is in part a search for truth, but it is only partly a search for truth. The mantle of innocence is flung over the defendant to such an extent that he is safeguarded by rules of evidence which frequently keep out absolute truth, much to the chagrin of juries. Nevertheless, this has been a part of our system since our laws were taken from the laws of England and over these many years has been found to best protect a balance between the rights of the individual and the rights of society.

* * *

The effectiveness of counsel is only as great as the confidentiality of its client-attorney relationship. If the lawyer cannot get all the facts about the case, he can only give his client half of a defense. This, of necessity, involves the client telling his attorney everything remotely connected with the crime.

Apparently, in the instant case, after analyzing all the evidence, and after hearing of the bizarre episodes in the life of their client, they decided that the only possibility of salvation was in a defense of insanity. For the client to disclose not only everything about this particular crime but also everything about other crimes which might have a bearing upon his defense, requires the strictest confidence in, and on the part of, the attorney.

When the facts of the other homicides became public, as a result of the defendant's testimony to substantiate his claim of insanity, "Members of the public were shocked at the apparent callousness of these lawyers, whose conduct was seen as typifying the unhealthy lack of concern of most lawyers with the public interest and with simple decency." A hue and cry went up from the press and other news media suggesting that the attorneys should be found guilty of such crimes as obstruction of justice or becoming an accomplice after the fact. From a layman's standpoint, this certainly was a logical conclusion. However, the constitution of the United States of America attempts to preserve the dignity of the individual and to do that guarantees him the services of an attorney who will bring to the bar and to the bench every conceivable protection from the inroads of the state against such rights as are vested in the constitution for one accused of crime. Among those substantial constitutional rights is that a defendant does not have to incriminate himself. His attorneys were bound to uphold that concept and maintain what has been called a sacred trust of confidentiality.

The following language from the brief of the Amicus Curiae further points up the statements just made:

> "The client's Fifth Amendment rights cannot be violated by his attorney. There is no viable distinction between the personal papers and criminal evidence in the hands or mind of the client. Because the discovery of the body of Alicia Hauck would have presented 'a significant link in a chain of evidence tending to establish his guilt' [c], Garrow was constitutionally exempt from any statutory requirement to disclose the location of the body. And Attorney Belge, as Garrow's attorney, was not only equally exempt, but under a positive stricture precluding such disclosure. Garrow, although constitutionally privileged against a requirement of compulsory disclosure, was free to make such a revelation if he chose to do so. Attorney Belge was affirmatively required to withhold disclosure. The criminal defendant's self-incrimination rights become completely nugatory if compulsory disclosure can be exacted through his attorney."

* * *

In the case at bar we must weigh the importance of the general privilege of confidentiality in the performance of the defendant's duties as an attorney, against the inroads of such a privilege, on the fair administration of criminal justice as well as the heart tearing that went on in the victim's family by reason of their uncertainty as to the whereabouts of Alicia Hauck. In this type situation the Court must balance the rights of the individual against the rights of society as a whole. There is no question but Attorney Belge's failure to bring to the attention of the authorities the whereabouts of Alicia Hauck when he first verified it, prevented bringing Garrow to the immediate bar of justice for this particular murder. This was in a sense, obstruction of justice. This duty, I am sure, loomed large in the mind of Attorney Belge. However, against this was the Fifth Amendment right of his client, Garrow, not to incriminate himself. If the Grand Jury had returned an indictment charging Mr. Belge with obstruction of justice under a proper statute, the work of this Court would have been much more difficult than it is.

There must always be a conflict between the obstruction of the administration of criminal justice and the preservation of the right against self-incrimination which permeates the mind of the attorney as the alter ego of his client. But that is not the situation before this Court. We have the Fifth Amendment right, derived from the constitution, on the one hand, as against the trivia of a pseudo-criminal statute on the other, which has seldom been brought into play. Clearly the latter is completely out of focus when placed alongside the client-attorney privilege. * * *

It is the decision of this Court that Francis R. Belge conducted himself as an officer of the Court with all the zeal at his command to protect the constitutional rights of his client. Both on the grounds of a privileged communication and in the interests of justice the Indictment is dismissed.

People v. Belge
376 N.Y.S.2d 771, 50 A.D.2d 1088 (S. Ct. App. Div. 1975)

MEMORANDUM:

We affirm the Order of the Trial Court which properly dismissed the indictments laid against defendant for alleged violations of § 4200 (duty of a decent burial) and § 4143 (requirement to report death occurring without medical attendance) of the Public Health Law. We believe that the attorney-client privilege attached insofar as the communications were to advance a client's interests, and that the privilege effectively shielded the defendant-attorney from his actions which would otherwise have violated the Public Health Law.

In view of the fact that the claim of absolute privilege was proffered, we note that the privilege is not all-encompassing and that in a given case there may be conflicting considerations. We believe that an attorney must protect his client's interests, but also must observe basic human standards of decency, having due regard to the need that the legal system accord justice to the interests of society and its individual members.

We write to emphasize our serious concern regarding the consequences which emanate from a claim of an absolute attorneyclient privilege. Because the only question presented, briefed and argued on this appeal was a legal one with respect to the sufficiency of the indictments, we limit our determination to that issue and do not reach the ethical questions underlying this case.

Order affirmed.

Notes

1. Is it easier to justify the refusal to disclose the location of the dead bodies in this case than the existence of the plaintiff's aneurism in *Spaulding*? Should the defendant's attorneys have revealed the location of the bodies? Could the district attorney have used the fact that the lawyers knew where the bodies were buried as evidence that Garrow committed the murders? Could the district attorney have used physical evidence from the bodies in seeking to convict Garrow?

2. The *Belge* decisions have been criticized for failing to acknowledge the competing moral claims for disclosure:

> When the father of one of the girls directly asked one attorney if he knew anything about the missing daughter, the lawyer did not answer. The attorney then avoided a meeting with the father of the second girl because he could not face the father's grief and anguish.

> * * *

> The grief of the parents has always been an aspect of the Lake Pleasant bodies case, yet in legal ethics it is rarely identified as the central feature of the story. Instead, the events are usually viewed from the perspective of the lawyer: the focus is on the professional responsibilities of her role. Belge and Armani employed such a perspective. The lawyer has a duty to protect client confidences. If a client has a right not to incriminate himself, he should not be incriminated by his statements to his lawyers. The bodies might have contained information that could implicate Garrow in two more murders, so their location could not be revealed.

> * * *

> The courts dismissed the indictment against the attorneys without ever reaching the question of the lawyers' responsibility to the parents of the

missing girls. The case's central moral question, then, fell outside the bounds of the court's technical legal analysis. Armani captured the conflicts of this situation in an interview given years after the events.

[Armani]: This was something that was really momentous for us because of the conflict within us. Your mind screaming one way `Relieve these parents!' You know—what is your responsibility? Should you report this? Shouldn't you report it? One sense of morality wants you to relieve the grief.

[Interviewer]: And the other?

[Armani]: The other is your sworn duty.

[Interviewer]: Didn't you think that there was a factor of just common decency here?

[Armani]: I can't explain it—but to me it was a question of which was the higher moral good.

[Interviewer]: Between what?

[Armani]: The question of the Constitution, the question of even a bastard like him having a proper defense, having adequate representation, being able to trust his lawyer as to what he says.

[Interviewer]: Against what?

[Armani]: As against the fact that I have a dead girl, the fact that her body's there. As against the breaking hearts of her parents. But they are—. It's a terrible thing to play God at that moment, but in my judgment—and I still feel that way—that their suffering is not worth jeopardizing my sworn duty or my oath of office or the Constitution.

Leslie Griffin, "The Lawyer's Dirty Hands," 8 *Geo. J. Legal Ethics* 219 (1995) *quoting* Ethics on Trial (WETA-TV, video 1987), *reprinted in* David J. Luban, "Freedom and Constraint in Legal Ethics: Some Mid-Course Corrections to Lawyers and Justice," 49 *Md. L. Rev.* 424, 425-26 (1990). For a fuller account of the *Belge* case from the perspective of one of the defendant's lawyers, *see* Tom Alibrandi & Frank H. Armani, *Privileged Information* (1984).

3. Other commentators have criticized the basic premise that the client's right to avoid self-incrimination shields the lawyer from a duty to disclose:

A murderer has no moral right whatever to escape incrimination by concealing the victim's body, although it would be wrong to compel him or her to reveal where it is. To the extreme wickedness of the original crime there has been added the wickedness of obstructing justice, of calculated cruelty to the victim's family and friends, and of desecrating a human body. That the legal right against self-incrimination should entitle the murderer to enlist professional associates in that obstruction, cruelty, and desecration is monstrous as moral theory. A morally decent attorney can be the client's alter ego only in actions that he or she believes the client may possibly have a moral right to do. That there are good moral reasons why a client should not be coerced into refraining from a wrong does not exculpate his attorney in also committing that wrong.

Alan Donagan, "Justifying Legal Practice in the Adversary System," in *The Good Lawyer: Lawyers' Roles and Lawyers' Ethics* 123, 143 (David Luban Ed., 1983).

Confidentiality Rules and Injury to Third Parties

The duty of confidentiality when a lawyer learns (1) that the client intends to commit a crime or (2) that the client has used the lawyer's services to commit a fraud, has been the subject of great controversy. The relevant provisions of the 1969 ABA Model Code originally provided:

DR 4-101   Preservation of Confidences and Secrets of a Client

(A) A lawyer may reveal:

(1) The intention of his client to commit a crime and the information necessary to prevent the crime.

*   *   *

DR 7-102   Representing a Client Within the Bounds of the Law

*   *   *

(B) A lawyer who receives information clearly establishing that:

(1) His client has, in the course of the representation, perpetrated a fraud upon a person or tribunal shall promptly call upon his client to rectify the same, and if his client refuses or is unable to do so, he shall reveal the fraud to the affected person or tribunal.

*   *   *

In 1982, the Kutak Commission (which drafted the Model Rules) proposed the following rule:

Kutak Commission Proposed Model Rule 1.6
(Revised Final Draft, June 30, 1982):

* * *

(b) A lawyer may reveal [confidential] information to the extent the lawyer reasonably believes necessary:

(1) to prevent the client from committing a criminal or fraudulent act that the lawyer reasonably believes is likely to result in death or substantial bodily harm, or in substantial injury to the financial interests or property of another;

(2) to rectify the consequences of a client's criminal or fraudulent act in the furtherance of which the lawyer's services had been used;

* * *

How did the Kutak proposal compare with the Model Code provisions?

In one of its most controversial actions, the ABA House of Delegates in 1983 altered the Kutak proposal, rejecting any provision for lawyer disclosure of client intent to cause financial injury or client fraud. How does the ABA's MR 1.6 compare with the Kutak Commission's proposed MR 1.6? With the related Model Code provisions? Which rules are preferable?

Model Rule 1.6's provisions concerning the intent of a client to injure a third party have not proven to be very popular with the states. As of February 2001, twenty-eight states had retained Model Code-type language permitting lawyers to reveal the intent of a client to commit any crime, two states (Florida and Virginia) *required* lawyers to reveal the intent of a client to commit a crime; nine jurisdictions required lawyers to reveal the intent of a client to commit a crime likely to cause death or serious bodily injury; sixteen jurisdictions had Model Rule-type provisions permitting lawyers to reveal only the intent of a client to commit a crime likely to cause death or serious bodily injury; and one jurisdiction (California) *prohibited* lawyers from revealing the intent of a client to commit any crime. Sixteen jurisdictions had Kutak Commission-type provisions permitting lawyers to disclose that their services have been used to commit a crime or fraud; thirty-three had

Model Rule-type rules prohibiting such disclosure; and two jurisdictions (Hawaii and Ohio) had original Model Code-type provisions requiring disclosure.[2]

The Restatement (Third) of the Law Governing Lawyers § 66 allows lawyers to disclose confidential information in order to "prevent reasonably certain death or serious bodily injury." As to financial harm, the Restatement allows greater disclosure than is permitted under MR1.6, but imposes conditions that were not contained in the Kutak proposal.

Restatement (Third) of the Law Governing Lawyers § 67 Using Or Disclosing Information To Prevent, Rectify, Or Mitigate Substantial Financial Loss

(1) A lawyer may use or disclose confidential client information when the lawyer reasonably believes that its use or disclosure is necessary to prevent a crime or fraud, and:

    (a) the crime or fraud threatens substantial financial loss;

    (b) the loss has not yet occurred;

    (c) the lawyer's client intends to commit the crime or fraud either personally or through a third person; and

    (d) the client has employed or is employing the lawyer's services in the matter in which the crime or fraud is committed.

(2) If a crime or fraud described in Subsection (1) has already occurred, a lawyer may use or disclose confidential client information when the lawyer reasonably believes its use or disclosure is necessary to prevent, rectify, or mitigate the loss.

(3) Before using or disclosing information under this Section, the lawyer must, if feasible, make a good-faith effort to persuade the client not to act. If the client or another person has already acted, the lawyer must, if feasible, advise the client to warn the victim or to take other action to prevent, rectify, or

---

[2]   *See* Attorneys' Liability Assurance Society, Inc., "Ethics Rules on Client Confidences," *in* Thomas D. Morgan & Ronald D. Rotunda, *2002 Selected Standards on Professional Responsibility* 134-144 (2002) for a summary of each state's rules on this subject. This summary is updated each year in the Morgan & Rotunda *Standards*.

mitigate the loss. The lawyer must, if feasible, also advise the client of the lawyer's ability to use or disclose information as provided in this Section and the consequences thereof.

* * *

The Ethics 2000 proposals followed the Restatement in allowing disclosure "to prevent reasonably certain death or serious bodily injury" and to prevent client fraud. The ABA accepted the "death or serious bodily injury" rule, but rejected the client fraud rule.

Which approach represents the proper balance of the lawyer's duty to a client and the general duty of every person to avoid assisting in fraud?

Though the Model Rules do not explicitly create an exception to the confidentiality rules for the use of a lawyer's services in the commission of a crime or fraud, as the following article indicates, it may be that under the comments to MR 1.6, attorneys have a means of notifying third parties that their work has been used to commit a fraud.

Notes

1. The original version of MR 1.6 stated that, an attorney *may* reveal a client confidence "to prevent the client from committing a criminal act that the lawyer believes is likely to result in imminent death or substantial bodily injury." In *Belge*, what if, instead of finding the girls dead bodies, Garrow's lawyers discovered the victims while they were still breathing? What would be the result under the current version of MR 1.6? In *Krist v. State*, 227 Ga. 85, 85-88, 179 S.E.2d 56, 57-59 (1970) the defendant had kidnapped and buried his victim in a wooden box equipped with a mechanism that permitted her to breathe. What if the defendant had disclosed this to his lawyer while the victim was still alive, yet prior to the police discovering her location? Would disclosure be permitted under either version of MR 1.6? *See* Harry I. Subin, "The Lawyer as Superego: Disclosure of Client Confidences to Prevent Harm," 70 *Iowa L. Rev.* 1091, 1103-04 (1985) (using this hypothetical to examine the limits of the client's right to expect confidentiality).

2. The Model Rule makes disclosure of the intent to commit certain future criminal acts discretionary. Under the law of torts, however, the courts might not treat such disclosures as a matter of discretion. In *Tarasoff v. The Regents of the University of California*, 17 Cal. 3d 425, 551 P.2d 334, 131 Cal. Rptr. 14 (1976), the California

Supreme Court subjected a psychiatrist to liability for the failure to disclose a patient's threat to kill the woman who was the object of the client's affections. Might an attorney be subject to similar liability? *See* Vanessa Merton, "Confidentiality and the 'Dangerous' Patient: Implications of *Tarasoff* for Psychiatrists and Lawyers," 31 *Emory L. J.* 263, 328-33 (1982) criticizing the Kutak proposal as encouraging the creation of a *Tarasoff* duty for lawyers.

3.   What is the proper course of conduct for the lawyer when a client is contemplating fraud? As the following article indicates, it may be that, even absent an explicit exception allowing disclosure under MR 1.6, attorneys have a means of notifying third parties that their clients propose to engage in a fraudulent act, or that the attorney's work has been used to commit a fraud.

Ronald D. Rotunda, "The Notice of Withdrawal and the New Model Rules of Professional Conduct: Blowing the Whistle and Waving the Red Flag"
63 *Ore. L. Rev.* 455, 474-84 (1984)
* * *

* * * You are a lawyer who has prepared for the client the necessary papers for a financial deal. The client is selling limited partnership interests to local doctors, dentists, and other professionals in your town. Relying on the papers that you have prepared, individuals, including some of your best friends and close relatives, prepare to invest. On the eve of closing the deal, you learn that your client is really planning to engage in massive financial fraud and that you, the lawyer, have been the unwitting tool of the client. You urge the client to stop the scheme to defraud your friends. The client laughs and says, "Quit if you want to, but with or without your participation, my plan will go through tomorrow."

What should you do? Under the * * * Model Code, there is some confusion, but it appears that the lawyer may reveal the client's intention to commit a crime and the information necessary to prevent it [see DR 4-101 quoted above].

* * *

Under the law of evidence, the long-held and uniform [attorney-client privilege] rule is that the lawyer has no privilege to keep client information confidential if the client communication furthers client fraud or crime. Whether the lawyer knew of the client's criminal or fraudulent purpose at the time that the lawyer's services were used or only learned of the improper purpose at a later date makes no difference. Similarly, under the law of agency the lawyer as agent has no right to keep confidential the principal's crimes or frauds committed in the course of the representation. Further, neither the law of torts nor the law of agency allows the lawyer to commit any tort on behalf of the principal.

* * *

This basic principle of law is not surprising. Courts, and the Restatement (Second) of Torts, have imposed liability on professionals such as accountants for the negligent preparation of an audit report that harms a third party who reasonably and foreseeably relies on that report. This basic principle of tort law logically can apply to lawyers as well as to accountants.

Of course, some fear that if a lawyer may disclose the client's plan to commit a serious fraud or crime, or the client's plan to use the lawyer's services to commit such acts, such a breach of confidence would prevent any client from ever again trusting his or her lawyer. The case law of torts and agency rejects this domino theory.

The theory also finds little support from experience under the prior ethical standards governing the legal profession. [The rules in most jurisdictions have either mandated or permitted disclosure.]

One must take with a grain of salt the protestations of those who fear that the sky will fall if the lawyer must reveal fraud. Such predictions ignore the other exceptions to the confidentiality rule adopted by the [ABA in MR 1.6]. These exceptions allow a lawyer to breach confidentiality to defend himself or herself against a charge of wrongful conduct, to collect a fee, or to undo perjury before a tribunal. If these inroads to the duty of confidentiality—and particularly these first two self-serving inroads—do not cause the sky to fall, neither will disclosure of the client's intent to defraud upset the heavens.

* * *

[Following the adoption by the ABA House of Delegates of MR 1.6, the ABA was highly criticized for the breadth of the confidentiality rule. In response, the ABA made] an addition to the Comment to Rule 1.6, governing confidentiality. This Comment, which serves as a "guide" to interpretation of the Rule, indicates that there is no breach of confidence if the lawyer notifies anyone that he or she has withdrawn his or her work product and has withdrawn from further representation of the (former) client. Even if the client tells the lawyer to keep secret the withdrawal, the lawyer need not respect this request. This Comment provides:

> Neither this rule [1.6] nor Rule 1.8(b) nor Rule 1.16(d) prevents the lawyer *from giving notice of the fact of withdrawal*, and the lawyer may *also withdraw or disaffirm any opinion, document, affirmation, or the like.*

The cross references in this Comment emphasize the breadth of this new power to give a notice of withdrawal. Rule 1.8(b) provides that a lawyer cannot use a client's secret to disadvantage the client. Rule 1.16(d) requires the withdrawing lawyer to "take steps to the extent reasonably practicable to protect a client's interests." Neither of these subsections impinge on this power to send a notice of withdrawal.

* * * While the lawyer may not tell the third party or government agency the reason for the withdrawal (only the client may do that), the recipients of the notice of withdrawal are certain to be put on notice that something is wrong.

* * * This notice of withdrawal appears to amount to disclosure and thus accomplishes indirectly what the original Kutak draft sought to accomplish directly. The lawyer need not withdraw silently. To prevent being held liable to those injured by the client's wrongful conduct, the lawyer has every incentive to file a noisy notice of withdrawal with all relevant parties.

* * *

Filing a notice of withdrawal, state the Model Rules, is a discretionary rather than obligatory act. Nothing "prevents" the lawyer from giving such a notice, and the lawyer "may withdraw" prior papers. The "Scope" section of the Model Rules emphasizes this point: the lawyer's decision not to disclose information under Rule 1.6 should not be subject to reexamination.

However, this hope expressed in the Model Rules may not come to pass. Just as the Model Code (and now the Model Rules) expressed the hope, to no avail, that violation of the ethics provisions would not lead to civil liability, this latest caveat will probably have little effect. When other law requires disclosure, and the Model Code or the Model Rules do not mandate confidentiality, the lawyer cannot seek protection in the discretionary aspects of the lawyer's ethical duty. The discretion to reveal, coupled with the duty to reveal expressed in other law, means that the lawyer must disclose or be held liable for damages to injured third parties. Thus, filing a notice of withdrawal may at times be a duty, rather than a subject of unreviewable discretion.

* * *

The responsibility of a lawyer to blow the whistle, or to withdraw silently or noisily, or to continue representation as if nothing had happened, is an important matter for the courts and practitioners. The Model Rules tell us that a lawyer need not be a hired gun. Nor is the lawyer a Pontius Pilate, who tries to wash his or her hands of the whole affair and silently walk away. Nor is the lawyer a fifth columnist or an undercover cop on the beat. Instead, the Model Rules in this area attempt to balance complex and competing interests and to steer between disclosure and silence in order to assure that zealous representation does not become overzealous representation.

Notes

1. Rotunda says that "the recipients of the notice of withdrawal are certain to be put on notice that something is wrong." Recipients who are lawyers are likely to be put on notice that something is wrong, but what of recipients that are not lawyers? Would the investors in the partnership described in the hypothetical that Rotunda presents at the beginning of his article be likely to understand the import of such a notice? Or would they likely say, "What do I care if the lawyer has quit?"

2. In ABA Formal Opinion 92-366 a majority of the ABA Committee opined that a lawyer who had drafted an opinion letter based upon fraudulent representations made by the client could advise the recipient of the letter that the lawyer disaffirmed the letter and no longer represented the client. The dissenting members of the Committee agreed that withdrawal was required when a client insisted upon pursuing a fraudulent scheme, but that the lawyer could not disaffirm the previously issued opinion letter since the passage of time would make current or future reliance upon the letter unreasonable. Therefore, the dissent reasoned, the only purpose disaffirmance served was to convey the information that the letter was fraudulent, and that was an impermissible disclosure of past wrongs. Should lawyers be able to disaffirm a prior statement? Does your answer depend in part upon whether the lawyer can be liable to the intended recipient of the statement?

3. Attorneys can be liable to non-clients on the basis of fraud or misrepresentation. In order to prevail the plaintiff must show that the attorney made a material misrepresentation which was known to be false, with the intention of inducing the plaintiff to act, which the plaintiff did to his detriment. A duty can arise from a half-truth. *See generally* Ronald E. Mallen & Jeffery M. Smith, *Legal Malpractice*, 5th Ed. §§ 6.7 and 8.10. This is consistent with MR 4.1 which prohibits lawyers from making false statements.

4. Attorneys can also be liable to non-clients for negligent misrepresentation when the lawyer or the lawyer's client invites the non-client to rely upon the attorney's opinion or legal advice. Restatement (Third) of the Law Governing Lawyers § 51 (2000). Yet MR 4.1(b) specifically limits the lawyer's obligation to disclose material facts to those facts which are not confidential under MR 1.6. Should compliance with 4.1 be a defense to an action by a non-client for negligent misrepresentation?

Fred C. Zacharias, "Rethinking Confidentiality"
74 *Iowa L. Rev.* 351, 358-61, 363-70 (1989)

* * *

A. The Justifications for Confidentiality

The primary argument in favor of attorney-client confidentiality in civil cases rests on a three-step syllogism. First, for the adversary system to operate, citizens must use lawyers to resolve disputes and the lawyers must be able to represent clients effectively. Second, attorneys can be effective only if they have all the relevant facts at their disposal. Third, clients will not employ lawyers, or at least will not provide them with adequate information, unless all aspects of the attorney-client relationship remain secret. Thus, the systemic argument goes, attorney-client confidentiality is the foundation of orderly and effective adversarial justice.

The bar, however, has relied on other justifications for confidentiality. By encouraging clients to communicate information they would otherwise withhold from their lawyers, confidentiality enhances the quality of legal [sic] representation and thus helps produce accurate legal verdicts. Proponents also claim that confidentiality improves the attorney-client relationship. It can foster aspects of lawyer and client "dignity." And, in theory, confidentiality helps lawyers discover improprieties that the client plans, advise against them, and ultimately stop the misconduct.

Undoubtedly, each of these justifications has played some role in convincing code drafters to favor rules preserving secrecy. But in many ways, strict confidentiality also serves personal interests of segments of the bar. For example, the rules relieve some lawyers from the psychological costs of having to make difficult ethical decisions * * * Strict confidentiality absolves the lawyer from deciding between betraying her client's (perhaps capricious) wishes and letting an innocent victim suffer.

Confidentiality rules also may benefit an attorney financially. * * * A lawyer forbidden to disclose need not fear repercussions if her affiliation with the client's actions later becomes public. When questioned about the propriety of assisting the client, the attorney can hide behind the nondisclosure rules. A smile or "no comment," suggesting that the questioner would act like the lawyer "if he only knew," enables the attorney to avoid the cost of bad publicity and community disapproval of her conduct. In contrast, when silence subjects lawyers to accusations of wrongdoing, most codes authorize lawyers to speak.

Strict confidentiality provisions promote and reinforce American society's perception of lawyers as hired guns. Public acceptance of the hired gun model enables the lawyers in the hypothetical cases to take on (and accept payment for) distasteful cases. Indeed, the presence of confidentiality may explain why clients are willing to pay high fees to lawyers when non-lawyers might be able to provide similar services more cheaply.

The extent to which the profession's personal or economic interests have influenced the scope of confidentiality rules can never be known. Yet their mere existence leads one to wonder whether the attorney-drafters of the strict codes—perhaps even unintentionally—have overemphasized the systemic justifications for confidentiality or undervalued the social benefits of less restrictive rules. A code that explicitly acknowledges lawyers' right to follow their own moral instincts despite a financial risk might produce a more ethical bar that can serve society better. The following sections thus evaluate the strength of the traditional justifications for strict confidentiality and the societal costs of avoiding exceptions.

B. Are the Traditional Justifications Sound in Theory?

* * *

1. Confidentiality's Systemic Justification

To accept the modern systemic arguments in favor of confidentiality, one must reach one of two conclusions: first, that clients would use lawyers significantly less if more exceptions existed; second, that clients who employ lawyers would reveal substantially less information. Both conclusions are questionable.

The proponents of confidentiality posit that in this complex, litigious society, our need for "trained [legal] technicians to advise men how to order their conduct" militates in favor of artificial rules that encourage the use of lawyers. Yet in theory, this very need suggests that potential clients will use lawyers even if confidentiality is circumscribed. As matters become complex, laypersons have no choice but to consult the experts. The threat of being sued or the need to sue for redress of grievances necessarily drives clients to lawyers. When litigation is not involved, the inability to understand or deal with a legal matter is usually the catalyst.

The notion that clients may, absent the promise of full confidentiality, withhold important information from their attorneys is intuitively more palatable. A client who expects the lawyer to reveal embarrassing or damaging facts may not be willing to tell all. Again, however, for the strictness of confidentiality rules to be significant in assuaging client fears, several premises about the actual practice of law must hold true. Attorneys must regularly inform clients of the rules, or clients must learn of them from independent sources. Clients must understand the explanation of confidentiality's scope. The rules must be sufficiently clear that clients can know which of their statements will remain secret. For if these premises do not hold true, hesitant clients will withhold information despite the existence of firm confidentiality guarantees.

Supporting the premises may be difficult. Even if a lawyer makes a good faith effort to explain the rules to clients, the clients are likely to remain confused at least as to details. Many aspects of confidentiality are ambiguous. A few universal exceptions to confidentiality exist, some of which are subject to hot debate. Often the distinction between disclosable communications and secrets rests on "vague and open-textured criteria." To the extent clients learn of confidentiality from sources other than their lawyers—such as television, literature, or friends—the explanations they receive are likely to ignore details or distinctions among the various jurisdictions' codes.

As a practical matter, clients thus probably end up with only a general understanding that attorney-client conversations usually remain confidential but occasionally may be revealed. If that is the case, creating limited additional disclosure exceptions is unlikely to affect a client's decision to confide. Absent supporting empirical evidence, it is problematic to assume that clients would avoid lawyers to any significant degree merely because they cannot speak in absolute secrecy.

2. Enhancing the Quality of Legal Representation and Maintaining Adversarial "Truth-seeking"

Stated broadly, the claim that lawyers can be effective only when informed of all relevant facts is simply untrue. Attorneys do without information in a broad variety of contexts. To make sense, the argument in support of confidentiality must thus be redefined as follows: Lawyers whose clients hide information are likely to perform less ably. By encouraging client disclosure through secrecy guarantees, the state protects clients who otherwise would jeopardize their case by withholding information.

Professor Morgan long ago questioned the need to protect uncooperative or deceitful clients. The client who receives bad advice because he fails to inform the lawyer has only himself to blame. Alternatively, if the client lies to the lawyer and later finds himself confronted by the truth, the government has little reason to aid the client. The law should probably not be written for the benefit of liars or perjurers.

Morgan's position, however, does not do full justice to one type of client: the genuinely confused client who needs advice and representation, but unthinkingly hesitates to confide for fear his secrets will become public. Yet by definition, this category of client feels sufficiently troubled to seek legal advice. He is unlikely to undermine that advice by withholding information, particularly when told by the lawyer that full disclosure is important.

If the client does withhold particularly embarrassing items, it is not clear that the representation will be significantly affected. In some settings, lawyers actually would prefer not to be told everything the client knows. Even a lawyer who ideally would like to know all relevant facts often can provide good legal advice based on partial information. Studies suggest that criminal defendants rarely are frank with their lawyers. Yet the criminal justice system relies on the presumption that these clients are nevertheless fairly and well represented.

I do not suggest that confidentiality rules have no effect on client forthrightness or the quality of representation. But in the abstract, it is difficult to determine the extent of any effect. If the number of clients needing and deserving the protection of absolute rules are indeed few, the interest in "assuring effective representation" may be outweighed by society's alternative interests in allowing limited disclosures.

3. Client Dignity and the Trust Relationship

Absolute confidentiality can enhance lawyer client relations. It often makes the client *feel* as if the lawyer is a true fiduciary, with loyalty to no one other than the client. It also avoids the unseemly situation in which a lawyer induces the client to be open and then informs on the client.

But these considerations alone do not justify the strictest of rules. In an ideal world, the government would promote the relationship between clients and all agents. But that does not mean it is essential to preserve confidentiality to an extreme degree. Even if we accept client "autonomy" as an important value, there are limits to how comfortable we want clients to be in the belief that their lawyers will never take a stand against them. Arguably, client distrust will increase if the lawyer insists that she will always act in accord with the client's wishes. So long as the attorney informs the client at the outset of the relationship that she may feel compelled to disclose particular types of information, subsequent disclosures are not unseemly. The client may more readily accept her as an ally *within the defined boundaries*, both because the lawyer has exhibited integrity and because the limitations on the alliance make the total package more believable.

The argument that confidentiality gives "appropriate regard" to client dignity is equally vulnerable. For one, the same argument applies to all professions. More importantly, too much secrecy can be counterproductive. As the Supreme Court implicitly recognized in approving a lawyer's threat to disclose a client's proposed perjury, the lawyer who contributes to the notion that the client can get away with anything demeans the client as a moral individual.

4. Preventing Client Misconduct

The most appealing secondary justification for attorney-client confidentiality is that helping lawyers obtain information enables them to advise clients against committing improper acts or filing frivolous claims. Yet the same empirical questions that plague the systemic justification for strict confidentiality are present here. Confidentiality probably does allow some lawyers to prevent some misconduct before it occurs. But adding limited exceptions might not *substantially* affect lawyers' ability to dissuade improper acts.

Moreover, it is unclear that strict confidentiality is what provokes client candor about potential improprieties. In most cases, lawyers impress upon clients the importance of full disclosure to the lawyer's ability to evaluate the case. This warning alone may procure the type of information lawyers need to prevent misconduct. As a factual matter, the additional disclosures strict confidentiality fosters may only marginally improve the lawyer's ability to enforce the law.

Enabling clients to discuss planned misconduct with impunity sometimes might even promote misconduct. In consulting with clients, lawyers often serve the function of psychiatrist, social worker, or priest-confessor. They provide some clients with a psychological outlet that *helps* the clients persist in misconduct. Empirical research might show that lawyers play this role only rarely, that the risk of promoting misconduct deserves little weight. Yet proponents of the dissuading misconduct rationale have not relied on such evidence; they do not even consider strict confidentiality's possible costs.

* * *

Notes

1. Are the exceptions for attorney self-protection and fee collection (MR 1.6(b)(3)) consistent with the ABA's assertions concerning the importance of confidentiality?

2. Professor Monroe Freedman is one of the strongest supporters of a comprehensive rule on confidentiality. He would recognize exceptions only when human life is at stake, when necessary to avoid presenting a case before a tainted jury or judge, or (grudgingly) when

necessary to defend against formal charges of wrong-doing by the lawyer. Monroe H. Freedman, *Understanding Lawyers' Ethics* 102-03 (1990). In support of confidentiality, Professor Freedman cites the case of the battered wife accused of killing her husband, who reveals that the killing occurred as the husband advanced threateningly, only after becoming convinced that the lawyer would not reveal her "damaging" secret. Without the promise of confidentiality, Freedman argues that the lawyer would never learn of the client's self-defense claim. Does this example answer Professor Zacharias' statement that the client "is unlikely to undermine that advice [of the lawyer] by withholding information, particularly when told by the lawyer that full disclosure is important"?

3. What does Zacharias mean when he writes "the lawyer who contributes to the notion that the client can get away with anything demeans the client as a moral individual"?

The Attorney-Client Privilege

As noted previously, the attorney-client privilege is different from the duty of confidentiality. The attorney-client privilege is a rule of evidence rather than a rule of professional responsibility. A frequently quoted definition of the attorney-client privilege is found in United States v. United Shoe Mach. Corp., 89 F. Supp. 357, 358 (D. Mass. 1950):

> The privilege applies only if (1) the asserted holder of the privilege is or sought to become a client; (2) the person to whom the communication was made (a) is a member of the bar of a court, or his subordinate and (b) in connection with this communication is acting as a lawyer; (3) the communication relates to a fact of which the attorney was informed (a) by his client (b) without the presence of strangers (c) for the purpose of securing primarily either (i) an opinion on law or (ii) legal services or (iii) assistance in some legal proceeding, and not (d) for the purpose of committing a crime or tort; and (4) the privilege has been (a) claimed and (b) not waived by the client.

Note that the rule of confidentiality is broader than the attorney-client privilege in two respects. First, the rule of confidentiality applies in all situations, whereas the privilege applies only when the lawyer is called on to testify. Second, the rule of confidentiality applies to a broader range of information; under MR 1.6, the duty of confidentiality applies to "information relating to representation of a client," whereas, the attorney-client privilege covers only communications from the client under fairly narrowly defined circumstances. In what other respects does the attorney-client privilege differ from the duty of confidentiality?

State v. Hansen
122 Wash.2d 712, 862 P.2d 117 (1993)

GUY, Justice.

* * *

In January 1988, Michael Hansen was convicted of a felony and was sentenced to 24 months in prison by King County Superior Court Judge Robert Dixon. Several months after his release from prison. Hansen began contacting attorneys in order to bring a civil action against the State, Judge Dixon, and Hansen's defense attorney and the prosecutor from the earlier trial.

On March 6, 1990, Hansen telephoned Chris Youtz, an attorney whose name he had obtained from the Seattle-King County Bar Association Lawyer Referral Service, with the stated desire that Youtz would take his case. Hansen explained to Youtz that he felt he had been conspired against, calling the trial a "kangaroo court." During this discussion, Hansen identified by name the prosecutor and public defender, but did not name the judge. Youtz explained to Hansen that he would not take the case and that Hansen might want to seek another attorney with more experience in criminal law. At this point in the conversation, Hansen became upset. Hansen explained that Youtz was the third lawyer he had talked to about the possible action, and he stated that the bar was not helping out with his cause. Hansen then stated: When you say I am not going to get any help from the Bar, I am not going to get any help from anybody . . . What am I going to do . . . I am going to get a gun and blow them all away, the prosecutor, the judge and the public defender. [C]. Youtz continued to talk to Hansen and finally explained to Hansen that there was nothing else he could do for him.

Youtz, concerned about the "serious threat" that Hansen had made, consulted with a Washington State Bar Association representative and his law partner as to whether it was proper to disclose what Hansen had communicated to him. In order to determine the name of the threatened judge, Youtz contacted the named prosecutor and described his conversation with Hansen. The prosecutor informed Youtz that it was Judge Dixon who had heard the case. Upon learning the judge's identity, Youtz telephoned Judge Dixon and discussed with him what had taken place. Youtz testified during the trial that he "was convinced that some action very well could be taken against these individuals, the prosecutor, the judge and the public defender, and that I was—it was that concern that helped me call them and warn them." [C].

The Seattle Police Department conducted an investigation and subsequently arrested Hansen and charged him with the crime of intimidating a judge [c]. Hansen was convicted of intimidation of a judge and was sentenced to 24 months in prison.

* * *

[The court first held that under the statute, the defendant did not have to intend or know that the communications would reach the judge.]

ATTORNEY-CLIENT PRIVILEGE

Hansen next argues that he should not be subject to culpability due to his reasonable belief that he was engaged in a confidential and privileged conversation when he made the threat. Hansen asserts there was no evidence presented of Youtz telling him that the conversation between Youtz and himself was not privileged or confidential.

* * *

* * * An attorney-client relationship is deemed to exist if the conduct between an individual and an attorney is such that the individual subjectively believes such a relationship exists. In re McGlothlen, 99 Wash.2d 515, 522, 663 P.2d 1330 (1983). However, the belief of the client will control only if it "is reasonably formed based on the attending circumstances, including the attorney's words or actions." Bohn v. Cody, 119 Wash.2d 357, 363, 832 P.2d 71 (1992).

In this case, the "attending circumstances" cannot form the basis for a subjective belief that an attorney-client relationship existed. Hansen's total contact with Youtz consisted of one phone call. The conversation consisted of Hansen expressing a desire to bring certain individuals to trial, to which Youtz explained that he would not take Hansen's case and that Hansen might be better off finding another attorney. There was no evidence which could have led Hansen to believe that an attorney-client relationship existed. Arguendo, even if an attorney-client relationship had existed, it would have ended when

Youtz explained to Hansen that he should seek another attorney. Therefore, on the record before us, there are not sufficient grounds to find that an attorney-client relationship existed.

If an attorney-client relationship could have been found to exist when Hansen made the threat against the judge, the prosecutor, and the public defender, the privilege would still not apply. The attorney-client privilege is not applicable to a client's remarks concerning the furtherance of a crime, fraud, or to conversations regarding the contemplation of a future crime. * * * Hansen's statement that he was going to blow away the judge, prosecutor and public defender falls under this exception to the attorney-client privilege.

Under the Rules of Professional Conduct, an attorney is permitted to reveal information concerning a client's intent to commit a crime. "A lawyer may reveal ... confidences or secrets to the extent the lawyer reasonably believes necessary ... [t]o prevent the client from committing a crime." RPC 1.6(b)(1).

To decide this case, we must determine whether an attorney has an affirmative duty to warn judges of true threats made by his or her client or by third parties. Whether a threat is a true or real threat is based on whether the attorney has a reasonable belief that the threat is real. We hold that attorneys, as officers of the court, have a duty to warn of true threats to harm members of the judiciary communicated to them by clients or by third parties.

* * *

Notes

1.   The Washington rule permitted disclosure of client confidences when the confidence related to the client's intent to commit a crime. How does this differ from MR 1.6?

2.   The Restatement summarizes the crime/fraud exception to the attorney-client privilege as follows:

The attorney-client privilege does not apply to a communication occurring when a client:

(a) consults a lawyer for the purpose, later accomplished, of obtaining assistance to engage in a crime or fraud or aiding a third person to do so, or

(b) regardless of the client's purpose at the time of consultation, uses the lawyer's advice or other services to engage in or assist a crime or fraud.

Restatement (Third) of the Law Governing Lawyers, § 82 (2000).

3. Were Hansen's threats made for the "purpose of securing primarily * * * legal services"?

One of the more difficult issues for courts has been the applicability of the attorney-client privilege to communications made within the corporation. Two rules have evolved. Under the "control group" test, communications are protected if they are between the corporation's lawyer and its senior management. *City of Philadelphia* v. *Westinghouse Elec. Corp.*, 210 F. Supp. 483 (E.D. Pa. 1962). Under the "subject matter" test, communications between attorney and employees are protected if "the subject matter of the communication is within the scope of the employee's corporate duties * * *." *See Diversified Industries, Inc.* v. *Meredith*, 572 F.2d 596, 609 (8th Cir. 1977).

Upjohn Co. v. United States
449 U.S. 383, 101 S. Ct. 677, 66 L. Ed. 2d 584 (1981)

Justice REHNQUIST delivered the opinion of the Court.

We granted certiorari in this case to address important questions concerning the scope of the attorney-client privilege in the corporate context * * *.

* * *

I

Petitioner Upjohn Co. manufactures and sells pharmaceuticals here and abroad. In January 1976 independent accountants conducting an audit of one of Upjohn's foreign subsidiaries discovered that the subsidiary made payments to or for the benefit of foreign government officials in order to secure government business. The accountants so informed petitioner Mr. Gerard Thomas, Upjohn's Vice President, Secretary, and General Counsel. Thomas is a member of the Michigan and New York Bars, and has been Upjohn's General Counsel for 20 years. He consulted with outside counsel and R. T. Parfet, Jr., Upjohn's Chairman of the Board. It was decided that the company would conduct an internal investigation of what were termed "questionable payments." As part of this investigation the attorneys prepared a letter containing a questionnaire which was sent to "All Foreign General and

Area Managers" over the Chairman's signature. The letter began by noting recent disclosures that several American companies made "possibly illegal" payments to foreign government officials and emphasized that the management needed full information concerning any such payments made by Upjohn. The letter indicated that the Chairman had asked Thomas, identified as "the company's General Counsel," "to conduct an investigation for the purpose of determining the nature and magnitude of any payments made by the Upjohn Company or any of its subsidiaries to any employee or official of a foreign government." The questionnaire sought detailed information concerning such payments. Managers were instructed to treat the investigation as "highly confidential" and not to discuss it with anyone other than Upjohn employees who might be helpful in providing the requested information. Responses were to be sent directly to Thomas. Thomas and outside counsel also interviewed the recipients of the questionnaire and some 33 other Upjohn officers or employees as part of the investigation.

On March 26, 1976, the company voluntarily submitted a preliminary report to the Securities and Exchange Commission on Form 8-K disclosing certain questionable payments. A copy of the report was simultaneously submitted to the Internal Revenue Service, which immediately began an investigation to determine the tax consequences of the payments. Special agents conducting the investigation were given lists by Upjohn of all those interviewed and all who had responded to the questionnaire. On November 23, 1976, the Service issued a summons pursuant to 26 U.S.C. § 7602 demanding production of:

> "All files relative to the investigation conducted under the supervision of Gerard Thomas to identify payments to employees of foreign governments and any political contributions made by the Upjohn Company or any of its affiliates * * *.

> "The records should include but not be limited to written questionnaires sent to managers of the Upjohn Company's foreign affiliates, and memorandums or notes of the interviews conducted in the United States and abroad with officers and employees of the Upjohn Company and its subsidiaries." [C].

The company declined to produce the documents * * * on the grounds that they were protected from disclosure by the attorney client privilege * * *. [The Court of Appeals for the Sixth Circuit held] that the privilege did not apply "[t]o the extent that the communications were made by officers and agents not responsible for directing Upjohn's actions in response to legal advice. . . for the simple reason that the communications were not the 'client's.'" [C]. The court reasoned that accepting petitioners' claim for a broader application of the privilege would encourage upper-echelon management to ignore unpleasant facts and create too broad a "zone of silence." Noting that Upjohn's counsel had interviewed officials such as the Chairman and President, the Court of Appeals remanded to the District Court so that a determination of who was within the "control group" could be made. * * *

II

Federal Rule of Evidence 501 provides that "the privilege of a witness. . . shall be governed by the principles of the common law as they may be interpreted by the courts of the United States in light of reason and experience." The attorney-client privilege is the oldest of the privileges for confidential communications known to the common law. 8 J. Wigmore, Evidence § 2290 (McNaughton rev. 1961). Its purpose is to encourage full and frank communication between attorneys and their clients and thereby promote broader public interests in the observance of law and administration of justice. The privilege recognizes that sound legal advice or advocacy serves public ends and that such advice or advocacy depends upon the lawyer's being fully informed by the client. * * *

* * * The first case to articulate the so-called "control group test" adopted by the court below, *Philadelphia* v. *Westinghouse Electric Corp.*, 210 F. Supp. 483, 485 (ED Pa.), petition for mandamus and prohibition denied *sub nom. General Electric Co.* v. *Kirkpatrick*, 312 F. 2d 742 (CA3 1962), cert. denied, 372 U. S. 943 (1963), reflected a similar conceptual approach:

> "Keeping in mind that the question is, 'Is it the corporation which is seeking the lawyer's advice when the asserted privileged communication is made?,' the most satisfactory solution, I think, is that if the employee making the communication, of whatever rank he may be, is in a position to control or even to take a substantial part in a decision about any action which the corporation may take upon the advice of the attorney, . . . then, in effect, *he is* (*or personifies*) *the corporation* when he makes his disclosure to the lawyer and the privilege would apply." (Emphasis supplied.)

Such a view, we think, overlooks the fact that the privilege exists to protect not only the giving of professional advice to those who can act on it but also the giving of information to the lawyer to enable him to give sound and informed advice. [C]. The first step in the resolution of any legal problem is ascertaining the factual background and sifting through the facts with an eye to the legally relevant. See ABA Code of Professional Responsibility, Ethical Consideration 4-1 [*Cf.* Comment to MR 1.6, *discussed supra*]:

> "A lawyer should be fully informed of all the facts of the matter he is handling in order for his client to obtain the full advantage of our legal system. It is for the lawyer in the exercise of his independent professional judgment to separate the relevant and important from the irrelevant and unimportant. The observance of the ethical obligation of a lawyer to hold inviolate the confidences and secrets of his client not only facilitates the full development of facts essential to proper representation of the client but also encourages laymen to seek early legal assistance."

* * *

The control group test adopted by the court below thus frustrates the very purpose of the privilege by discouraging the communication of relevant information by employees of the client to attorneys seeking to render legal advice to the client corporation. * * *

The narrow scope given the attorney-client privilege by the court below not only makes it difficult for corporate attorneys to formulate sound advice when their client is faced with a specific legal problem but also threatens to limit the valuable efforts of corporate counsel to ensure their client's compliance with the law. * * *

* * *

The Court of Appeals declined to extend the attorney-client privilege beyond the limits of the control group test for fear that doing so would entail severe burdens on discovery and create a broad "zone of silence" over corporate affairs. Application of the attorney-client privilege to communications such as those involved here, however, puts the adversary in no worse position than if the communications had never taken place. The privilege only protects disclosure of communications; it does not protect disclosure of the underlying facts by those who communicated with the attorney:

> "[T]he protection of the privilege extends only to *communications* and not to facts. A fact is one thing and a communication concerning that fact is an entirely different thing. The client cannot be compelled to answer the question, 'What did you say or write to the attorney?' but may not refuse to disclose any relevant fact within his knowledge

merely because he incorporated a statement of such fact into his communication to his attorney." *Philadelphia* v. *Westinghouse Electric Corp.*, 205 F. Supp. 830, 831 (ED Pa. 1962).

[Cc]. Here the Government was free to question the employees who communicated with Thomas and outside counsel. * * *

* * *

Notes

1.   What does the Court mean by "[the privilege] does not protect disclosure of the underlying facts by those who communicated with the attorney"?

2.   The control group test is a natural corollary to the adoption of an entity theory of corporation representation. The entity theory treats corporations as a separate being from the managers and owners of the corporation. The control group test recognizes that only certain "agents" of the entity speak for the corporation, and therefore the privilege covers only those agents. Other employees are treated as non-client witnesses, and can be questioned concerning their conversations with the entity's lawyers. Why does the Court reject the control group test?

3.   Should corporations and other organizations be afford confidentiality and attorney-client privilege, or should the duty of confidentiality and the privilege apply only to the individuals who act on behalf of the organizations?

4.   *Work Product* - In addition to the duty of confidentiality and the attorney-client privilege, the work product doctrine also protects some information that an attorney learns during legal representation. Under the work product rule, materials prepared by a lawyer in anticipation of litigation are immune from pretrial discovery. The work product doctrine is broader than the attorney-client privilege in that it applies to information gained from those other than the client. The doctrine is narrower than the attorney-client privilege in that it applies only to information gathered in anticipation of litigation. In addition, the opposing side can avoid the rule and discover information that an attorney has obtained if it can show extreme necessity, for example that a witness that the attorney has interviewed is no longer available and that the information is critically important. Under all circumstances, however, the doctrine protects a lawyer's mental impressions, opinions, and theories. For a fuller discussion of the work product doctrine, *see*

Hickman v. Taylor, 329 U.S. 495, 67 S.Ct. 385, 91 L.Ed. 451 (1947), Charles W. Wolfram, *Modern Legal Ethics* § 6.6 (1986), FRCP 26(b)(3), and Restatement (Third) of the Law Governing Lawyers, §§ 87-93 (2000). In the *Upjohn* case, the Supreme Court held that the notes of the Upjohn attorneys were protected by the work product doctrine. *See Upjohn, supra,* 449 U.S. 383 (1981).

Chapter Four

CONFLICTS OF INTEREST

A. Conflicting Interests With Other Clients and With Third Parties

Read Model Rules 1.7 to 2.4[1]

Hotz v. Minyard
304 S.C. 225, 403 S.E.2d 634 (1991)

GREGORY, Chief Justice:

This appeal is from an order granting respondents summary judgment on several causes of action. We reverse in part and affirm in part.

Respondent Minyard (Tommy) and appellant (Judy) are brother and sister. Their father, Mr. Minyard, owns two automobile dealerships, Judson T. Minyard, Inc. (Greenville Dealership), and Minyard-Waidner, Inc. (Anderson Dealership). Tommy has been the dealer in charge of the Greenville Dealership since 1977. Judy worked for her father at the Anderson Dealership beginning in 1983; she was also a vice-president and minority shareholder. In 1985, Mr. Minyard signed a contract with General Motors designating Judy the successor dealer of the Anderson Dealership.

Respondent Dobson is a South Carolina lawyer practicing in Greenville and a member of respondent Dobson & Dobson, P.A. (Law Firm). * * *

Dobson did legal work for the Minyard family and its various businesses for many years. On October 24, 1984, Mr. Minyard came to Law Firm's office to execute a will with his wife, his secretary, and Tommy in attendance. At this meeting he signed a will which left Tommy the Greenville Dealership, gave other family members bequests totalling $250,000.00, and divided the remainder of his

---

[1]   For MR 1.7, *Cf.*, DR 5-101(A), 5-105; EC 5-14, 5-16; Cal. Rules 3-310. For MR 2.3 there is no counterpart in the Model Code or the Cal. Rules.

estate equally between Tommy and a trust for Judy after his wife's death. All present at the meeting were given copies of this will. Later that afternoon, however, Mr. Minyard returned to Dobson's office and signed a second will containing the same provisions as the first except that it gave the real estate upon which the Greenville dealership was located to Tommy outright. Mr. Minyard instructed Dobson not to disclose the existence of the second will. He specifically directed that Judy not be told about it.

In January 1985, Judy called Dobson requesting a copy of the will her father had signed at the morning meeting on October 24, 1984. At Mr. Minyard's direction, or at least with his express permission, Dobson showed Judy the first will and discussed it with her in detail.

Judy testified she had the impression from her discussion with Dobson that under her father's will she would receive the Anderson Dealership and would share equally with her brother in her father's estate. According to Dobson, however, he merely explained Mr. Minyard's intent to provide for Judy as he had for Tommy when and if she became capable of handling a dealership. Dobson made a notation to this effect on the copy of the will he discussed with Judy. Judy claimed she was led to believe that the handwritten notes were part of her father's will.

In any event, Judy claims Dobson told her the will she was shown was in actuality her father's last will and testament. Although Dobson denies ever making this express statement, he admits he never told her the will he discussed with her had been revoked.

In January 1986, Mr. Minyard was admitted to the hospital for various health problems. In April 1986, he suffered a massive stroke. Although the date of the onset of his mental incompetence is disputed, it is uncontested he is now mentally incompetent.

Judy and Tommy agreed that while their father was ill, Judy would attend to his daily care and Tommy would temporarily run the Anderson Dealership until Judy returned. During this time, Tommy began making changes at the Anderson Dealership. Under his direction, the Anderson Dealership bought out another dealership owned by Mr. Minyard, Judson Lincoln-Mercury, Inc., which was operating at a loss. Tommy also formed a holding company which assumed ownership of Mr. Minyard's real estate leased to the Anderson Dealership. Consequently, rent paid by the dealership was greatly increased.

Judy questioned the wisdom of her brother's financial dealings. When she sought to return to the Anderson Dealership as successor dealer, Tommy refused to relinquish control. Eventually, in August 1986, he terminated Judy from the dealership's payroll.

Judy consulted an Anderson law firm concerning her problems with her brother's operation of the Anderson Dealership. As a result, on November 15, 1986, Mr. Minyard executed a codicil removing Judy and her children as beneficiaries under his will. Judy was immediately advised of this development by letter. In March 1987, Judy met with Tommy, her mother, and Dobson at the Law Firm's office. She was told if she discharged her attorneys and dropped her plans for a lawsuit, she would be restored under her father's will and could work at the Greenville Dealership with significant fringe benefits. Judy testified she understood restoration under the will meant she would inherit the Anderson Dealership and receive half her father's estate, including the real estate, as she understood from her 1985 meeting with Dobson. Judy discharged her attorneys and moved to Greenville. Eventually, however, Tommy terminated her position at the Greenville Dealership.

As a result of the above actions by Tommy and Dobson, Judy commenced this suit alleging various causes of action. The causes of action against Tommy for tortious interference with contract, a shareholder derivative suit for wrongful diversion of corporate profits, and fraud survived summary judgment and are not at issue here. Judy appeals the trial judge's order granting summary judgment on the remaining causes of action against Tommy, Dobson, and the professional associations. We address only the trial judge's ruling on the cause of action against Dobson for breach of fiduciary duty. Judy also appeals the dismissal of Minyard-Waidner, Inc. as a party defendant.

ANALYSIS

Judy's complaint alleges Dobson breached his fiduciary duty to her by misrepresenting her father's will in January 1985. As a result, in March 1987 she believed she would regain the Anderson Dealership if she refrained from pursuing her claim against her brother. This delay gave Tommy additional time in control of the Anderson Dealership during which he depleted its assets. Law Firm and

Accounting Firm are charged with vicarious liability for Dobson's acts.

The trial judge granted Dobson, Law Firm, and Accounting Firm summary judgment on the ground Dobson owed Judy no fiduciary duty because he was acting as Mr. Minyard's attorney and not as Judy's attorney in connection with her father's will. We disagree.

We find the evidence indicates a factual issue whether Dobson breached a fiduciary duty to Judy when she went to his office seeking legal advice about the effect of her father's will. Law Firm had prepared Judy's tax returns for approximately twenty years until September 1985 and had prepared a will for her she signed only one week earlier. Judy testified she consulted Dobson personally in 1984 or 1985 about a suspected misappropriation of funds at one of the dealerships and as late as 1986 regarding her problems with her brother. She claimed she trusted Dobson because of her dealings with him over the years as her lawyer and accountant.

A fiduciary relationship exists when one has a special confidence in another so that the latter, in equity and good conscience, is bound to act in good faith. [C]. An attorney/client relationship is by nature a fiduciary one. [C]. Although Dobson represented Mr. Minyard and not Judy regarding her father's will, Dobson did have an ongoing attorney/client relationship with Judy and there is evidence she had "a special confidence" in him. While Dobson had no duty to disclose the existence of the second will against his client's (Mr. Minyard's) wishes, he owed Judy the duty to deal with her in good faith and not actively misrepresent the first will. We find there is a factual issue presented whether Dobson breached a fiduciary duty to Judy. We conclude summary judgment was improperly granted Dobson on this cause of action. [C].

* * *

Notes

1. The trial court found that Dobson was acting only as Mr. Minyard's attorney in connection with the will. Why does the appellate court disagree?

2. How would this case have been resolved if Dobson had not been Judy's attorney? Does liability for his conduct depend upon the existence of an attorney-client relationship with the injured party?

3. Dobson supervised the execution of the first will in the morning in the presence of the Mr. Minyard's wife, secretary and son. Later, that same day, Dobson supervised the execution of a second will by Mr. Minyard, and agreed to keep the existence of the second will a secret. Did Dobson violate any Rules of Professional Conduct?

4. When Judy asked Dobson to advise her concerning the terms of her father's will, Dobson had two conflicting duties: a duty to maintain the confidences of Mr. Minyard, and a duty to give all relevant information to Judy. How could Dobson honor Mr. Minyard's wish to conceal the existence of a second will, while dealing with Judy "in good faith"? If Dobson had refused to discuss the first will, would his refusal violate his duty of confidentiality? Recall Professor Rotunda's discussion of "waving the red flag" of withdrawal in Chapter 3.

5. In deciding that Judy was Dobson's client, the court noted that Dobson prepared a will which she had signed one week prior to the meeting concerning her father's will. It is common practice for lawyers to prepare wills for several members of the same family. Yet as *Hotz* illustrates, interests of individual family members may be in conflict. Should lawyers represent more than one family member for estate planning? *See* Teresa S. Collett, "The Ethics of Intergenerational Representation," 62 *Fordham L.Rev.* 1453 (1994).

6. John Smith and his wife Mary go to a lawyer who has handled some minor legal matters for John to make their wills prior to going on a trip abroad.

John tells his lawyer what disposition he and his wife desire to make of their estates, and the lawyer prepares separate wills for them to sign prior to their departure. After John has signed his will, the lawyer suggests to John that he would like to be alone with Mary before she signs. John withdraws to another office. The lawyer asks Mary if the will is as she would have made it had her husband not been present at the conference and if the will were to be secret from her husband.

She says no, that her will as drawn contains several provisions that are contrary to her wishes, and that she would change if her husband were not to know the ultimate disposition of her estate. However, she says that she would not be willing to precipitate the domestic discord and confrontation that would occur if her husband were to learn that she had drawn a will contrary to his wishes and in accordance with her own desires.

Mary asks the lawyer if he will write one page of her will to provide that certain persons benefiting by her will as drawn will be replaced by certain other persons. The lawyer states that under the circumstances he does not think that he can in fairness represent her in making these changes but suggests that she go ahead and sign this will and then, as soon as possible, go to some other lawyer and have her will rewritten in accordance with her true wishes.

Legal Ethics Forum, "The case of the unwanted will," 65 *A.B.A. J.* 484 (conducted by Stanley A. Kaplan 1979). Has the lawyer acted ethically in accepting John's directions concerning the contents of Mary's will? Can the lawyer ethically allow Mary to sign a will that the lawyer knows does not represent Mary's desires concerning the distribution of her property at her death? What obligation does the lawyer owe to John under these circumstances? *See* Thomas L. Shaffer, "The Legal Ethics of Radical Individualism," 65 *Tex. L. Rev.* 963 (1987), and Teresa S. Collett, "And the Two Shall Be as One . . . Until the Lawyers Are Done," 7 *Notre Dame J.L. Ethics & Pub. Pol'y* 101 (1993). Compare the facts of A v. B, 726 A.2d 924 (N.J. 1999) in which a law firm that jointly represented husband and wife in planning their estates sought to disclose the existence of husband's illegitimate child to wife.

Employers Casualty Company v. Tilley
496 S.W.2d 552 (Tex. 1973)

DANIEL, Justice.

This is a declaratory judgment action filed on January 22, 1971, by Employers Casualty Company, the insurer, against 'Joe Tilley, d/b/a Joe's Rental Tools and/or Oil City Casing Crews, Joe's Rental Tools Company, a corporation,' the insured, seeking a determination that a policy violation by the insured (late notice) relieved the insurer of any obligation to defend a personal injury suit instituted by Douglas Starky against the insured on September 19, 1969. Tilley and the corporations named above will be referred to collectively as 'Tilley'.

Prior to filing the instant suit, Employers on October 6, 1969 * * * engaged an attorney to represent Tilley as his attorney in the Starky personal injury suit. For a period of nearly 18 months, the attorney not only performed such services for Tilley in defending against Starky, but he also performed services for Employers which were adverse to Tilley on the question of coverage. Tilley claimed that he had no knowledge of the Starky accident which occurred on

November 25, 1967, until he was sued on September 19, 1969. This was his excuse for not notifying Employers before the suit was filed.

Knowing of Tilley's contention, the attorney did not advise him of the apparent conflict of interest between Tilley and Employers. Instead, he continued to act as Tilley's attorney while actively working against him in developing evidence for Employers on the coverage question. Such evidence subsequently became the basis for this suit, filed by another attorney for Employers against Tilley, seeking to deny coverage on the grounds of late notice. Tilley filed a cross-action, alleging among other things waiver and estoppel.

[Douglas Starky] was an employee of Prudential Drilling Company at the time of his injury on a Prudential well site on November 25, 1967. Tilley, as an independent contractor was furnishing tools and employees for the lifting of casing pipe off a Prudential platform. Starky had tied the 'catline' to a casing pipe immediately prior to the pipe slipping and falling upon him, causing injuries which subsequently resulted in the loss of his right arm. It was Tilley's equipment and crew which were lifting the pipe after it had been supposedly secured to the catline by Starky. Grady Fore was Tilley's foreman in charge of the Tilley crew and operating the lift at the time the pipe slipped. He said the accident was due to the manner in which Starky tied the catline to the pipe rather than to the manner in which he lifted the pipe. It is undisputed that Fore knew of the occurrence, but it is disputed as to whether he or anyone else told Tilley of the accident or whether Tilley had actual notice of it before Starky filed suit against Tilley on September 19, 1969.

Employers concedes its coverage and duty to defend Tilley, unless as now contended in this suit, Tilley had actual or imputed knowledge of the accident when or soon after it occurred. If so, Employers contends that Tilley has lost coverage for failure to comply with the following provision of the policy:

'4. INSURED'S DUTIES IN THE EVENT OF OCCURRENCE, CLAIM OR SUIT: (a) In the event of an occurrence, written notice, containing particulars sufficient to identify the insured and also reasonably obtainable information with respect to the time, place and circumstances thereof, and the names and addresses of the injured and of available witnesses, shall be given by or for the insured to the company or any of its authorized agents as soon as practicable.'

While Employers alleges that Tilley had actual notice of the 'occurrence' soon after the accident in 1967, its motion for summary judgment was based solely upon undisputed proof that Tilley's foreman, Grady Fore, was present and had knowledge of the occurrence on November 25, 1967; its contention that this knowledge was imputed to Tilley; and that failure of Tilley to give notice for 20 months was, as a matter of law, a breach of the notice provisions of the policy. * * *

[Tilley's motion for summary judgment alleged:]

5. During the period that Employers Casualty purported to offer a defense to Tilley, the company without any warning or notice to Tilley of any conflict of interests committed the following acts in breach of their fiduciary duty through its agents and attorneys:

(a) The attorney engaged by Employers to represent Tilley took a statement from Tilley's foreman to establish that Tilley had notice through the foreman of the accident.

(b) The attorney took four other statements from Tilley employees seeking to establish that they had informed Tilley of the accident, knowing at the time that this was contrary to Tilley's position.

(c) The same attorney briefed the legal question of late notice for Employers without advising Tilley of his actions or his findings.

(d) The attorney interviewed two other persons at the request of Employers to establish the late notice defense now asserted by Employers against Tilley.

(e) The attorney, over a period of a year and one-half wrote numerous letters and engaged in numerous oral conversations with the insurance company pertaining to developing its coverage defense, suggesting additional investigation, and advising as to the legal possibilities of establishing such defense.

* * *

[We are] confronted with the undisputed proof that it was the attorney furnished by Employers to represent Tilley in the Starky suit who at the same time worked for Employers adversely to Tilley in developing the evidence upon which this suit for denial of coverage is based; that the development of evidence and briefing against Tilley on the coverage question was sought and paid for by Employers, without Tilley being informed of the conflict of services being performed by his attorney; that Employers, through this attorney, continued to represent Tilley for nearly 18 months before withdrawing; and the forceful argument that such conduct constituted a waiver of the policy defense and was so contrary to public policy that Employers is estopped as a matter of law from denying its responsibility for the defense of the Starky case. * * *

These are serious questions involving legal ethics and public policy with which this Court has not dealt under like circumstances. Counsel for both parties apparently concede that similar situations often confront insurers and attorneys employed by them to represent insureds under comprehensive liability insurance policies and that guidelines from this Court would be welcomed, even though the parties disagree as to what the guidelines and consequences should be. At the outset, it should be stated that the impeccable reputation of the attorney engaged by Employers to represent Tilley, Mr. Dewey Gonsoulin, and the fact that his conduct may be representative of the customary conduct of counsel employed by insurance companies in similar situations, is not questioned by counsel for Tilley nor by this Court. However, as stated by courts of other jurisdictions which have dealt with the problem, custom, reputation, and honesty of intention and motive are not the tests for determining the guidelines which an attorney must follow when confronted with a conflict between the insurer who pays his fee and the insured who is entitled to his undivided loyalty as his attorney of record. [Cc]

Duties of Insurers and Attorneys Employed to Represent Insureds

Under the policy in question (comprehensive liability) the insurance company's obligation to defend the insurer provides that the attorney to represent the insured is to be selected, employed and paid by the insurance company. Nevertheless, such attorney becomes the attorney of record and the legal representative of the insured, and as such he owes the insured the same type of unqualified loyalty as if he had been originally employed by the insured. If a conflict arises between the interests of the insurer and the insured, the attorney owes a duty to the insured to immediately advise him of the conflict.

* * *

[Ethical Consideration 5—16 of the Code of Professional Responsibility provides:]

'EC 5–16. In those instances in which a lawyer is justified in representing two or more clients having differing interests, it is nevertheless essential that each client be given the opportunity to evaluate his need for representation free of any potential conflict and to obtain other counsel if he so desires. Thus before a lawyer may represent multiple clients, he should explain fully to each client the implications of the common representation and should accept or continue employment only if the clients consent. If there are present other circumstances that might cause any of the multiple clients to question the undivided loyalty of the lawyer, he should also advise all of the clients of those circumstances.'

The American Bar Association National Conference of Lawyers and Liability Insurers made a careful study of this recurring problem and issued a list of 'guiding principles' for the guidance of liability insurers furnishing legal counsel for their insureds. [CC] Two of the principles which are relevant here read in part as follows:

'IV. CONFLICTS OF INTEREST GENERALLY–DUTIES OF ATTORNEY. In any claim or in any suit where the attorney selected by the company to defend the claim or action becomes aware of facts or information which indicate to him a question of coverage in the matter being defended or any other conflict of interest between the company and the insured with respect to the defense of the matter, the attorney should promptly inform both the company and the insured, preferably in writing, of the nature and extent of the conflicting interest. . . .'

'V. CONTINUATION BY ATTORNEY EVEN THOUGH THERE IS A CONFLICT OF INTERESTS. Where there is a question of coverage or other conflict of interest, the company and the attorney selected by the company to defend the claim or suit should not thereafter continue to defend the insured in the matter in question unless, after a full explanation of the coverage question, the insured acquiesces in the continuation of such defense. . . .'

We approve the above quoted 'guiding principles' as conforming to the public policy of this State heretofore enunciated by this Court in our Canons of Ethics. * * *

* * *

The subsequent conduct of Employers through the same attorney it had engaged to represent Tilley was clearly in violation of the public policy set forth in the above 'guiding principles.' An attorney employed by an insurer to represent the insured simply cannot take up the cudgels of the insurer against the insured as was done in the Starky case at Employers' behest. * * *

Effect of Subsequent Conduct of Employers and Attorney

Even when no violation of public policy is involved, an estoppel may arise from silence, where there is a duty to speak, and failure to do so worsens or prejudices the position of the party to whom the duty is owed. [CC] Employers contends that no prejudice has been shown as a matter of law to have occurred by reason of its conduct or silence. We disagree. Tilley was led to make his employees available for statements, sometimes on his own time and at his own expense, with no reason to think that his attorney was working other than in his own interest. The second statement taken from his foreman, Grady Fore, on March 12, 1970, admittedly had as one of its purposes the development of late notice evidence against Tilley. * * *

* * *

Employers argues that this work and gathering of evidence by the Employers-- Tilley attorney was not prejudicial because it could have been developed just as easily by one of Employers' agents, investigators or other attorneys. * * * Whether Employers would have been as successful in gathering evidence through other attorneys as it was through the attorney that Tilley and his employees thought to be looking after nothing but Tilley's defense, is a matter of speculation. It falls in the realm of what might have been. We are here concerned with what actually occurred–the means by which Employers actually developed the evidence of Grady Fore's knowledge and Tilley's alleged knowledge of the accident which occurred on November 25, 1967, on which the present declaratory judgment suit is based.

It is undisputed that the work of the Employers--Tilley attorney on the coverage issue now involved in this law suit was not on his own initiative or merely incidental to his defense of Tilley; it was at the instance and request of Employers and for its benefit against Tilley. As indicated, both Employers and the Employers--Tilley attorney owed an obligation to immediately notify Tilley of the conflict on the specific coverage question which was known to them on or soon after October 9, 1969. Their failure to do so for nearly 18 months can be attributed only to Employers' desire to strengthen its position in preparation for the filing of the instant suit. We think prejudice to Tilley in the Starky case and in this case has been shown as a matter of law.

Under the undisputed facts and circumstances of this case, it would be untenable to permit Employers to disclaim liability for the defense of Tilley in the Starky suit on account of the late notice defense. Its conduct being violative of the guiding principles and public policy heretofore discussed, we hold that Employers is estopped as a matter of law from denying the responsibilities under its policy for defense of the Starky suit.

Accordingly, for the reasons stated in this opinion, the judgment of the Court of Civil Appeals is affirmed.

SAM D. JOHNSON, Justice (concurring).

* * *

[The Canons of this court's Code of Professional Responsibility were formulated to govern attorneys, they are directed to lawyers, they set the proscriptive limits for members of the legal profession. The fourth Canon speaks to the fiduciary relationship between a lawyer and his client and the principle that the confidence of a client must be held inviolate; the fifth recites that the lawyer's professional judgment is to be used solely for the benefit of his client and that no conflicting interest shall dilute such loyalty. [Cf. MR 1.6-1.8 and Comments]

If the representation from the record described by the opinion of the majority is to be considered as a representation of two or more clients, the ethical considerations enumerated under the Interests of Multiple Clients are controlling.

'EC 5–14. Maintaining the independence of professional judgment required of a lawyer precludes his acceptance or continuation of employment that will adversely affect his judgment on behalf of or dilute his loyalty to a client. This problem arises whenever a lawyer is asked to represent two or more clients who may have differing interests, whether such interest be conflicting, inconsistent, diverse, or otherwise discordant.

'EC 5–15. If a lawyer is requested to undertake or to continue represen-tation of multiple clients having potentially differing interests, he must weigh carefully the possibility that his judgment may be impaired or his loyalty divided if he accepts or continues the employment. He should resolve all doubts against the propriety of the representation. A lawyer should never represent in litigation multiple clients with differing interests; and there are few situations in which he would be justified in representing in litigation multiple clients with potentially differing interests. . . .'

* * *

These two parties, Tilley and Employers Casualty, had differing interests and this was known to the attorney either at the outset or after only a very few days from the attorney's employment. Even with such knowledge there was no withdrawal by the attorney; there was no information or explanation concerning the conflict given to Tilley. To the contrary, the record strongly suggests concealment of the conflict from Tilley for the purpose of ultimately promoting the interest and position of Employers Casualty over that of Tilley; by providing a defense for Employers Casualty whereby it would have no obligation to Tilley.

The representation provided by the attorney more appropriately should be construed as representation of a single client, Tilley. The majority opinion of this court recites that the policy in question provides that the attorney to represent the insured is to be selected, employed and paid by Employers Casualty but that such attorney is to be the attorney of record and legal representative of the insured (Tilley) and owes to him the same type of unqualified loyalty as if he had been originally employed by him. The 'unqualified loyalty' of the attorney to his client (Tilley) tolerates no comparison against those factual recitals made in the majority opinion. Such conduct must be measured by the first of the ethical considerations enumerated under Canon 5 which relates to the lawyer's duty, obligation and loyalty to his client.

> 'EC 5–1. The professional judgment of a lawyer should be exercised, within the bounds of the law, solely for the benefit of his client and free of compromising influences and loyalties. Neither his personal interests, the interests of other clients, nor the desires of third persons should be permitted to dilute his loyalty to his client.'

The Ethical Considerations under Canon 5 make it clear that situations where the cost of legal services are borne by a third party are ethically proper only so long as control remains in the client and the responsibility of the lawyer is solely to the client. [Cf. MR 1.8(f)]

This court's majority opinion has concluded that the attorney's actions, as in the present instance, affect the rights of the two parties to this action as against each other. The 'guiding principles' should not be concepts which have not been considered or approved by the bench and bar of this state; the 'guiding principles' should be this court's Code of Professional Responsibility which speaks precisely and directly to the permissible actions of attorneys. This court should not be considering the ethical obligation, whatever it may be, which is required of a commercial enterprise to its customer; this court should be considering the fiduciary relationship inherent in the attorney-client relationship and the effect of its transgression upon the rights of the parties hereto.

Notes

1.   In cases where an attorney represents the insured, the identity of the client is often contested. Many jurisdictions hold that the lawyer has two clients, both the insurance company and the policy holder. Charles Silver & Kent Syverud, "The Professional Responsibilities of Insurance Defense Lawyers," 45 Duke L.J. 255, 273 (1995). A smaller number hold that defense counsel represents only the insured. E.g. Atlanta Int'l Ins. Co. v. Bell, 475 N.W.2d 294 (Mich. 1991). In ABA Formal Opinion 96-403 (1996) (Obligations Of A Lawyer Representing An Insured Who Objects To A Proposed Settlement Within Policy Limits), the Committee observed, "[t]he Model Rules of Professional Conduct offer virtually no guidance as to whether a lawyer retained and paid by an insurer to defend its insured represents the insured, the insurer, or both." ABA Comm. on Professional Ethics and Professional Responsibility, Formal Op. 01-421 (2001).

2.   The lawyer's duty of loyalty to the client under the Model Code of Professional Responsibility continues under the Model Rules. See MR 1.7. When someone other than the client pays a lawyer, MR 1.8(f) requires that the client consent to such payment, that there be no interference with the client-lawyer relationship, and that information relating to the representation remain confidential.

3.   Generally, liability insurance contracts require the insurance company to defend the policy holder and to pay for liability (up to a limit). Such contracts often give the insurance company the right to control the defense. Attorneys who are hired by liability insurance companies to represent policy holders face several potential conflicts of interest. In addition to the coverage and policy waiver problems discussed in *Tilley*, there may be settlement problems. For example, the insured may want to settle the case for the policy limits, and the insurance company may want to litigate. On the other hand, under a professional malpractice policy, the insured may want to establish that

he or she did not commit malpractice, and the company may want to settle. See Rogers v. Robson, Masters, Ryan, Brumund, & Belom, 407 N.E.2d 47 (Ill. 1980).

4. In an effort to reduce legal expenses, many insurance companies have imposed litigation cost limits and management guidelines. In Formal Opinion 01-421, the ABA Standing Committee on Ethics and Professional Responsibility instructed lawyers that when representing insured clients, they should not allow these limits and guidelines to compromise their professional judgment or result in an inability to provide competent representation of the insured.

5. What practical effect would the dual client or single client designation have? Cf. MRs 1.7 and 1.8(f). For discussion of the issues raised above and others, see Charles W. Wolfram, *Modern Legal Ethics* §8.4 (1986) and Restatement (Third) of the Law Governing Lawyers §134, comment f (2000).

B. Constitutional Considerations in Criminal Cases

In the context of criminal litigation, conflicts of interest raise constitutional concerns.

Mickens v. Taylor
122 S. Ct. 1237, 152 L.Ed. 2d 291 (2002)

Justice SCALIA delivered the opinion of the Court.

The question presented in this case is what a defendant must show in order to demonstrate a Sixth Amendment violation where the trial court fails to inquire into a potential conflict of interest about which it knew or reasonably should have known.

I

[On March 20, 1992, Bryan Saunders was appointed to be the attorney for Timothy Hall, who was charged with assault. Saunders met with Hall once for 15 to 20 minutes sometime the following week. On March 30, Hall was murdered. "[F]our days later a juvenile court judge dismissed the charges against [Hall], noting on the docket sheet that Hall was deceased. The one-page docket sheet also listed Saunders as Hall's counsel. On April 6, 1992, the same judge appointed Saunders to represent petitioner [Mickens who was charged with murdering Hall]. Saunders did not disclose to the court, his co-counsel, or petitioner that he had previously represented Hall." A Virginia jury convicted Mickens of premeditated murder during or following the commission of an attempted sodomy. Finding the murder outrageously and wantonly vile, it sentenced petitioner to death. Mickens sought habeas corpus relief alleging that he was denied effective assistance of counsel because Hall had a conflict of interest.]

The Sixth Amendment provides that a criminal defendant shall have the right to "the assistance of counsel for his defense." This right has been accorded, we have said, "not for its own sake, but because of the effect it has on the ability of the accused to receive a fair trial." [C]. It follows from this that assistance which is ineffective in preserving fairness does not meet the constitutional mandate, see *Strickland v. Washington*, 466 U.S. 668, 685-686, 104 S.Ct. 2052, 80 L.Ed.2d 674 (1984); and it also follows that defects in assistance that have no probable effect upon the trial's outcome do not establish a constitutional violation. As a general matter, a defendant alleging a Sixth Amendment violation must demonstrate "a reasonable probability that, but for counsel's unprofessional errors, the result of the proceeding would have been different." *Id.*, at 694, 104 S.Ct. 2052.

There is an exception to this general rule. We have spared the defendant the need of showing probable effect upon the outcome, and have simply presumed such effect, where assistance of counsel has been denied entirely or during a critical stage of the proceeding. When that has occurred, the likelihood that the verdict is unreliable is so high that a case-by-case inquiry is unnecessary. [Cc] But only in "circumstances of that magnitude" do we forgo individual inquiry into whether counsel's inadequate performance undermined the reliability of the verdict. [C]

We have held in several cases that "circumstances of that magnitude" may also arise when the defendant's attorney actively represented conflicting interests. The nub of the question before us is whether the principle established by these cases provides an exception to the general rule of *Strickland* under the circumstances of the present case. To answer that question, we must examine those cases in some detail.

In *Holloway v. Arkansas*, 435 U.S. 475, 98 S.Ct. 1173, 55 L.Ed.2d 426 (1978), defense counsel had objected that he could not adequately represent the divergent interests of three codefendants. *Id.*, at 478-480, 98 S.Ct. 1173. Without inquiry, the trial court had denied counsel's motions for the appointment of separate counsel * * *. The

Holloway Court deferred to the judgment of counsel regarding the existence of a disabling conflict, recognizing that a defense attorney is in the best position to determine when a conflict exists, that he has an ethical obligation to advise the court of any problem, and that his declarations to the court are "virtually made under oath." *Id.,* at 485-486, 98 S.Ct. 1173 * * * [*Holloway*] creates an automatic reversal rule only where defense counsel is forced to represent codefendants over his timely objection, unless the trial court has determined that there is no conflict. *Id.,* at 488, 98 S.Ct. 1173 ("[W]henever a trial court improperly requires joint representation over timely objection reversal is automatic").

In *Cuyler v. Sullivan*, 446 U.S. 335, 100 S.Ct. 1708, 64 L.Ed.2d 333 (1980), the respondent was one of three defendants accused of murder who were tried separately, represented by the same counsel. Neither counsel nor anyone else objected to the multiple representation, and counsel's opening argument at Sullivan's trial suggested that the interests of the defendants were aligned. *Id.,* at 347-348, 100 S.Ct. 1708. We declined to extend *Holloway* 's automatic reversal rule to this situation and held that, absent objection, a defendant must demonstrate that "a conflict of interest actually affected the adequacy of his representation." 446 U.S., at 348-349, 100 S.Ct. 1708. In addition to describing the defendant's burden of proof, *Sullivan* addressed separately a trial court's duty to inquire into the propriety of a multiple representation, construing *Holloway* to require inquiry only when "the trial court knows or reasonably should know that a particular conflict exists," 446 U.S., at 347, 100 S.Ct. 1708--which is not to be confused with when the trial court is aware of a vague, unspecified possibility of conflict, such as that which "inheres in almost every instance of multiple representation," *id.,* at 348, 100 S.Ct. 1708. In *Sullivan,* no "special circumstances" triggered the trial court's duty to inquire. *Id.,* at 346, 100 S.Ct. 1708.

* * *

Petitioner's proposed rule of automatic reversal when there existed a conflict that did not affect counsel's performance, but the trial judge failed to make the *Sullivan*-mandated inquiry, makes little policy sense. As discussed, the rule applied when the trial judge is not aware of the conflict (and thus not obligated to inquire) is that prejudice will be presumed only if the conflict has significantly affected counsel's performance--thereby rendering the verdict unreliable, even though *Strickland* prejudice cannot be shown. [C]. The trial court's awareness of a potential conflict neither renders it more likely that counsel's performance was significantly affected nor in any other way renders the verdict unreliable. * * *

* * *

Since this was not a case in which (as in *Holloway)* counsel protested his inability simultaneously to represent multiple defendants; and since the trial court's failure to make the *Sullivan*-mandated inquiry does not reduce the petitioner's burden of proof; it was at least necessary, to void the conviction, for petitioner to establish that the conflict of interest adversely affected his counsel's performance. The Court of Appeals having found no such effect [C], the denial of habeas relief must be affirmed.

* * *

Lest today's holding be misconstrued, we note that the only question presented was the effect of a trial court's failure to inquire into a potential conflict upon the *Sullivan* rule that deficient performance of counsel must be shown. The case was presented and argued on the assumption that (absent some exception for failure to inquire) *Sullivan* would be applicable--requiring a showing of defective performance, but *not* requiring in addition (as *Strickland* does in other ineffectiveness-of-counsel cases), a showing of probable effect upon the outcome of trial. That assumption was not unreasonable in light of the holdings of Courts of Appeals, which have applied *Sullivan* "unblinkingly" to "all kinds of alleged attorney ethical conflicts," [C]. They have invoked the *Sullivan* standard not only when (as here) there is a conflict rooted in counsel's obligations to *former* clients [Cc], but even when representation of the defendant somehow implicates counsel's personal or financial interests, including a book deal [C], a job with the prosecutor's office [C], the teaching of classes to Internal Revenue Service agents [C], a romantic "entanglement" with the prosecutor [C], or fear of antagonizing the trial judge [C].

It must be said, however, that the language of *Sullivan* itself does not clearly establish, or indeed even support, such expansive application. "[U]ntil," it said, "a defendant shows that his counsel *actively represented* conflicting interests, he has not established the constitutional predicate for his claim of ineffective assistance." 446 U.S., at 350, 100 S.Ct. 1708 (emphasis added). Both *Sullivan* itself, see *id.,* at 348-349, 100 S.Ct. 1708, and *Holloway,* see 435 U.S., at 490-491,

98 S.Ct. 1173, stressed the high probability of prejudice arising from multiple concurrent representation, and the difficulty of proving that prejudice. [Cc]. Not all attorney conflicts present comparable difficulties. * * *

This is not to suggest that one ethical duty is more or less important than another. The purpose of our *Holloway* and *Sullivan* exceptions from the ordinary requirements of *Strickland,* however, is not to enforce the Canons of Legal Ethics, but to apply needed prophylaxis in situations where *Strickland* itself is evidently inadequate to assure vindication of the defendant's Sixth Amendment right to counsel. [C]. In resolving this case on the grounds on which it was presented to us, we do not rule upon the need for the *Sullivan* prophylaxis in cases of successive representation. Whether *Sullivan* should be extended to such cases remains, as far as the jurisprudence of this Court is concerned, an open question.

* * *

For the reasons stated, the judgment of the Court of Appeals is *Affirmed.*

Justice STEVENS, dissenting.

* * *

* * * In retrospect, it seems obvious that the death penalty might have been avoided by acknowledging Mickens' involvement, but emphasizing the evidence suggesting that their sexual encounter was consensual. Mickens' habeas counsel garnered evidence suggesting that Hall was a male prostitute, [Cc]; that the area where Hall was killed was known for prostitution, [C]; and that there was no evidence that Hall was forced to the secluded area where he was ultimately murdered. An unconflicted attorney could have put forward a defense tending to show that Mickens killed Hall only after the two engaged in consensual sex, but Saunders offered no such defense. This was a crucial omission--a finding of forcible sodomy was an absolute prerequisite to Mickens' eligibility for the death penalty. * * *

* * *

If the defendant is found guilty of a capital offense, the ensuing proceedings that determine whether he will be put to death are critical in every sense of the word. At those proceedings, testimony about the impact of the crime on the victim, including testimony about the character of the victim, may have a critical effect on the jury's decision. [C].   Because a lawyer's fiduciary relationship with his deceased client survives the client's death, [C], Saunders necessarily labored under conflicting obligations that were irreconcilable. He had a duty to protect the reputation and confidences of his deceased client, and a duty to impeach the impact evidence presented by the prosecutor.

* * *

Mickens had a constitutional right to the services of an attorney devoted solely to his interests. That right was violated. The lawyer who did represent him had a duty to disclose his prior representation of the victim to Mickens and to the trial judge. That duty was violated. When Mickens had no counsel, the trial judge had a duty to "make a thorough inquiry and to take all steps necessary to insure the fullest protection of" his right to counsel. [C]. Despite knowledge of the lawyer's prior representation, she violated that duty.

We will never know whether Mickens would have received the death penalty if those violations had not occurred nor precisely what effect they had on Saunders' representation of Mickens. [C]. We do know that he did not receive the kind of representation that the Constitution guarantees.   If Mickens had been represented by an attorney-impostor who never passed a bar examination, we might also be unable to determine whether the impostor's educational shortcomings "'actually affected the adequacy of his representation.'" [C]. We would, however, surely set aside his conviction if the person who had represented him was not a real lawyer. * * *

* * *

Justice BREYER, with whom Justice GINSBURG joins, dissenting.

The Commonwealth of Virginia seeks to put the petitioner, Walter Mickens, Jr., to death after having appointed to represent him as his counsel a lawyer who, at the time of the murder, was representing the very person Mickens was accused of killing. I believe that, in a case such as this one, a categorical approach is warranted and automatic reversal is required.   To put the matter in language this Court has previously used: By appointing this lawyer to represent Mickens, the Commonwealth created a "structural defect affecting the framework within which the trial [and sentencing] proceeds, rather than simply an error in the trial process itself." [C].

* * *

* * * [T]his is the kind of representational incompatibility that is egregious on its face. Mickens was represented by the murder victim's lawyer; that lawyer had represented the victim on a criminal matter; and that lawyer's representation of the victim had continued until one business day before the lawyer was appointed to represent the defendant.

* * * [T]he conflict is exacerbated by the fact that it occurred in a capital murder case. In a capital case, the evidence submitted by both sides regarding the victim's character may easily tip the scale of the jury's choice between life or death. Yet even with extensive investigation in post-trial proceedings, it will often prove difficult, if not impossible, to determine whether the prior representation affected defense counsel's decisions regarding, for example: which avenues to take when investigating the victim's background; which witnesses to call; what type of impeachment to undertake; which arguments to make to the jury; what language to use to characterize the victim; and, as a general matter, what basic strategy to adopt at the sentencing stage. Given the subtle forms that prejudice might take, the consequent difficulty of proving actual prejudice, and the significant likelihood that it will nonetheless occur when the same lawyer represents both accused killer and victim, the cost of litigating the existence of actual prejudice in a particular case cannot be easily justified. [C].

* * * [T]he Commonwealth itself *created* the conflict in the first place. Indeed, it was the *same judge* who dismissed the case against the victim who then appointed the victim's lawyer to represent Mickens one business day later. In light of the judge's active role in bringing about the incompatible representation, I am not sure why the concept of a judge's "duty to inquire" is thought to be central to this case. No "inquiry" by the trial judge could have shed more light on the conflict than was obvious on the face of the matter, namely, that the lawyer who would represent Mickens today is the same lawyer who yesterday represented Mickens' alleged victim in a criminal case.

This kind of breakdown in the criminal justice system creates, at a minimum, the appearance that the proceeding will not "'reliably serve its function as a vehicle for determination of guilt or innocence,'" and the resulting "'criminal punishment'" will not "'be regarded as fundamentally fair.'" [C]. This appearance, together with the likelihood of prejudice in the typical case, are serious enough to warrant a categorical rule--a rule that does not require proof of prejudice in the individual case.

The Commonwealth complains that this argument "relies heavily on the immediate visceral impact of learning that a lawyer previously represented the victim of his current client." [C]. And that is so. The "visceral impact," however, arises out of the obvious, unusual nature of the conflict. It arises from the fact that the Commonwealth seeks to execute a defendant, having provided that defendant with a lawyer who, only yesterday, represented the victim. In my view, to carry out a death sentence so obtained would invariably "diminis[h] faith" in the fairness and integrity of our criminal justice system. [Cc]. That is to say, it would diminish that public confidence in the criminal justice system upon which the successful functioning of that system continues to depend.

I therefore dissent.

Notes

1.   In criminal matters, defense counsel's conflict of interest can be raised by counsel, the defendant, the prosecutor, or the judge.

> [B]oth the prosecutor and the trial judge have a responsibility to assure a fair trial for each defendant. When a defense lawyer would be required to assume an adverse position with respect to one or more clients, the conflict is nonconsentable [c]. Efficient operation of the judicial system requires that a verdict not be vulnerable to contentions that a defendant was disadvantaged in by an undisclosed conflict of interest. A prosecutor might object to joint-representation arrangements to assure that a conflict possibility is resolved before trial. Even without objection by the prosecutor or defendant, the tribunal may raise the issue on its own initiative and refuse to permit joint representation where there is a significant threat to the interest in the finality of judgments.

Restatement (Third) of the Law Governing Lawyers § 129 cmt c (2000).

2.   In Wheat v. United States, 486 U.S. 153, 108 S. Ct. 1692, 100 L. Ed. 2d 140 (1988), the government objected to the lawyer's representation of codefendants. The district court rejected the defendant's waiver of the conflict and required the defendant to obtain another attorney. The Supreme Court upheld the actions of the judge, stating:

> The District Court must recognize a presumption in favor of petitioner's counsel of choice, but that presumption may be overcome not only by

a demonstration of actual conflict but by a showing of a serious potential for conflict. The evaluation of the facts and circumstances of each case under this standard must be left primarily to the informed judgment of the trial court.

3.   If a conflict of interest is waived by the defendant, most courts hold that the defendant is bound by the waiver. Absent a timely objection and actual prejudice, the conviction will stand. *See, e. g., United States v. Bradshaw*, 719 F.2d 907 (7th Cir. 1983); *United States v. Zajac*, 677 F.2d 61 (11th Cir. 1982).

4.   In *The Florida Bar v. Vernell*, 374 So.2d 473 (Fla. 1979) a lawyer was suspended from the practice of law for six months, in part due to his suggestion to clients that they plead guilty to a criminal charge, and if they received harsh sentences, appeal on the basis of his joint representation.

5.   If a lawyer represents codefendants in a criminal action in which there is a conflict of interest, should the client have a claim for malpractice? Professor Susan Koniak has observed:

> [W]e do find what amounts to special immunity for criminal defense lawyers to perform incompetently. Most state courts make it significantly more difficult for criminal defendants to bring malpractice actions against their lawyers than for civil plaintiffs or defendants to do so.

She notes that many state courts require criminal defendants to establish their innocence of the criminal charges in order to recover against their attorneys for malpractice. Pennsylvania requires not only a showing of innocence, but also a showing that the attorney's conduct was reckless or in wanton disregard of the client's interest. Susan P. Koniak, "Through the Looking Glass of Ethics and the Wrong with Rights We Find There," 9 *Geo. J. Legal Ethics* 1, 6, 10 (1995). *Stevens v. Bispham*, 316 Or. 221, 851 P. 2d 556 (1993), provides a comprehensive overview of the existing law governing attorney malpractice by criminal defense lawyers.

C. Conflicting Interests Between Client and Lawyer

Read Model Rule 1.8[2]

Rule 1.8 addresses specific instances where the interests of lawyers are likely to conflict with the interests of their clients. Rule 1.8(d), like its predecessor DR 5-104(B), governs agreements concerning literary and media rights. These rights may have significant financial value, particularly in highly publicized cases.

Maxwell v. Superior Court of Los Angeles County
30 Cal. 3d 606, 639 P. 2d 248, 180 Cal.Rptr. 177 (1982)

NEWMAN, J.—One due process requirement is that an individual charged with serious crime be represented by competent and independent counsel. Another is that courts generally must not interfere with defendant's informed conclusions as to how his defense ought to be conducted. In this lawsuit, which involves an indigent defendant accused of capital murder, those two requirements appear to conflict; and we must decide which one commands more deference.

*　*　*

Petitioner is charged with four counts of robbery (Pen. Code, § 211) and ten of murder (§ 187), some of which involve special circumstances raising the possibility that he will be sentenced to death (§ 190.2). He retained attorneys who seem to be experienced criminal defense lawyers.

The contract provides that irrevocably he assigns to counsel, as their fee, "any and all right, title, and interest, of any kind, nature and description throughout the world in and to the story of [his] entire life . . ." including all entertainment and commercial exploitation rights. He is to receive 15 percent of the "net amount" realized by the exploitation. He promises to cooperate in the exploitation efforts and not to disclose his story to others except with counsel's consent or as required by law or his defense.

*　*　*

---

[2]   *Cf.* DR 4-101(B)(3), 5-103, 5-104, 5-106, 5-107(A)(1), 6-102(A); EC 5-2 to -7; Cal. Rules 3-120, 3-300, 3-310(C), (E), 3-320, 3-400, 4-210.

The contract reflects extensive disclosure of possible conflicts and prejudice. It declares that counsel may wish to (1) create damaging publicity to enhance exploitation value, (2) avoid mental defenses because, if successful, they might suggest petitioner's incapacity to make the contract, and (3) see him convicted and even sentenced to death for publicity value. But a catch-all paragraph—after reciting that other, unforeseen conflicts may also arise—reads: "*The Lawyers will raise every defense which they, in their best judgment based upon their experience feel is warranted by the evidence and information at their disposal and which, taking into consideration the flow of trial and trial tactics, is in Maxwell's best interests. The Lawyers will conduct all aspects of the defense of Maxwell as would a reasonably competent attorney acting as a diligent conscientious advocate.*" (Italics added.)

* * *

After considering the psychiatric reports submitted in confidence by counsel, the judge ruled that (1) petitioner knowingly and willingly had chosen not to seek outside advice and was satisfied with his representation and the contract, and (2) counsel's competency was not at issue, but (3) counsel nonetheless must be disqualified because of the inherent conflict created. * * *

* * *

Protection of a defendant's right to loyal counsel is essential. This court has said that trial judges assume the burden of ensuring that their appointments of counsel for indigent defendants do not "result in a denial of effective counsel because of some possible conflict . . . ." [Cc]. * * *

Yet effective assistance is linked closely to representation by counsel of choice. When clients and lawyers lack rapport and mutual confidence the quality of representation may be so undermined as to render it an empty formality. Hence many precedents recognize that the constitutional right to counsel includes a reasonable opportunity for those defendants who have the necessary resources to control the designation of their legal representatives. [Cc].

* * *

People v. *Crovedi* (1966) 65 Cal. 2d 199 [53 Cal.Rptr. 284, 417 P.2d 868] held that a court abused its discretion by denying a continuance during retained counsel's temporary incapacity. "[T]hough it is clear," said *Crovedi*, "that a defendant has no *absolute* right to be represented by a particular attorney [fn. omitted], still the courts should make all reasonable efforts to ensure that a defendant financially able to retain an attorney of his own choosing can be represented by that attorney. . . .[¶]. . . [T]he state should keep to a necessary minimum its interference with the individual's desire to defend himself in whatever manner he deems best, *using any legitimate means within his resources*—and . . . that desire can constitutionally be forced to yield only when it will result in *significant prejudice* to the defendant himself or in a disruption of the orderly processes of justice unreasonable under the circumstances of the particular case." (Pp. 207-208, first italics original.)

* * *

It is argued that life-story fee contracts are inherently prejudicial, unethical, and against public policy and that the judge has power and the duty to protect the integrity of the trial and, thus, confidence in the judicial process. Do those concerns perhaps outweigh a single defendant's interest in chosen counsel?

Contracts of this kind are widely criticized. It is said they tempt lawyers, consciously or subconsciously and adversely to the client's interests, to tilt the defense for commercial reasons. * * *

* * *

* * * We now conclude, however, that, with exceptions set forth in this opinion, the mere possibility of a conflict does not warrant pretrial removal of competent counsel in a criminal case over defendant's informed objection. When the possibility of significant conflict has been brought to the court's attention and the danger of proceeding with chosen counsel has been disclosed generally to defendant, he may insist on retaining his attorneys if he waives the conflict knowingly and intelligently for purposes of the criminal trial. To the extent *People* v. *Municipal Court* (*Wolfe*) (1977) 69 Cal.App.3d 714, 719-720 [138 Cal.Rptr. 235] suggests a contrary conclusion it is disapproved.

* * *

In this case, extensive pretrial disclosures about conflicts arising from the fee contract were made on the record to both petitioner and court. Yet petitioner insisted on proceeding with his counsel. Did that insistence constitute an adequate waiver, precluding counsel's removal? We believe that it did.

*   *   *

The trial court's procedure here, we think, sufficiently established that petitioner was competent to waive his rights. The judge examined a psychiatric evaluation, and the record suggests neither mental nor emotional incapacity. * * *

*   *   *

BIRD, C. J., Concurring and Dissenting. * * *

In our criminal justice system, the poor have basically two choices. They can accept court-appointed counsel or make some arrangement with private counsel that ensures that counsel will receive some remuneration for the services rendered. One of the problems this case underscores is the fact that our courts do not properly or completely compensate appointed counsel for the work they perform. As a result, if an attorney in the private practice of the law accepts a court appointment, it usually means that the attorney will be less than fully compensated for his or her work.

In a complex and serious case such as the one before the court, it may not be economically feasible for counsel to accept a court appointment. Therefore, the only way in which an indigent may be able to secure counsel of his choice may be through a "life story" arrangement. For this court to hold *any* "life story" agreement, regardless of its contents, impermissible would be to foreclose to the indigent perhaps the only opportunity he may have to secure counsel of his choice. * * *

*   *   *

RICHARDSON, J., Dissenting. * * *

*   *   *

The scope of the conflicts "built in" to the agreement exceeds those acknowledged by the attorneys themselves in paragraph 14. The real vice of the arrangement appears most clearly in considering certain tactical decisions which may confront trial counsel. Suppose that before trial, through a plea bargain, defendant's life may be saved by an informed entry of a guilty plea to certain of the multiple counts, including murder, with which he is charged. Should counsel recommend such a bargain? Perhaps they should, but *would* they, knowing that the sales value of a book or television manuscript would decline if there was no dramatic trial testimony elicited? How really objective will counsel be in exploring the opportunities for avoiding trial without any attendant publicity if the commercial value of defendant's life story is thereby reduced or destroyed? If defendant is tried, should he be called as a witness to tell his "story," or exercise his constitutional right to remain silent, thereby putting "the prosecution to its proof"? Surely, the sales value of defendant's story would be affected by the decision. If defendant takes the stand during trial would the areas of his direct examination be affected, however subtly, perhaps unknowingly, by counsel's financial interest in the drama and salability of his testimony? * * *

* * *

Accordingly, I would sustain the action of the trial court in relieving counsel for defendant's protection.

Notes

1.   The court's opinion does not deal with the prohibition of life-story fee contracts in the ethics code because California's rules have no such provision. Is the holding of *Maxwell* a better rule than MR 1.8(d)?

2.   As the trial judge, would you approve representation based upon such an agreement?

3.   The majority opinion bases its approval of life-story fee contracts in large part upon the indigent defendant's inability to obtain and compensate counsel in any other way. Yet a fundamental premise of contract law is that the parties to a contract each begin with some bargaining power. The law provides safeguards against overreaching by the more powerful party. In the *Maxwell* opinion, the majority relied upon the extensive pretrial disclosures about the conflicts inherent in such contracts, as well as the evidence establishing mental capacity of the defendant at the time the contract was entered into. Do you believe these are adequate safeguards against overreaching by lawyers? *See* Mark R. McDonald, "Literary-Rights Fee Agreements in California: Letting the Rabbit Guard the Carrot Patch of Sixth Amendment Protection and Attorney Ethics?," 24 *Loyola of L.A. L. Rev.* 365 (1991). For an examination of the issues presented by prosecutors' use of information for literary purposes, *see* Rita M. Glavin, Note, "Prosecutors Who Disclose Prosecutorial Information for Literary or Media Purposes: What About the Duty of Confidentiality?," 63 *Fordham L. Rev.* 1809 (1995).

4. Would you agree to a life-story fee contract if you were poor and charged with committing a felony?

5. The 2002 amendments to the Model Rules added MR 1.8(j), prohibiting lawyers from having sexual relations with clients. Is this any business of the ABA? What interests are at stake? When a similar rule (Cal. Rules 3-120) was proposed in California, a young, big-firm Los Angeles lawyer stated that with her busy practice, she never saw anyone but lawyers and clients, and that she did not like any of the lawyers she knew.

D. Conflicting Interests Between Present and Former Clients

Read Model Rule 1.9[3]

When a lawyer faces a conflict of interest between present clients the applicable rules are based on the duty of loyalty. The rules concerning conflicts of interests between current and former clients are based only in part on a continuing duty of loyalty. What other concerns are evidenced by Rule 1.9?

Westinghouse Elec. Corp. v. Gulf Oil Corp.
588 F.2d 221 (7th Cir. 1978)

[Plaintiff Westinghouse alleged that Gulf and other defendants were part of an international cartel which had fixed and increased the price of uranium.]

SPRECHER, Circuit Judge.

In this case we review the propriety of a district court's refusal to grant a motion to disqualify opposing counsel. The issues presented are whether there is a sufficient relationship between matters presented by the pending litigation and matters which the lawyers in question worked on in behalf of the party now seeking disqualification and whether the party seeking disqualification has given legally sufficient consent to the dual representation.

* * *

---

[3] *Cf.* DR 4-101(B)-(C), 5-105(C); EC 4-6; Cal. Rules 3-310(E).

* * * During a five year period of representation from 1971 through 1976, the Bigbee firm through nine of its twelve attorneys performed numerous services for Gulf including the patenting of fifty-nine mining claims, drafting leases required for uranium exploration, representing Gulf in litigation involving title disputes, counseling Gulf in relation to the resolution of certain problems relating to mine waters, and lobbying on behalf of Gulf in front of the New Mexico state legislature on tax and environmental matters. * * *

Gulf argued before the district court that these matters on which Bigbee represented Gulf were substantially related to the matters raised in the Westinghouse litigation. Gulf delineated this relationship by arguing that since the Mt. Taylor properties constituted Gulf's largest supply of uranium and was not currently in production, the reasons for Gulf's failure to produce from this property would be material to the allegation of the Westinghouse suit that Gulf, as well as the other defendants, withheld uranium supplies from the market. * * *

The district court accepted Gulf's argument of actual adverseness but nonetheless declined to disqualify the Bigbee firm. The court concluded that Bigbee "certainly did gain knowledge of Gulf's uranium properties during its work" but reasoned that nevertheless there was not a substantial relationship between the matters encompassed by the prior representation and those of the Westinghouse litigation, because the prior representation "focused on real estate transactions connected with Gulf's untapped and undeveloped uranium reserves," whereas the "heart of the complaint" details a price-fixing conspiracy, the evidence of which "will focus on meetings and communications among the alleged co-conspirators, as well as evidence on uranium prices, terms and conditions of sale, and market availability." Thus, the court concluded that there was no substantial relationship between the matters. [C].

* * *

The substantial relationship rule embodies the substance of Canons 4 and 9 of the A.B.A. Code of Professional Responsibility. Canon 4 provides that "a lawyer should preserve the confidences and secrets of a client," [*Cf.* MR 1.6] and Canon 9 provides that "a lawyer should avoid even the appearance of professional impropriety." As a result it is clear that the determination of whether there is a substantial relationship turns on the possibility, or appearance thereof, that confidential information might have been given to the attorney in relation to the subsequent matter in which disqualification is sought. The rule thus does not necessarily involve any inquiry into the imponderables involved in the degree of relationship between the two matters but instead involves a realistic appraisal of the possibility that confidences had been disclosed in the one matter which will be harmful to the client in the other. The effect of the Canons is necessarily to restrict the inquiry to the possibility of disclosure; it is not appropriate for the court to inquire into whether actual confidences were disclosed.

* * * The evidence need only establish the scope of the legal representation and not the actual receipt of the allegedly relevant confidential information. Then only where it is clearly discernible, "that the issues involved in a current case do not relate to matters in which the attorney formerly represented the adverse party will the attorney's present representation be treated as measuring up to the standard of legal ethics." *Fleischer v. A. A. P., Inc.,* 163 F.Supp. 548, 553 (S.D.N.Y.1958). * * *

[S]ubstantial relationship "is determined by asking whether it could reasonably be said that during the former representation [that] attorney might have acquired information related to the subject matter of the subsequent representation." 398 F.Supp. at 223. The opinion in *T. C. Theatre* continued "[i]f so, then the relationship between the two matters is sufficiently close to bring the later representation within the prohibition of . . . [the canons]." 113 F.Supp. at 269. Essentially then, disqualification questions require three levels of inquiry. Initially, the trial judge must make a factual reconstruction of the scope of the prior legal representation. Second, it must be determined whether it is reasonable to infer that the confidential information allegedly given would have been given to a lawyer representing a client in those matters. Finally, it must be determined whether that information is relevant to the issues raised in the litigation pending against the former client.

Although the district court properly identified this rule of law, it erred in its application. First, we accept Judge Marshall's factual reconstruction of the scope of Bigbee's prior representation. * * *

* * * [W]e think it is clearly reasonable to presume that the information regarding quantity and quality of uranium was given. Indeed, it seems difficult to believe that Bigbee would not have acquired rather

detailed information relating to the quantity and quality of the uranium reserves in the course of its filing of mining patents and resolution of conflicting claims. Judge Marshall concluded that the firm "did gain knowledge of Gulf's uranium properties during its work." 448 F.Supp. at 1312.

Having established the presumption that this information was given, disqualification must result if that information is relevant to the issues in the suit pending against Gulf. Relevance must be gauged by the violations alleged in the complaint and assessment of the evidence useful in establishing those allegations. * * *

* * * [A]n agreement to restrict the production of uranium unquestionably is a price fixing arrangement. "Price fixing" is a characterization which extends to all conspiracies designed to manipulate the price of goods. [Cc] In fact, all serious attempts to establish a supracompetitive price must necessarily include an agreement to restrict output.   Otherwise the monopoly price could never be maintained. Thus, the lower court's view that conspiracy to fix prices and conspiracy to restrict output are distinct offenses is in error. * * *

* * *

Most price fixing conspiracies are established through circumstantial evidence.   Proof that Gulf was restricting its output of uranium would be highly relevant circumstantial evidence if its competitors were behaving in a parallel fashion. * * *

* * *

The district court is reversed and the motion of Gulf Oil Corporation to disqualify Bigbee, Stephenson, Carpenter & Crout from representing United Nuclear Corporation in *Westinghouse Electric Corporation v. Rio Algom Limited, et al.*, is granted.

REVERSED AND REMANDED.

Notes

1.   In determining whether a disqualifying conflict of interest exists, the *Westinghouse* court articulated a three-step analysis:

Initially, the trial judge must make a factual reconstruction of the scope of the prior legal representation. Second, it must be determined whether it is reasonable to infer that the confidential information allegedly given would have been given to a lawyer representing a client in those matters. Finally, it must be determined whether that information is relevant to the issues raised in the litigation pending against the former client.

This test is used by a majority of courts and has been referred to as the "particularized examination of issues" test. Charles Wolfram, *Modern Legal Ethics* § 7.4 (1986).

2. Alternative tests are described by the court in *Chrispens v. Coastal Ref. & Mktg., Inc.*, 257 Kan. 745, 751-52, 897 P.2d 104, 111 (1995):

> Three separate approaches regarding the substantial relationship test have been used throughout the country. The first approach indicates that the comparison of the former and current representations should center on the facts of each case. The second approach, advanced by the Second Circuit, insists that the inquiry should focus on legal issues and requires the issues involved in the former representation to be "identical" to or "essentially the same" as those presented in the current representation. The relationship under the second approach must be "patently clear." *Government of India v. Cook Industries, Inc.*, 569 F.2d 737, 739-40 (2d Cir. 1978). This approach has not been a view widely adopted. See Nelson, *Conflicts in Representation: Subsequent Representations in a World of Mega Law Firms*, 6 Geo. J. Legal Ethics 1023, 1031 (1993). The third approach is set forth in the case of *Westinghouse Elec. Corp. v. Gulf Oil Corp.*, 588 F.2d 221 (7th Cir.1978).

3. Protecting client confidences is one motivating force behind Rule 1.9. How can client confidences be protected while insuring that the former client has a legitimate objection to the attorney's representation of the new client?

> The irrebuttable presumption [that the attorney received relevant confidential information] prevents the former client-present adversary from being put into the dilemma of having to reveal confidences in order to obtain a disqualification. *See Government of India v. Cook Industries, Inc.*, 569 F.2d 737, 741 (2d Cir.197 8) (Mansfield, J., concurring). However, in some cases where an attorney can show that no confidential information was gained, the former client's interest may be outweighed by the attorney's interest in maintaining the attorney's reputation, which may needlessly suffer unless counsel is given an opportunity to clear counsel's name. *Id.* Therefore, it has been argued that trial courts should have the discretion in an appropriate case to permit the door to be opened for rebuttal of the presumption through the use of *in camera* or other protective devices to safeguard the interest of the former client . . . . Despite the flexibility and appeal of this approach, the prevailing rule is that the presumption is irrebuttable. . .

In re Stokes, 156 B.R. 181, 186 n.3 (Bankr. E.D.Va. 1993).

E. Imputed Conflicts of Interest

Once it is determined that the interests of multiple clients or the attorney are in conflict, the lawyer must either obtain the consent of the clients or withdraw from representation. If the lawyer must withdraw, is it possible for a member of the same firm to undertake the representation? According to Model Rule 1.10(a), the answer is generally "no." But what about representation that is adverse to the interests of a former client, by a lawyer who is no longer a member of the firm? May the lawyer undertake the new representation? May the lawyer's new firm handle the representation? May another lawyer, who has never been a member of the firm which represented the former client, undertake the new representation?

Read Model Rules 1.10 to 1.12[4]

LaSalle Nat'l Bank v. County of Lake
703 F.2d 252 (7th Cir. 1983)

CUDAHY, Circuit Judge.

This case confronts us with some of the ethical problems involved when a former government attorney takes up the practice of law with a large law firm. Lake County, Illinois, one of the parties to this appeal, is the former employer of an attorney now practicing law with the firm representing the plaintiffs-appellants. Lake County moved to disqualify the plaintiffs' law firm because of the County's former relationship with one of the firm's associates. The district court granted the motion, finding that the past association gave rise to an appearance of impropriety and holding that both the attorney and the entire law firm must be disqualified. * * *

* * *

Marc Seidler, the attorney upon whose career our attention must focus in this case, served as an Assistant State's Attorney in Lake County from 1976 until January 31, 1981. . . . As such, he had general supervisory responsibility with respect to all civil cases handled by the State's Attorney's office. On February 2, 1981, Mr. Seidler joined the

---

[4]

    For MR 1.10 *cf.*, DR 5-105(D); there is no direct counterpart in the Cal. Rules. For MR 1.11 *cf.*, DR 8-101(B); EC 9-3; there is no direct counterpart in the Cal. Rules. For MR 1.12 *cf.*, DR 8-101(A); EC 5-20; there is no direct counterpart in the Cal. Rules.

Chicago law firm of Rudnick & Wolfe as an associate, working in the firm's Northbrook, Illinois office.

* * *

[The court found that Seidler had a conflict of interest.]

Having found that Mr. Seidler was properly disqualified from representation of the plaintiffs in this case, we must now address whether this disqualification should be extended to the entire law firm of Rudnick & Wolfe. . . . [T]he knowledge possessed by one attorney in a law firm is presumed to be shared with the other attorneys in the firm. . . . The question arises here whether this presumption may be effectively rebutted by establishing that the "infected" attorney was "screened," or insulated, from all participation in and information about a case, thus avoiding disqualification of an entire law firm based on the prior employment of one member.

Although this court has rejected screening in a situation involving simultaneous representation of adverse interests by different offices of a large law firm, *Westinghouse Electric Corp. v. Kerr-McGee Corp.*, 580 F.2d 1311, 1321 (7th Cir. 1978), it has never directly confronted this issue in a situation such as that presented here. Other circuits, however, have begun to address the problems which arise when attorneys leaving government service join large law firms. If past employment in government results in the disqualification of future employers from representing some of their long-term clients, it seems clearly possible that government attorneys will be regarded as "Typhoid Marys." Many talented lawyers, in turn, may be unwilling to spend a period in government service, if that service makes them unattractive or risky for large law firms to hire. In recognition of this problem, several other circuits have begun either explicitly or implicitly to approve the use of screening as a means to avoid disqualification of an entire law firm by "infection." The Second Circuit has expressed its approval of the use of screening in a situation where the law firm's continued representation of a client results in no threat of a taint to the trial process. *Armstrong v. McAlpin*, 625 F.2d 433, 445 (2d Cir.1980) (en banc), *vacated on other grounds*, 449 U.S. 1106, 101 S.Ct. 911, 66 L.Ed.2d 835 (1981). * * *

In 1975 the Committee on Ethics and Professional Responsibility of the American Bar Association turned its attention to the acceptability of screening in its Formal Opinion No. 342. The specific question under consideration was whether Disciplinary Rule 5-105(D) ("If a lawyer is required to decline employment or to withdraw from employment under a disciplinary rule, no partner, or associate, or any other lawyer affiliated with him or his firm, may accept or continue such employment") applied in the case of the many former government attorneys now in private practice. The Committee stated that it did not interpret DR 5-105(D) to require disqualification of an entire law firm if the former government attorney had been screened from any direct or indirect participation in the matter. ABA, Comm. on Ethics and Professional Responsibility, Formal Op. 342 (1975) at 11 [*Cf.* MR 1.11]. * * *

* * *

The screening arrangements which courts and commentators have approved, however, contain certain common characteristics. The attorney involved in the *Armstrong v. McAlpin* case, for example, was denied access to relevant files and did not share in the profits or fees derived from the representation in question; discussion of the suit was prohibited in his presence and no members of the firm were permitted to show him any documents relating to the case; and both the disqualified attorney and others in his firm affirmed these facts under oath. * * *

In the case at hand, by contrast, Mr. Seidler joined the firm of Rudnick & Wolfe on February 2, 1981; yet screening arrangements were not established until the disqualification motion was filed in August 1981. [C]. Although Mr. Seidler states in his affidavit that he did not disclose to any person associated with the firm any information about the validity of the Agreement or the County's strategy on any matter relevant to this litigation, no specific institutional mechanisms were in place to insure that information was not shared, even if inadvertently, between the months of February and August. Recognizing that this is an area in which the relevant information is singularly within the ken of the party defending against the motion to disqualify and in which the reputation of the bar as a whole is implicated, we hold that the district court did not abuse its discretion in extending the disqualification of Marc Seidler to the entire firm of Rudnick & Wolfe. The district court order is therefore

AFFIRMED.

Notes

1.   The *LaSalle* case deals with the problem of a lawyer moving from government service to a private law firm. This is known as the "revolving door" problem, referring to lawyer mobility both into and away from government service. Model Rule 1.11 is the controlling rule. By its terms Rule 1.11 permits continued representation in cases where the firm screens the prior government lawyer from participation.

2.   The *LaSalle* court affirms the disqualification because no screening arrangement was in place from the time that Seidler joined the firm. Other cases have referred to screening procedures as "Chinese Walls" or "cones of silence." Denying access to relevant files and prohibiting all members of the firm from discussing the matter with the screened attorney are two of the procedures that courts have required before denying motions to disqualify. What evidence should be required to establish the existence of a screen?

3.   Courts have split over the question whether screening will cure a conflict of interest when lawyers move between private law firms. *Compare Cheng v. GAF Corp.*, 631 F.2d 1052 (2d Cir. 1980) (permitting screens when it could be shown that the screen was implemented in an effective manner) *with Tessier v. Plastics Surgery Specialists, Inc.* 731 F. Supp. 724 (E.D. Va. 1990) (expressing skepticism over the effectiveness of such devices).

4.   The Restatement (Third) of the Law Governing Lawyers § 124 takes the position that screening will cure the problem of imputed disqualification when a lawyer moves from firm-to-firm, so long as "any confidential client information communicated to the personally prohibited lawyer is unlikely to be significant in the subsequent matter." The Ethics 2000 Commission also proposed that screening cure the firm's disqualification when a lawyer moves from firm-to-firm, but the ABA House of Delegates rejected this proposal.

Monroe Freedman, "The Ethical Illusion of Screening; Pretending that a Lawyer Can Switch Sides on a Case and be 'Screened' off from that Case Represents a Serious Ethical Breakdown"
Legal Times (November 20, 1995)

We stand at the dawn of a new error. Not long ago, it was universally recognized that when a lawyer left government service to join a private law firm, two things followed. First, the lawyer was disqualified from opposing the government in any matter in which the lawyer had been substantially involved when in government service. Second, the lawyer's new firm was similarly disqualified through "imputed disqualification."

The old error was to allow a government lawyer who switches sides in a case to be "screened" from communicating with her new firm about the case, thereby avoiding disqualification of the firm.

The ethical breakdown that permits screening of former government lawyers began in the mid-1970s and culminated in the American Bar Association's 1983 Model Rules of Professional Conduct. Under Rule 1.11, the law firm can avoid disqualification by screening the former government lawyer from participation in the case and by giving written notice to the government agency.

The new error is to extend the screening scam from former government lawyers and apply it to lawyers who switch sides in cases by moving from one private law firm to another. That is, despite the former client's objections, a lawyer switching sides can be screened, and his new firm can then represent the former client's adversary in the same case.

The traditional conflict-of-interest rules on switching sides were designed to protect the former clients' confidences, even at the expense of reducing lawyers' employment mobility. The evasion of these rules through screening jeopardizes client confidences in order to increase lawyers' job opportunities. This, of course, makes a monkey of the claim that the law is a profession and not a business.

Here is a basic illustration: Attorney is with firm A&B and is heavily involved in representing Plaintiff. In the middle of the litigation, Attorney switches to firm Y&Z, which is representing Defendant in the same case. As noted earlier, the traditional rule of ethics has been that both Attorney and firm Y&Z are disqualified from representing Defendant in that case. The rule relies on presumptions that are based upon common sense and the practicalities of proof.

The first presumption is that Attorney learned confidences from Plaintiff while serving as its lawyer. This presumption is justified in part by Attorney's ethical obligation to learn everything that might be relevant to Plaintiff's case. Moreover, the presumption that Attorney learned confidences from Plaintiff avoids making Plaintiff reveal its confidences in order to protect them.

The second presumption is that Attorney, having switched sides, might use Plaintiff's confidences on behalf of Defendant. This presumption is based in part on the fact that Attorney, in representing Defendant, would be ethically required to be loyal to Defendant, to act zealously on its behalf, and to communicate to Defendant all information material to the representation.

If only unconsciously, Attorney might violate Plaintiff's confidences in representing Defendant. Thus, the traditional rule of disqualification recognizes that Plaintiff could reasonably suspect that its confidences were being betrayed, and the rule respects this legitimate client concern.

The disqualification of firm Y&Z (called imputed disqualification) is also based upon common sense and practicalities of proof. Even if Attorney is not personally representing Defendant at his new firm, there is a reasonable possibility that Attorney, having switched allegiances, might disclose Plaintiff's confidences to his new partners.

IMPOSSIBLE TO POLICE

As observed in "Developments in the Law—Conflicts of Interest in the Legal Profession," 94 Harvard Law Review 1244 (1981), Attorney's new colleagues have a "significant incentive" to elicit the confidences, and Attorney has a similar incentive to prove his allegiance to his new firm by cooperating. Thus, there is a "distinctive danger" that Attorney will reveal Plaintiff's confidences to Defendant's lawyers. Moreover, such violations would be virtually impossible to police. A brief conversation in someone's office, or during a private dinner, or in a phone call to Attorney's home, would be hard to expose and to prove.

In short, the traditional presumption underlying imputed disqualification is based upon a high level of temptation, a low level of visibility, and a near-impossible burden if Plaintiff were required to prove an actual breach of its confidences.

Of course, Plaintiff might consent to Attorney's representation of Defendant, or might consent to Y&Z's continued representation of Defendant with the understanding that Attorney would not be involved in that representation. Plaintiff might be willing to consent, for example, in order to avoid delaying the case. And if Plaintiff does consent, there's no need for disqualification.

But what if Plaintiff, understandably, refuses to consent? Until quite recently, there has been no disagreement about the result— unless Plaintiff consents, both Attorney and firm Y&Z are disqualified from representing Defendant.

Enter Defendant's lawyers, carrying a screen. (Or, perhaps, carrying a wall. Screening used to be called a "Chinese Wall," a term coined to suggest impregnability, but misperceived as an ethnic slur and, therefore, in disfavor these days.) A screen consists simply of assurances by the lawyers at Y&Z that Attorney will not work on the case or talk about it with the lawyers who represent Defendant. Nothing else changes.

The temptations to violate Plaintiff's confidences are still high, violations are still virtually impossible to police, and Plaintiff's ability to prove a violation is still practically nil. The only thing that has changed is that the lawyers at Y&Z—where, by hypothesis, there is a plausible possibility that Plaintiff's confidences will be disclosed—have given assurances to Plaintiff. But Plaintiff is still objecting.

'TRUST US. WE'RE LAWYERS'

Supporters of screening contend, of course, that objections to screening reflect skepticism, even cynicism, about lawyers. That may be. There is, sad to say, some skepticism about lawyers out there. A major purpose of the conflict-of-interest rules is to allay that skepticism, and an unpoliceable assurance of screening by a law firm is not likely to do the job. Imagine the scene. Plaintiff gets a letter from Y&Z, whom he thinks of as The Enemy. The letter says, "Your lawyer, Attorney, now works for us. But we won't talk with him about your case. Trust us. We're lawyers."

Notes

1.   Charles Wolfram also questions whether "screening-lawyer foxes" (the partners in the new firm) will carefully guard the "screened-lawyer chickens." Charles Wolfram, *Modern Legal Ethics* § 7.6.4 (1986).

2.   When lawyers in one office of a law firm have a conflict of interest with a client of another office of the firm that is located in a different city, should screening remedy the conflict? *See Westinghouse Elec. Corp. v. Kerr-McGee Corp.*, 580 F.2d 1311 (7th Cir. 1978) and *Harrison v. Fisons Corp.*, 819 F.Supp. 1039 (M.D.Fla., 1993).

F. Organizational Clients

Read Model Rule 1.13[5]

Ellen Joan Pollock, "Limited Partners: Lawyers for Enron Faulted Its Deals, Didn't Force Issue; Vinson & Elkins Rejects Idea Firm Should Have Taken Doubts to Client's Board,"

The Wall Street Journal (Wednesday, May 22, 2002)

Early in the morning [on October 23, 2001], Ronald Astin, a partner at the Houston law firm Vinson & Elkins, joined Enron Corp. executives in a meeting room next to Chairman Kenneth Lay's office. A conference call with analysts was about to begin, and the group needed to script an explanation for Enron's unfolding troubles, which included mysterious partnerships that appeared to be keeping big chunks of debt hidden away.

The tense mood soon grew worse. Mr. Astin had drafted a section saying that Enron Chief Financial Officer Andrew Fastow initially presented the idea of the partnerships to the board. According to people at the meeting, Mr. Fastow began shouting that he wasn't responsible for forming the partnerships.

It was the climax of a beneath-the-surface struggle between the outside lawyer and the Enron executive. Over five years, as Mr. Fastow structured ever-more-complex deals for the big energy and trading company, Mr. Astin and other Vinson & Elkins lawyers sometimes objected, saying the deals posed conflicts of interest or weren't in Enron's best interests.

But Vinson & Elkins didn't blow the whistle. Again and again, its lawyers backed down when rebuffed by Mr. Fastow or his lieutenants, expressing their unease to Enron's in-house attorneys but not to its most senior executives or to its board. And when asked to assess Enron manager Sherron Watkins' warning to Mr. Lay last summer of potential accounting scandals, Vinson & Elkins delivered to Enron a report that largely downplayed the risks.

Now, deals that troubled some Vinson & Elkins lawyers are central to investigations of the collapse of Enron. But while the mantle of heroine has fallen on Ms. Watkins, Vinson & Elkins is on the defen-

---

5   *Cf.* EC 5-18; Cal. Rules 3-600.

sive. One of the country's most powerful law firms, with some 850 lawyers in nine cities, Vinson & Elkins now faces lawsuits from Enron shareholders and Enron employees. And a report of a special investigation done for Enron's board has criticized the law firm for an "absence" of "objective and critical professional advice."

The firm's bind casts a stark light on the central issue law firms face when they represent large corporations: Just what are their obligations to the client and the client's shareholders? In terms of legal ethics, outside lawyers have a clear ethical duty to withdraw from transactions in which clients are obviously breaking the law. But many situations are murkier. At what point should the lawyers speak up, and to whom, when the legality of planned corporate moves is merely questionable? And what about when individual executives are planning steps that appear not in the interests of the client company itself?

Vinson & Elkins' managing partner, Joseph Dilg, has told a congressional panel probing Enron that so long as a transaction isn't illegal and has been approved by the client company's management, outside lawyers may advise on the transaction. "In doing so, the lawyers are not approving the business decisions that were made by their clients," he said.

But others, such as Boston University law professor Susan Koniak, say lawyers must do more. They have a duty to make sure a client's managers aren't "breaching their duties to the corporation," says Ms. Koniak, who testified before a Senate hearing on Enron and accountability issues in February. She believes Vinson & Elkins lawyers should have taken their concerns to Enron directors.

But she adds that what the firm actually did "is not any different from what most lawyers in most big firms would have done. This is how law is practiced. . . . It's a game of musical chairs, and Vinson & Elkins got caught standing up."

Vinson & Elkins' former managing partner, Harry Reasoner, says, "We were giving our advice to the people we were instructed to give it to under their protocol, the in-house lawyers." Enron's executives and in-house lawyers were aware of the risks of the transactions, he says, adding: "The implication that we should have gone around their in-house lawyers and their executives directly to the board, I would say we had no basis for believing such an extraordinary action would have been appropriate or necessary."

Exactly what Vinson & Elkins did and when in the Enron matter isn't easy to determine, and the law firm wouldn't make most partners available for interviews. Some details can be gleaned from interviews done for the special report to Enron's board, conducted by the Washington law firm Wilmer, Cutler & Pickering.

The stakes for Vinson & Elkins were high. The firm's partners and Enron were intertwined in Houston's corporate community. They shared causes ranging from the United Negro College Fund to electing George W. Bush. Kenneth and Linda Lay traveled the Houston social and charity circuit with Mr. Reasoner and his wife, Macey. The friendship dated from a case Mr. Reasoner handled in 1976 for a former Lay employer, Florida Gas.

Enron was Vinson & Elkins' biggest client, pouring roughly $35.6 million into the firm's coffers in 2001, 7.8% of its revenue.

But by 1997, when Enron proposed the first of its now-notorious partnership deals, Vinson & Elkins hold on Enron business was weakening as the company increasingly used other law firms as well. It was retaining Houston's Andrews & Kurth and Bracewell & Patterson. New York powerhouse Skadden, Arps, Slate, Meagher & Flom also did work for Enron and won even more after it opened a Houston office. Enron General Counsel James Derrick was interested in giving work to a lot of different firms.

They needed little persuading. "Every large law firm in the country in one form or another tried to get Enron's business," says an Enron staffer. "Enron became innovative and sexy and a nice client to have in your stable."

Against this backdrop, Enron in 1997 called on Vinson & Elkins, and specifically its Mr. Astin, to help it set up a novel partnership. Though not a star at the law firm, the Utah-born Mr. Astin, now 54 years old, enjoyed increasing stature as Enron's finance group kept calling on him. Enron staffers thought of him as rather scholarly and attributed his occasional bursts of temper to the pressures of the job.

This deal did nothing to ease those pressures. Enron planned to buy out the 50% stake that California Public Employees' Retirement System, or Calpers, held in an Enron investment partnership called JEDI -- and then immediately sell that stake to a new entity called Chewco. Chewco was designed to be independent, so that several hundred million dollars of debt associated with JEDI wouldn't have to appear on Enron's balance sheet.

When a draft memorandum to solicit investors in Chewco landed on Mr. Astin's desk, he grew concerned. It appeared that Mr. Fastow, then a fast-rising finance executive, would manage Chewco and be allowed to invest in it. Mr. Astin thought this a clear conflict of interest, according to Mr. Reasoner, then Vinson & Elkins' managing partner. Mr. Reasoner served as a spokesman for Mr. Astin, who declined to be interviewed.

Mr. Astin discussed his concerns with Mr. Dilg, who was Vinson & Elkins' partner in charge of the Enron account. Mr. Dilg agreed that the Fastow role could create conflicts, and also created an obligation for disclosure on the proxy statement, according to a summary of an interview of an Enron in-house lawyer, Kristina Mordaunt, conducted for the report to Enron's board. She said she and Mr. Dilg agreed to bring the matter up with Mr. Fastow. Three Vinson & Elkins lawyers, several Enron lawyers and Mr. Fastow then met on Sept. 8, 1997, according to Mr. Astin's account for the board report.

Mr. Astin told Mr. Fastow that Enron's conflict-of-interest policy might be an issue, that letting certain employees invest in Chewco could exacerbate rivalries among Enron business units, and that if Mr. Fastow invested in Chewco this had to have approval of senior Enron executives, according to Mr. Astin's account.

Mr. Fastow replied that investment banks compensate employees with equity interests in companies, so why not Enron, according to Mr. Astin. The Vinson & Elkins lawyer said his own response to that was to point out that Enron wasn't a bank and to urge Mr. Fastow to consider Enron's interest as a whole. Mr. Fastow declined through a spokesman to comment on his dealings with the law firm.

Eventually Mr. Fastow was convinced, according to an account Ms. Mordaunt gave for the report to the board. According to Mr. Astin, she told him several days later that, based on Vinson & Elkins' advice, the Chewco memorandum for potential investors wouldn't state that Mr. Fastow was to be Chewco's manager, nor that Enron employees could invest in Chewco.

Mr. Astin's victory was short-lived. In November 1997, he realized that although Chewco's manager wouldn't be Mr. Fastow, it would be a protege of his at Enron: Michael Kopper. Because of Mr. Kopper's lower rank, proxy disclosure was no longer an issue. But Mr. Astin felt that conflict-of-interest issues remained, and law-firm attorneys talked about "the fact that Kopper would benefit personally from the Chewco deal," according to the summary of Mr. Astin's interview for the report to the board. He said he knew Enron staffers were gossiping that Mr. Kopper's role showed favoritism by Mr. Fastow.

Mr. Astin also said that Mr. Kopper, concerned about the appearance of a conflict, had sought his advice, and that Mr. Astin told Mr. Kopper conflicts needed approval from both Mr. Fastow and Enron's board.

Mr. Astin said he then urged Mr. Kopper to get advice on the conflict issue from Kirkland & Ellis, the law firm that did much of the paperwork on the Chewco deal. But that firm, since it represented only Chewco, wouldn't have had an obligation to look after Enron's interests. Citing attorney-client confidentiality, it declined to comment. So did Mr. Kopper's lawyer.

Mr. Astin indicated to those preparing the report to the board that after that, he didn't follow up on Mr. Kopper's situation.

Chewco, to be independent and keep debt off Enron's books under accounting rules, needed to have outside equity equal to at least 3% of its total capital. What came to light last November was that Chewco never met this test. The principal outside investors were paper entities that never had enough money in Chewco to satisfy the accounting rules. In acknowledging this last year, Enron also acknowledged that as a result of Chewco it had improperly inflated its earnings over several years by some $400 million.

After Chewco, Mr. Fastow in 1999 set up two other partnerships, LJM and then LJM2, that also helped Enron greatly inflate its reported financial results. Mr. Fastow, by then chief financial officer, became general partner of both and invested in LJM2.

Enron's board approved his involvement in the LJM partnerships. To do that, the board took the extraordinary step of twice adopting resolutions that, in effect, waived the company's conflict-of-interests policy. Vinson & Elkins was not consulted on the decisions to do this, according to two partners of the law firm. Enron "didn't seek our advice and didn't get our advice" about the waivers, says Vinson & Elkins partner John Murchison. "It was presented to us as a fait accompli."

Lawyers at both Enron and Vinson & Elkins often speculated about how much Mr. Fastow earned from the LJM partnerships, but no one knew, several lawyers told the people preparing the report to Enron's board. They worried that he was enriching himself at Enron's expense.

Vinson & Elkins partners represented Enron in a series of off-balance-sheet transactions with the LJM partnerships. They were complex. In some, Enron sold assets to the partnerships, only to have the assets later sold back.

Some deals required that a law firm write "true sale" opinions certifying that assets were being properly transferred to the partnerships. Mr. Astin and another Vinson & Elkins partner, Mark Spradling, weren't always satisfied that the deals met the conditions necessary for them to write such an opinion, according to people familiar with the legal work. Vinson & Elkins partners "would battle among themselves about giving opinions, about what they could say," an Enron staffer says. "They tried to work by committee, and it was always frustrating for us. . . . We knew that there were chasms among the five partners about certain legal issues." Vinson & Elkins ultimately didn't give opinions on some deals, says a lawyer at the law firm.

Indeed, "there was a view at Enron that transactions were difficult to close with V&E," says a summary of a board-report interview with one Enron in-house lawyer, Joel Ephross. "Such view was based on V&E's concerns that their opinions . . . were being improperly relied upon by Anderson," Enron's auditor.

Sometimes Enron turned instead to Andrews & Kurth. "There were things that Andrews & Kurth looked at differently than Vinson & Elkins. Andrews & Kurth was a bit more flexible," says an Enron staffer, and had "an attitude of 'let's reach solutions here' rather than 'I'm going to create impediments.'"

Andrews & Kurth says it isn't "aware of doing any work at the request of Enron on any transaction that another law firm had declined to work on." The firm says it "takes its ethical obligations to its clients and profession seriously." It didn't specifically address the idea that it was more flexible about approving Enron maneuvers.

Vinson & Elkins did draw up documents for Enron deals known as the Raptors, in which LJM2 invested. In these complex deals, Enron stock was used to offset declines in some of Enron's investments, and Enron was able to avoid reporting almost $1 billion of those losses. Mr. Astin later told those who prepared the report to Enron's board that he worried about the Raptor deals and conveyed his worry more than once to an Enron in-house lawyer, Rex Rogers.

* * *

Ms. Koniak, the Boston University professor, believes that when Enron's board allowed Mr. Fastow to manage and invest in the LJMs, Vinson & Elkins should have made sure the directors understood the legal implications. They should have "said to the board, 'This is a big legal risk you're taking. Let's be clear about this. If anything starts going wrong, that's going to be evidence'" in any resulting court fight, Ms. Koniak says.

Roger Cramton, professor and former dean of Cornell Law School, says that with some of the deals Enron did, lawyers should have started "to be suspicious about whether these transactions are legal in the sense of fiduciary responsibility to the shareholders, to the board of directors and whether they are illegal in other senses."

But Mr. Cramton says a lawyer can't substitute his or her business judgment for the client's, and whether to take legal concerns up a client's chain of a command is a complex judgment call. If the client is at material legal risk, the lawyer should "go to managers first and try to get them to listen. If they sugar-coat it over and they clearly don't want to know about them," going to the board or a board committee could be appropriate, he says.

Vinson & Elkins' share of Enron's legal pie continued to shrink – to 20% of work Enron farmed out in 2001, by Mr. Reasoner's estimate. But Vinson & Elkins remained the firm Enron went to first with its most sensitive projects, such as the 2001 proxy statement. The issue: Must Mr. Fastow's compensation from partnerships be disclosed in a footnote about related-party transactions?

Few knew what that compensation was, and it was understood that Mr. Fastow wasn't eager to have it disclosed. Enron finally decided not to make the disclosure, relying on advice from Mr. Astin, who said this advice was technically correct because not all the LJM transactions were completed and thus the compensation was hard to calculate.

Mr. Mintz, the Enron in-house lawyer, wasn't happy about the decision and wrote a memo about it to Mr. Fastow – who was his boss. The decision "was a close call; arguably, the more conservative approach would have been to disclose the amount of your interest," Mr. Mintz wrote, adding that the rationale for not making the disclosure might not be applicable in future filings.

Two people say Mr. Astin reviewed drafts of the memo before it was sent. Asked by Enron general counsel Mr. Derrick whether he was comfortable with the decision, Mr. Astin said he was, according to the account Mr. Derrick gave for the report to the board.

Last fall, Mr. Fastow finally revealed his partnership compensation: $45 million. Lawyers and Enron staffers alike were stunned. The report to Enron's board said that Vinson & Elkins should have pressed Mr. Fastow to disclose the figure, because the amount needed to be taken into account in determining whether a proxy disclosure was necessary. "The lawyers apparently searched for and embraced a technical rationale to avoid that disclosure," the report to the board asserts, adding that the law firm "should have brought a stronger, more objective and more critical voice to the disclosure process."

Most criticism of Vinson & Elkins has focused on one of its last assignments for Enron. After Ms. Watkins warned Mr. Lay last summer of "accounting scandals," Enron hired the law firm to investigate. Despite the firm's own qualms about some of the deals, it agreed to limit the inquiry's scope. And in mid-October, just before Enron unraveled, it sent a nine-page report that raised no serious alarms.

Vinson & Elkins warned that because of "bad cosmetics" involving the LJM deals, there was "a serious risk of adverse publicity and litigation," but suggested that a deeper investigation wasn't warranted. As for proxy disclosures, "one can always argue in hindsight" that disclosures are inadequate, it said. After Enron filed for bankruptcy in early December, the firm stopped representing the company.

Now the firm has been forced into an odd corner. Though it had strong misgivings about some of Enron's deal-making and disclosures, it isn't in a position to talk about those misgivings because it, too, faces lawsuits and investigations. At a congressional hearing in March, Mr. Dilg, who oversaw the Enron account for Vinson & Elkins, deflected many questions, prompting an exasperated Rep. Clifford B. Stearns of Florida to ask, "You're saying that you, as counsel for Enron, never saw anything egregious about anything they did during the entire relationship you had with Enron?" Mr. Dilg answered, "Yes, sir."

Notes

1. Based on this report, does it appear that Vinson & Elkins attorneys complied with the requirements of MR 1.13? What, if anything, should Vinson & Elkins have done differently?

2. In assessing the conduct of Vinson & Elkins, is it relevant that much of Vinson & Elkins' legal advice was given to Enron's in-house legal department of over 250 lawyers, many of whom were partners at large law firms prior to joining Enron? Comment c to §§ 20 of the Restatement (Third) of the Law Governing Lawyers says "a standard of reasonableness under all the circumstances determines the appropriate measure of consultation." One of the circumstances to be considered is "the client's sophistication."

3. Representatives of the Andrews & Kurth law firm say the firm was not "aware of doing any work at the request of Enron on any transaction that another law firm had declined to work on." Should that be relevant to Andrews & Kurth's decision to accept representation?

4. Following this and other corporate scandals in the early 2000s, Congress enacted a statute instructing the Securities and Exchange Commission to require attorneys to report "evidence of a material violation of securities law or breach of fiduciary duty or similar violation by the company or any agent thereof" to the senior lawyer or executive at the company. If that person fails to "appropriately respond," the attorney must report the evidence to the board of directors. Sarbanes-Oxley Act of 2002, Pub. L. No. 107-204, § 304 (2002). A lawyer who fails to comply risks being barred from practice before the SEC. Is this Act consistent with MR 1.13? Can they be reconciled? Critics of the Act, including the ABA President argued that it infringes on the right of states to control the practice of law. Is the Act justified?

5. Many commentators believe that the lawyer for a close corporation owes duties to the corporation's shareholders as well as the entity. This may be proper because the managers and the owners of close corporation are often the same people. Lawyers for close corporations often represent the individual shareholders in other matters, such as estate planning or family disputes. Even in cases where the legal representation is limited to corporate interests, it is argued that the corporate officers reasonably expect the lawyer to protect their individual interests as well as the corporation's interest.

See In re Banks, 283 Or. 459 584 P.2d 284 (1978) (in banc). This issue is explored in greater detail in Lawrence E. Mitchell, "Professional Responsibility and the Close Corporation: Toward a Realistic Ethic," 74 *Cornell L. Rev.* 466 (1989) and Note, "An Expectations Approach to Client Identity," 106 *Harv. L. Rev.* 687 (1993).

6.   Model Rule 1.13 treats organizations as if they exist separate from the individuals from which they are composed. This is known as the "entity theory," and has a substantial impact upon the nature of lawyer's duties. When representing an organization the lawyer owes loyalty to the entity, rather than the individuals directing the representation. The lawyer's duty to give information and maintain confidences is controlled by the lawyer's determination of what is in the best interest of the organization. Contrast this with the "aggregate" or "group theory" of representation. Under the aggregate theory, lawyers owe duties to each individual that directs the representation of the organization. Confidentiality and the duty to give information run to each member of the group.

Chapter Five

LAWYER ADVOCACY AND ITS LIMITS

A. Advocacy and Moral Responsibility

Read Model Rules 1.16 and 2.1[1]

Lon L. Fuller and John D. Randall, "Professional Responsibility: Report of the Joint Conference"
44 *A.B.A. J.* 1159, 1160-61 (December 1958)

* * *

The lawyer appearing as an advocate before a tribunal presents, as persuasively as he can, the facts and the law of the case as seen from the standpoint of his client's interest. It is essential that both the lawyer and the public understand clearly the nature of the role thus discharged. Such an understanding is required not only to appreciate the need for an adversary presentation of issues, but also in order to perceive truly the limits partisan advocacy must impose on itself if it is to remain wholesome and useful.

In a very real sense it may be said that the integrity of the adjudicative process itself depends upon the participation of the advocate. This becomes apparent when we contemplate the nature of the task assumed by any arbiter who attempts to decide a dispute without the aid of partisan advocacy.

Such an arbiter must undertake, not only the role of judge, but that of representative for both of the litigants. Each of these roles must be played to the full without being muted by qualifications derived from the others. When he is developing for each side the most effective statement of its case, the arbiter must put aside his neutrality and permit himself to be moved by a sympathetic identification sufficiently intense to draw from his mind all that it is capable of giving,—in analysis,

---

[1]   For MR 1.16, *cf.* DR 2-109, 2-110; EC 2-32; Cal. Rules 2-400; 3-200; 3-700. For MR 2.1, *cf.* EC 7-8. There is no direct counterpart to MR 2.1 in the Cal. Rules.

patience and creative power. When he resumes his neutral position, he must be able to view with distrust the fruits of this identification and be ready to reject the products of his own best mental efforts. The difficulties of this undertaking are obvious. If it is true that a man in his time must play many parts, it is scarcely given to him to play them all at once.

It is small wonder, then, that failure generally attends the attempt to dispense with the distinct roles traditionally implied in adjudication. What generally occurs in practice is that at some early point a familiar pattern will seem to emerge from the evidence; an accustomed label is waiting for the case and, without awaiting further proofs, this label is promptly assigned to it. It is a mistake to suppose that this premature cataloguing must necessarily result from impatience, prejudice or mental sloth. Often it proceeds from a very understandable desire to bring the hearing into some order and coherence, for without some tentative theory of the case there is no standard of relevance by which testimony may be measured. But what starts as a preliminary diagnosis designed to direct the inquiry tends, quickly and imperceptibly, to become a fixed conclusion, as all that confirms the diagnosis makes a strong imprint on the mind, while all that runs counter to it is received with diverted attention.

An adversary presentation seems the only effective means for combatting this natural human tendency to judge too swiftly in terms of the familiar that which is not yet fully known. The arguments of counsel hold the case, as it were, in suspension between two opposing interpretations of it. While the proper classification of the case is thus kept unresolved, there is time to explore all of its peculiarities and nuances.

* * *

* * * It is only through the advocate's participation that the hearing may remain in fact what it purports to be in theory: a public trial of the facts and issues. Each advocate comes to the hearing prepared to present his proofs and arguments, knowing at the same time that his arguments may fail to persuade and that his proofs may be rejected as inadequate. It is a part of his role to absorb these possible disappointments. The deciding tribunal, on the other hand, comes to the hearing uncommitted. It has not represented to the public that any fact can be proved, that any argument is sound, or that any particular way of stating a litigant's case is the most effective expression of its merits.

The matter assumes a very different aspect when the deciding tribunal is compelled to take into its own hands the preparations that must precede the public hearing. In such a case the tribunal cannot truly be said to come to the hearing uncommitted, for it has itself appointed the channels along which the public inquiry is to run. If an unexpected turn in the testimony reveals a miscalculation in the design of these channels, there is no advocate to absorb the blame. The deciding tribunal is under a strong temptation to keep the hearing moving within the boundaries originally set for it. The result may be that the hearing loses its character as an open trial of the facts and issues, and becomes instead a ritual designed to provide public confirmation for what the tribunal considers it has already established in private. When this occurs adjudication acquires the taint affecting all institutions that become subject to manipulation, presenting one aspect to the public, another to knowing participants.

These, then, are the reasons for believing that partisan advocacy plays a vital and essential role in one of the most fundamental procedures of a democratic society. But if we were to put all of these detailed considerations to one side, we should still be confronted by the fact that, in whatever form adjudication may appear, the experienced judge or arbitrator desires and actively seeks to obtain an adversary presentation of the issues. Only when he has had the benefit of intelligent and vigorous advocacy on both sides can he feel fully confident of his decision.

Viewed in this light, the role of the lawyer as a partisan advocate appears not as a regrettable necessity, but as an indispensable part of a larger ordering of affairs. The institution of advocacy is not a concession to the frailties of human nature, but an expression of human insight in the design of a social framework within which man's capacity for impartial judgment can attain its fullest realization.

When advocacy is thus viewed, it becomes clear by what principle limits must be set to partisanship. The advocate plays his role well when zeal for his client's cause promotes a wise and informed decision of the case. He plays his role badly, and trespasses against the obligations of professional responsibility, when his desire to win leads him to muddy the headwaters of decision, when, instead of lending a needed perspective to the controversy, he distorts and obscures its true nature.

* * *

Note

Is Fuller and Randall's description of decision-making consistent with your experience? Do you generally resolve decisions based on your first instinct?

Seymour Wishman, *Confessions of a Criminal Lawyer*
3-7 (1981)

IT WAS PAST TEN on a sweaty summer night when I accompanied the sister of a client to the emergency ward of Newark City Hospital. I had successfully defended her brother against a mugging charge about a year before, and was scheduled to begin a new armed robbery trial for him. The date of the trial was now in doubt because of the wounds he had received in a "disturbance" at the jail. I was rushing to see how he was, and to prevent him from saying anything incriminating to a nurse, doctor, or worse, the police, about the fight he had just lost with a guard—the guard would probably claim my client had attacked him, regardless of what had actually happened.

My client's sister and I joined the parade of wounded and mutilated bodies staggering through the swinging doors. Across the lobby, a heavy but not unattractive woman in a nurse's uniform suddenly shrieked, "Get that motherfucker out of here!" Two women rushed forward to restrain her. "That's the lawyer, that's the motherfuckin' lawyer!" she shouted.

I looked around me. No one else resembled a lawyer. Still screaming, she dragged her two restrainers toward me. I was baffled. As the only white face in a crowd of forty, I felt a growing sense of anxiety.

"That's the son of a bitch that did it to me!" she screamed.

I didn't know what she was talking about.

"Kill him and that nigger Horton!"

Larry Horton. . . of course. Larry Horton was a client of mine. Six months before, I had represented him at his trial for sodomy and rape. At last I recognized the woman's face. She had testified as the "complaining" witness against Horton.

WISHMAN: Isn't it a fact that after you met the defendant at a bar, you asked him if he wanted to have a good time?

LEWIS: No! That's a lie!

WISHMAN: Isn't it true that you took him and his three friends back
           to your apartment and had that good time?

LEWIS: No!

WISHMAN: And, after you had that good time, didn't you ask for
           money?

LEWIS: No such way!

WISHMAN: Isn't it a fact that the only reason you made a complaint
           was because you were furious for not getting paid?

LEWIS: No! No! That's a lie!

WISHMAN: You claim to have been raped and sodomized. As a
           nurse, you surely have an idea of the effect of such an
           assault on a woman's body. Are you aware, Mrs. Lewis,
           that the police doctor found no evidence of force or
           trauma?

LEWIS: I don't know what the doctors found. . .

* * *

Weighing on me more heavily than the possibility that I had helped
a guilty man escape punishment was the undeniable fact that I had
humiliated the victim—alleged victim—in my cross-examination of
her. But, as all criminal lawyers know, to be effective in court I had to
act forcefully, even brutally, at times. I had been trained in law school
to regard the "cross" as an art form. In the course of my career I had
frequently discredited witnesses. My defense of myself had always
been that there was nothing personal in what I was doing. This woman
was obviously unwilling to dismiss my behavior as merely an aspect of
my professional responsibility; instead of an effective counsel, she saw
me simply as a "motherfucker."

* * *

Notes

1.   [T]he model put forth by supporters of partisan
advocacy—well-prepared and effective advocates on each side,
effective judge and jury—is an ideal case. In many cases, the
adversary system does not work so well. Often the parties do not
have equal resources and lawyers do not have equal abilities. One
side is not as well represented as the other. Most people in North
America cannot afford protracted services from a lawyer. Even

when both lawyers are effective advocates, the judge or jury may be ineffective.

Thomas L. Shaffer & Robert F. Cochran, Jr., *Lawyers, Clients, and Moral Responsibility* 11 (1994).

2.　　The argument for the adversary ethic is based on a courtroom model: a judge or jury will be prepared to make wise decisions after the arguments of advocates. Therefore the lawyer is morally obligated to give the best possible argument for the client in order to facilitate the decision-making of the judge or jury. This argument may be persuasive for litigation-related work, but does the adversary ethic apply outside the courtroom, where there is no neutral third party to choose between the arguments of advocates? For example, should it apply when a lawyer is drafting a contract? Professor Monroe Freedman argues that it should:

> [A]ny lawyer who counsels a client, negotiates on a client's behalf, or drafts a legal document for a client must do so with an actual or potential adversary in mind. When a contract is negotiated, there is a party on the otherside. A contract, will, or a form submitted to a government agency may well be read at some later date with an adversary's eye, and could become the subject of litigation. The advice given to a client and acted upon today may strengthen or weaken the client's position in litigation next year.

Monroe H. Freedman, *Understanding Lawyers' Ethics* 66 (1990). Do you find this argument persuasive? For a contrary view, *see* Murray Schwartz, "The Professionalism and Accountability of Lawyers," 66 *Cal. L.Rev.* 669 (1978).

Richard Wasserstrom, "Lawyers as Professionals: Some Moral Issues"
5 Human Rights 1, 5-9, 12, 15 (1975)

* * *

* * * Conventional wisdom has it that where the attorney-client relationship exists, the point of view of the attorney is properly different—and appreciably so—from that which would be appropriate in the absence of the attorney-client relationship. For where the attorney-client relationship exists, it is often appropriate and many times even obligatory for the attorney to do things that, all other things being equal, an ordinary person need not, and should not do. What is characteristic of this role of a lawyer is the lawyer's required indifference to a wide variety of ends and consequences that in other contexts would be of undeniable moral significance. Once a lawyer represents a client, the lawyer has a duty to make his or her expertise fully available in the realization of the end sought by the client, irrespective, for the most part, of the moral worth to which the end will be put or the character of the client who seeks to utilize it. Provided that the end sought is not illegal, the lawyer is, in essence, an amoral technician whose peculiar skills and knowledge in respect to the law are available to those with whom the relationship of client is established. * * *

* * *

And in each case, the role-differentiated character of the lawyer's way of being tends to render irrelevant what would otherwise be morally relevant considerations. Suppose that a client desires to make a will disinheriting her children because they opposed the war in Vietnam. Should the lawyer refuse to draft the will because the lawyer thinks this a bad reason to disinherit one's children? Suppose a client can avoid the payment of taxes through a loophole only available to a few wealthy taxpayers. Should the lawyer refuse to tell the client of a loophole because the lawyer thinks it an unfair advantage for the rich? Suppose a client wants to start a corporation that will manufacture, distribute and promote a harmful but not illegal substance, *e.g.*, cigarettes. Should the lawyer refuse to prepare the articles of incorporation for the corporation? In each case, the accepted view within the profession is that these matters are just of no concern to the lawyer *qua* lawyer. * * *

* * * In this way, the lawyer as professional comes to inhabit a simplified universe which is strikingly amoral—which regards as morally irrelevant any number of factors which nonprofessional citizens might take to be important, if not decisive, in their everyday lives.* * *

* * *

* * * Nonetheless, for most lawyers, most of the time, pursuing the interests of one's clients is an attractive and satisfying way to live in part just because the moral world of the lawyer is a simpler, less complicated, and less ambiguous world than the moral world of ordinary life. There is, I think, something quite seductive about being able to turn aside so many ostensibly difficult moral dilemmas and decisions with the reply: but that is not my concern; my job as a lawyer is not to judge the rights and wrong of the client or the cause; it is to defend as best I can my client's interests. For the ethical problems that can arise within this constricted point of view are, to say the least,

typically neither momentous nor terribly vexing. Role-differentiated behavior is enticing and reassuring precisely because it does constrain and delimit an otherwise often intractable and confusing moral world.

* * *

* * * I am inclined to think that we might all be better served if lawyers were to see themselves less as subject to role-differentiated behavior and more as subject to the demands of the moral point of view. * * *

* * *

* * * [E]ven if on balance the role-differentiated character of the lawyer's way of thinking and acting is ultimately deemed to be justifiable within the system on systemic instrumental grounds, it still remains the case that we do pay a social price for that way of thought and action. For to become and to be a professional, such as a lawyer, is to incorporate within oneself ways of behaving and ways of thinking that shape the whole person. It is especially hard, if not impossible, because of the nature of the professions, for one's professional way of thinking not to dominate one's entire adult life.

* * * The nature of the professions—the lengthy educational preparation, the prestige and economic rewards, and the concomitant enhanced sense of self—makes the role of professional a difficult one to shed even in those obvious situations in which that role is neither required nor appropriate. In important respects, one's professional role becomes and is one's dominant role, so that for many persons at least they become their professional being. This is at a minimum a heavy price to pay for the professions as we know them in our culture, and especially so for lawyers. * * *

* * *

Wasserstrom is concerned with lawyers who play a role in their professional lives that is at odds with the morality that controls their lives outside of the office. They live divided lives. Lawyers who are controlled by a morality that is not their own are at moral risk. Much of the moral life is a matter of habit. The danger is that if moral sensitivity has no place in lawyers' daily lives, their moral sensitivity will atrophy. Even worse is the danger that the adversary life of the lawyer will infect the rest of the lawyer's life. But, as the following case illustrates, there are dangers when the lawyer's morals control his or her actions in the law office.

The Florida Bar v. Betts
530 So.2d 928 (Fla. 1988)

PER CURIAM.

* * *

* * * [R]espondent was retained to prepare the will of his client, Claude Fairfield. Subsequently, two codicils were prepared during a time when Fairfield was in a rapidly deteriorating physical and mental state. In the first codicil, Fairfield removed his daughter and son-in-law as beneficiaries. Respondent spoke with his client on several occasions in an effort to persuade him to reinstate his daughter.

Subsequently, respondent prepared the second codicil to reach this result. However, when the codicil was presented to Fairfield, he was in a comatose state. In his findings, the referee determined that the second codicil was not read to Fairfield, that Fairfield made no verbal response when respondent presented the codicil to him, and that the codicil was executed by an X that respondent marked on the document with a pen he placed and guided in Fairfield's hand.

* * * [T]he referee recommended that respondent be found guilty of violating Disciplinary Rule 1-102(A)(5) (engaging in conduct that is prejudicial to the administration of justice) and Disciplinary Rule 1-102(A)(6) (conduct that adversely reflects on his fitness to practice law) of the Code of Professional Responsibility [*Cf.* MR 8.4(c) & (d)]. The referee further recommended that respondent be given a private reprimand for his actions, and recommended that he be placed on probation for a period of one year.

* * *

We adopt the findings of fact of the referee, which are not contested by either party. The sole dispute is over the severity of the discipline.

We agree with the Bar that the recommendation of the referee is inappropriate. Improperly coercing an apparently incompetent client into executing a codicil raises serious questions both of ethical and legal impropriety, and could potentially result in damage to the client or third parties. It is undisputed that respondent did not benefit by his action and was merely acting out of his belief that the client's family should not be disinherited. Nevertheless, a lawyer's responsibility is to execute his client's wishes, not his own.

The Florida Bar asks that a public reprimand be imposed, and we concur. * * *

* * *

Note

Assume the client in *Betts* disinherited his daughter because she joined a different religion or a different political party or because she married someone of a different race. Would anything justify the lawyer's actions in this case? In a case in which the client is asking the lawyer to do something that the lawyer believes is wrong, what should the lawyer do?

Monroe H. Freedman and Abbe Smith, *Understanding Lawyers' Ethics*
52-56, 69-70 (2d ed. 2002)

* * *

The phrase "role differentiation" is used by critics of zealous, client-centered lawyering to express the idea that lawyers will do things on behalf of their clients that the lawyers themselves would be unwilling to do if they were not acting in their role as lawyers. These critics contend that role differentiation causes lawyers to act in ways that are amoral and even immoral. Rejecting that criticism, the position taken here is that role differentiation is essential to any rational moral system and that it is entirely appropriate that lawyers' moral judgments take account of the fact that they have voluntarily assumed fiduciary responsibilities to their clients.

A leading critic of role differentiation is Professor Richard Wasserstrom. In an article that has been widely cited with approval, Wasserstrom recalls John Dean's list of those involved in the Watergate coverup. Dean placed an asterisk next to the names of each of the lawyers on the list, because he had been struck by the fact that so many of those implicated in wrongdoing were lawyers. Wasserstrom concludes that the involvement of lawyers in Watergate was "natural, if not unavoidable," the "likely if not inevitable consequence of their legal acculturation." * * * "For at best," Wasserstrom asserts, "the lawyer's world is a simplified moral world; often it is an amoral one; and more than occasionally perhaps, an overtly immoral one."

Wasserstrom considers "role-differentiated behavior" to be the root of the problem. As he says, the "nature of role-differentiated behavior

. . . often makes it both appropriate and desirable for the person in a particular role to put to one side considerations of various sorts—and especially various moral considerations—that would otherwise be relevant if not decisive." Illustrative of how Wasserstrom thinks lawyers should make moral considerations relevant is his suggestion that a lawyer should refuse to advise a wealthy client of a tax loophole provided by the legislature for only a few wealthy taxpayers. If that case were to be generalized, it would mean that the legal profession can properly regard itself as an oligarchy, whose duty is to nullify decisions made by the people's duly elected representatives. That is, if lawyers believed that particular clients (wealthy or poor) should not have been given certain rights, the lawyers would be morally (and professionally?) bound to circumvent the legislative process and to forestall the judicial process by the simple device of keeping their clients in ignorance of tempting rights.

Nor is that a caricature of Wasserstrom's position. The role-differentiated amorality of the lawyer is valid, he says, "only if the enormous degree of trust and confidence in the institutions themselves (that is, in the legislative and judicial processes) is itself justified." "[W]e are today," he asserts, "certainly entitled to be quite skeptical both of the fairness and of the capacity for self-correction of our larger institutional mechanisms, including the legal system."

If that is so, it seems to be a *non sequitur* to suggest that we should place that same trust and confidence in the morality of lawyers, individually or collectively. A common complaint, implicit in much of what Wasserstrom says, is that lawyers have too much influence in our public life. In that view, lawyers should not be entrusted, or encouraged, to override democratic institutions as well as their clients' rights to self-governance.

* * *

"There is something quite seductive," adds Wasserstrom, "about [lawyers] being able to turn aside so many ostensibly difficult moral dilemmas with the reply that my job is not to judge my client's cause, but to represent my client's interest." Surely, though, it is at least as seductive to be able to say, "my moral judgement—or my professional responsibility—requires that I be your master. Therefore, you will conduct yourself as I direct you to do."

* * *

* * *[S]uppose that you are going about some pressing matter when your arm is suddenly seized by an old man with a long gray beard, a wild look in his eye, and what appears to be an enormous dead bird hanging around his neck, and the old man launches into a tale of a bizarre adventure at sea. If he is a stranger and you are alone on a poorly lighted street, you may well call the police. If he is a stranger, but you decide that he is harmless, you may simply go on to your other responsibilities. If he is a friend or member of your family, you may feel obligated to spend some time listening to the ancient mariner, or even to confer with others as to how to care for him. If you are a psychiatric social worker, you may act in yet some other way, and that action may depend upon whether you are on duty at your place of employment, or hurrying so that you will not be late to a wedding—and in the latter case, your decision may vary depending upon whether the wedding is someone else's or your own.

Surely there can be no moral objection to those radically different courses of conduct, or to the fact that they are governed substantially by personal, social, and professional context, that is, by role-differentiation. One simply cannot be expected, in any rational moral system, to react to every stranger in the same way in which one may be obligated to respond to a member of one's family or to a friend.

Client Autonomy

Thus, in an interesting and thought-provoking article, Professor Charles Fried has analogized the lawyer to a friend—a "special-purpose" or "limited-purpose" friend "in regard to the legal system." The lawyer, thereby, is seen to be "someone who enters into a personal relation with you—not an abstract relation as under the concept of justice." That means, Fried says, that "like a friend [the lawyer] acts in your interests, not his own; or rather he adopts your interests as his own."

The moral foundation upon which Fried justifies that special-purpose friendship is the sense of self, the moral concepts of "personality, identity, and liberty." He notes that social institutions are so complex that without the assistance of an expert adviser, an ordinary lay person cannot exercise the personal autonomy to which he or she is morally and legally entitled within the system. "Without such an adviser, the law would impose constraints on the lay citizen (unequally at that) which it is not entitled to impose explicitly." The limited purpose of the lawyer's friendship, therefore, is "to preserve and foster the client's autonomy within the law."

* * *

One of the essential values of a just society is respect for the dignity of each member of that society. Essential to each individual's dignity is the free exercise of his autonomy. Toward that end, each person is entitled to know his rights with respect to society and other individuals, and to decide whether to seek fulfillment of those rights through the due processes of law.

The lawyer, by virtue of her training and skills, has a legal and practical monopoly over access to the legal system and knowledge about the law. The lawyer's advice and assistance are often indispensable, therefore, to the effective exercise of individual autonomy.

Accordingly, the attorney acts both professionally and morally in assisting clients to maximize their autonomy, that is, by counseling clients candidly and fully regarding the clients' legal rights and moral responsibilities as the lawyer perceives them, and by assisting clients to carry out their lawful decisions. Further, the attorney acts unprofessionally and immorally by depriving clients of their autonomy, that is, by denying them information regarding their legal rights, by otherwise preempting their moral decisions, or by depriving them of the ability to carry out their lawful decisions.

* * *

Notes

1. Freedman uses the story of the ancient mariner to illustrate that our responsibilities to people may differ, depending on our relationship to them. He argues that our responsibilities differ to family, friends, and strangers. If everyone is responsible for everyone, no one is responsible for anyone. Freedman cites Charles Fried's analogy between lawyers and friends. Both Freedman and Fried ground their proposed role for the attorney in the importance of client autonomy. But should client autonomy trump all interests of those who would be affected by decisions made in the law office?

Freedman's and Fried's analogies miss the central issue, which is what lawyers *should* do for clients. Your duty as friend or sister to the ancient mariner might be to listen to and counsel him. It might not be to attack someone for him. As to Fried's friendship analogy, Gerald

Postema says:

> The impersonalism and moral detachment characteristic of the lawyer's role under the standard conception [of lawyer advocacy] are not found in relations between friends. Loyalty to one's friend does not call for disengagement of one's moral personality.

Gerald J. Postema, "Moral Responsibility in Professional Ethics," 55 *N.Y.U. L. Rev.* 63, 81 (1980). Dauer and Leff point to other distinctions between the lawyer-client relationship and friendship in Edward A. Dauer & Arthur A. Leff, "Correspondence: The Lawyer as Friend," 86 *Yale L.J.* 573, 578-79 (1977).

2.   Thomas Shaffer and Robert Cochran, in the article below, suggest that the friendship analogy, as traditionally understood, is a good one for analyzing the way that lawyers should address moral issues with clients, but their lawyer-as-friend is not Fried's lawyer-as-friend. Shaffer and Cochran are attracted to Aristotle's understanding of friendship. For Aristotle, friendship was a moral relationship. Friends are concerned with one another's character. Friends will not play the guru and control a friend's decision, but neither will they play the hired gun and aid a friend in doing wrong. Friends raise moral issues, wrestle with them together, and seek to discover the good. Both the Wasserstrom and the Freedman articles assume that the client will be a moral problem for the lawyer. It might be that the client can serve as a source of moral wisdom for the lawyer.

Thomas L. Shaffer and Robert F. Cochran, Jr., "Lawyers, Clients, and Moral Responsibility"
adapted from their book, *Lawyers, Clients, and Moral Responsibility* (West, 1994)

Decisions made in law offices are important. They are important because they affect people, and people are important. Some law office decisions are controlled in substance by the law; most are not. In a tort dispute, will the client assert or resist a claim? In a divorce, will the client take actions that will harm a child or spouse? In structuring a business deal, or writing a will, who will benefit? Who will lose? Will the officers of a corporation consider the effects of its actions on workers, on consumers, on competitors, on the environment, on the community?

As to all of these decisions, lawyers and clients have substantial discretion. They are all decisions that raise moral concerns. But, what is the place of moral values in the law office? We can examine that issue by asking two questions:

(1) Who controls substantive decisions during legal representation? and
(2) Are the interests of people other than the client taken into consideration?

We would like to examine those questions in the context of the story of a law suit that arose in Boston in the early part of this century.

The Warren family was one of the most prominent families in Boston. Mr. Warren died and left the family business in a trust for the benefit of his widow and five children. Sam, the oldest son, had had the most experience in business, and had the trust of everyone in the family. He was placed in charge of the business and the family trust. Ned, a younger brother, moved to England and lived off of his trust income.

After many years, there were difficulties with the business and Ned began to suspect his older brother Sam of bad faith. Ned went to one of Boston's finest lawyers and shared his suspicions. His lawyer filed a complaint in equity, charging Sam with a breach of trust. On the same day on which the complaint was filed, Ned wrote Sam a letter in which he stated:

The phrases are such as in a legal document I have felt obliged to sign, but are very far from representing my feelings toward you ...
Let us try to agree; it would be much pleasanter.
Your affectionate brother, E.P. Warren

As you might imagine, Sam was deeply offended by the allegations in the complaint. The two brothers went to court. During the trial, Sam was subjected to rigorous cross examination. After several days on the witness stand, he committed suicide. The effect of the litigation on Sam was dramatic and unusual, but it illustrates the stress and anxiety that people go through in our adversary system.

The Lawyer as Hired Gun - We often hear lawyers referred to as "hired guns." In some respects, Ned's lawyer acted as the hired gun of our classic westerns--he attacked someone for the client. But in other respects, Ned's lawyer was different, and more dangerous, than the hired gun. The hired gun acts at the direction of the boss--the boss assumes responsibility for what the hired gun does. If Ned's lawyer had acted as hired gun, he would have looked to Ned to control the representation. But Ned's letter indicates that, though he had misgivings about the suit, he deferred to his lawyer.

The Lawyer as Godfather - Ned's lawyer did not act as a hired gun lawyer; he more closely resembled another classic figure from American film, the Godfather. Like Don Corleone, Ned's lawyer controlled the action and ignored the interests of other people.

Ned deferred to his lawyer; it is likely that the lawyer deferred to his role as an advocate. Note that no one dealt with the moral issue: Should they accuse Sam of a breach of trust? Ned turned the problem over to the lawyer, the lawyer deferred to his role as advocate.

This is not an uncommon role for lawyers. In Douglas Rosenthal's classic study of lawyer-client relations, he interviewed one client who had suffered fairly minor injuries in a traffic accident. The lawyer persuaded the client to embellish his claim for damages. The client said:

> [T]he lawyer is a reassuring presence who takes away your guilt feelings. He says, "Hey, this is the way the game is played; you take as much as you can get; it's what they expect; it's the way it's done." [The lawyer] takes upon his own shoulders the burden of your guilt--he's the professional.

Note the great danger that arises when the lawyer assumes this role. No one assumes moral responsibility for what may be very damaging activity.

The Adversary System - Hired gun lawyers and godfather lawyers are likely to defend their attacks on others with arguments based on their role in the adversary system– if both sides have aggressive lawyers who present their cases well, judges and juries will be able to decide wisely. It is a theory that works well in many cases, but, as every lawyer knows, it does not work well in many other cases. Often lawyers are not equally effective, and, increasingly, one side to a conflict is unable to afford the expense of a lawyer. In addition, many people who are not in court are affected by decisions made during litigation, and, of course, most legal work is done in the office, where the judge is not present as an arbiter of justice.

The other argument for lawyer advocacy is that lawyer advocacy protects client autonomy. But what of other people who are affected by lawyer advocacy? What of their autonomy? What about communities that are damaged by the pursuit of client autonomy? Aggressive representation may protect the client's autonomy at the expense of people who have no lawyer to protect them. There are places for aggressive advocacy. Our argument is that lawyer and client cannot put blinders on and assume that advocacy will always yield justice.

Indiscriminate lawyer advocacy not only harms other people; it harms clients and lawyers. Clients are deprived of the opportunity for moral reflection about the issues they face. Lawyers either distance themselves from what they do or suffer moral pain. In an interview conducted by Rand Jack and Dana Crowley Jack, a lawyer, Diana Cartwright, reports, "I have to contradict myself depending on the role I'm taking. . . . It's sort of professional prostitution." Some lawyers try to live divided lives, with one set of morals for the office and another set for home, but life at the office is likely to infect our lives at home.

The Lawyer as Guru - An alternative to the injustice and moral schizophrenia yielded by unreflective lawyer advocacy is presented by the traditional American lawyer. David Hoffman, who in the 1830s drafted the first guidelines for American lawyers, said, "[The client] shall never make me a partner in his knavery." Judge Clement Haynsworth, a modern gentleman-lawyer put it, "[T]he lawyer must never forget that he is the master. He is not there to do the client's bidding. It is for the lawyer to decide what is morally and legally right. . . ."

The traditional lawyer acts as guru, taking control of the representation and making decisions based on what he or she thinks to be right. Such lawyers do not live divided lives. As Atticus Finch of *To Kill a Mockingbird* said, "I can't live one way in town and another way in my home." He was a wise papa in both places.

But, whereas there is no place in the office of the godfather or the hired gun lawyer for the morals of the lawyer, there is no place in the office of the guru lawyer for the morals of the client. Guru lawyers start off (as most bar association discussions of legal ethics do) with the assumption that the client will be a moral problem for the client. Guru lawyers assume that they can be a source of moral wisdom for the client. A Guru lawyer in the Warren case would have told Ned that he should not sue his brother. Such lawyers show admirable concern for others and for client rectitude, but they show little respect for the client and little recognition that clients can be a source of moral wisdom for the lawyer. Humility is justified when approaching the moral issues that arise in the law office. These issues are likely to be difficult. People disagree over what sound ethics require. We do not suggest that there are not objective moral standards, but none of us has perfect ability to discern those standards or to determine how they should apply. There is a danger that lawyers will be confident of their moral judgment when confidence is not justified. As we argue in the following section, two consciences, in conversation, are more likely to get to moral truth than one.

The Lawyer as Friend - Our preferred alternative for lawyers is the lawyer as friend, based on Aristotle's notion of friendship as a virtue. We are not saying that lawyers can be close friends to all of their clients, but that lawyers might raise moral issues with clients in the way that they would raise them with a close friend. Friends raise moral concerns with friends, not in a condemning fashion, but as a question, in a tentative fashion, as something that the friend might want to consider. Aristotle said friends collaborate in the good. A friend is unlikely to impose his or her will on a friend, but neither will a friend sit by and let a friend go down a wrong path. A lawyer as friend will raise and discuss moral issues with clients in a way that takes those issues seriously, without imposing the lawyer's values on the client. One of the best ways to raise such issues is by asking questions which come naturally in the course of decision-making. As to each alternative under consideration, the lawyer should ask the client, "What will be its effect on other people?"

There are two places, in particular, in the client counseling process where we believe the interests of other people should be considered. The first is the point where the lawyer and client are considering the potential consequences of various alternative courses of action. Some suggest that the lawyer and client consider only consequences to the client. We suggest that the lawyer and client consider the consequences to other people as well. Decisions should be made based on a recognition of the effects of one's actions on others. The lawyer and client should consider all of the consequences that might arise from various alternatives. This can be as simple as the lawyer asking the client what affects various alternatives will have on other people.

The second place where the lawyer should raise the interests of other people is at the point of decision-making. Once the alternatives are identified, the client must choose between them. Among the many questions that the lawyer should ask at this point, one is, "What would be fair?" Note that this question does not impose the lawyers values on clients; it calls on clients to draw on their own sources of moral values.

Most decisions made in the law office are decisions over which reasonable people might disagree. So long as the client does not ask the lawyer to do something that the lawyer believes to be wrong, we believe that the lawyer should defer to the client. If the client asks the lawyer to do something which the lawyer believes to be wrong, we believe that the lawyer should withdraw from representing the client. But we think that that will be the unusual case. We suspect that in most cases, as lawyer and client discuss the issues they face, they will reach agreement as to the direction to take. It may not be the direction that either of them would have taken alone, but it will be a decision, a moral decision, that they will make together.

B. Litigation and Other Proceedings

Read Model Rules 3.1, 3.2, and 3.4[2]

Washington State Physicians Ins. Exch. & Ass'n v. Fisons Corp.
122 Wash. 2d 299, 858 P.2d 1054 (1993)

ANDERSEN, Chief Justice.

FACTS OF CASE

We are asked in this case to decide whether a physician has a cause of action against a drug company for personal and professional injuries which he suffered when his patient had an adverse reaction to a drug he had prescribed. The physician claimed the drug company failed to warn him of the risks associated with the drug. * * * We are also asked to rule that the trial court erred in denying sanctions against the drug company for certain abuses in the discovery process.

The physician's action began as part of a malpractice and product liability suit brought on behalf of a child who was the physician's patient. On January 18, 1986, 2-year-old Jennifer Pollock suffered seizures which resulted in severe and permanent brain damage. It was determined that the seizures were caused by an excessive amount of

---

[2]   For MR 3.1, *cf.* DR 7-102(A); EC 7-4; Cal. Rule 3-200; CAL. BUS. & PROF. CODE § 6068(c) (West 1995). For MR 3.2, *cf.* DR 7-101(A)(1); there is no counterpart to MR 3.2 in the Cal. Rules. For MR 3.4, *cf.* DR 7-102(A)(6), 7-104(A)(2), 7-106(A), 7-106(C)(1)-(5), (7), 7-109(A)-(C); EC 7-6, 7-24, 7-27 to -28; Cal. Rules 3-210, 5-220, 5-310(A)-(B).

theophylline in her system. The Pollocks sued Dr. James Klicpera (Jennifer's pediatrician), who had prescribed the drug, as well as Fisons Corporation (the drug manufacturer and hereafter drug company) which produced Somophyllin Oral Liquid, the theophylline-based medication prescribed for Jennifer.

Dr. Klicpera cross-claimed against the drug company both for contribution and for damages and attorneys' fees under the Consumer Protection Act as well as for damages for emotional distress.

In January 1989, after nearly 3 years of discovery, Dr. Klicpera, his partner and the Everett Clinic settled with the Pollocks. * * *

More than 1 year after this settlement, an attorney for the Pollocks provided Dr. Klicpera's attorney a copy of a letter received from an anonymous source. The letter, dated June 30, 1981, indicated that the drug company was aware in 1981 of "life-threatening theophylline toxicity" in children who received the drug while suffering from viral infections. The letter was sent from the drug company to only a small number of what the company considered influential physicians. The letter stated that physicians needed to understand that theophylline can be a "capricious drug."

The Pollocks and Dr. Klicpera contended that their discovery requests should have produced the June 1981 letter and they moved for sanctions against the drug company. The request for sanctions was initially heard by a special discovery master, who denied sanctions, but who required the drug company to deliver all documents requested which related to theophylline. * * *

The day after the hearing on sanctions, the drug company delivered approximately 10,000 documents to Dr. Klicpera's and Pollocks' attorneys. Among the documents provided was a July 10, 1985 memorandum from Cedric Grigg, director of medical communications for the drug company, to Bruce Simpson, vice president of sales and marketing for the company.

This 1985 memorandum referred to a dramatic increase in reports of serious toxicity to theophylline in early 1985 and also referred to the current recommended dosage as a significant "mistake" or "poor clinical judgment". The memo alluded to the "sinister aspect" that the physician who was the "pope" of theophylline dosage recommendation was a consultant to the pharmaceutical company that was the leading manufacturer of the drug and that this consultant was "heavily into [that company's] stocks". The memo also noted that the toxicity reports were not reported in the journal read by those who most often prescribed the drug and concluded that those physicians may not be aware of the "alarming increase in adverse reactions such as seizures, permanent brain damage and death." The memo concluded that the "epidemic of theophylline toxicity provides strong justification for our corporate decision to cease promotional activities with our theophylline line of products." The record at trial showed that the drug company continued to promote and sell theophylline after the date of this memo.

On April 27, 1990, shortly after the 1985 memo was revealed, the drug company settled with the Pollocks for $6.9 million. * * *

[At the trial of Dr. Klicpera's claim against the drug company] [t]he jury awarded Dr. Klicpera $150,000 for loss of professional consultations, $1,085,000 for injury to professional reputation, and $2,137,500 for physical and mental pain and suffering. * * *

* * *

The drug company sought direct review by this court and we accepted review. Dr. Klicpera and his insurer (WSPIE) cross appeal from the trial court's refusal to award discovery sanctions for the alleged discovery violations.

* * *

* * * The two documents, dubbed the "smoking guns" by the doctor, show that the drug company knew about, and in fact had warned selected physicians about, the dangers of theophylline toxicity in children with viral infections at least as early as June 1981, 4 years before Jennifer Pollock was injured.

Although interrogatories and requests for production should have led to the discovery of the "smoking gun" documents, their existence was not revealed to the doctor until one of them was anonymously delivered to his attorneys.

* * *

Both documents contradicted the position taken by the drug company in the litigation, namely, that it did not know that theophylline based medications were potentially dangerous when given to children with viral infections.

* * *

CR 26(g) was added to our civil rules in 1985; it provides as follows:

Every request for discovery or response or objection thereto made by a party represented by an attorney shall be signed by at least one attorney of record in his individual name, whose address shall be stated. A party who is not represented by an attorney shall sign the request, response, or objection and state his address. The signature of the attorney or party constitutes a certification that he has read the request, response, or objection, and that to the best of his knowledge, information, and belief formed after a reasonable inquiry it is: (1) consistent with these rules and warranted by existing law or a good faith argument for the extension, modification, or reversal of existing law; (2) not interposed for any improper purpose, such as to harass or to cause unnecessary delay* * *.

CR 26(g) has not yet been interpreted by this court. The rule parallels Fed.R.Civ.P. 26(g) (Rule 26(g)) and, like its federal counterpart and like CR 11, CR 26(g) is aimed at reducing delaying tactics, procedural harassment and mounting legal costs. Such practices "tend to impose unjustified burdens on other parties, frustrate those who seek to vindicate their rights in the courts, obstruct the judicial process, and bring the civil justice system into disrepute." Schwarzer, *Sanctions Under the New Federal Rule 11—A Closer Look*, 104 F.R.D. 181, 182 (1985) (hereinafter Schwarzer).

* * * The federal advisory committee notes describe the discovery process and problems that led to the enactment of Rule 26(g) as follows:

Excessive discovery and evasion or resistance to reasonable discovery requests pose significant problems. . . .

The purpose of discovery is to provide a mechanism for making relevant information available to the litigants. * * *

* * * *Rule 26(g) is designed to curb discovery abuse by explicitly encouraging the imposition of sanctions. . . . The term "response" includes answers to interrogatories and to requests to admit as well as responses to production requests. . . .*

Concern about discovery abuse has led to widespread recognition that there is a need for more aggressive judicial control and supervision. Sanctions to deter discovery abuse would be more effective if they were diligently applied "not merely to penalize those whose conduct may be deemed to warrant such a sanction, but to deter those who might be tempted to such conduct in the absence of such a deterrent." . . . *Thus the premise of Rule 26(g) is that imposing sanctions on attorneys who fail to meet the rule's standards will significantly reduce abuse by imposing disadvantages therefor.*

(Citations omitted. Italics ours.) *Amendments to the Federal Rules of Civil Procedure,* Advisory Committee Note, 97 F.R.D. 166, 216-19 (1983).

* * *

The trial court * * * denied sanctions, in part because: * * * (3) the conduct of the drug company and its counsel was consistent with the customary and accepted litigation practices of the bar of Snohomish County and of this state; * * *

* * *Conduct is to be measured against the spirit and purpose of the rules, not against the standard of practice of the local bar. * * *

* * *

The drug company was persistent in its resistance to discovery requests. Fair and reasoned resistance to discovery is not sanctionable. Rather it is the misleading nature of the drug company's responses that is contrary to the purposes of discovery and which is most damaging to the fairness of the litigation process.

The specific instances alleged to be sanctionable in this case involve misleading or "non" responses to a number of requests which the doctor claims should have produced the smoking gun documents themselves or a way to discover the information they contained. The two smoking gun documents reportedly were contained in files which related to Intal, a cromolyn sodium product, which was manufactured by Fisons and which competed with Somophyllin. The manager of medical communications had a thorough collection of articles, materials and other documents relating to the dangers of theophylline and used the information from those materials to market Intal, as an alternative to Somophyllin Oral Liquid. The drug company avoided production of these theophylline-related materials, and avoided identifying the manager of medical communications as a person with information about the dangers of theophylline, by giving evasive or misleading responses to interrogatories and requests for production.

* * *

[The following are a few of many examples cited by the court:]

In November 1986 the doctor served his first requests for production on the drug company. Four requests were made. Three asked for documents concerning Somophyllin. Request 3 stated:

3.   Produce genuine copies of any letters sent by your company to physicians concerning theophylline toxicity in children.

The drug company's response was:

> Such letters, *if any*, regarding Somophyllin Oral Liquid will be produced at a reasonable time and place convenient to Fisons and its counsel of record.

Clerk's Papers, at 8458.

Had the request, as written, been complied with, the first smoking gun letter (exhibit 3) would have been disclosed early in the litigation. That June 30, 1981 letter concerned theophylline toxicity in children; it was sent by the drug company to physicians.

*   *   *

When the child or the doctor attempted to see information from the files of other products, the drug company objected. For example:

> *Request for Production No. 1*: All documents contained in all files from the regulating department, marketing department, drug surveillance department, pharmaceutical development department, product manager department and the medical departments regarding all cromolyn [Intal] products of Fisons Corporation. Regarding this request for production all documents should include from inception of file to the present.

> *Answer*: Defendant Fisons objects to this discovery request as not reasonably calculated to lead to the discovery of admissible evidence, as overbroad in time, and as incredibly burdensome and harassing. This discovery request encompasses approximately *eighty-five* percent of *all* documents in the subject files and departments—millions of pages of documents. *Neither cromolyn (which should be referred to as cromolyn sodium), nor any cromolyn product, nor the properties or efficacy of cromolyn is at issue in this litigation.* Furthermore, Fisons objects to this discovery request as calling for the production of extremely sensitive trade secret and proprietary material.

*   *   *

The drug company's responses and answers to discovery requests are misleading. The answers state that all information *regarding* Somophyllin Oral Liquid which had been requested would be provided. They further imply that all documents which are relevant to the plaintiffs' claims were being produced. * * *

It appears clear that no conceivable discovery request could have been made by the doctor that would have uncovered the relevant documents, given the above and other responses of the drug company.

The objections did not specify that certain documents were not being produced. Instead the general objections were followed by a promise to produce requested documents. These responses did not comply with either the spirit or letter of the discovery rules and thus were signed in violation of the certification requirement.

* * *

* * * [T]he drug company argues that the smoking gun documents and other documents relating to theophylline were not documents *regarding* Somophyllin Oral Liquid because they were intended to market another product. No matter what its initial purpose, and regardless of where it had been filed, under the facts of this case, a document that warned of the serious dangers of the primary ingredient of Somophyllin Oral Liquid is a document *regarding* Somophyllin Oral Liquid.

* * *

[T]he drug company's attorneys claim they were just doing their job, that is, they were vigorously representing their client. The conflict here is between the attorney's duty to represent the client's interest and the attorney's duty as an officer of the court to use, but not abuse the judicial process.

[V]igorous advocacy is not contingent on lawyers being free to pursue litigation tactics that they cannot justify as legitimate. The lawyer's duty to place his client's interests ahead of all others presupposes that the lawyer will live with the rules that govern the system. Unlike the polemicist haranguing the public from his soapbox in the park, the lawyer enjoys the privilege of a professional license that entitles him to entry into the justice system to represent his client, and in doing so, to pursue his profession and earn his living. He is subject to the correlative obligation to comply with the rules and to conduct himself in a manner consistent with the proper functioning of that system.

Schwarzer, *Sanctions Under the New Federal Rule 11—A Closer Look*, 104 F.R.D. 181, 184 (1985).

Like CR 11, CR 26(g) makes the imposition of sanctions mandatory, if a violation of the rule is found. Sanctions are warranted in this case. What the sanctions should be and against whom they should be imposed is a question that cannot be fairly answered without further factual inquiry, and that is the trial court's function. While we recognize that the issue of imposition of sanctions upon attorneys is a difficult and disagreeable task for a trial judge, it is a necessary one if our system is to remain accessible and responsible.

Misconduct, once tolerated, will breed more misconduct and those who might seek relief against abuse will instead resort to it in self-defense.

Schwarzer, 104 F.R.D. at 205.

In making its determination, the trial court should use its discretion to fashion "appropriate" sanctions. The rule provides that sanctions may be imposed upon the signing attorney, the party on whose behalf the response is made, or both.

* * *

* * * In the present case, sanctions need to be severe enough to deter these attorneys and others from participating in this kind of conduct in the future.

The trial court's denial of sanctions is reversed and the case is remanded for a determination of appropriate sanctions.

* * *

Notes

1. The plaintiff in this matter received a copy of the first "smoking gun" letter through "an anonymous source." Assume that the anonymous source was a troubled associate with the law firm that represented Fisons. Were his actions justified? What should he have done? If the lawyers had asked the defendant in *Spaulding v. Zimmerman, see* Chapter Three, to allow disclosure of the aneurysm to the plaintiff, and the defendant had refused, would defense counsel be justified in sending a copy of the doctor's report anonymously to the lawyer for the plaintiff?

2. Rule 37 of the Federal Rules of Civil Procedure was amended effective December 1, 1993. Under amended Rule 37, sanctions against the party or attorney for failure to disclose pursuant to the discovery rules (including giving "an evasive or incomplete disclosure") are limited to the reasonable expenses, including attorney's fees, of the moving party. Would the outcome of *Fisons* be different if it had been resolved under the amended Federal Rules?

3. Even in the absence of formal sanctions, courts and other lawyers can exert significant pressure on lawyers to "do the right thing." Informal sanctions can be more effective than formal sanctions. Lawyers develop reputations within local bar associations for trustwor-

thiness, or lack thereof. Even in large cities, lawyers within specialties develop reputations for honesty or dishonesty. The informal pressure that judges can apply is illustrated by the following story from an Oklahoma court:

During a motion docket of a state civil trial court, two lawyers were arguing the enforceability of an agreement regarding the discovery schedule. The lawyer insisting on strict compliance with the original schedule admitted that he had orally agreed to a more lenient schedule, but he sought enforcement of the original timetable under a local court rule that required all agreements of counsel to be in writing. The lawyer seeking additional time argued the unfairness of this change in position.

The judge felt compelled to order compliance with the original schedule in light of the court rule. However, after rendering his ruling on the schedule, he ordered both attorneys to turn and face the courtroom. Because this was a general docket call, the courtroom was packed with lawyers from most of the firms in town. The judge then asked his bailiff to get everyone's attention. When all eyes were focused on the bench the judge introduced the two lawyers, and announced "I just want everyone to know how Mr. X practices law. He orally agreed to postpone certain discovery matters, but now is before this court arguing that his word is not enforceable because the agreement wasn't in writing as required by the local court rules. Take a good look at him now so you will know who you are dealing with in the future."

4. Consider also the following order from the United States District Court in Oklahoma:

Defendant's Motion to Dismiss or in the Alternative to Continue Trial is denied. If the recitals in the briefs from both sides are accepted at face value, neither side has conducted discovery according to the letter and spirit of the Oklahoma County Bar Association Lawyer's Creed. This is an aspirational creed not subject to enforcement by this Court, but violative conduct does call for judicial disapprobation at least. If there is a hell to which disputatious, uncivil, vituperative lawyers go, let it be one in which the damned are eternally locked in discovery disputes with other lawyers of equally repugnant attributes.

It is so ordered this __ day of February, 1989.

Krueger v. Pelican Production Corp. (No. CIV-87-2385-A) (D.Ct. Ok. 1989). Did the judge exceed his authority?

In re Ryder
263 F. Supp. 360 (E.D. Va. 1967)

PER CURIAM.

This proceeding was instituted to determine whether Richard R. Ryder should be removed from the roll of attorneys qualified to practice before this court. Ryder was admitted to this bar in 1953. He formerly served five years as an Assistant United States Attorney. He has an active trial practice, including both civil and criminal cases.

In proceedings of this kind the charges must be sustained by clear and convincing proof, the misconduct must be fraudulent, intentional, and the result of improper motives. [C]. We conclude that these strict requirements have been satisfied. Ryder took possession of stolen money and a sawed-off shotgun, knowing that the money had been stolen and that the gun had been used in an armed robbery. He intended to retain this property pending his client's trial unless the government discovered it. He intended by his possession to destroy the chain of evidence that linked the contraband to his client and to prevent its use to establish his client's guilt.

On August 24, 1966 a man armed with a sawed-off shotgun robbed the Varina Branch of the Bank of Virginia of $7,583. Included in the currency taken were $10 bills known as "bait money," the serial numbers of which had been recorded.

On August 26, 1966 Charles Richard Cook rented safety deposit box 14 at a branch of the Richmond National Bank. Later in the day Cook was interviewed at his home by agents of the Federal Bureau of Investigation, who obtained $348 from him. Cook telephoned Ryder, who had represented him in civil litigation. Ryder came to the house and advised the agents that he represented Cook. He said that if Cook were not to be placed under arrest, he intended to take him to his office for an interview. The agents left. Cook insisted to Ryder that he had not robbed the bank. He told Ryder that he had won the money, which the agents had taken from him, in a crap game. At this time Ryder believed Cook.

Later that afternoon Ryder telephoned one of the agents and asked whether any of the bills obtained from Cook had been identified as a part of the money taken in the bank robbery. The agent told him that some bills had been identified. Ryder made inquiries about the number of bills taken and their denominations. The agent declined to give him specific information but indicated that several of the bills were recorded as bait money.

The next morning, Saturday, August 27, 1966, Ryder conferred with Cook again. He urged Cook to tell the truth, and Cook answered that a man, whose name he would not divulge, offered him $500 on the day of the robbery to put a package in a bank lock box. Ryder did not believe this story. Ryder told Cook that if the government could trace the money in the box to him, it would be almost conclusive evidence of his guilt. He knew that Cook was under surveillance and he suspected that Cook might try to dispose of the money.

That afternoon Ryder telephoned a former officer of the Richmond Bar Association to discuss his course of action. He had known this attorney for many years and respected his judgment. The lawyer was at home and had no library available to him when Ryder telephoned. In their casual conversation Ryder told what he knew about the case, omitting names. He explained that he thought he would take the money from Cook's safety deposit box and place it in a box in his own name. This, he believed, would prevent Cook from attempting to dispose of the money. The lawyers thought that eventually F.B.I. agents would locate the money and that since it was in Ryder's possession, he could claim a privilege and thus effectively exclude it from evidence. This would prevent the government from linking Ryder's client with the bait money and would also destroy any presumption of guilt that might exist arising out of the client's exclusive possession of the evidence.

* * *

[Ryder prepared a document giving himself power of attorney, had Cook sign it, and took the power of attorney] to the Richmond National Bank. He rented box 13 in his name with his office address, presented the power of attorney, entered Cook's box, took both boxes into a booth, where he found a bag of money and a sawed-off shotgun in Cook's box. The box also contained miscellaneous items which are not pertinent to this proceeding. He transferred the contents of Cook's box to his own and returned the boxes to the vault. He left the bank, and neither he nor Cook returned.

* * *

On September 7, 1966 Cook was indicted for robbing the Varina Branch of the Bank of Virginia. A bench warrant was issued and the next day Ryder represented Cook at a bond hearing. Cook was identified as the robber by employees of the bank. He was released on bond. Cook was arraigned on a plea of not guilty on September 9, 1966.

On September 12, 1966 F.B.I. agents procured search warrants for Cook's and Ryder's safety deposit boxes in the Richmond National Bank. They found Cook's box empty. In Ryder's box they discovered $5,920 of the $7,583 taken in the bank robbery and the sawed-off shotgun used in the robbery.

* * *

At the outset, we reject the suggestion that Ryder did not know the money which he transferred from Cook's box to his was stolen. We find that on August 29 when Ryder opened Cook's box and saw a bag of money and a sawed-off shotgun, he then knew Cook was involved in the bank robbery and that the money was stolen. The evidence clearly establishes this. Ryder knew that the man who had robbed the bank used a sawed-off shotgun. He disbelieved Cook's story about the source of the money in the lockbox. He knew that some of the bills in Cook's possession were bait money.

* * *

We also find that Ryder was not motivated solely by certain expectation the government would discover the contents of his lockbox. He believed discovery was probable. In this event he intended to argue to the court that the contents of his box could not be revealed, and even if the contents were identified, his possession made the stolen money and the shotgun inadmissible against his client. He also recognized that discovery was not inevitable. His intention in this event, we find, was to assist Cook by keeping the stolen money and the shotgun concealed in his lockbox until after the trial. His conversations, and the secrecy he enjoined, immediately after he put the money and the gun in his box, show that he realized the government might not find the property.

We accept his statement that he intended eventually to return the money to its rightful owner, but we pause to say that no attorney should ever place himself in such a position. Matters involving the possible termination of an attorney-client relationship, or possible subsequent proceedings in the event of an acquittal, are too delicate to permit such a practice.

* * *

It was Ryder, not his client, who took the initiative in transferring the incriminating possession of the stolen money and the shotgun from

Cook. Ryder's conduct went far beyond the receipt and retention of a confidential communication from his client. Counsel for Ryder conceded, at the time of argument, that the acts of Ryder were not within the attorney-client privilege.

* * *

* * * [T]his proceeding is not concerned with the concealment of Cook's papers or other articles of an evidentiary nature. Neither Cook nor his attorney could be compelled to produce merely evidentiary articles nor could such articles be seized in a legal search. [Cc] In Harris v. United States, 331 U. S. 145, 154, 67 S. Ct. 1098, 1103, 91 L. Ed. 1399 (1947), Mr. Chief Justice Vinson said:

> "This Court has frequently recognized the distinction between merely evidentiary materials, on the one hand, which may not be seized either under the authority of a search warrant or during the course of a search incident to arrest, and on the other hand, those objects which may validly be seized including the instrumentalities and means by which a crime is committed, the fruits of crime such as stolen property, weapons by which escape of the person arrested might be effected, and property the possession of which is a crime."

Ryder, an experienced criminal attorney, recognized and acted upon the fact that the gun and money were subject to seizure while in the possession of Cook.

* * *

In Clark v. State, 159 Tex. Cr. R. 187, 261 S.W.2d 339 (1953), cert. denied, reh. denied sub nom. Clark v. Texas, 346 U. S. 855, 905, 74 S. Ct. 69, 98 L. Ed. 369 (1953), a lawyer's advice to get rid of a gun used to commit a murder was admissible in evidence. The court observed the conversation was not within the realm of legitimate professional conduct and employment. [C]. In argument, it was generally conceded that Ryder could have been required to testify in the prosecution of Cook as to the transfer of the contents of the lockbox.

* * *

The money in Cook's box belonged to the Bank of Virginia. [A Virginia statute provides that one who receives or conceals stolen goods is guilty of larceny.]* * * No canon of ethics or law permitted Ryder to conceal from the Bank of Virginia its money to gain his client's acquittal.

Cook's possession of the sawed-off shotgun was illegal. 26 U.S.C. § 5851. Ryder could not lawfully receive the gun from Cook to assist

Cook to avoid conviction of robbery. Cook had never mentioned the shotgun to Ryder. When Ryder discovered it in Cook's box, he took possession of it to hinder the government in the prosecution of its case, and he intended not to reveal it pending trial unless the government discovered it and a court compelled its production. No statute or canon of ethics authorized Ryder to take possession of the gun for this purpose.

Canon 15 [of the ABA Canons of Professional Ethics] [*Cf.* MRs 1.2(d) and 3.4(a)] states in part:

> "* * * [T]he great trust of the lawyer is to be performed within and not without the bounds of law. The office of attorney does not permit, much less does it demand of him for any client, violation of law or any manner of fraud or chicane. He must obey his own conscience and not that of his client."

In helping Cook to conceal the shotgun and stolen money, Ryder acted without the bounds of law. He allowed the office of attorney to be used in violation of law. The scheme which he devised was a deceptive, legalistic subterfuge—rightfully denounced by the canon as chicane.

There is much to be said, however, for mitigation of the discipline to be imposed. Ryder intended to return the bank's money after his client was tried. He consulted reputable persons before and after he placed the property in his lockbox, although he did not precisely follow their advice. Were it not for these facts, we would deem proper his permanent exclusion from practice before this court. In view of the mitigating circumstances, he will be suspended from practice in this court for eighteen months effective October 14, 1966.

* * *

Notes

1.   Can you distinguish Ryder's failure to disclose the location of the shotgun and money from Belge's failure to disclose the location of the dead bodies (see Chapter Three)?

2.   When lawyers come into possession of the fruits or instrumentalities or other physical evidence of a crime, they have the duty to turn them over to the prosecutor. Morrell v. State, 575 P.2d 1200 (Alaska 1978) ("kidnapping plan" drawn by client); People v. Meredith, 29 Cal. 3d 682, 631 P.2d 46, 175 Cal. Rptr. 612 (1981) (victim's partially burned wallet removed from trash can by lawyer's investiga-

tor). However, if the source of the evidence is the client, information concerning the source is generally treated by the courts as protected by the attorney client privilege. People v. Nash, 418 Mich. 196, 341 N.W.2d 439 (1983); State *ex rel*. Sowers v. Olwell, 64 Wash. 2d 828, 394 P.2d 681 (1964). For a critical review of cases dealing with the lawyer's obligations in these situations, see Norman Lefstein, "Incriminating Physical Evidence, the Defense Attorney's Dilemma, and the Need for Rules, 64 N.C.L.Rev. 897 (1986).

Read Model Rule 3.3[3]

Nix v. Whiteside
475 U.S. 157, 106 S. Ct. 988, 89 L. Ed.2d 123 (1986)

Chief Justice BURGER delivered the opinion of the Court.

We granted certiorari to decide whether the Sixth Amendment right of a criminal defendant to assistance of counsel is violated when an attorney refuses to cooperate with the defendant in presenting perjured testimony at his trial.

* * *

Whiteside was convicted of second-degree murder by a jury verdict which was affirmed by the Iowa courts. The killing took place on February 8, 1977, in Cedar Rapids, Iowa. Whiteside and two others went to one Calvin Love's apartment late that night, seeking marijuana. Love was in bed when Whiteside and his companions arrived; an argument between Whiteside and Love over the marijuana ensued. At one point, Love directed his girlfriend to get his "piece," and at another point got up, then returned to his bed. According to Whiteside's testimony, Love then started to reach under his pillow and moved toward Whiteside. Whiteside stabbed Love in the chest, inflicting a fatal wound.

Whiteside was charged with murder, and when counsel was appointed he objected to the lawyer initially appointed, claiming that he felt uncomfortable with a lawyer who had formerly been a prosecutor. Gary L. Robinson was then appointed and immediately began an investigation. Whiteside gave him a statement that he had stabbed

---

[3]   *Cf.* DR 7-102(A)(3)-(5), 7-102(B)(1), 7-106(B)(1); EC 7-23, 7-26, 7-27; Cal. Rule 5-200; CAL.BUS. & PROF. CODE §§ 6068(d), 6128(a).

Love as the latter "was pulling a pistol from underneath the pillow on the bed." Upon questioning by Robinson, however, Whiteside indicated that he had not actually seen a gun, but that he was convinced that Love had a gun. No pistol was found on the premises; shortly after the police search following the stabbing, which had revealed no weapon, the victim's family had removed all of the victim's possessions from the apartment. Robinson interviewed Whiteside's companions who were present during the stabbing, and none had seen a gun during the incident. Robinson advised Whiteside that the existence of a gun was not necessary to establish the claim of self-defense, and that only a reasonable belief that the victim had a gun nearby was necessary even though no gun was actually present.

Until shortly before trial, Whiteside consistently stated to Robinson that he had not actually seen a gun, but that he was convinced that Love had a gun in his hand. About a week before trial, during preparation for direct examination, Whiteside for the first time told Robinson and his associate Donna Paulsen that he had seen something "metallic" in Love's hand. When asked about this, Whiteside responded:

> "[I]n Howard Cook's case there was a gun. If I don't say I saw a gun, I'm dead."

Robinson told Whiteside that such testimony would be perjury and repeated that it was not necessary to prove that a gun was available but only that Whiteside reasonably believed that he was in danger. On Whiteside's insisting that he would testify that he saw "something metallic" Robinson told him, according to Robinson's testimony:

> "[W]e could not allow him to [testify falsely] because that would be perjury, and as officers of the court we would be suborning perjury if we allowed him to do it; . . . I advised him that if he did do that it would be my duty to advise the Court of what he was doing and that I felt he was committing perjury; also, that I probably would be allowed to attempt to impeach that particular testimony." [C].

Robinson also indicated he would seek to withdraw from the representation if Whiteside insisted on committing perjury.

Whiteside testified in his own defense at trial and stated that he "knew" that Love had a gun and that he believed Love was reaching for a gun and he had acted swiftly in self-defense. On cross-examination, he admitted that he had not actually seen a gun in Love's hand. * * *

* * *

The United States Court of Appeals for the Eighth Circuit* * * directed that the writ of habeas corpus be granted. * * *[T]he court reasoned that an intent to commit perjury, communicated to counsel, does not alter a defendant's right to effective assistance of counsel and that Robinson's admonition to Whiteside that he would inform the court of Whiteside's perjury constituted a threat to violate the attorney's duty to preserve client confidences. * * *

* * *

We turn next to the question presented: the definition of the range of "reasonable professional" responses to a criminal defendant client who informs counsel that he will perjure himself on the stand. We must determine whether, in this setting, Robinson's conduct fell within the wide range of professional responses to threatened client perjury acceptable under the Sixth Amendment.

In *Strickland*, we recognized counsel's duty of loyalty and his "overarching duty to advocate the defendant's cause." *Ibid*. Plainly, that duty is limited to legitimate, lawful conduct compatible with the very nature of a trial as a search for truth. Although counsel must take all reasonable lawful means to attain the objectives of the client, counsel is precluded from taking steps or in any way assisting the client in presenting false evidence or otherwise violating the law. * * *

* * *

* * * The more recent Model Rules of Professional Conduct (1983) similarly admonish attorneys to obey all laws in the course of representing a client:

"*RULE 1.2* Scope of Representation

.   .   .   .   .

"(d) A lawyer shall not counsel a client to engage, or assist a client, in conduct that the lawyer knows is criminal or fraudulent. . . ."

Both the Model Code of Professional Responsibility and the Model Rules of Professional Conduct also adopt the specific exception from the attorney-client privilege for disclosure of perjury that his client intends to commit or has committed. DR 4-101(C)(3) (intention of client to commit a crime); Rule 3.3 (lawyer has duty to disclose falsity of evidence even if disclosure compromises client confidences). Indeed, both the Model Code and the Model Rules do not merely *authorize* disclosure by counsel of client perjury; they *require* such disclosure. See Rule 3.3(a)(4); DR 7-102(B)(1); [C]

* * *

It is universally agreed that at a minimum the attorney's first duty when confronted with a proposal for perjurious testimony is to attempt to dissuade the client from the unlawful course of conduct. * * * [T]he Model Rules and the commentary, as well as the Code of Professional Responsibility adopted in Iowa, expressly permit withdrawal from representation as an appropriate response of an attorney when the client threatens to commit perjury. Model Rules of Professional Conduct, Rule 1.16(a)(1), Rule 1.6, Comment (1983) * * *.

The Court of Appeals' holding that Robinson's "action deprived [Whiteside] of due process and effective assistance of counsel" is not supported by the record since Robinson's action, at most, deprived Whiteside of his contemplated perjury. * * * We see this as a case in which the attorney successfully dissuaded the client from committing the crime of perjury.

* * *

Whatever the scope of a constitutional right to testify, it is elementary that such a right does not extend to testifying *falsely*.

* * *

Whiteside's attorney treated Whiteside's proposed perjury in accord with professional standards, and since Whiteside's truthful testimony could not have prejudiced the result of his trial, the Court of Appeals was in error to direct the issuance of a writ of habeas corpus and must be reversed.

Reversed.

Note

When a criminal defendant wants to commit perjury, two alternatives to the Model Rule's disclosure requirement have been proposed. At one time, the ABA took the position that the attorney should allow the client to make the perjurious statement in narrative form, on the grounds that a criminal defendant has a constitutional right to testify. Under this proposal, the attorney would not disclose the perjury, but the attorney also would not aid the client with questions during the perjurious portion of the direct examination and the attorney would make no mention of the perjurious testimony during closing argument. ABA Standards for Criminal Justice Defense Function, Standard 7.7(c)(1971 ed.).

Monroe Freedman has argued that the lawyer should counsel the client not to perjure himself, but if the client insists on testifying, the lawyer should call the client to testify. If the client lies on the stand, the lawyer should act as if the lawyer believes the testimony to be truthful. Freedman argues that any other position undercuts the right to confidentiality, betrays the client's trust, and will discourage clients from fully disclosing information to the attorney. Monroe Freedman, "Professional Responsibility of the Criminal Defense Lawyer: The Three Hardest Questions," 64 *Mich. L.Rev.* 1469 (1966). For a critical response, see Teresa S. Collett, "Understanding Freedman's Ethics," 33 *Ariz. L.Rev.* 455 (1991).

In People v. Guzman, 755 P.2d 917 (Cal. 1988), the California Supreme Court rejected the Freedman position, holding that the defendant did not have the right to the assistance of a lawyer in presenting perjury. The Court appeared to approve the old ABA position under which the defendant is allowed to testify without the assistance of the lawyer. However, the Court did not identify this as the only way to deal with client perjury.

Read Model Rules 3.5 and 3.6[4]

United States v. Cutler
58 F.3d 825 (2d Cir. 1995)

* * *

BACKGROUND

John Gotti was arrested on December 11, 1990, on racketeering charges. The murder of Paul Castellano, a rival mobster, was one of many predicate acts. This marked the fourth time that the government tried to end Gotti's criminal career, the previous attempts having failed. The then-United States Attorney, Andrew Maloney, announced the indictment at a press conference, where he called Gotti a "murderer, not a folk hero" and boasted that this time the government's case, which

---

[4] For MR 3.5, *cf.* DR 7-108, 7-110(B), 7-106(C)(6); Cal. Rule 5-300. For MR 3.6, *cf.* DR 7-107, California has no comparable provision.

included extensive wiretap evidence, was much stronger than in the prior trials.

Gotti's lawyer, Bruce Cutler, a member of the New York Bar, countered by calling the prosecutors "publicity-hungry" and on a vendetta to frame his client. He was quoted in New York's four major newspapers--the *Daily News, Newsday,* the *New York Post,* and the *New York Times.* He also gave an interview on *Prime Time Live,* a nationally-broadcast television show, where he emphatically denied that Gotti was a mob boss.

A. *Local Rule 7* [Cf. MR 3.6]

Cutler's and Maloney's comments seemed to be in tension with Local Rule 7, to phrase it charitably. That rule provides:

> It is the duty of the lawyer or law firm not to release or authorize the release of information or opinion which a reasonable person would expect to be disseminated by means of public communication, in connection with pending or imminent criminal litigation with which a lawyer or law firm is associated, if there is a reasonable likelihood that such dissemination will interfere with a fair trial or otherwise prejudice the due administration of justice....
>
> From the time of arrest, issuance of an arrest warrant or the filing of a complaint, information or indictment, in any criminal matter until the commencement of trial or disposition without trial, a lawyer or law firm associated with the prosecution or defense shall not release or authorize the release of any extrajudicial statement which a reasonable person would expect to be disseminated by means of public communication, relating to that matter and concerning:
>
> (1) The prior criminal record (including arrests, indictments or other charges of crime) or the character or reputation of the accused, except that the lawyer or law firm may make a factual statement of the accused's name, age, residence, occupation and family status; and if the accused has not been apprehended, a lawyer associated with the prosecution may release any information necessary to aid in the accused's apprehension or to warn the public of any dangers the accused may present;
>
> ....
>
> (4) The identity, testimony or credibility of prospective witnesses, except that the lawyer or law firm may announce the identity of the victim if the announcement is not otherwise prohibited by law;
>
> ....

(6) Any opinion as to the accused's guilt or innocence or as to the merits of the case or the evidence in the case.

E.D.N.Y.Crim.R. 7(a).

B. *The December 20, 1990 "Admonition"*

When a detention hearing was scheduled, the district court granted Gotti's motion to close the hearing and seal all evidentiary submissions, including transcripts from the wiretaps. [C].

On December 20, 1990, after the hearing, Judge Glasser admonished the parties (and Cutler in particular) to try the case only in the courtroom, not in the press [Cc].

* * *

Undeterred, Cutler held a press conference outside the courthouse. He declaimed that the government had "thrown the Constitution out the window," mocked the government's witnesses as "bums," and erroneously described the government's tape recordings of wiretapped conversations as the same ones used in earlier prosecutions. Cutler's performance at the press conference made the local news that night and the tabloids the next morning.

C. *The January 9, 1991 Order*

Three weeks later, the parties again appeared before Judge Glasser. The judge was not pleased with the continuing swirl of publicity, and again he instructed both parties to comply with Local Rule 7 * * *. Nonetheless, the very next day, *Newsday* quoted Cutler about the tapes. He said the tapes contained denials by Gotti of involvement in the murder of Paul Castellano.

* * *

[C]utler continued to ignore the court's direction to comply with Local Rule 7. He was quoted in February, March, and July in all four major New York dailies. In addition, he gave a long interview to *Interview Magazine,* a glossy magazine, in which he repeated his allegations about government vendettas and accused the government of suborning perjury. He also showed up on *60 Minutes,* praising Gotti for his loyalty, integrity, and honesty, denying the existence of the mob, comparing the prosecutors to Senator Joseph McCarthy, and deprecating the tapes. Finally, he appeared on a local television news program, *Thirteen Live,* where he accused the government of persecuting Gotti.

D. *The July 22, 1991 Order*

After four letters of complaint from the government about Cutler's extrajudicial statements, the parties appeared before Judge Glasser a third time on July 22, 1991. Judge Glasser once again ordered counsel to follow Local Rule 7: "Local Rule 7 ... is, in essence, a kind of gag order. The thing you ought to say is, there is a case pending, the rules of this Court say I can't comment on it." Judge Glasser made clear he wanted no more comments to the press.

Days later, the district court disqualified Cutler [and a colleague] primarily because they were likely to be called as witnesses at Gotti's trial, [C]. Two days after that, the court unsealed the tapes played at Gotti's detention hearing, noting that Cutler had called into question the integrity of the court and finding that any "[a]dditional publicity which may flow from unsealing the record *at this time* would ... not give rise to a probability, substantial or otherwise, that the defendants' right to a fair trial will be prejudiced." [C]

In the following week, stories about Gotti adorned the front pages of New York's dailies, together with excerpts from the transcripts of the wire-tapped conversations. In addition, television news programs obtained copies of the tapes of the conversations and repeatedly broadcast portions of them, allowing potential jurors to hear Gotti describe murders and other crimes.

Although he no longer represented Gotti in connection with the racketeering charges, Cutler countered with a media barrage of his own. The *pièce de résistance* came on August 13, 1991, a mere month before the scheduled trial date. (Gotti's new lawyers expected Judge Glasser to adjourn the trial to give them more time to prepare, but an adjournment had not yet been granted.) That day, Cutler appeared on a one-hour live television show called *9 Broadcast Plaza*. His performance, aptly summarized by the district court, included the following:

> wherever Gotti lives, there is no problem with drugs and crime in the neighborhood; Gotti is not a danger to any community other than federal prosecutors; Gotti has "admirable qualities[,"] including being courageous, loyal, sincere, selfless and devoted to his family; Gotti is a "good man" and an "honorable man"; Gotti is not a "ruthless man"; Gotti is one of "the most compassionate men" Cutler knows; Gotti is "deadly against drugs"[;] .... the prosecutors "are doing everything they can to destroy John Gotti" and are "dealing in vendettas[,"] "on a witch hunt[,"] and "framing people"; the Government "threw the Constitution out the window" and is on a "vendetta" against Gotti; the prosecution is an "example of McCarthyism";

Gotti was being "persecuted" because of his "lifestyle" and "friends"; the prosecutors want to "destroy" Gotti "because of his popularity" and because "he's deadly against drugs"; the "evidence is phony"; the "tapes are phony"[;] .... the Government is "creating cases against individuals they target" by "giving freedom to drug dealers and murderers if they will sing the government's tune against the likes of John Gotti"; and ... jurors realize that "the witnesses lie" and that "even the federal investigators lie" and that is why they vote "not guilty unabashedly."[C]

E. *The Contempt Proceedings*

Not surprisingly, the *9 Broadcast Plaza* interview provoked yet another government letter complaining about Cutler. This time, Judge Glasser had had enough. He issued an order to show cause why Cutler should not be held in criminal contempt, in violation of 18 U.S.C. § 401(3). The order cited twenty-five instances of media coverage stemming from Cutler's public comments about the upcoming trial (the vast majority coming after the January 9 order), in which a common theme emerged: Gotti would be vindicated again; the prosecutors were a "sick and demented lot"; and the government's tapes were "snippets deliberately taken out of context." The highlight was Cutler's performance on *9 Broadcast Plaza.*

After appointing a special prosecutor, Judge Glasser recused himself, and the matter was reassigned to then-Chief Judge Platt for trial. * * *

Meanwhile, voir dire of the Gotti jury pool began. Of the 215 jurors interviewed, 214 had read or heard something about Gotti. Only forty-seven had formed an opinion about Gotti's guilt or innocence. Of these, forty-six thought he was guilty; only one believed he was innocent, based on things he had heard in his neighborhood. (Gotti was subsequently convicted and sentenced to life imprisonment; we affirmed.[Cc].)

Cutler's contempt trial lasted five days. [Cc].

The district court found Cutler guilty of criminal contempt of two specific orders--those of January 9, 1991, and July 22, 1991--in violation of 18 U.S.C. § 401(3). * * *

At sentencing, the district court imposed three years' probation on Cutler * * *

Cutler now appeals.

* * *

II. *Sufficiency of the Evidence*

Before turning to the elements of the contempt conviction, we must clarify our scope of review. The orders here prohibited Cutler from discussing the merits of the Gotti case with the media only if his comments were reasonably likely to "interfere with a fair trial or otherwise prejudice the due administration of justice." E.D.N.Y. Crim.R. 7(a). As prior restraints, these orders implicate the First Amendment. [Cc].

As eight Justices of the Supreme Court have noted, in First Amendment cases, we independently review "the whole record in order to make sure that the judgment does not constitute a forbidden intrusion on the field of free expression." *Gentile v. State Bar,* 501 U.S. 1030, 1038, 111 S.Ct. 2720, 2726, 115 L.Ed.2d 888 (1991) (quotation marks and citations omitted) (Kennedy, J., dissenting in part, joined by Marshall, Blackmun, and Stevens, JJ.); *accord id.* at 1079, 111 S.Ct. at 2747 (Rehnquist, C.J., dissenting in part, joined by White, Scalia, and Souter, JJ.). [Cc].

We need not limn the precise contours of the constitutional fact doctrine. Suffice it to say that in First Amendment cases, we must scrutinize carefully the lower court's *application* of the relevant standards to the facts at hand. * * * In contempt cases involving media coverage critical of the administration of criminal justice in pending cases, we review *de novo* whether the coverage presents a "threat of clear and present danger to the impartiality and good order of the courts." *See Pennekamp v. Florida,* 328 U.S. 331, 335, 66 S.Ct. 1029, 1032, 90 L.Ed. 1295 (1946). These issues resemble mixed questions of law and fact, which we review *de novo.*

* * *

B. *Violations of the Orders*

* * * Cutler mounts a two-pronged challenge to the finding that he violated the orders. He argues that: (1) even when comments fall within the six categories specifically mentioned in Local Rule 7, the rule proscribes them only if they are reasonably likely to prejudice the proceedings; and (2) none of the comments cited in the order to show cause were reasonably likely to prejudice the proceedings. The first argument has merit; the second does not.

Local Rule 7 proscribes generally any statements by counsel that "a reasonable person would expect to be disseminated by means of public communication, in connection with pending or imminent criminal litigation . . ., if there is a reasonable likelihood that such dissemination will interfere with a fair trial or otherwise prejudice the due administration of justice."　The rule then enumerates several specific categories of forbidden speech, but without repeating the "reasonable likelihood" standard.　For example, an attorney cannot offer his opinion as to his client's guilt or innocence, or as to the merits of the case.　E.D.N.Y. Crim.R. 7(a)(6).　Reasoning that the reasonable likelihood standard did *not* apply to comments within the six categories, the district court held that if a comment fell within a category and if a reasonable person would expect that the comment would be disseminated by the press, the comment was prohibited. [Cc].　This goes too far.

　　　Were we writing on a completely clean slate, we might adopt the district court's approach.　But, the Fourth Circuit has already rejected it.　*See Hirschkop,* 594 F.2d at 365-68.　Reviewing a local rule virtually identical to Local Rule 7, the *Hirschkop* court held that a *per se* proscription of certain types of speech was overbroad and violated the First Amendment.　To pass muster, speech that fell within a proscribed category had to be reasonably likely to interfere with a fair trial or otherwise prejudice the due administration of justice.　*See id.* at 367-68.

　　　We see no need to adopt an interpretation of Local Rule 7 that might offend the Constitution.　Accordingly, we conclude that speech falling within the six categories violates Local Rule 7 only if it is also reasonably likely to interfere with a fair trial or the administration of justice. [C].

　　　That said, we believe there is a strong, albeit rebuttable, presumption that speech falling within the six categories violates Local Rule 7, as these categories "furnish the context in which the 'reasonable likelihood' standard is intended to operate." [Cc].

　　　Despite our different approach to Local Rule 7, we need not disturb the result reached by the district court.　The district court, at the government's request, made findings of fact under the assumption that the reasonable likelihood standard did apply to speech that fell within proscribed categories, and concluded that, under that standard, Cutler had still violated the orders.　Cutler challenges this finding on several grounds.　They all lack merit.

First, he contends that the district court ignored his expert witnesses' testimony. We disagree. The experts, criminal trial lawyers, stated their opinion that Cutler's extensive comments could have had no prejudicial effect. The court characterized this testimony as self-serving and worthy of little weight, given that as defense lawyers, the experts shared an inherent bias. Thus, the court did not ignore the testimony; it simply discounted its probative value, which was well within its discretion. [Cc].

Next, Cutler argues that the voir dire of the Gotti jury venire demonstrates that his comments were not reasonably likely to prejudice the proceedings. Again, we disagree. True, evidence that the Cutler-generated publicity did not in fact taint the jury pool may be relevant to the issue whether those statements were likely to interfere with a fair trial. *See Gentile,* 501 U.S. at 1047, 111 S.Ct. at 2730-31 (Kennedy, J., dissenting in part, joined by Marshall, Blackmun, and Stevens, JJ.). But *Gentile* never said that such evidence was dispositive, nor did *Gentile* require that actual prejudice be shown. Instead, Local Rule 7's "standard for controlling pretrial publicity must be judged at the time a statement is made." *Id.; see id.* at 1081, 111 S.Ct. at 2748 (Rehnquist, C.J., dissenting in part, joined by White, Scalia, and Souter, JJ.) (rejecting argument that attorney could not be sanctioned for statements to media if no prejudice actually resulted).

Finally, Cutler chastises the district court for taking his comments out of context. He notes that Gotti's trial received more press coverage and publicity than any other trial in New York history. He contends that in the midst of a veritable firestorm of anti-Gotti publicity, the few cinders he added could not possibly have tainted the proceedings. He adds that the timing of his comments--made five months before the trial began--underscores their relative harmlessness. We are not persuaded, however, by Cutler's Uriah Heep pose.

Cutler vastly understates the effect defense lawyers can have on prospective jurors. As *Gentile* cautions, "lawyers' statements are likely to be received as especially authoritative" because "lawyers have special access to information through discovery and client communications." *Id.* at 1074, 111 S.Ct. at 2744-45 (majority opinion). Indeed, *Gentile* affirmed the very portion of Nevada's pre-trial publicity rule that considered statements of the sort Cutler made as "ordinarily" likely to have a "substantial likelihood of materially prejudicing" a pending criminal proceeding. *See id.* at 1065-76, 111 S.Ct. at 2740-46; *id.* at 1081-82, 111 S.Ct. at 2748-49 (O'Connor, J., concurring).

Moreover, although the timing of Cutler's comments may be significant, *see id.* at 1044, 111 S.Ct. at 2729 (Kennedy, J., dissenting in part, joined by Marshall, Blackmun, and Stevens, JJ.) (when comments preceded trial by six months, "only the most damaging information could give rise to any likelihood of prejudice"), this factor does not necessarily weigh in Cutler's favor. Our review of the record makes clear that his "statements were timed to have a maximum impact, when public interest in the case was at its height immediately after" the disqualification briefs and record were unsealed. *Id.* at 1079, 111 S.Ct. at 2747 (Rehnquist, C.J., dissenting in part, joined by White, Scalia, and Souter, JJ.).

Finally, we note that in *Gentile,* four Justices were prepared to hold that relatively innocuous statements made at a single press conference some six months before trial in the midst of extensive and sensationalized publicity were *substantially* likely to materially prejudice the proceedings. *See id.* at 1076-81, 111 S.Ct. at 2745-48. In contrast, Cutler spoke repeatedly and heatedly to the press in the months preceding Gotti's trial. Given the more lenient "reasonable likelihood" standard here, coupled with Cutler's performance on *9 Broadcast Plaza* alone, we do not doubt that a majority of the *Gentile* Court would find that Cutler violated the orders. [Cc].

We thus find that Cutler's comments were reasonably likely to prejudice the Gotti proceedings.

C. *Willfulness*

Criminal contempt generally "requires a specific intent to consciously disregard an order of the court." [C]. Cutler contends that he did not willfully disobey the orders because he did not know the comments listed in the order to show cause were reasonably likely to prejudice the proceedings. This argument taxes the most generous credulity.

We hold attorneys to a higher standard of conduct than we do lay persons. [C]. Accordingly, we may infer Cutler's willfulness from his "'reckless disregard for his professional duty.'" [C]. Cutler's persistent attempts to try Gotti's case in the media, despite Judge Glasser's repeated warnings, belie any notion that he did not intend these particular comments to prejudice the proceedings, or that he did not recklessly disregard the orders.

Any doubt about this is dispelled by Cutler's participation in a Brooklyn Law School symposium on April 25, 1991, before the Gotti trial began. There, he expounded upon the virtues of a friendly press:

> ... I've really grown to appreciate and respect Anthony DeStefano from *New York Newsday*[,] Pete Bowles for *New York Newsday,* Lenny Buder for *The New York Times,* and Arnie Lubasch from *The New York Times* and some of the other reporters who I think do a conscientious job. Do I have selfish reasons? I have honest reasons that I don't want to alienate them, *that I want the prospective veniremen out there to feel that I mean what I say and say what I mean, and if that can spill over and help my client, then I feel it's important for me to do that.*

[C] (emphasis added). With a smoking gun like this, we cannot fault the district court for finding that the government proved Cutler's willfulness "not only beyond any reasonable doubt, but beyond any possible doubt." [C].

In short, the record amply supports findings that the orders were specific, and that Cutler's comments were reasonably likely to prejudice prospective jurors and were willfully made with the intent of prejudicing prospective jurors. Accordingly, we affirm Cutler's criminal contempt conviction.

* * *

CONCLUSION

We have considered all of Cutler's arguments, and find them without merit. We recognize that Cutler did not singlehandedly generate the media circus that threatened the fairness of the final Gotti trial; federal prosecutors and law enforcement officials deserve their share of the blame. Moreover, we sympathize with the plight of a defense lawyer torn between his duties to act as an officer of the court and to zealously defend his client. Nonetheless, a lawyer, of all people, should know that in the face of a perceived injustice, one may not take the law into his own hands. Defendant did, and now he must pay the price.

In some quarters, doubtless, this affirmance will elicit thunderbolts that we are chilling effective advocacy. Obviously, that is neither our intention nor our result. The advocate is still entitled--indeed encouraged--to strike hard blows, but not unfair blows. Trial practice, whether criminal or civil, is not a contact sport. And, its tactics do not include eye-gouging or shin-kicking.

In this case, a conscientious trial judge tried mightily to limit the lawyers to press statements that were accurate and fair. The defendant's statements were dipped in venom and were deliberately couched to poison the well from which the jury would be selected. Such conduct goes beyond the pale, by any reasonable standard, and cannot be condoned under the rubric of "effective advocacy."

We are not unaware that it has become *de rigueur* for successful criminal defense lawyers to cultivate cozy relationships with the media. [Cc]. Indeed, in this very case, defendant urged law students to do just that. As Seneca once observed, "quae fuerant vitia mores sunt" ("what once were vices are now the manners of the day"). L. Annaeus Seneca, *Epistulae ad Lucilium,* Epis. xxxix, at ¶ 6. The Bruce Cutler case must now stand as a caution that enough of the "old ethics" survive to bar flouting the Canons of Professional Conduct. [Cc].

Lord Henry Brougham, who defended Queen Caroline on a criminal charge of adultery, was an early apostle of what today would be known as Rambo litigation tactics. In his argument before the House of Lords, he summed up his view of the advocate's role: "the first great duty of an advocate [is] to reckon everything subordinate to the interests of his client." Twenty-three years later, at a dinner for barristers, with the eighty-six-year-old Lord Brougham in the audience, Chief Justice Alexander Cockburn responded--to loud cheers from the distinguished assembly--

> "[t]he arms which an advocate wields he ought to use as a warrior, not as an assassin. He ought to uphold the interests of his clients *per fas,* not *per nefas.* He ought to know how to reconcile the interests of his clients with the eternal interests of truth and justice."

The Times (London), Nov. 9, 1864, *quoted in 5 Encyclopedia Britannica* 941 (1947).

The judgment of conviction and sentence are AFFIRMED.

Notes

1. Criminal defense attorneys are in a difficult position when prosecutors, police officers (who are not bound by lawyer professional responsibility rules), or anonymous sources release information that is

prejudicial to their clients. In 1994, the ABA amended MR 3.6 to permit a lawyer to make:

> [A] statement that a reasonable lawyer would believe is required to protect a client from the substantial undue prejudicial effect of recent publicity not initiated by the lawyer or the lawyer's client.

MR 3.6(c). At the same time, the ABA amended MR 3.8 to prohibit prosecutors from "making extrajudicial comments that have a substantial likelihood of heightening public condemnation of the accused." MR 3.8(g). Did the publicity in the *Gotti* case justify Cutler's actions? Would Cutler be subject to discipline under MR 3.6? Should the state bar discipline him in light of the punishment the court imposed?

2. Does it matter that Cutler made some of the comments after he had been disqualified and was no longer serving as Gotti's lawyer? Would it make a difference if Cutler had not been involved in the case, but made the same statements as a legal commentator for a television program?

3. In *Office of Disciplinary Counsel v. Grimes*, 614 N.E.2d 740 (Ohio 1993), a lawyer was publicly reprimanded for calling a judge a "son-of-a-bitch" in a conversation with a newspaper reporter. Justice Pfeifer of the Ohio Supreme Court dissented.

> I would dismiss the complaint against the respondent. The conduct at issue was not only out of character but was also inconsequential.

> Which of us who have ever practiced law has not muttered a choice epithet about our favorite judge? More important, which of us who are judges has not done something to earn an occasional raspberry? It is obvious in this case that the respondent did not expect his mild outburst to be quoted in the newspaper. Respondent self-administered the appropriate disciplinary measure by publicly apologizing to Judge Heydinger.

* * *

> Finally, I am always concerned to see a lawyer reprimanded for his speech. Our legal system relies upon vigorous advocacy, which occasionally leads to spirited interplay between lawyers and judges. We ought not rule in a way that may affect that friction.

Id. at 742. In *Grimes*, the lawyer was found to have violated DR 1-102(A)(6) of the Model Code of Professional Responsibility, which prohibits a lawyer from engaging in "conduct that adversely reflects on his fitness to practice law." This was an all-purpose provision of the Model Code, which enabled judges to discipline lawyers for conduct that did not fit within a specific provision of the Code. Under the

Model Rules, a court might discipline a lawyer who called a judge such a name under MR 8.4(d) for engaging in "conduct that is prejudicial to the administration of justice. . ." Should the First Amendment protect a lawyer who makes such comments about a judge?

Read Model Rules 3.7 to 3.9[5]

MR 3.8(d) requires prosecutors to:

[M]ake timely disclosure to the defense of all evidence or information known to the prosecutor that tends to negate the guilt of the accused or mitigates the offense * * *

A criminal defendant is entitled to the same information, upon request, as a matter of Constitutional law under Brady v. Maryland, 373 U.S. 83, 83 S. Ct. 1194, 10 L. Ed. 2d 215 (1963). The following case raises a *Brady* issue, as well as other issues of prosecutorial responsibility.

United States v. Kojayan
8 F.3d 1315 (9th Cir. 1993)

KOZINSKI, Circuit Judge:

* * *

Chake Kojayan, a middle-aged Lebanese woman, came to Los Angeles from Lebanon on June 13, 1991, with $100,000 worth of heroin sewn into a bag. There's no dispute about that, or about a lot of other things. She had been given the bag by an acquaintance * * *. In the meantime, Krikor Nourian was arranging a sale of the heroin to people who turned out to be DEA agents. On June 26, [codefendant] Hratch Kalfayan drove Kojayan to the Airport Hilton Hotel, where they met Nourian and DEA Special Agent Alleva, who was posing as a buyer. After a conversation, part in English and part in Armenian—a language Agent Alleva didn't understand —Kalfayan gave the bag to Alleva. Kalfayan, Kojayan and Nourian were then arrested. Kalfayan and Kojayan were indicted for conspiracy to possess heroin with intent to distribute, [C], and possession with intent to distribute, [C]. Nourian

---

[5]   For MR 3.7, *cf.* DR 5-101(B), 5-102(A)-(B); EC 5-9, 5-10; Cal. Rule 5-210. For MR 3.8, *cf.* DR 7-103; EC 7-13; Cal. Rule 5-110. For MR 3.9, *cf.* EC 7-15 to -16, 8-5; there is no Cal. Rule counterpart to MR 3.9.

was whisked away by the government, never to be seen again by Kalfayan and Kojayan.

The dispute at trial was about knowledge. Kojayan admitted she was given the bag for safekeeping, but claimed she had no idea what was in it; it was Kalfayan who was in on the deal. Kalfayan claimed the opposite: He was just chauffeuring Kojayan to where she wanted to go; the seemingly incriminating things he said at the hotel were only his translations of Kojayan's statements. The government claimed both defendants knew what was going on. It went about proving this largely through Agent Alleva, who testified about what Nourian and to some extent Kalfayan told him just before the arrest. * * * Nourian didn't appear at trial. Instead, the government introduced his statements (both taped and untaped) [C] as the statements of a co-conspirator.

Long before the start of the trial, the defendants had tried hard—citing, among other things, *Brady v. Maryland*, 373 U.S. 83, 83 S.Ct. 1194, 10 L.Ed.2d 215 (1963)—to learn Nourian's whereabouts and whether he'd agreed to cooperate with the government. [C]. The government responded brusquely: "There is no discovery obligation for the government to inform defendant whether or not her unindicted co-conspirator is cooperating with the government subsequent to his arrest in this case. The government has complied with its discovery obligations; it is not required to be defendant's investigator." [C] * * *

Nevertheless, the defense attorneys—experienced criminal lawyers—had a strong hunch Nourian must have cut a deal pursuant to which he promised to testify if the government called him. At trial, they decided to make hay out of the government's failure to do so: They argued that, because the prosecution (and only the prosecution) could have called Nourian to the stand but didn't, the jurors should infer that his testimony would have undercut the government's case. This wouldn't have been a remarkably strong inference, but it would have been a permissible one: When the government can call a key percipient witness, but relies instead on out-of-court statements and on testimony by an agent who didn't understand half the critical conversation, a jury could conclude that the witness's "testimony, if produced, would [have been] unfavorable" to the prosecution. [C].

* * * Though they urged the jury to infer the existence of a deal from the circumstances, without any direct evidence of an agreement, their claims naturally seemed weak. As the Assistant United States Attorney

[AUSA] forcefully argued to the jury, the defense's contentions appeared to be:

> a classic example of asking the jury to speculate. . . . The government can't force someone to talk. They have to agree to talk after they've been arrested.
>
> Well, you can figure out defendant Nourian was arrested. He has Fifth Amendment rights. *He has the right to remain silent.* The government can't force anyone to talk. It is against their Fifth Amendment rights. *Don't be misled that the government could have called Nourian.*

[C] If the AUSA was telling the truth, the jury would have had no basis for inferring what the defense wanted them to infer. And apparently it didn't: After two days of deliberation, it convicted both defendants on all counts.

II

The AUSA, however, was not telling the truth. Defense counsel had guessed right—Nourian had entered into a cooperation agreement with the government and had promised to "truthfully testify . . . at any trial or other court proceeding with respect to any matters about which [the government] may request his testimony." [C] * * *

* * * In this context, telling the jury that "Nourian . . . has the right to remain silent," and that "the government can't force someone to talk" was highly misleading. Adding "[d]on't be misled that the government *could* have called Nourian" was simply false: The government could have called Nourian, and could have done so with a very great deal of confidence that he would testify.

* * *

[The defendant raised the propriety of the prosecutor's statement in an objection at trial, in a motion for a new trial, and on appeal. Through all of this, the prosecutor never revealed that there had been a plea agreement with Nourian and that he could have testified. It was not until oral argument before the Circuit Court, under the persistent questioning of the court, that the prosecutor disclosed the plea agreement:]

[Q]:   Was there a cooperation agreement?

AUSA: Well, your honor, that is not something that's in the record.

[Q]:   I understand. Was there a cooperation agreement?

AUSA: There was an agreement with the Southern District of New York and [Nourian], yes.

* * *

[Following this disclosure, the government filed a supplementary brief. The government seeks "to minimize the prosecutor's misconduct and place the blame for it on opposing counsel."]

While the government refers to defense counsel's allegedly improper conduct eight times, it never explains what defense counsel did wrong. As we read the record, all that happened was this: Defense counsel said "Nourian was arrested. I submit to you that the government could have called him as a witness." [C] The first part of the statement was certainly a fact in the record; Nourian *was* arrested, as the government argued to the jury, [C]. The second was well within the realm of proper argument; it invited the jury to infer that, since the government had taken physical possession of Nourian's body, it probably had ways of getting him into court if it wanted to. Our case law and model jury instructions specifically authorize counsel to argue such a theory to the jury. [C]. The introductory phrase "I submit" was an important flag in alerting the jurors that defense counsel was not stating a fact, but asking them to use their common sense in drawing an inference. *See United States v. Necoechea*, 986 F.2d 1273, 1279 (9th Cir. 1993) ("These 'I submit' statements do not constitute vouching. . . [They are] simply an inference from evidence in the record. [They are not] a reference to extra-record facts. . .").

* * *

We fail to see how any of this is even remotely improper. Lawyers are supposed to invite the jury to infer things from the evidence. When a prosecutor asks jurors to deduce a defendant's guilt from circumstantial evidence, for example, he's urging them to take a leap beyond the record, to use their common sense in reaching a conclusion not explicitly spelled out by the evidence. This is the very essence of jury summation.

While casting aspersions at opposing counsel, the government's supplemental brief overlooks two significant differences between defense counsel's argument and its own. First, unlike defense counsel, the prosecutor went well beyond asking the jury to *infer* matters outside the record. He actually made unsupported factual claims. When a lawyer asserts that something not in the record is true, he is, in effect, testifying. He is telling the jury: "Look, I know a lot more about this case than you, so believe me when I tell you X is a fact." This is definitely improper.

Defense counsel also asked the jury to infer only things that he believed in good faith *might* be true. While defense counsel didn't know that Nourian had a cooperation agreement [C], he had no reason to doubt it. The government's lawyer, by contrast, made factual assertions he well knew were untrue. This is the difference between fair advocacy and misconduct. [C].

* * *

As disappointing as what is said in the government's supplemental brief is what is not said. While the government condemns opposing counsel for speculating about the existence of the cooperation agreement, the government lawyers who supposedly took a detached and independent look at the problem never once mention *why* it became necessary for defense counsel to speculate. After all, the defense had made a *Brady* request about whether Nourian had signed a cooperation agreement, and the government had a continuing obligation to provide *Brady* materials to the defense. * * * When defense counsel later requested [an instruction that from the failure of the prosecution to call Nourian, the jury could infer that his testimony would be unfavorable to the prosecution] and their request foundered because they were unaware of the government's agreement with Nourian, the government was required, under *Brady*, to disclose this evidence. *Brady*, 373 U.S. at 87, 83 S.Ct. at 1196-97. The evidence was "favorable to [the] accused" because it might have convinced the court to give the instruction. *Id.* The instruction, in turn, would have told the jury that Nourian was not only available but that the prosecution could compel his appearance if it so chose. This might have led the jury to infer that his testimony would have been unfavorable to it. Even if the court refused to give the instruction, evidence of Nourian's agreement would have strengthened defense counsel's argument to the jury that his live testimony would have explained away his hearsay testimony. This case was close, and we find a "reasonable probability" that, had this evidence been disclosed, the result would have been different; the evidence was therefore material. [C].

* * *

III

Prosecutors are subject to constraints and responsibilities that don't apply to other lawyers. *See, e.g., Berger v. United States*, 295 U.S. 78, 88, 55 S.Ct. 629, 633, 79 L.Ed. 1314 (1935). While lawyers representing private parties may—indeed, must—do everything ethically permissible to advance their clients' interests, lawyers representing the government in criminal cases serve truth and justice first. The prosecutor's job isn't just to win, but to win fairly, staying well within the rules. *See United States v. Hill*, 953 F.2d 452, 458 (9th Cir.1991); Barbara Allen Babcock, *Fair Play: Evidence Favorable to an Accused and Effective Assistance of Counsel*, 34 Stan.L.Rev. 1133, 1141 (1982). As Justice Douglas once warned, "[t]he function of the prosecutor under the Federal Constitution is not to tack as many skins of victims as possible to the wall. His function is to vindicate the right of people as expressed in the laws and give those accused of crime a fair trial." *Donnelly v. DeChristoforo*, 416 U.S. 637, 648-49, 94 S.Ct. 1868, 1874, 40 L.Ed.2d 431 (1974) (Douglas, J., dissenting).

The government here has strayed from this responsibility. Quite aside from the major and minor trespasses and evasions catalogued above, we must ask the broader question: How did all this come about? The answer isn't particularly edifying: It is because the government's lawyer made a strategic decision to present Nourian's evidence by way of hearsay, and then did everything he could to keep the defense from learning Nourian's whereabouts and the existence and nature of the cooperation agreement. While we're in no position to second-guess the government's decision not to bring Nourian to court, we see no justification for the prosecutor's refusal to give the defense whatever information he had about Nourian—the status of his criminal case, the nature and extent of any cooperation agreement. The government has never articulated why it withheld this information, saying only that "[t]he government. . . is not required to be defendant's investigator." [C]. Such hard-bitten litigation tactics are unbecoming a prosecutor. *See* Monroe H. Freedman, *Understanding Lawyers' Ethics* (Chapter 11— "Prosecutors' Ethics") (1990).

Turning to the remedy, the government vigorously argues that whatever error may have been committed by its lawyer, it was minor and harmless, and that defendants would have been convicted anyhow. We are less sanguine. This was a close case: The jury deliberated for over two days after a one-and-a-half-day trial. [C]. Evidence of Nourian's plea agreement might well have helped convince the jury to reach a not guilty verdict for one or both of the defendants. Had the prosecutor done his job—had he disclosed to the defendants that Nourian was cooperating, as required by *Brady*, had he stuck to the truth in his arguments—the verdict could well have been different.

Evidence matters; closing argument matters; statements from the prosecutor matter a great deal. The government deprived the defendants of an opportunity to put on what could have been a powerful defense. *See United States v. Agurs*, 427 U.S. 97, 103, 96 S. Ct. 2392, 2397, 49 L. Ed. 2d 342 (1976) (where prosecutor knowingly uses perjured testimony, error isn't harmless unless there's no reasonable likelihood that the misconduct influenced the verdict).

Having determined the convictions must be reversed, we must next consider whether to allow the government to retry the defendants. The normal rule, of course, is that where prejudicial error is committed at trial, the case will be sent back for a retrial. But where, as here, the error is one of prosecutorial misconduct, we must take into account considerations beyond this case. Quite as important as assuring a fair trial to the defendants now before us is assuring that the circumstances that gave rise to the misconduct won't be repeated in other cases.

Much of what the United States Attorney's office does isn't open to public scrutiny or judicial review. [C]. It is therefore particularly important that the government discharge its responsibilities fairly, consistent with due process. The overwhelming majority of prosecutors are decent, ethical, honorable lawyers who understand the awesome power they wield, and the responsibility that goes with it. But the temptation is always there: It's the easiest thing in the world for people trained in the adversarial ethic to think a prosecutor's job is simply to win. [Cc].

* * *

The prosecutorial misconduct in this case deprived the defendants of due process of law. It contaminated their trial, and we cannot say it was harmless. [Cc]. In a situation like this, the judiciary—especially the court before which the primary misbehavior took place—may exercise its supervisory power to make it clear that the misconduct was serious, that the government's unwillingness to own up to it was more serious still and that steps must be taken to avoid a recurrence of this chain of events. We therefore VACATE the judgment of conviction and REMAND for the district court to determine whether to retry the defendants or dismiss the indictment with prejudice as a sanction for the government's misbehavior. [Cc].

Notes

1.   In Berger v. United States, 295 U.S. 78, 88, 55 S. Ct. 629, 79 L. Ed. 1314 (1935), the Court said:

> The United States Attorney is the representative not of an ordinary party to a controversy, but of a sovereignty whose obligation to govern impartially is as compelling as its obligation to govern at all; and whose interest, therefore, in a criminal prosecution is not that it shall win a case, but that justice shall be done. As such, he is in a peculiar and very definite sense the servant of the law, the twofold aim of which is that guilt shall not escape or innocence suffer. He may prosecute with earnestness and vigor—indeed, he should do so. But, while he may strike hard blows, he is not at liberty to strike foul ones. It is as much his duty to refrain from improper methods calculated to produce a wrongful conviction as it is to use every legitimate means to bring about a just one.

2.   At one point in his opinion in *Kojayan*, Judge Kozinski says:

> Prosecutors are subject to constraints and responsibilities that don't apply to other lawyers. [C]. While lawyers representing private parties may—indeed, must—do everything ethically permissible to advance their clients' interests, lawyers representing the government in criminal cases serve truth and justice first.

Kojayan, 8 F.3d at 1323. Why not require "lawyers representing private parties" to "serve truth and justice first?"

3.   Prosecutors have enormous power. Former prosecutor, Irving Younger, said, "[a] prosecutor's power to damage or destroy anyone he chooses to indict is virtually limitless."[6] An indictment, even if later dismissed or if the defendant is later found not guilty, can destroy a person's reputation and subject her to great expense. Standard 3-3.9 of the ABA's *Standards for Criminal Justice* provides that a prosecutor should not indict someone "in the absence of sufficient admissible evidence to support a conviction." Is this standard preferable to MR 3.8(a)'s "probable cause" standard?

4.   Widespread perception that prosecutors often call defense counsel as witnesses in order to disqualify counsel led to the adoption of Model Rule 3.8(e) which requires prosecutors to obtain judicial approval prior to issuing a subpoena to a defendant's lawyer. The application of 3.8(e) to federal prosecutors has been successfully

---

[6]   Irving Younger, *Memoir of a Prosecutor*, Commentary, vol. 62, no. 4, p. 66 (Oct. 1976) *quoted in* Monroe H. Freedman, *Understanding Lawyers' Ethics* 216 (1990).

challenged on the grounds that application of state ethics rules would violate the Supremacy Clause. *Baylson v. Disciplinary Bd. of Sup. Ct. of Pa.,* 975 F.2d 102 (3d Cir. 1992), *cert. denied,* 113 S. Ct. 1578 (1993). Federal prosecutors remain subject to Department of Justice guidelines requiring departmental approval prior to subpoenaing a lawyer.

C. Transactions With Those Other Than the Client

Read Model Rules 4.1 to 4.4[7]

Slotkin v. Citizens Casualty Co. of N. Y.
614 F.2d 301 (2d Cir. 1979)

[Appellants here are Steven Slotkin and his mother, Charlotte Slotkin. Mrs. Slotkin, a diabetic, gave birth to Steven at Brookdale Hospital Center on November 16, 1963. Steven sustained brain damage at birth which his doctors diagnosed as congenital cerebral palsy. As a result of the brain damage, he is paralyzed, confined to a wheelchair, and will require constant care for the rest of his life. Plaintiffs claimed, and the jury in the action below subsequently found, that the hospital's failure properly to administer insulin to Mrs. Slotkin during the period immediately preceding delivery caused Steven's brain damage.

The Slotkins commenced a state court action against the hospital, which was insured by appellee, Citizens Casualty Co. Citizens provided $200,000 of primary liability insurance coverage. Lloyd's of London underwrote $1 million worth of excess insurance. The hospital was represented by Christopher McGrath and John McGrath, of the law firm of McGrath, Cohen & McGrath.

On March 4, 1971, just shortly before the close of plaintiffs' case, the parties held a settlement conference before the judge. At that conference Christopher McGrath stated on the record that the total insurance coverage was $200,000 and that he knew that the Hospital did not have additional insurance with other companies. The specific

---

[7]   For MR 4.1, *cf.* DR 7-102(A)(3), (5); there is no Cal. Rules counterpart to MR 4.1. For MR 4.2, *cf.* DR 7-104(A)(1); EC 7-18; Cal. Rule 2-100. For MR 4.3, *cf.* DR 7-104(A)(2); EC 7-18; there is no Cal. Rules counterpart to MR 4.3. For MR 4.4, *cf.* DR 7-102(A)(1), 7-106(C)(2), 7-108(D)-(E); EC 7-10, 7-29 to -30; Cal. Rule 3-200.

representations of Christopher McGrath and John McGrath are more fully laid out in the court's opinion below. The parties agreed to a settlement of $185,000.]

The parties drafted a stipulation of settlement that was read into the record; the settlement provided in pertinent part:

> It is further stipulated and agreed that the settlement of $185,000 is hereby approved by the trial judge * * *

> It is further stipulated that the attorney for the defendant represents that the total insurance coverage of the defendant is the sum of $200,000, under a policy with Citizens Casualty, and to the best of his knowledge there are no other policies covering this event.

[Though appellee Christopher McGrath stipulated that to the best of his knowledge there was only $200,000 worth of coverage, he had access to documents that demonstrated otherwise. In the Citizens' files, which were in the possession of the McGraths' firm, there were letters from an attorney who represented the excess insurer, which clearly indicated that there was excess coverage.

A week to ten days after the parties entered into the stipulation, an attorney for the hospital told Christopher McGrath of the excess coverage. Christopher McGrath advised the trial judge and the plaintiff's attorney that there was $1 million in excess coverage and that the representations as to insurance coverage had been erroneous. At this point the judge had not yet signed an order allocating the sums paid in settlement.

The $185,000 settlement was approved by the state court and paid. The Slotkins then sued the McGraths, Citizens, and the attorney for the hospital, in the federal district court in the instant diversity action, alleging fraud. The jury found Citizens and the McGraths liable for misrepresenting the insurance coverage. The jury awarded damages in the amount of $680,000, representing the difference between the actual settlement in the state action and a likely settlement amount had there been no misrepresentation of the coverage. The District Court Judge granted the defendants judgment notwithstanding the verdict on the grounds that plaintiffs learned of the excess insurance before the final order and "had not significantly changed their position before learning the truth."]

OAKES, Circuit Judge:

* * *

A. *Judgment Notwithstanding the Verdict*

* * *

* * * [I]t was the settlement stipulation entered into *before* the plaintiffs knew of the excess coverage that was the contract induced by appellees' misrepresentations; and as a result of the stipulation plaintiffs terminated the state court jury trial without a verdict. [C] The law of New York is clear that one who has been induced by fraudulent misrepresentation to settle a claim may recover damages without rescinding the settlement. [Cc].

Even if the underlying premises of this New York rule allowing rescission on the one hand or ratification and suit for damages on the other were unsound, we would of course nevertheless be bound by that rule. The premises for the rule, however, are quite sound. If all that will result from a misrepresentation is a new trial, then the party making it has everything to gain and nothing to lose. The plaintiffs would be placed at a disadvantage by a new trial; the defendants would not. If anything, defendants would benefit by having a preview of plaintiffs' case. As McCormick notes in the case of willful fraud:

> [I]f the defendant by willful falsehood has cozened the plaintiff into risking his property upon a bargain, which, upon the information given by the defendant, would have been profitable, a remedy which merely seeks to place the plaintiff back in the position he was in before seems hardly adequate. The plaintiff might well be given the value of the expected bargain. A willful fraud should cost as much as a broken promise. If the cheat can anticipate that the worst that can happen is that he shall be called upon to pay back his profit upon the trade, he may be encouraged to defraud.

C. McCormick, Handbook on the Law of Damages § 121, at 453 (1935). Thus the New York rule serves to deter fraud. Moreover, the rule does not present a problem of double recovery. In this case, for example, Judge Pollack appropriately instructed the jury that in fixing damages it should deduct from the "fair settlement value" the $185,000 received under the settlement. [C].

* * *

B. *The Liability of the Parties*

Because we believe that the jury could properly have found, as it did under appropriate instructions, [c], that fraudulent misrepresentations made to plaintiffs amounted to legal fraud, and that they did not waive their right to sue for the injury that they suffered as a result of those representations, we address the remaining principal question on appeal of who was responsible and who is therefore liable.

1. Christopher McGrath

We believe that the jury could properly find that Christopher McGrath's conduct rendered him liable under New York law, as charged. McGrath was [initially] in charge of the settlement negotiations * * * ; all the while McGrath's position of authority heightened the impact of his representations as to the insurance coverage. McGrath stipulated that "to the best of his knowledge" there was only $200,000 worth of coverage in spite of the information in the documents in his possession. [C]. McGrath's insistence that the policy limit was $200,000, [c], renders him liable under the New York definition of scienter as "a reckless indifference to error," "a pretense of exact knowledge," or "[an] assertion of a false material fact `susceptible of accurate knowledge' but stated to be true on the personal knowledge of the representer." [C]. This, of course, attunes with the classic formulation of Judge Cardozo in the touchstone case of *Ultramares Corp. v. Touche, Niven & Co.*, 255 N.Y. 170, 174 N.E. 441, 449-50 (1931).

* * *

[4. John McGrath

"Although he may have been only minimally at fault," John McGrath is also subject to liability.] There was evidence that John McGrath gave the appearance of personal knowledge when he specifically ratified his brother's misrepresentation: "What Chris told you is true. . . . All the coverage there is on the case is $200,000 . . . . That's it. How many times do you want to hear it?" * * * There was evidence that John McGrath participated in the drafting of the March 4 stipulation which contained explicit representations as to the coverage limit. Moreover, the letters from the excess insurer's counsel were in his firm's file. * * *

Finally, even though the case was not tried on a partnership theory, as a matter of law John McGrath was liable for his partner's tort. [Cc].

* * *

* * * We hold that the $680,000 verdict against Citizens, [the hospital's attorney] and both McGraths, jointly and severally, may be reinstated.

Note

A misrepresentation may subject a lawyer to greater personal risks than other types of improper conduct. As Judge Van Graafeiland notes in his dissent in *Slotkin*:

> As a general rule, malpractice policies do not insure against fraudulent acts or omissions. *See*, e. g., *St. Paul Fire & Marine Insurance Co. v. Clarence-Rainess & Co.*, 70 Misc.2d 1082, 1083, 335 N.Y.S.2d 169 (1972), *aff'd*, 41 A.D.2d 604, 340 N.Y.S.2d 587 (1973). The McGraths' policy so provides, and they are being defended by their insurance carrier pursuant to a stipulation that the carrier will not be responsible for the payment of any judgment against them which sounds in fraud.

Slotkin, 614 F.2d 301, at 318 n.2 (Van Graafielard, J., dissenting).

ABA Comm. on Ethics and Professional Responsibility, Informal Op. 1518 (1986)
"Notice to Opposing Counsel of Inadvertent Omission of Contract Provision"

A and B, with the assistance of their lawyers, have negotiated a commercial contract. After deliberation with counsel, A ultimately acquiesced in the final provision insisted upon by B, previously in dispute between the parties and without which B would have refused to come to overall agreement. However, A's lawyer discovered that the final draft of the contract typed in the office of B's lawyer did not contain the provision which had been in dispute. The Committee has been asked to give its opinion as to the ethical duty of A's lawyer in that circumstance.

The Committee considers this situation to involve merely a scrivener's error, not an intentional change in position by the other party. A meeting of the minds has already occurred. The Committee concludes that the error is appropriate for correction between the lawyers without client consultation.[8]

---

[8]   [ABA's note 1]. Assuming for purposes of discussion that the error is "information relating to [the] representation," under Rule 1.6 [Confidentiality] disclosure would be "impliedly authorized in order to carry out the representation." The Comment to Rule 1.6 points out that a lawyer has implied authority to make "a disclosure that facilitates a satisfactory conclusion"—in this case completing the commercial contract already agreed upon and left to the lawyers to memorialize. We do not here reach the issue of the lawyer's

A's lawyer does not have a duty to advise A of the error pursuant to any obligation of communication under Rule 1.4 of the ABA Model Rules of Professional Conduct (1983). "The guiding principle is that the lawyer should fulfill reasonable client expectations for information consistent with the duty to act in the client's best interests and the client's overall requirements as to the character of representation." Comment to Rule 1.4. In this circumstance there is no "informed decision," in the language of Rule 1.4, that A needs to make; the decision on the contract has already been made by the client. Furthermore, the Comment to Rule 1.2 points out that the lawyer may decide the "technical" means to be employed to carry out the objective of the representation, without consultation with the client.

The client does not have a right to take unfair advantage of the error. The client's right pursuant to Rule 1.2 to expect committed and dedicated representation is not unlimited. Indeed, for A's lawyer to suggest that A has an opportunity to capitalize on the clerical error, unrecognized by B and B's lawyer, might raise a serious question of the violation of the duty of A's lawyer under Rule 1.2(d) not to counsel the client to engage in, or assist the client in, conduct the lawyer knows is fraudulent. In addition, Rule 4.1(b) admonishes the lawyer not knowingly to fail to disclose a material fact to a third person when disclosure is necessary to avoid assisting a fraudulent act by a client, and Rule 8.4(c) prohibits the lawyer from engaging in conduct involving dishonesty, fraud, deceit, or misrepresentation.

* * *

Notes

1.   Compare MR 4.1(b) (requiring truthfulness to others) with MR 3.3(a)(1) (requiring truthfulness to the court). As originally drafted by the Kutak Commission, the requirements were the same. The ABA added the exception to MR 4.1(b) for confidential information. Why provide less protection to third parties than to courts?

2.   Compare MR 4.1(b) (attorney must disclose material fact to avoid assisting a client in committing a fraud, unless information is confidential) with MR 1.2(d) (attorney may not assist client in committing a fraud). The provisions appear to be inconsistent. Failure to disclose confidential information when necessary to avoid assisting

---

duty if the client wishes to exploit the error.

a fraud would violate MR 1.2(d). Disclosure of the information would violate MRs 1.6 and 4.1(b). How does the ABA avoid the conflict in Informal Opinion 86-1518? *See* the ABA's footnote 1.

3.   Professor Ronald Rotunda reconciles the inconsistency between MRs 4.1(b) and 1.2(d) as follows:

> [Model Rule 4.1] provides, in subsection (b), that while representing a client the lawyer may not knowingly "fail to disclose a material fact. . . when disclosure is necessary to avoid assisting a criminal or fraudulent act by a client, *unless disclosure is prohibited by Rule 1.6.*" Rule 4.1 appears to state that when disclosure is prohibited by Rule 1.6, the lawyer must keep secret material facts even if such nondisclosure would assist a client's criminal or fraudulent act. But if the lawyer does assist in such an act through his or her nondisclosure, the lawyer will be held liable by other law. Such nondisclosure also appears to violate Rule 1.2(d). The Comment to Rule 1.2 makes clear that a "lawyer may not continue assisting a client in conduct that the lawyer originally supposes is legally proper but then discovers is criminal or fraudulent. Withdrawal from the representation, therefore, may be required." The remedy for the apparent inconsistency may be found in the concept of filing a notice of withdrawal [with those who might be injured by the fraud, *see* the Comment to MR 1.6 discussed *supra* Chapter Three].
>
> Thus, while the lawyer cannot assist criminal or fraudulent client conduct under Rule 1.2(d), under Rule 4.1(b) the lawyer must keep the client's secrets, protected by Rule 1.6, even if doing so assists the client's fraud or crime. The only possible solution to this dilemma between Rule 1.2(d) and Rule 4.1(b) is to withdraw, and then file a notice of withdrawal in order to alert the victims of the client's wrongdoing.

Ronald D. Rotunda, "The Notice of Withdrawal and the New Model Rules of Professional Conduct: Blowing the Whistle and Waving the Red Flag," 63 *Ore. L. Rev.* 455, 483 (1984). *See* Chapter Three *supra* for a substantial excerpt from Rotunda's article.

4.   What should the lawyer do when the lawyer learns after the fact that the client has used the lawyer's services to perpetrate a fraud. In ABA Formal Opinion 92-366, the Committee opined:

> When a lawyer's services have been used in the past by a client to perpetrate a fraud, but the fraud has ceased, the lawyer may but is not required to withdraw from further representation of the client; in these circumstances a "noisy" withdrawal is not permitted.

In the event that the fraud is not complete or has not ceased, the opinion, over a vigorous dissent, directed the lawyer to withdraw and permitted the lawyer to "disaffirm documents prepared in the course of the representation that are being, or will be, used in the furtherance of the fraud, even though such a 'noisy' withdrawal may have the collateral effect of inferentially revealing client confidences."

Brooks v. Zebre
792 P.2d 196 (Wyo. 1990)

THOMAS, Justice.

* * *

This dispute centers upon the lease of a ranch in Sweetwater County that included an option to purchase. The ranch, a viable livestock raising enterprise, was developed by Isaac Brooks who died in the spring of 1983, leaving a substantial estate that included the ranch. Isaac Brooks's wife, Patricia, was appointed the personal representative of the estate, and she, of course, was among the heirs. In addition to his wife, Isaac Brooks was survived by their four natural children and a daughter of Mrs. Brooks whom Isaac had adopted. One son was in quite delicate health, having already had a colostomy and a brain shunt at a relatively early age.

About two months after Isaac Brooks's death, members of the Arambel family, neighbors and long-time friends, began a series of almost daily visits with Mrs. Brooks. In the course of these visits, she expressed an interest in leasing the ranch. She also manifested an overriding concern for the future of her ill son. The record demonstrates that the additional duties required of her as personal representative, which included management of the ranch, when added to her usual responsibilities as the mother of five young children, created an extremely difficult burden for Brooks, who had not received much formal education and had little business experience. She exhibited indications of stress including drinking as much as a case of beer per day.

Not long after she expressed an interest in leasing the ranch, the Arambels arranged a meeting with Brooks in the law offices of [their attorney John A.] Zebre for the purpose of discussing and arranging a possible lease. Zebre was acquainted with Brooks, and the record discloses he visited in her home during Isaac Brooks's last illness. At that time, he reviewed Isaac Brooks's will, in her presence, and offered some suggestions as to improvement of the dispositive scheme. Despite this earlier acquaintance, however, and despite whatever knowledge Zebre possessed of the Isaac Brooks will and estate, there is no question on the part of any party that Zebre represented only the Arambels.

At the meeting in Zebre's office, Brooks advised him that another attorney was handling the probate of the estate of her deceased husband, and she suggested to all who were present that the estate attorney be involved in the negotiations. Later, she testified that, in response to this suggestion, John Arambel told her, "[y]ou don't need to talk to [the attorney] because he won't let you do it because he wants all the money." She further testified that Zebre said to her, "[d]on't tell [the attorney] because he'll just tell you not to lease that ranch." Zebre claims to have made several attempts to contact the attorney for the Brooks estate, but the record does not demonstrate that any contact ever was made or that the estate attorney was informed of these matters until after all negotiations had been completed and the agreement had been executed. The meeting at which the contract provisions were agreed upon was conducted with neither Brooks, nor her children, nor the estate being represented by an attorney or any other person knowledge-able in either business or law.

* * *

Brooks's testimony with respect to this meeting was that she was not able to comprehend much of the discussion. Her recollections of the meeting, and the discussion relating to the lease and the option, were extremely vague. She testified that she did not remember any conversation concerning an option to purchase the ranch, a forty-year lease, a sale of all the cattle and sheep, or other essential terms and conditions of the agreement finally reached. Zebre recalls, on the other hand, that Brooks was "very poised, confident" and that "she was very certain and very positive, confident about what she was there about, what was happening."

* * *

Subsequently, an action was instituted by the Arambels for a declaration of their rights under the agreement. Brooks and the estate counterclaimed for rescission of the contract, and they caused Zebre to be named as a "third-party defendant." The product of that action was that the court ruled that the agreement was unconscionable and ordered rescission and appropriate restitution. The claims against Zebre were not resolved at that time. Later, all parties agreed to a mutually satisfactory arrangement to settle the matter except for the claims against Zebre. Zebre then moved for, and was granted, a summary judgment by the court. This appeal is taken by Brooks and the Bank, claiming that the district court erred in granting summary judgment because Zebre, even though representing the Arambels, is responsible for damages on the tort theories of negligence, gross negligence, and fraud.

In order to recover for negligence or gross negligence, the plaintiff is required to demonstrate all necessary elements of the tort including the element of a legal duty owed by the defendant to the plaintiff. [Cc]. The issue of whether a duty is owed is strictly a question of law. [Cc]. With respect to questions of law, we do not defer to the decision of the lower court. [C]. When we determine, however, that no legal duty exists from a defendant to the plaintiff, a summary judgment with respect to claims of negligence is appropriate and must be affirmed. [C].

From the record, it is indisputable that Zebre owed his professional duty to the Arambels. They were his clients, and an attorney assumes the very highest of duties with respect to zealous representation of his clients. [C]. Brooks's interests with respect to the transaction were adverse to those of the Arambels, and it is fundamental that Zebre could not have assumed a duty to Brooks without violating his primary duty to the Arambels. [C]. The situation emphasizes scriptural wisdom. "No servant can serve two masters. For he will either hate the one and love the other, or he will cling to the one and despise the other." *Luke 16:13* (Richmond Lattimore Translation). * * *

* * *

[W]e agree with the district court and hold that an attorney owes no actionable duty to an adverse party emanating from the zealous representation of his own client. [Cc]. Any infringement upon this proposition, in our judgment, results in an irreconcilable conflict of interest working extreme violence to the adversarial process as we know it. [C]. Because it is undisputed in the record that Zebre was representing only the Arambels, Brooks and the Bank present no genuine issue of material fact germane to this rule. Consequently, the claims of negligence and gross negligence against Zebre must fail, as a matter of law, and the summary judgment as to those issues must be affirmed.

* * *

We turn then to the contention of Brooks and the Bank that they are entitled to a cause of action arising out of an asserted violation of the rules adopted by this court relating to ethical conduct of attorneys. The clear rule is that no private cause of action in favor of a non-client can be found attributable to violations of the disciplinary rules relating to attorneys. [Cc]. We hold that no claim will lie on behalf of Brooks and the Bank founded upon any violation of the disciplinary rules relating to attorneys.

* * *

Since the record, and the law, establish that no legal duty flowed from Zebre to Brooks in this instance, the claims for recovery for negligence and gross negligence must fail. Furthermore, in the absence of any evidence of fraud, the claim of Brooks and the Bank to recover for fraud must fail. We affirm the summary judgment entered by the trial court in Zebre's favor.

* * *

URBIGKIT, Justice, dissenting.

I regretfully but strongly dissent. The result of this holding permits predation by an attorney so long as the defrauded victim is not a client. I am unconvinced by the majority's rationale that any other result would do "extreme violence to the adversarial process." This fraud did not occur within the context of an adversarial process and I find such an explanation misplaced. It is non-adversarial if only one attorney directs the events. [C].

John Arambel appeared to be close friends of Isaac and Patricia Brooks. The Arambels and the Brooks were neighboring ranchers. When Isaac Brooks died, John Arambel and his son Peter found use for John Zebre and his license to practice law. The three joined together and quickly convinced the recently widowed Patricia Brooks to sign an agreement after repeatedly advising her not to consult her attorney before she signed. Whether disoriented by grief or blinded by the trust of old friends during a time of enormous personal pain and anxiety, Patricia Brooks signed an agreement she should never have signed. That agreement essentially gave away the ranch.

* * *

It should be recognized that no case as egregious as this has been found where civil immunity has been provided for misconduct under the mantle of zealous advocacy. [Cc]. Zebre used his legal license to commit a fraud not only on a recently widowed, unsophisticated individual, but on the court system and the minor heirs who had a direct interest. This fraud was accomplished by excluding the estate attorney who could have provided some usable information. The estate attorney described his consternation and anger in detail at trial as he described his initial interviews with the defrauded widow[. He estimated that the contract would have sold a five million dollar ranch for consideration worth one million dollars.]

* * *

The majority allows the notion of privity to drive this result and ignores a pre-eminence of Wyoming's ethical standards for legal conduct. We could and should do better if the public respect we seek for the legal profession is to be achieved.

> [T]o the extent that disciplinary violations go unpunished, the application of codified ethical standards in legal malpractice proceedings may be an additional deterrent against unethical conduct. In fact, in some cases, a monetary penalty in civil litigation may be a more meaningful sanction than a private admonition or reprimand in the disciplinary system. [C].

> *The basis for defining this case is the admitted and accepted violation of one of the fundamental tenants of legal practice: "You do not negotiate ex parte with another lawyer's client." "Hoffman's Resolution XLIII was: 'I will never enter into any conversation with my opponent's client relative to his claim or defense, except with the consent and in the presence of his counsel.'" [C].*

* * *

Zebre assumed the responsibility of an advising attorney when he advised Patricia Brooks to exclude her counsel. Since Zebre undertook to advise, direct, and control the negotiations, he assumed responsibility to both parties. When he said he would not cheat the estate and Patricia Brooks, we need only enforce that bargain by requiring a compensatory payment equal to the losses his legal activities precipitated. * * *

* * *

In the preamble to Wyoming's Rules of Professional Conduct for Attorneys at Law [Wyoming's version of the Model Rules], there is required among other responsibilities:

> [1] A lawyer is a representative of clients, an officer of the legal system and a public citizen having special responsibility for the quality of justice.

* * *

[7]   A lawyer's responsibilities as a representative of clients, an officer of the legal system and a public citizen are usually harmonious. Thus, when an opposing party is well represented a lawyer can be a zealous advocate on behalf of a client and at the same time assume that justice is being done. So also, a lawyer can be sure that preserving client confidences ordinarily serves the public interest because people are more likely to seek legal advice, and thereby heed their legal obligations, when they know their communications will be private.

[8]   In the nature of law practice, however, conflicting responsibilities are encountered. Virtually all difficult ethical problems arise from conflict between a lawyer's responsibilities to clients, to the legal system and to the lawyer's own interest in remaining an upright person while earning a satisfactory living. The Rules of Professional Conduct prescribe terms for resolving such conflicts. Within the framework of these Rules many difficult issues of professional discretion can arise. Such issues must be resolved through the exercise of sensitive professional and moral judgment guided by the basic principles underlying the Rules.

* * *

Provisions of the Rules of Professional Conduct for Attorneys at Law further include:

Rule 4.1. Truthfulness in statements to others.

In the course of representing a client a lawyer shall not knowingly:

(a) make a false statement of material fact or law to a third person; or

(b) fail to disclose a material fact to a third person when disclosure is necessary to avoid assisting a criminal or fraudulent act by a client, unless disclosure is prohibited by Rule 1.6.

Rule 4.2. Communication with person represented by counsel.

In representing a client, a lawyer shall not communicate about the subject of the representation with a party the lawyer knows to be represented by another lawyer in the matter, unless the lawyer has the consent of the other lawyer or is authorized by law to do so.

* * *

The majority denies that fraud is visible, although many others may see it without squinting, when Zebre convinced Patricia Brooks to rely on his advice that she need not consult the estate attorney and then secured her signature to an unconscionable sales contract. Fraud is not one of those elusive concepts.

An intentional perversion of truth [*you do not need to consult your attorney because I would not cheat you*] for the purpose of inducing another in reliance [*trust me*] upon it to part with some valuable thing [*a ranch and an inheritance*] belonging to him or to surrender a legal right.

* * *

A fraud case was clearly presented here and, in denial of that right to the defrauded estate, the district court and this majority committed a terrible error.

VI

CONCLUSION

We leave this case as we began. A grossly unconscionable contract was negotiated with an untrained, modestly educated, recently widowed woman after she was talked into excluding her attorney. A direct participant was an attorney who purported to protect her in a hurriedly negotiated transaction while violating fundamental professional ethics by ensuring that her attorney, who could have protected the widow, was not available. * * * Contrary to statements made by Zebre's counsel at oral argument before this court (whether actually representing his interest or otherwise) that justice should be found through disciplinary proceedings (which could include disbarment), I see in this case a responsibility for compensation in damage done. Anything else is not real justice to the defrauded estate and its beneficiaries and, consequently, I most strongly and with great anguish dissent.

* * *

Notes

1.   Can you reconcile this case with *Slotkin*?

2.   In his dissent, Justice Urbigkit says:

This fraud did not occur within the context of an adversarial process and I find such an explanation misplaced. It is non-adversarial if only one attorney directs the events.

Brooks, 792 2d at 203. Is the negotiation of a lease "an adversarial process"? Should different rules apply to attorneys who are negotiating rather than litigating? To attorneys who are negotiating with a party that is not represented?

3.   This was, of course, an action for damages against Zebre. What provisions of MRs 4.1 to 4.4 did Zebre violate? In his dissent,

Justice Urbigkit also said:

> Where the Wyoming State Bar in its disciplinary obligations and procedures was during this entire course of events is not disclosed. As a matter of judicial fact and notice, serious reprimand, or possibly disbarment, should have occurred but did not. Whether complaint was made and why appropriate action was not taken are questions to which answers are not provided.
>
> The seriousness of an attorney's conduct when negotiating an unsupportable deal directly with another attorney's client is surely not unknown to the Wyoming State Bar grievance organization.

Brooks, 792 P.2d at 203, n.2 (Urbigkit, J., dissenting). Does the risk of Zebre's disbarment provide sufficient protection for the Patricia Brooks of this world?

Chapter Six

BUSINESS PROBLEMS IN THE PRACTICE
OF LAW

Most lawyers not only practice law, they make their living practicing law—law practice is both a profession and a business. This chapter deals with two prominent business problems in the practice of law: power and money. The first section deals with power relationships within organizations. Many lawyers practice in law firms[1] or as in-house counsel in corporations.[2] They supervise and are supervised by others. Practicing law in law firms and corporations may create special ethical pressures (and opportunities) for lawyers, as the cases in the following section suggest. The second section of this chapter deals with the problems of billing and legal fees.

A.   Power and Responsibility in Law Firms and Corporations

Read Model Rules 5.1 to 5.3[3]

Steven Brill, "When A Lawyer Lies"
Esquire 23-24 (Dec. 19, 1978)

Eighteen months ago, Joseph Fortenberry, Harvard College '66 and Yale Law '69, was on the perfect big-time lawyer's career

---

[1]   An important part of the history of the practice of law in the United States has been the growth of law firms. In the 1800s almost all lawyers were general practitioners and practiced alone or in small partnerships. In 1872, only 3 law firms in the nation had five or more lawyers; in 1898, 67 firms had five or more; and in 1915, 240 firms had five or more. Richard L. Abel, *American Lawyers* 182 (1989). "In 1959, there were . . . 32 firms with more than 50 lawyers; in 1979, . . . 90 [firms] had more than 100." *Id.* "Although no firm had more than 200 lawyers in 1979, forty firms were larger than that in 1987." *Id.* at 183. Baker & McKenzie went over 1000 in 1987. *Id.*

[2]   *See* David S. Machlowitz, "Lawyers Move In-house," 75 *A.B.A. J.* 66 (May 1989).

[3]   For MR 5.1 *cf.* Cal. Rules 3-110, discussion. There is no Model Code counterpart, or a direct parallel in the Cal. Rules. There is no Model Code or California Rules counterpart to MR 5.2. There is no Model Code or Cal. Rules counterpart to MR 5.3, but see DR 4-101(D); Discussion to Cal. Rule 3-110.

path. At thirty-three, he had a federal court of appeals clerkship under his belt and was senior associate at the New York law firm of Donovan Leisure Newton & Irvine working on the all-important antitrust case that Kodak was defending against Berkey Photo.

His prospects for being made a partner at the prestige firm the following year were excellent: He was regarded not only as brilliant but also as engaging and enjoyable to work with; Kodak was the firm's biggest case (occupying twenty lawyers full time, with gross billings of some $4 million a year); and he was working hand in hand with Mahlon Perkins Jr., one of the firm's most respected partners.

Then came April 20, 1977. That morning, in the middle of one of hundreds of depositions (on-the-record question-and-answer sessions with a witness prior to the trial) that he had sat through for months, Joe Fortenberry's career unraveled.

Alvin Stein, the lawyer for Berkey Photo, was questioning a Kodak "expert witness," Yale economics professor Merton Peck, about files and other materials the professor had received from Kodak in order to prepare his testimony. In such suits, each side is allowed to obtain—or "discover"—almost any documents that the other side has used to prepare and bolster its case. Such materials can often be used to attack the credibility of witnesses.

Peck told Berkey lawyer Stein that he had shipped all the materials back to Perkins of Donovan Leisure earlier that year. What happened, then, to the documents, Stein asked Perkins. I threw them out as soon as I got them, the Donovan Leisure partner replied.

Perkins was lying. He'd saved all the documents in a suitcase, frequently taking them back and forth between his office at the firm and a special office he'd leased near the federal courthouse for the trial. And Joe Fortenberry, sitting at Perkins' side during this deposition, knew his boss was lying. He'd worked with the suitcase full of documents, and at least once he'd carried it between Perkins' two offices. Two weeks later, Perkins submitted a sworn statement to the court confirming he'd destroyed the documents.

In January of 1978, Perkins' perjury came to light when Stein, at the end of the Kodak-Berkey trial, asked Peck about any reports he had submitted prior to the trial to Kodak's lawyers. This led back to more probing questions about the materials Peck had used to prepare his testimony. Then—in what has since become a much-reported, pinstriped soap opera—on the Sunday night before the last week of the trial, a frightened Perkins broke down and confessed to Kodak lead lawyer John Doar that he'd never destroyed the documents but had actually hid them in a cupboard in his office. Perkins told the judge the next day, then resigned from the firm; Stein used Donovan Leisure's withholding of documents to help convince the jury of Kodak's bad faith and guilt; Kodak lost the case in a spectacular $113 million verdict (since reduced to $87 million); Kodak dropped Donovan Leisure; and Perkins was convicted of contempt of court for his perjury and sentenced to a month in prison.

But what about Joe Fortenberry?

The rules by which the bar disciplines lawyers—the Code of Professional Responsibility—require that "a lawyer who receives information clearly establishing that . . . a person other than his client has perpetrated a fraud upon a tribunal shall promptly reveal the fraud to the tribunal." Moreover, the code requires that a lawyer who knows that another lawyer has engaged in dishonesty, deceit, or misrepresentation must report the offending lawyer to proper prosecutorial authorities. [*Cf.* MR 8.3(a)]

In short, Fortenberry was obligated to speak up when Perkins lied. Instead, he said nothing to anyone. To be sure, Perkins, perhaps thinking he was helping Fortenberry, told the federal prosecutors who later investigated the case that Fortenberry had whispered in his ear and reminded him of the existence of the documents when Perkins told Stein he'd destroyed them. Fortenberry denies this. What's undisputed, and more relevant, is that Fortenberry never said a word about Perkins' lie to the judge, as he was obligated to, or even to any other Donovan Leisure partner.

Throw the book at him, right? Wrong. Law firms teach young associates that they are apprentices to the partners, not whistle blowers. The partners, after all, are supposed to be the ones with the experience and standing to make decisions about right and wrong. Fortenberry had worked for Perkins for more than six months. In an environment like Donovan Leisure, this means that he respected the fifty-nine year old "Perk," as his admiring partners called him, for the well-liked senior litigator that he was. It also means that he was intimidated by Perkins and, of course, that he knew Perkins was his ticket to a partnership when the firm partners would decide in the following year which of the associates at Fortenberry's level would be offered that golden prize. "What happened to Joe" says a close associate "was that he saw Perk lie and really couldn't believe it. And he just had no idea what to do. I mean, he knew Perkins was lying, but he kept thinking that there must be a reason. Besides, what do you do? The guy was his boss and a great guy!"

As stung as Donovan Leisure is by the Perkins affair, the firm's partners have treated Fortenberry with the compassion that suggests that they understand his dilemma. They've paid for him to retain his own lawyer for the investigation that resulted in Perkins' guilty plea and for possible bar-association disciplinary action. (Federal prosecutors say there's no evidence of criminal misconduct on Fortenberry's part, but the Association of the Bar of the City of New York never comments on its own investigations regarding possible violations of the Lawyers Code of Professional Responsibility, even to the point of acknowledging whether there is one going on.) And they've kept him on at the firm and gone out of their way with signs ranging from work assignments to lunch invitations to show that they hold him blameless. In many ways, it hasn't helped. Friends say that Fortenberry—"a well-liked, personable genius," as one puts it—has been severely hurt emotionally by the Perkins episode. "He just looks and acts like a beaten man," as another associate explained.

There's one thing that Donovan Leisure could do to revive Fortenberry. They could make him a partner this June, when the decision on partners of his seniority is normally made. The odds are he'd have been made a partner had the Perkins affair never happened; so if, as Samuel Murphy of the firm's management committee told me recently, "in judging Joe for partnership, we're not going to hold the tragedy with Perk against him in any way," it stands to reason that he will get the offer. Then again, how does Donovan Leisure look, its reputation already hurt by the Perkins affair, offering a partnership to the man who apparently violated the Code of Professional Responsibility and kept quiet while Perkins perpetrated his fraud on the court?

With Donovan Leisure beginning to recover from the Perkins affair * * * the upcoming decision on what to do with Fortenberry may be the one last hurdle they have to pass. (A once-feared malpractice suit by Kodak is now unlikely, a source at the camera maker says.)

But there are larger questions, too, that Fortenberry's sad situation should raise. Donovan Leisure senior partner Murphy says that "the firm is trying to create an atmosphere in which associates in positions like Fortenberry's will feel free to take the story of one partner acting improperly to another partner." But Perkins' impropriety—a clear, deliberate lie—is an easy call. What about an associate who thinks his partner is filing a frivolous motion or is bilking a client? "You know, when you come to work at a big firm you do give up independence," Murphy concedes. "And a young lawyer's idea about what is frivolous, for example, can't always be accepted, though we do encourage them to tell the partners they're working for what they think."

And what about firms other than Donovan Leisure that haven't been clubbed by a Perkins disaster into thinking about "open doors" and the like? I asked eight different associates, ages twenty-seven to thirty-two, at major firms around the country what they'd do in Fortenberry's situation. None said that they'd speak up to the judge in the case as their Code of Professional Responsibility requires; only four suggested that there was another partner at the firm they'd feel free to go to if their boss did something like that; and one told a story of watching a partner bill a client (a major utility) for three times the hours worked and, not knowing what to do, doing nothing.

Judge Marvin E. Frankel, the trial judge in the Kodak-Berkey case, was highly critical of Donovan Leisure's conduct during the trial and so outraged by Perkins' lie that he personally called it to the attention of the federal prosecutors. Frankel has since left the bench and become a partner at the midtown firm of Proskauer Rose Goetz & Mendelsohn. An associate there told me last week he'd "have no idea" what to do in a Perkins situation. "There isn't any way for an associate to handle that problem," Frankel concedes. Yet, unexplainably, the once-outraged judge shifts the direct responsibility from the individual law firms, where it belongs, to the organized bar generally: "All firms, including this one, should push the bar association to evolve procedures so that an associate doesn't have to be a hero to do what's ethical."

Every year more and more of the best brains in our society go from law school to firms like Donovan Leisure. And every year these firms get larger—and more competitive. Without some real effort from those at the top, this is an environment that is destined to make automatons out of those who get by and tragedies out of those, like Fortenberry, who have the bad luck to get tripped up.

NOTE

Fortenberry's role in the scandal had nothing to do with his failure to be made a partner. The firm had actually passed him over two months before the Perkins matter ever came to light, partners there say. It later concealed its decision so as to enhance Fortenberry's chances of getting another job, keeping him working so that prospective employers would not see his immediate dismissal from the firm and conclude that Fortenberry was indeed implicated in Perkins' wrong-doing. Even so, Fortenberry was not hired by any private law firm to which he applied for a job.

Ironically, Perkins may have emerged relatively well. In the fall of 1978, he appeared in federal district court and pleaded guilty to a reduced misdemeanor charge of contempt of court. His lawyer, Harold Tyler, commented at sentencing that "there, possibly but for the grace of God, go I, because of the pressures which come upon men and women who practice law in big cases." Though Perkins spent 27 days in jail (where he served as assistant to the chaplain), he received a pension payment from Donovan Leisure and has never been disbarred. Since his release, Perkins has traveled extensively in the Far East, where he taught English to Japanese students for some time. Since his return, he has devoted himself to his duties as president of the Greenwich, Connecticut, Philharmonic Orchestra. He has little contact with his former partners at Donovan Leisure, but one lawyer who spoke with him in late 1980 describes him as "happier, I believe, than he had been as a practicing lawyer."

J. Stewart, "Kodak and Donovan Leisure: The Untold Story," *The American Lawyer* 62 (Jan. 1983), *quoted in* Deborah L. Rhode & David Luban, *Legal Ethics* 381 (1992).

Wieder v. Skala
80 N.Y.2d 628, 609 N.E.2d 105, 593 N.Y.S.2d 752 (1992)

HANCOCK, Judge.

* * *

* * *[P]laintiff alleges that he was a commercial litigation attorney associated with defendant law firm from June 16, 1986 until March 18, 1988. In early 1987, plaintiff requested that the law firm represent him in the purchase of a condominium apartment. The firm agreed and assigned a fellow associate (L.L.) "to do 'everything that needs to be done'". For several months, L.L. neglected plaintiff's real estate transaction and, to conceal his neglect, made several "false and fraudulent material misrepresentations." In September 1987, when plaintiff learned of L.L.'s neglect and false statements, he advised two of the firm's senior partners. They conceded that the firm was aware "that [L.L.] was a pathological liar and that [L.L.] had previously lied to [members of the firm] regarding the status of other pending legal matters." When plaintiff confronted L.L., he acknowledged that he had lied about the real estate transaction and later admitted in writing that he had committed "several acts of legal malpractice and fraud and deceit upon plaintiff and several other clients of the firm."

The complaint further alleges that, after plaintiff asked the firm partners to report L.L.'s misconduct to the Appellate Division Disciplinary Committee as required under DR 1-103(A) of the Code of Professional Responsibility [*Cf.* MR 8.3(a)], they declined to act. Later, in an effort to dissuade plaintiff from making the report himself, the partners told him that they would reimburse his losses. Plaintiff nonetheless met with the Committee "to discuss the entire matter." He withdrew his complaint, however, "because the [f]irm had indicated that it would fire plaintiff if he reported [L.L.'s] misconduct." Ultimately, in December 1987—as a result of plaintiff's insistence–the firm made a report concerning L.L.'s "numerous misrepresentations and [acts of] malpractice against clients of the [f]irm and acts of forgery of checks drawn on the [f]irm's account." Thereafter, two partners "continuously berated plaintiff for having caused them to report [the] misconduct." The firm nevertheless continued to employ plaintiff "because he was in charge of handling the most important litigation in the [f]irm." Plaintiff was fired in March 1988, a few days after he filed motion papers in that important case.

Plaintiff asserts that defendants wrongfully discharged him as a result of his insistence that L.L.'s misconduct be reported as required by DR 1-103(A). * * *

* * *

* * *[P]laintiff's performance of professional services for the firm's clients as a duly admitted member of the Bar was at the very core and, indeed, the only purpose of his association with defendants. Associates are, to be sure, employees of the firm but they remain independent officers of the court responsible in a broader public sense for their professional obligations. Practically speaking, plaintiff's duties and responsibilities as a lawyer and as an associate of the firm were so closely linked as to be incapable of separation. It is in this distinctive

relationship between a law firm and a lawyer hired as an associate that plaintiff finds the implied-in-law obligation on which he founds his claim.

We agree with plaintiff that in any hiring of an attorney as an associate to practice law with a firm there is implied an understanding so fundamental to the relationship and essential to its purpose as to require no expression: that both the associate and the firm in conducting the practice will do so in accordance with the ethical standards of the profession. Erecting or countenancing disincentives to compliance with the applicable rules of professional conduct, plaintiff contends, would subvert the central professional purpose of his relationship with the firm—the lawful and ethical practice of law.

The particular rule of professional conduct implicated here (DR 1-103[A]) [*Cf.* MR 8.3(a)], it must be noted, is critical to the unique function of self-regulation belonging to the legal profession. Although the Bar admission requirements provide some safeguards against the enrollment of unethical applicants, the Legislature has delegated the responsibility for maintaining the standards of ethics and competence to the Departments of the Appellate Division [Cc]. To assure that the legal profession fulfills its responsibility of self-regulation, DR 1-103(A) places upon each lawyer and Judge the duty to report to the Disciplinary Committee of the Appellate Division any potential violations of the Disciplinary Rules that raise a "substantial question as to another lawyer's honesty, trustworthiness or fitness in other respects". Indeed, one commentator has noted that, "[t]he reporting requirement is nothing less than essential to the survival of the profession" [Cc].

Moreover, as plaintiff points out, failure to comply with the reporting requirement may result in suspension or disbarment [C]. Thus, by insisting that plaintiff disregard DR 1-103(A) defendants were not only making it impossible for plaintiff to fulfill his professional obligations but placing him in the position of having to choose between continued employment and his own potential suspension and disbarment. * * *

It is the law that in "every contract there is an implied undertaking on the part of each party that he will not intentionally and purposely do anything to prevent the other party from carrying out the agreement on his part" [Cc]. * * *

Just such fundamental understanding, though unexpressed, was inherent in the relationship between plaintiff and defendant law firm [C]. Defendants, a firm of lawyers, hired plaintiff to practice law and this objective was the only basis for the employment relationship. Intrinsic to this relationship, of course, was the unstated but essential compact that in conducting the firm's legal practice both plaintiff and the firm would do so in compliance with the prevailing rules of conduct and ethical standards of the profession. Insisting that as an associate in their employ plaintiff must act unethically and in violation of one of the primary professional rules amounted to nothing less than a frustration of the only legitimate purpose of the employment relationship.

* * *We conclude, therefore, that plaintiff has stated a valid claim for breach of contract based on an implied-in-law obligation in his relationship with defendants.

* * *

Note

Does *Wieder* reflect the same concerns articulated by the Illinois court in *In re Himmel* (Chapter One, Part E)? How would the New York court resolve the controversy in *Himmel*? How would the Illinois court resolve the controversy in *Wieder*?

Balla v. Gambro, Inc.
145 Ill. 2d 492, 584 N.E.2d 104, 164 Ill. Dec. 892 (1991)

[Former "house counsel" attorney brought action against former employer for retaliatory discharge.]

Justice CLARK delivered the opinion of the court:

The issue in this case is whether in-house counsel should be allowed the remedy of an action for retaliatory discharge.

Appellee, Roger Balla, formerly in-house counsel for Gambro, Inc. (Gambro), filed a retaliatory discharge action against Gambro. * * *

Gambro is a distributor of kidney dialysis equipment manufactured by Gambro Germany. Among the products distributed by Gambro are dialyzers which filter excess fluid and toxic substances from the blood of patients with no or impaired kidney function. The manufacture and sale of dialyzers is regulated by the United States

Food and Drug Administration (FDA); [Cc].

Appellee, Roger J. Balla, is and was at all times throughout this controversy an attorney licensed to practice law in the State of Illinois. On March 17, 1980, appellee executed an employment agreement with Gambro which contained the terms of appellee's employment. Generally, the employment agreement provided that appellee would "be responsible for all legal matters within the company and for personnel within the company's sales office." * * *

* * *

In July 1985 Gambro Germany informed Gambro in a letter that certain dialyzers it had manufactured, the clearances of which varied from the package insert, were about to be shipped to Gambro. Referring to these dialyzers, Gambro Germany advised Gambro:

> "For acute patients risk is that the acute uremic situation will not be improved in spite of the treatment, giving continuous high levels of potassium, phosphate and urea/creatine. The chronic patient may note the effect as a slow progression of the uremic situation and depending on the interval between medical check-ups the medical risk may not be overlooked."

Appellee told the president of Gambro to reject the shipment because the dialyzers did not comply with FDA regulations. The president notified Gambro Germany of its decision to reject the shipment on July 12, 1985.

However, one week later the president informed Gambro Germany that Gambro would accept the dialyzers and "sell [them] to a unit that is not currently our customer but who buys only on price." Appellee contends that he was not informed by the president of the decision to accept the dialyzers but became aware of it through other Gambro employees. Appellee maintains that he spoke with the president in August regarding the company's decision to accept the dialyzers and told the president that he would do whatever necessary to stop the sale of the dialyzers.

On September 4, 1985, appellee was discharged from Gambro's employment by its president. The following day, appellee reported the shipment of the dialyzers to the FDA. The FDA seized the shipment and determined the product to be "adulterated within the meaning of section 501(h) of the [Federal Act]."

On March 19, 1986, appellee filed a four-count complaint in tort for retaliatory discharge seeking $22 million in damages. [The trial court granted Gambro's motion for summary judgment. On appeal, the Appellate Court held that an attorney is not barred as a matter of law from bringing an action for retaliatory discharge.]

We agree with the trial court that appellee does not have a cause of action against Gambro for retaliatory discharge under the facts of the case at bar. Generally, this court adheres to the proposition that "'an employer may discharge an employee-at-will for any reason or for no reason [at all].'" [The court's discussion of the development of retaliatory discharge is omitted.]

* * *

In this case it appears that Gambro discharged appellee, an employee of Gambro, in retaliation for his activities, and this discharge was in contravention of a clearly mandated public policy. Appellee allegedly told the president of Gambro that he would do whatever was necessary to stop the sale of the "misbranded and/or adulterated" dialyzers. In appellee's eyes, the use of these dialyzers could cause death or serious bodily harm to patients. As we have stated before, "[t]here is no public policy more important or more fundamental than the one favoring the effective protection of the lives and property of citizens." [Cc]. However, in this case, appellee was not just an employee of Gambro, but also general counsel for Gambro.

* * *

* * *[G]enerally, in-house counsel do not have a claim under the tort of retaliatory discharge. However, we base our decision as much on the nature and purpose of the tort of retaliatory discharge, as on the effect on the attorney-client relationship that extending the tort would have. In addition, at this time, we caution that our holding is confined by the fact that appellee is and was at all times throughout this controversy an attorney licensed to practice law in the State of Illinois. Appellee is and was subject to the Illinois Code of Professional Responsibility [C], adopted by this court. The tort of retaliatory discharge is a limited and narrow exception to the general rule of at-will employment [C]. The tort seeks to achieve "'a proper balance * * * among the employer's interest in operating a business efficiently and profitably, the employee's interest in earning a livelihood, and society's interest in seeing its public policies carried out.'" [Cc]. Further, as stated in *Palmateer*, "[t]he foundation of the tort of retaliatory discharge lies in the protection of public policy * * *." [C].

In this case, the public policy to be protected, that of protecting the lives and property of citizens, is adequately safeguarded without extending the tort of retaliatory discharge to in-house counsel. Appellee was required under the Rules of Professional Conduct to report Gambro's intention to sell the "misbranded and/or adulterated" dialyzers. Rule 1.6(b) of the Rules of Professional Conduct reads:

> "A lawyer *shall* reveal information about a client to the extent it appears necessary to prevent the client from committing an act that would result in death or serious bodily injury." (Emphasis added.) (134 Ill.2d R. 1.6(b).) [Contrast MR 1.6(b) ("may reveal")]

Appellee alleges, and the FDA's seizure of the dialyzers indicates, that the use of the dialyzers would cause death or serious bodily injury. Thus, under the above-cited rule, appellee was under the mandate of this court to report the sale of these dialyzers.

In his brief to this court, appellee argues that not extending the tort of retaliatory discharge to in-house counsel would present attorneys with a "Hobson's choice." According to appellee, in-house counsel would face two alternatives: either comply with the client/employer's wishes and risk both the loss of a professional license and exposure to criminal sanctions, or decline to comply with client/employer's wishes and risk the loss of a full-time job and the attendant benefits. We disagree. * * * In-house counsel do not have a choice of whether to follow their ethical obligations as attorneys licensed to practice law, or follow the illegal and unethical demands of their clients. In-house counsel must abide by the Rules of Professional Conduct. Appellee had no choice but to report to the FDA Gambro's intention to sell or distribute these dialyzers, and consequently protect the aforementioned public policy.

In addition, we believe that extending the tort of retaliatory discharge to in-house counsel would have an undesirable effect on the attorney-client relationship that exists between these employers and their in-house counsel. Generally, a client may discharge his attorney at any time, with or without cause. [C]. This rule applies equally to in-house counsel as it does to outside counsel. Further, this rule "recognizes that the relationship between an attorney and client is based on trust and that the client must have confidence in his attorney in order to ensure that the relationship will function properly." [Cc]. As stated in *Herbster*, "the attorney is placed in the unique position of maintaining a close relationship with a client where the attorney receives secrets, disclosures, and information that otherwise would not be divulged to intimate friends." [C]. We believe that if in-house counsel are granted the right to sue their employers for retaliatory discharge, employers might be less willing to be forthright and candid with their in-house counsel. Employers might be hesitant to turn to their in-house counsel for advice regarding potentially questionable corporate conduct knowing that their in-house counsel could use this information in a retaliatory discharge suit.

We recognize that under the Illinois Rules of Professional Conduct, attorneys shall reveal client confidences or secrets in certain situations (see 134 Ill.2d Rules 1.6(a), (b), (c)), and thus one might expect employers/clients to be naturally hesitant to rely on in-house counsel for advice regarding this potentially questionable conduct. However, the danger exists that if in-house counsel are granted a right to sue their employers in tort for retaliatory discharge, employers might further limit their communication with their in-house counsel. As stated in *Upjohn Co. v. United States* (1981), 449 U.S. 383, 389, 101 S. Ct. 677, 682, 66 L. Ed. 2d 584, 591, regarding the attorney-client privilege:

> "Its purpose is to encourage full and frank communication between attorneys and their clients and thereby promote broader public interests in the observance of law and administration of justice. The privilege recognizes that sound legal advice or advocacy serves public ends and that *such advice or advocacy depends upon the lawyer being fully informed by the client*." (Emphasis added.)

If extending the tort of retaliatory discharge might have a chilling effect on the communications between the employer/client and the in-house counsel, we believe that it is more wise to refrain from doing so.

Our decision not to extend the tort of retaliatory discharge to in-house counsel also is based on other ethical considerations. Under the Rules of Professional Conduct, appellee was required to withdraw from representing Gambro if continued representation would result in the violation of the Rules of Professional Conduct by which appellee was bound, or if Gambro discharged the appellee. (See 134 Ill.2d Rules 1.16(a)(2), (a)(4)) [*Cf.* MR 1.16(a)(1), (a)(3)]. In this case, Gambro did discharge appellee, and according to appellee's claims herein, his continued representation of Gambro would have resulted in a violation of the Rules of Professional Conduct. Appellee argues that such a choice of withdrawal is "simplistic and uncompassionate, and is completely at odds with contemporary realities facing in-house attorneys." These contemporary realities apparently are the economic ramifications of losing his position as in-house counsel. However difficult economically and perhaps emotionally it is for in-house counsel to discontinue representing an employer/client, we refuse to allow in-house counsel to sue their employer/client for damages because they obeyed their ethical obligations. In this case, appellee, in addition to being an employee at Gambro, is first and foremost an attorney bound by the Rules of Professional Conduct. These Rules of Professional Conduct hope to articulate in a concrete fashion certain values and goals such as defending the integrity of the judicial system, promoting the administration of justice and protecting the integrity of the legal profession. [C]. An attorney's obligation to follow these Rules of Professional Conduct should not be the foundation for a claim of retaliatory discharge.

We also believe that it would be inappropriate for the employer/client to bear the economic costs and burdens of their in-house counsel's adhering to their ethical obligations under the Rules of Professional Conduct. Presumably, in situations where an in-house counsel obeys his or her ethical obligations and reveals certain information regarding the employer/client, the attorney-client relationship will be irreversibly strained and the client will more than likely discharge its in-house counsel. In this scenario, if we were to grant the in-house counsel the right to sue the client for retaliatory discharge, we would be shifting the burden and costs of obeying the Rules of Professional Conduct from the attorney to the employer/client. The employer/client would be forced to pay damages to its former in-house counsel to essentially mitigate the financial harm the attorney suffered for having to abide by Rules of Professional Conduct. This, we believe, is impermissible for all attorneys know or should know that at certain times in their professional career, they will have to forgo economic gains in order to protect the integrity of the legal profession.

* * *

For the foregoing reasons, the decision of the appellate court is reversed, and the decision of the trial court is affirmed.

Appellate court reversed; circuit court affirmed.

Justice FREEMAN, dissenting:

I respectfully dissent from the decision of my colleagues. In concluding that the plaintiff attorney, serving as corporate in-house counsel, should not be allowed a claim for retaliatory discharge, the majority first reasons that the public policy implicated in this case, *i.e.*, protecting the lives and property of Illinois citizens, is adequately safeguarded by the lawyer's ethical obligation to reveal information about a client as necessary to prevent acts that would result in death or serious bodily harm (134 Ill.2d R. 1.6(b)). I find this reasoning fatally flawed.

The majority so reasons because, as a matter of law, an attorney cannot even contemplate ignoring his ethical obligations in favor of continuing in his employment. I agree with this conclusion "as a matter of law." However, to say that the categorical nature of ethical obligations is sufficient to ensure that the ethical obligations will be satisfied simply ignores reality. Specifically, it ignores that, as unfortunate for society as it may be, attorneys are no less human than nonattorneys and, thus, no less given to the temptation to either ignore or rationalize away their ethical obligations when complying therewith may render them unable to feed and support their families.

I would like to believe, as my colleagues apparently conclude, that attorneys will always "do the right thing" because the law says that they must. However, my knowledge of human nature, which is not much greater than the average layman's, and, sadly, the recent scandals involving the bench and bar of Illinois are more than sufficient to dispel such a belief. Just as the ethical obligations of the lawyers and judges involved in those scandals were inadequate to ensure that they would not break the law, I am afraid that the lawyer's ethical obligation to "blow the whistle" is likewise an inadequate safeguard for the public policy of protecting lives and property of Illinois citizens.

As reluctant as I am to concede it, the fact is that this court must take whatever steps it can, within the bounds of the law, to give lawyers incentives to abide by their ethical obligations, beyond the satisfaction inherent in their doing so. We cannot continue to delude ourselves and the people of the State of Illinois that attorneys' ethical duties, alone, are always sufficient to guarantee that lawyers will "do the right thing." In the context of this case, where doing "the right thing" will often result in termination by an employer bent on doing the "wrong thing," I believe that the incentive needed is recognition of a cause of action for retaliatory discharge, in the appropriate case.

The majority also bases its holding upon the reasoning that allowing in-house counsel a cause of action for retaliatory discharge will have a chilling effect on the attorney-client relationship and the free flow of information necessary to that relationship. This reasoning completely ignores what is very often one of the basic purposes of the attorney-client relationship, especially in the corporate client-in-house counsel setting. More importantly, it gives preeminence to the public policy favoring an unfettered right to discharge an attorney, although "[t]here is no public policy more important or more fundamental than the one favoring the effective protection of the lives and property of citizens." [C].

One of the basic purposes of the attorney-client relationship, especially in the corporate client-in-house counsel setting, is for the attorney to advise the client as to, exactly, what conduct the law requires so that the client can then comply with that advice. Given that purpose, allowing in-house counsel a cause of action for retaliatory discharge would chill the attorney-client relationship and discourage a corporate client from communicating freely with the attorney only where, as here, the employer decides to go forward with particular conduct, regardless of advice that it is contrary to law. I believe that, just as in-house counsel might reasonably so assume, this court is entitled to assume that corporate clients will rarely so decide. As such, to allow a corporate employer to discharge its in-house counsel under such circumstances, without fear of any sanction, is truly to give the assistance and protection of the courts to scoundrels.

Moreover, to recognize and sanction the corporate employer's freedom (as opposed to its "right") to discharge its in-house counsel under such circumstances, by denying the in-house counsel a cause of action for retaliatory discharge, is to exalt the at-will attorney-client contractual relationship above all other considerations, including the most important and fundamental public policy of protecting the lives and property of citizens. * * *

In holding as it does, the majority also reasons that an attorney's obligation to follow the Rules of Professional Conduct should not be the basis for a claim of retaliatory discharge.

Preliminarily, I would note that were an employee's desire to obey and follow the law an insufficient basis for a retaliatory discharge claim, *Palmateer* would have been decided differently. In this regard, I do not believe any useful purpose is served by distinguishing attorneys from ordinary citizens. It is incontrovertible that the law binds all men, kings and paupers alike. [C]. An attorney should not be punished simply because he has ethical obligations imposed upon him over and above the general obligation to obey the law which all men have. Nor should a corporate employer be protected simply because the employee it has discharged for "blowing the whistle" happens to be an attorney.

I find the majority's reasoning that an attorney's ethical obligations should not be the basis of a retaliatory discharge claim faulty for another reason. In so concluding, the majority ignores the employer's decision to persist in the questionable conduct which its in-house counsel advised was illegal. It is that conduct, not the attorney's ethical obligations, which is the predicate of the retaliatory discharge claim. That conduct is the true predicate of the claim because it is what required the attorney to act in compliance with his ethical obligations and thereby resulted in his discharge by the employer. As such, granting the attorney a claim for retaliatory discharge simply allows recovery against the party bent on breaking the law, rather than rewarding an attorney for complying with his ethical obligations.

Additionally, I cannot share the majority's solicitude for employers who discharge in-house counsel, who comply with their ethical obligations, by agreeing that they should not bear the economic burden which that compliance imposes upon the attorney. Unlike the majority, I do not believe that it is the attorney's compliance with his ethical obligations which imposes economic burdens upon him. Rather, those burdens are imposed upon him by the employer's persistence in conduct the attorney has advised is illegal and by the employer's wrongful termination of the attorney once he advises the employer that he must comply with those obligations.

Similarly, I do not believe that this case implicates any knowledge on an attorney's part that, in order to protect the integrity of the legal profession, he will have to forgo *prospective* economic gain. Plaintiff here did not merely forgo the prospect of economic gain in order to comply with his ethical obligations. Rather, he was wrongfully deprived of continued employment and its attendant benefits, economic and otherwise, simply because he sought to competently represent his client within the bounds of the law. 134 Ill.2d Preamble 472, Rules of Professional Conduct.

* * *

Ultimately, the court's decision in the instant case does nothing to encourage respect for the law by corporate employers nor to encourage respect by attorneys for their ethical obligations. [C]. Therefore, I must respectfully dissent.

Notes

1.   Can the holdings of *Wieder v. Skala* and *Balla v. Gambro Co.* be reconciled? Does the employment of in-house counsel contain an implied agreement that the lawyer will comply with the ethical standards of the legal profession?

2.   Should clients have an unlimited right to discharge their lawyers? For the lawyer's refusal to violate the law? Refusal to violate professional standards? Should clients be able to discharge a firm because it insists on assigning their cases to lawyers of a minority race or women lawyers? See MR 1.16(a)(3). Is the question whether the lawyer should be entitled to recover for retaliatory discharge or breach of contract a different issue?

3.   In Faretta v. California, 422 U.S. 806, 95 S. Ct. 2525, 45 L. Ed. 2d. 562 (1975) the Supreme Court held that a criminal defendant is not required to accept the assistance of counsel. The Court reasoned that compelling defendants to accept counsel over their objections limited the ability of clients to control their defense. Is this concern relevant when considering whether attorneys should be allowed to assert an action for wrongful discharge?

4.   In *Balla*, under Illinois' version of MR 1.6(b) the attorney was *required* to disclose information "to the extent it appears necessary to prevent the client from committing an act that would result in death or serious bodily injury." Under the ABA's version of MR 1.6(a), an attorney *may* reveal such information. How would the attorney's claim have been altered if he had been practicing in a jurisdiction that followed the ABA language?

5.   In General Dynamics v. Superior Court, 7 Cal. 4th 1164, 876 P.2d 487, 32 Cal.Rptr.2d 1 (1994), the California Supreme Court rejected *Balla* and held that in house counsel is entitled to bring a wrongful discharge claim.

Hull v. Celanese Corporation
513 F.2d 568 (2d Cir. 1975)

[Joan Hull brought this action against her employer, Celanese Corporation, alleging sex-based discrimination in employment in violation of Title VII of the Civil Rights Act of 1964. She was represented by the law firm of Rabinowitz, Boudin & Standard. Celanese denied the material allegations of the complaint.

Donata A. Delulio, an attorney on the corporate legal staff of Celanese, was assigned to work on the defense of the *Hull* case in February of 1973 and her work on the case continued until September 1973. Delulio characterized her work on the Hull case as follows:

"During the six months that I worked on that case I studied the general regulations of the Equal Employment Opportunities Commission, its procedures and the law on sex discrimination generally. I obtained specific information from the personnel department at the division concerning salaries and hiring practices. I attended on [sic] interview of the employee's [Hull's] superior, and attended one interview of another division employee. I participated in a conference with outside consultants hired by the corporation to prepare statistical information regarding employment within the division. I obtained inter-office memoranda and prepared a memorandum myself regarding the case."[4]

During September of 1973 Hull and Delulio met socially. Two months later Delulio approached Hull to ascertain the name of the law firm representing Hull. As a result of this conversation, Delulio contacted the Rabinowitz firm on November 9, and on November 15, 1973 the Rabinowitz firm filed sex discrimination charges on behalf of Delulio with the EEOC.

Delulio thereafter consulted with the Association of the Bar of the City of New York regarding the propriety of her intervention in the Hull action. By letter dated March 12, 1974, the Association advised Delulio against intervention. Subsequently, the Rabinowitz firm filed the motion herein seeking leave for Delulio and four other women to intervene as plaintiffs in the action. Celanese opposed the proposed intervention and sought the disqualification of the Rabinowitz firm based on the risk that confidential information received by Delulio as

---

[4]   [Court's note 9] Hull v. Celanese Corp., 1974 WL 3025, n.1 (S.D.N.Y.) quoting Delulio letter to Ass'n. of Bar, January 29, 1974. [The Committee advised Miss Delulio in writing that in its opinion she should neither intervene in the Hull action, nor prosecute her own action.]

Celanese's attorney might be used by the Rabinowitz firm against Celanese in the prosecution of the joint Hull-Delulio claims. The trial court denied Delulio's motion to intervene and subsequently ordered the disqualification of the Rabinowitz firm from representation of Hull.]

TENNEY, District Judge.

This Court today hears the appeal from an order of disqualification of plaintiff's counsel, the law firm of Rabinowitz, Boudin & Standard ("the Rabinowitz firm"). The question at issue is whether a law firm can take on, as a client, a lawyer for the opposing party in the very litigation against the opposing party. Factually, the case is novel and we approach it mindful of the important competing interests present. It is incumbent upon us to preserve, to the greatest extent possible, both the individual's right to be represented by counsel of his or her choice and the public's interest in maintaining the highest standards of professional conduct and the scrupulous administration of justice.

* * *

In the instant case we have a divergence from the more usual situation of the lawyer switching sides to represent an interest adverse to his initial representation [c]. Here, the in-house counsel for Celanese switched sides to become a plaintiff (rather than a lawyer) on the other side. Also, here the matter at issue is not merely "substantially related" to the previous representation, rather, it is exactly the same litigation. Thus, while the cases are factually distinguishable, the admonition of Canon 9 is equally appropriate here. This is, in short, one of those cases in which disqualification is "a necessary and desirable remedy . . . to enforce the lawyer's duty of absolute fidelity and to guard against the danger of inadvertent use of confidential information. . . ." [C].

The Rabinowitz firm argues that they had never worked for Celanese and therefore never had direct access to any confidences of Celanese. They maintain that they carefully cautioned Delulio not to reveal any information received in confidence as an attorney for Celanese, but rather to confine her revelations to them to the facts of her own case. This, they contend would avoid even an indirect transferral of confidential information. They conclude that since they never got any information either directly or indirectly, they could not use the information either consciously or unconsciously.

This argument, somewhat technical in nature, seems to overlook the spirit of Canon 9 as interpreted by this Court in *Emle*. We credit the efforts of the Rabinowitz firm to avoid the receipt of any confidence. Nonetheless, *Emle* makes it clear that the court need not "inquire whether the lawyer did, *in fact*, receive confidential information. . . ." *Emle Industries, Inc. v. Patentex, Inc., supra*, 478 F.2d at 571. Rather, "where 'it can reasonably be said that in the course of the former representation the attorney *might* have acquired information related to the subject matter of his subsequent representation,' *T.C. Theatre Corp., supra* [113 F.Supp.], at 269 (emphasis supplied), it is the court's duty to order the attorney disqualified." *Id.* at 571. The breach of confidence would not have to be proved; it is presumed in order to preserve the spirit of the Code.

The Rabinowitz firm had notice that Delulio had worked on the defense of the *Hull* case and should have declined representation when approached. Had Delulio joined the firm as an assistant counsel in the *Hull* case, they would have been disqualified. Here she joined them, as it were, as a client. The relation is no less damaging and the presumption in *Emle* should apply.

* * *

The novel factual situation presented here dictates a narrow reading of this opinion. This decision should not be read to imply that either Hull or Delulio cannot pursue her claim of employment discrimination based on sex. The scope of this opinion must, of necessity, be confined to the facts presented and not read as a broad-brush approach to disqualification.

The preservation of public trust both in the scrupulous administration of justice and in the integrity of the bar is paramount. Recognizably important are Hull's right to counsel of her choice and the consideration of the judicial economy which could be achieved by trying these claims in one lawsuit. These considerations must yield, however, to considerations of ethics which run to the very integrity of our judicial process.

Accordingly, the order of the district court is affirmed.

Notes

1.   The court's opinion suggests that Delulio may pursue her sex discrimination claim against Celanese with different counsel. Should Delulio be allowed to pursue her claim against Celanese? Even if

such pursuit requires the use of information that is confidential and subject to the attorney-client privilege?

2.   Model Rule 1.6 (confidentiality) is not violated by Delulio's use of the information obtained while she was representing Celenase. Do you see why? Does this mean that Delulio is free to disclose the information in the context of her case?

3.   Model Rule 1.6 would be violated if Delulio disclosed the information to Hull for use in Hull's lawsuit. Is there a principled way to distinguish the use of the information in Delulio's case from its use in Hull's case?

4.   Why can Delulio pursue her case, while Balla cannot pursue his claim?

B. Fees and Client Property

Read Model Rules 1.5 and 1.15[5]

Lisa G. Lerman, "Lying to Clients"
138 *U. Pa. L.Rev.* 659, 703-17 (1990)

* * *

I interviewed twenty lawyers to identify examples of lawyers deceiving clients. Most of these attorneys are in private practice, though a few work for the government or for other public service institutions. I spoke with people in various practices, including small firms, large firms, local practice, and national practice. The focus is on civil practice. The purpose of the study was not to expose egregious deception, but to probe the fabric of daily law practice to identify common types of deception.

* * *

1. Billing

Nearly all of the lawyers interviewed reported some amount of deception in practices relating to billing clients. In many instances the lawyers often failed to keep a running log of their time and estimated the number of hours they worked for their clients. Some attorneys

---

[5]   For MR 1.5, *cf.* DR 2-106, 2-107(A); EC 2-17 to 2-20, 2-22; Cal. Rule 4-200, 2-200; CAL. BUS. & PROF. CODE §§ 6147-6148 (Deering 1995). For MR 1.15, *cf.* DR 9-102; EC 9-5; Cal. Rule 4-100 and standards developed by the Board of Governors.

reported that they were too busy to keep detailed records. As long as any amounts added were trivial, most lawyers felt that there was nothing wrong with making good faith estimates of hours or with rounding off hours. Some believed that keeping accurate track of hours would result in more time billed to the clients. Therefore, they felt that this practice did not harm clients. If there was no harm, the lawyers often concluded that there was nothing wrong.

a. *Doing Nonessential Work—Running the Meter*

Several lawyers reported performing unnecessary work and then billing for it. This practice is deceptive if the lawyer conceals from the client what work is being done, or if the lawyer informs the client about the work but leads the client to believe that it is essential.

* * *

[Winston Hall reported:] "The most common [type of deception], by far, is makework that the client pays for but that didn't lead very directly to the result. That describes an enormous percentage of the activity that I think goes on in law firms." He described one conversation with a partner in his law firm, in which the partner explained that "law practice is somewhat supply-side driven. You can decide how heavily you are going to bill on a matter. There is a wide range of acceptability. If you've got the people, you do more work; if you don't have the people, then you don't." Hall contends that the problem with this phenomenon is twofold. First, the lawyer has too much discretion. "A business acquisition can cost anywhere between $20,000 and $100,000," depending on the lawyer's decisions about how to approach the work. Second, "the client can't even evaluate how [the lawyer] exercised that discretion after the fact."

Hall offered as an example one situation in which a company hired his firm and another firm to work on two very similar matters. His firm "did an exhaustive $100,000 job and produced a two-inch binder filled with memos. . . . [T]he other firm did a fifteen page memo that cost about $5,000." The client was "initially kind of horrified at the difference."

* * *

If clients understood the broad scope of the lawyer's discretion, they might exercise more control over what work was to be done. Hall elaborates:

The worst clients from the point of view of a lawyer are the expartners from the firm . . . who know damn well . . . [that lawyers do work to run the meter]. One lawyer . . . who [left to become general counsel of a client bank] would say, "I don't want a single memo written about this" . . . because he knew exactly what happens.

A few of the interviewees reported instances in which lawyers' pecuniary interests affected the settlement advice they gave to clients. David Larsen said that many solo practitioners are chronically short on cash and, consequently, have an added incentive to encourage settlement in contingent fee cases. Larsen described one situation in which a lawyer (who was representing his client's adversary) advised a client to settle a personal injury case worth $100,000 for a meager $4,700 to be paid over four years. The lawyer, a solo practitioner, had cash flow problems and needed money immediately.

In contrast, large firms that bill by the hour are more likely to run the meter. Madeline Stein, who worked in two firms in which most of the clients paid on an hourly basis, said: "From my experience it was more likely that a lawyer would attempt to deceive a client into continued litigation, including trial, by inflating the client's chances of success."

b. *Padding Bills and Double Billing*

One of the most significant types of billing deception reported was inflating or padding the bills of wealthy clients. Several different techniques were reported.

Some attorneys reported that the work performed did not always correspond to the hours billed. Michael Williams, characterizing a widespread attitude in his firm toward wealthy clients, said "some people in the firm feel like, 'well they are a rich client, they can pay, we can put a couple more hours down than we worked'. . . . Certainly that's deception, to the tune of tens of thousands."

* * *

Martin Richards, a former paralegal at a large law firm, reported that he had been ordered by a partner in the law firm to double-bill his time:

> In preparation for litigation and anticipated discovery on behalf of Client A, I was sent on a trip . . . to the client's HQ to review document files. . . .
> Meanwhile, a matter involving Client B was heating up. . . . The partner handling the Client B matter was also handling Client A. He asked that I take some of the [Client B] depositions with me and digest

them while on the road. He also said something to the effect, "Besides, it will give you something to do on the plane." Appraising the partner of the firm policy to bill transportation time to the client (in this case Client A), I asked how I should bill the time I spent digesting the depositions for Client B. He responded that I should bill the total transportation time to Client A and the time spent digesting depositions to Client B. In other words, double bill. . . .

[L]ater, in similar situations, the senior paralegal in charge of assignments let it be known that this is how billing was to be handled.

Richards found this experience somewhat disillusioning, because he had such respect for the integrity of the partner who gave him these instructions.

Mary Helen Murphy described one lawyer in her firm who would write his billing sheets three months after doing the work—without looking at his calendar. She said he did not need to look at his calendar because he only worked an average of two hours a day, but he billed twelve to sixteen hours per day. The hours billed usually were split between two clients. She reported this problem and numerous others to senior partners in the firm, but nothing was done to correct the problem. She also noted that the lawyer who was making up hours "had been threatened that if he didn't get his billing up, he would be fired."

Murphy spent months trying to get the law firm to pay attention to the incompetence and fraud that this senior associate was perpetrating. At one point he heard that she had been complaining about him. He came into her office and said:

"'You are not going to get away with this. Don't pull things like that on me.' And he closed the door and he started gesturing. . . his face was splotchy. . . . I said, 'Get out'. . . . I couldn't open the door . . . he had one fist up at me, and the other on the door. . . . I started to scream. One of the senior partners came down and said, 'We'll have to up his dose of lithium again and then the partner said to me 'Don't leave your scissor on that side of the desk.' That was their response to what this man had done. Murphy ultimately resigned from the law firm because of the unethical conduct that she observed there.

* * *

Another lawyer listed several reasons why padding of wealthy clients' bills is so common: (1) they can afford it, (2) one does so much work for them that it is easy to lose track, (3) padding is unlikely to be noticed because the bills are so large, (4) small clients have no money, and to keep hours up lawyers must bill the time to someone (which seems fair from a "Robin Hood" perspective), and (6) eventually the work done for one client is used for another.

David Larsen said he pads his bills to his clients to cover some related pro bono work. He does work for some states and for a non-profit group to which the state agencies belong. The state agency representatives have agreed (but have not told their superiors) that he should "fluff" his bills to the states to cover the work for the organization, thus subsidizing the organization. The "client" deceived by this practice is not the official who deals directly with the attorney, but the agency that employs the representative. The lawyer thinks that this practice is justifiable both because "the state benefits by it," and because he feels that his "client" is the person he is dealing with rather than the agency.

Most of the lawyers interviewed reported some relationship between the affluence of the client and their billing practices. Some mentioned that they were less scrupulous in recording hours worked for clients who were on retainer, while others reported that they were likely to round up their estimated hours if they knew the client could afford it. Many of the lawyers interviewed mentioned that they often under-billed clients who were friends or who were not in a position to pay large legal fees.

c. *Meeting Minimum Firm Hours Requirements*

Attorneys in many large, urban law firms are expected to bill up to 2500 hours a year. Consequently, they may bill hours that they have not worked.

Winston Hall said that his firm never established an explicit billing minimum. "The partners would say 1700 hours would be fine, which actually I thought was quite high. . . . The general impression that no partner ever tried to change [, however] was that 2000-2100 was expected."

Deborah Greenberg said that at her firm "the minimum for associates is 1700-1800 per year, or about 35 hours a week, not including administrative time and pro bono time. 1700-1800 used to be a target. Now it is a minimum." Although some lawyers inflated their hours to satisfy their firms' unreasonable demands, Alison Price, who works for a smaller firm, reported that she did not have enough work to bill the requisite number of hours. "The problem is that they want these many hours, and you're looking for work to do, and there is no work to do. You have to fudge."

d. *Premium Billing and Itemization*

Winston Hall explained that although many firms bill their clients by the hour, "premium billing"—adding substantial sums to the bills based on a subjective determination of the value of the work—is the latest innovation. Hall elaborates:

> The trend now in law firms is this concept of premium billing. Lawyers are on a feeding frenzy, and they are trying to figure out new ways to make money. So they pump up the hours of associates. There's got to be a limit to that; somewhere around 3000 hours, people start to die off.

> Billing rates are announced, and there are limits to how much you can charge. My guess is that my firm has increased 70-80 percent in 3-4 years, but I'm not sure. . . . When [lawyers] do a specially good job they want to bill extra money. Sometimes they tell clients that, and sometimes they don't. . . . It started in New York; Wachtel and Skadden invented it, and it has caught on in a big way. . . . Our firm tries to do it to the extent that they can. . . .

> Because that system [premium billing] has no apparent limits on money, it gets them tremendously excited, . . . this is how the firm is going to average, instead of half a million dollars a year, a million dollars a year per partner, by this premium billing. And then they point to investment bankers and say, investment bankers bill this way, why shouldn't we, we are smarter and we work harder. . . .

> This is using hours as a minimum, and taking further advantage of the information imbalances. . . . What it is moving toward is a vague notion of taking a larger share of the profits you earn for a client, but it is really taking advantage of the information unfairness.

Lawyers may be less than precise in billing practices with relative confidence that no one will ask too many embarrassing questions because the content of bills sent to clients offers little information on which to base questions. * * *

* * *

ABA Committee on Ethics and Professional Responsibility, Formal Opinion 379 (1993)
"Billing for Professional Fees, Disbursements and Other Expenses"

* * *

[The Committee has been asked to evaluate several billing practices.]

The first set of practices involves billing more than one client for the same hours spent. In one illustrative situation, a lawyer finds it possible to schedule court appearances for three clients on the same day. He spends a total of four hours at the courthouse, the amount of time he would have spent on behalf of each client had it not been for the fortuitous circumstance that all three cases were scheduled on the same day. May he bill each of the three clients, who otherwise understand that they will be billed on the basis of time spent, for the four hours he spent on them collectively? In another scenario, a lawyer is flying cross-country to attend a deposition on behalf of one client, expending travel time she would ordinarily bill to that client. If she decides not to watch the movie or read her novel, but to work instead on drafting a motion for another client, may she charge both clients, each of whom agreed to hourly billing, for the time during which she was traveling on behalf of one and drafting a document on behalf of the other? A third situation involves research on a particular topic for one client that later turns out to be relevant to an inquiry from a second client. May the firm bill the second client, who agreed to be charged on the basis of time spent on his case, the same amount for the recycled work product that it charged the first client?

* * *

[T]he lawyer who has agreed to bill on the basis of hours expended does not fulfill her ethical duty if she bills the client for more time than she actually spent on the client's behalf. In addressing the hypotheticals regarding (a) simultaneous appearance on behalf of three clients, (b) the airplane flight on behalf of one client while working on another client's matters and (c) recycled work product, it is helpful to consider these questions, not from the perspective of what a client could be forced to pay, but rather from the perspective of what the lawyer actually earned. A lawyer who spends four hours of time on behalf of three clients has not earned twelve billable hours. A lawyer who flies for six hours for one client, while working for five hours on behalf of another, has not earned eleven billable hours. A lawyer who is able to reuse old work product has not re-earned the hours previously billed and compensated when the work product was first generated. Rather than looking to profit from the fortuity of coincidental scheduling, the desire to get work done rather than watch a movie, or the luck of being asked the identical question twice, the lawyer who has agreed to bill solely on the basis of time spent is obliged to pass the benefits of these economies on to the client. The practice of billing several clients for the same time or work product, since it results in the earning of an unreasonable fee, therefore is contrary to the mandate of the Model Rules. Model Rule 1.5.

Moreover, continuous toil on or overstaffing a project for the purpose of churning out hours is also not properly considered "earning" one's fees. One job of a lawyer is to expedite the legal process. Model Rule 3.2. Just as a lawyer is expected to discharge a matter on summary judgment rather than proceed to trial if possible, so too is the lawyer expected to complete other projects for a client efficiently. A lawyer should take as much time as is reasonably required to complete a project, and should certainly never be motivated by anything other than the best interests of the client when determining how to staff or how much time to spend on any particular project.

* * *

Notes

1.   ABA formal opinion 93-379 also states:

[Lawyers must disclose the basis for future billing.] A corollary of the obligation to disclose the basis for future billing is a duty to render statements to the client that adequately apprise the client as to how that basis for billing has been applied. In an engagement in which the client has agreed to compensate the lawyer on the basis of time expended at regular hourly rates, a bill setting out no more than a total dollar figure for unidentified professional services will often be insufficient to tell the client what he or she needs to know in order to understand how the amount was determined. By the same token, billing other charges without breaking the charges down by type would not provide the client with the information the client needs to understand the basis for the charges.

2.   Hourly billing was noncontroversial until about 20 years ago when abuses like those described by Professor Lerman began to

surface. This has led to the creation of a new industry, legal fee audit firms. Many of these firms do nothing but review fee statements for abuse. Often the audit firms are compensated solely on the amount of savings a client receives from abuses identified.

3.   MR 1.5(a), Model Code DR 2-106(b), and California RPC 4-200 all list substantially the same factors that are to be considered in determining whether a lawyer's fee is proper. Yet under MR 1.5(a) the fee must "not be unreasonable"; under DR 2-106 the fee must be not "clearly excessive"; and under California RPC 4-200 the fee must not be "unconscionable." Which is the better standard? Does it matter?

———

Always controversial, contingent fees have been prohibited in every Western European nation. Many within the tort reform movement believe these fees encourage frivolous litigation. Defenders argue that this system of compensation enables people, who otherwise could not afford a lawyer, to obtain representation.

Committee on Legal Ethics of the West Virginia State Bar
v. Gallaher
180 W. Va. 332, 376 S.E.2d 346 (1988)

MILLER, Justice:

* * *

On February 14, 1985, sixty-four year old Neva Dillon was a passenger in a motor vehicle operated by her son, Junior M. Dillon. Mrs. Dillon was injured when her son's vehicle slid on icy roads and struck an approaching vehicle near Van, West Virginia. As a consequence of the collision, Mrs. Dillon incurred medical bills in excess of $2300.

Junior Dillon was insured under a liability policy issued by Mountaineer Fire and Casualty Insurance Company. * * * For approximately one month, Mrs. Dillon dealt directly with Mountaineer and rejected Mountaineer's initial settlement offer of $726.25.

On the recommendation of her son, Mrs. Dillon decided to retain a lawyer to represent her in further negotiations with Mountaineer. On March 25, 1985, she met with Mr. Gallaher at his office in

Fayetteville to discuss her case. Mrs. Dillon was not well educated, lacked prior experience with lawyers, and was unable to read or write.

Mr. Gallaher explained to Mrs. Dillon that it would be necessary to file a claim against Mountaineer, and possibly to file a civil suit against her son. Mrs. Dillon stated that she did not want to sue her son. Mr. Gallaher contends that he informed her that the possibility of recovery in the case was rather slim, but stated he would see what he could do. No written fee contract was executed at that time and fees were not discussed.

Mr. Gallaher's position is that his activities in preparing the case included obtaining a written medical authorization from Mrs. Dillon, reviewing pertinent medical records and bills, and forwarding such information to Mountaineer. By letter dated September 4, 1985, Mr. Gallaher made a formal settlement demand of $8,500. Almost three weeks later, Mountaineer responded with a settlement offer of $4,500. Mr. Gallaher immediately accepted this offer.

On September 26, 1985, Mr. Gallaher met with Mrs. Dillon at her home in Bob White, West Virginia. When her family inquired about Mountaineer's offer, Mr. Gallaher stated that $4,500 was the best settlement available under the circumstances. Mrs. Dillon assented to the settlement and executed a release of all claims. Mr. Gallaher stated at this time that his fee would be 50 percent of the settlement, or $2,250.

* * *

In justifying his 50 percent fee, Mr. Gallaher presented to the Committee an itemized time sheet showing 16.6 hours of work in the case. Two lawyers who practice in Fayette County were called by Mr. Gallaher to testify. One of the lawyers stated that the normal contingent fee in the vicinity was 33⅓ percent for cases settled prior to trial, and 40 percent for cases actually tried. Testimony by the other lawyer tended to show that the normal fee was 33⅓ percent for cases settled without suit, and 40 percent for cases in which suit was filed. There was also testimony that Mr. Gallaher's fee, the equivalent of $140 per hour, was not clearly excessive.

The Committee asserts that Mr. Gallaher's 50 percent contingent fee was clearly excessive in violation of DR 2-106 [*Cf.* MR 1.5]. It recommends a public reprimand and restitution to Mrs. Dillon of $450. For the reasons that follow, we adopt the Committee's recommendation of a public reprimand, but order restitution of $750.

* * *

[In Committee of Legal Ethics v. Tatterson, 352 S.E. 2d 107 (W.Va. 1986), we stated:]

> If an attorney's fee is grossly disproportionate to the services rendered and is charged to a client who lacks full information about all of the relevant circumstances, the fee is `clearly excessive' within the meaning of Disciplinary Rule 2-106(A) [Cf. MR 1.5(a) ("fee shall be reasonable")], even though the client has consented to such fee. The burden of proof is upon the attorney to show the reasonableness and fairness of the contract for the attorney's fee.

* * *

[W]e conclude that Mr. Gallaher's fee violated DR 2-106. There was never any anticipation that suit would be filed due to the family relationship. It was also clear that Mrs. Dillon was prepared to accept a modest settlement. This was confirmed by Mr. Gallaher's ability to accept Mountaineer's first offer of $4,500 without discussing the same with Mrs. Dillon. Furthermore, the lawyer's investment of time and skill was de minimus.

* * *

We readily acknowledge that the risk involved in Mrs. Dillon's case was substantial, and that a contingent fee was warranted. Nevertheless, we find the fee to be grossly disproportionate under *Tatterson.* Mr. Gallaher expended, at most, 16.6 hours in all aspects of the case. This time consisted principally of review of medical records, telephone conferences, and routine correspondence. No specialized skills were required and no novel questions were presented.

We find another fact to be of critical importance to the outcome of this case. * * * [T]he lawyer's fee was so great that the plaintiff was not made whole. It is significant that, after deduction of Mr. Gallaher's fee, the sum received by Mrs. Dillon was less than her uncontested special damages. We, therefore, conclude that the fee was clearly excessive in violation of DR 2-106.

* * *

Notes

1.   The Court is influenced by the fact that the client was not made whole. Is that relevant? Suppose liability was contested and the case was settled for less than the special damages.

2.   "If it were not for contingent fees, indigent victims of tortious accidents would be subject to the unbridled, self-willed partisanship of their tortfeasors. The person who has, without fault on his part, been injured and who, because of his injury, is unable to work, and has a large family to support, and has no money to engage a lawyer, would be at the mercy of the person who disabled him because, being in a superior economic position, the injuring person could force on his victim, desperately in need of money to keep the candle of life burning in himself and his dependent ones, a wholly unconscionable meager sum in settlement or even refuse to pay him anything at all. Any society, and especially a democratic one, worthy of respect in the spectrum of civilization, should never tolerate such a victimization of the weak by the mighty.

Richette v. Solomon, 187 A.2d 910, 919 (Pa. 1963).

3.   Under the typical contingency fee agreement, the lawyer agrees to represent a client in exchange for a percentage of any recovery received through settlement or successful completion of litigation. Many people associate such agreements with lawyers representing plaintiffs in personal injury litigation. However, as clients have become more dissatisfied with hourly billing, contingency fee agreements are being used to compensate lawyers for defending litigation or doing the legal work for transactions. When used to pay defense counsel, the fee is calculated on the basis of the money saved by a successful defense. When used to pay transactional lawyers, the fee may represent a percentage of the value of the transaction.

4.   Critics of contingency fees have argued that contingency fees are unethical, since lawyers will suggest or agree to a contingency fee over an hourly rate only where recovery is virtually certain. The lawyer gets a percentage of the portion of the recovery that is not a product of the lawyer's work. Under such circumstances, it is suggested that the premium inherent in contingency fees is unearned and represents overreaching by the lawyers.[6] Supporters argue that fees earned in cases where recovery is virtually certain compensate lawyers for the cases they accept where recovery is more tenuous. The ABA Standing Committee on Ethics and Professional Responsibility recently concluded that contingency fees are ethical if the client

---

[6]   Lester Brinkman, "ABA Regulation of Contingency Fees: Money Talks, Ethics Walks," 65 *Fordham L. Rev.* 247 (1996).

is fully informed about alternative billing systems, and agrees to the contingency fee.[7]

5.   There is a danger that contingency fees will affect the advice a lawyer gives to a client. When the lawyer has a personal stake in the outcome of the representation, it can be more difficult to render the independent judgment the client is entitled to under MR 2.1. Recall an example from Chapter 2:

> Assume that you are representing a poor plaintiff in a personal injury action. You estimate that there is a 90 percent chance that she will win a $100,000 verdict. She is afraid of going to trial, both because of the risk that she will lose and because she fears the stress of cross-examination. She has received a $15,000 settlement offer and she is inclined to take it. What do you do?

Assuming a contingency fee of one-third, the lawyer will receive $5,000 if she settles and $33,333 if she wins at trial. As you can see, the economics of the contingency fee alter the system of incentives and disincentives experienced by lawyers. In other contingency fee cases lawyers may profit more from quickly settling a case, than from diligently litigating it. Hourly fees create different incentives. What are they?

6.   Several jurisdictions place caps on contingency fees in some types of cases. This has been a common response to the "litigation explosion" in recent years. Are such caps on contingency fees justified? What are the problems with caps on contingency fees?

7.   MR 1.5(d) prohibits fees that are contingent on the securing of a divorce or upon the amount of alimony in a domestic relations matter and prohibits all contingent fees in criminal cases. Why do you think contingent fees in such cases are prohibited?

8.   *Client Trust Accounts*—Model Rule 1.15 requires lawyers to keep clients' money and property separate from their own, to keep adequate records, and to notify clients when they receive money or property that belongs to the client. The requirement that lawyers keep client funds in a separate account is a common source of lawyer discipline. When lawyers receive money that belongs to the client, they should immediately place it in a client trust account, an account that is separate from the lawyer's and law firm's funds.

---

[7]   ABA Formal Ethics Opinion 94-389 (1994).

Chapter Seven

PROVISION OF LEGAL SERVICES

A. Public Service and Representation of the Poor

The following is from an address that Louis Brandeis gave to the Harvard Ethical Society in 1905. What parts of Brandeis' speech might be written today?

Louis D. Brandeis, "The Opportunity in the Law"
Business: A Profession 313, 321-27 (1914)
* * *

It is true that at the present time the lawyer does not hold as high a position with the people as he held seventy-five or indeed fifty years ago; but the reason is not lack of opportunity. It is this: Instead of holding a position of independence, between the wealthy and the people, prepared to curb the excesses of either, able lawyers have, to a large extent, allowed themselves to become adjuncts of great corporations and have neglected the obligation to use their powers for the protection of the people. We hear much of the "corporation lawyer," and far too little of the "people's lawyer." The great opportunity of the American Bar is and will be to stand again as it did in the past, ready to protect also the interests of the people.

* * *

The leading lawyers of the United States have been engaged mainly in supporting the claims of the corporations; often in endeavoring to evade or nullify the extremely crude laws by which legislators sought to regulate the power or curb the excesses of corporations.

Such questions as the regulation of trusts, the fixing of railway rates, the municipalization of public utilities, the relation between capital and labor, call for the exercise of legal ability of the highest order. Up to the present time the legal ability of a high order which has been expended on those questions has been almost wholly in opposition to the contentions of the people. The leaders of the Bar, without any preconceived intent on their part, and rather as an incident to their professional standing, have, with rare exceptions, been ranged on the side of the corporations, and the people have been represented, in the main, by men of very meager legal ability.

If these problems are to be settled right, this condition cannot continue. Our country is, after all, not a country of dollars, but of ballots. The immense corporate wealth will necessarily develop a hostility from which much trouble will come to us unless the excesses of capital are curbed, through the respect for law, as the excesses of democracy were curbed seventy-five years ago. There will come a revolt of the people against the capitalists, unless the aspirations of the people are given some adequate legal expression; and to this end cooperation of the abler lawyers is essential.

For nearly a generation the leaders of the Bar have, with few exceptions, not only failed to take part in constructive legislation designed to solve in the public interest our great social, economic and industrial problems; but they have failed likewise to oppose legislation prompted by selfish interests. They have often gone further in disregard of common weal. They have often advocated, as lawyers, legislative measures which as citizens they could not approve, and have endeavored to justify themselves by a false analogy. They have erroneously assumed that the rule of ethics to be applied to a lawyer's advocacy is the same where he acts for private interests against the public, as it is in litigation between private individuals.

The ethical question which laymen most frequently ask about the legal profession is this: How can a lawyer take a case which he does not believe in? The profession is regarded as necessarily somewhat immoral, because its members are supposed to be habitually taking cases of that character. As a practical matter, the lawyer is not often harassed by this problem; partly because he is apt to believe, at the time, in most of the cases that he actually tries; and partly because he either abandons or settles a large number of those he does not believe in. But the lawyer recognizes that in trying a case his prime duty is to present his side to the tribunal fairly and as well as he can, relying upon his adversary to present the other side fairly and as well as he can. Since the lawyers on the two sides are usually reasonably well matched, the judge or jury may ordinarily be trusted to make such a decision as justice demands.

But when lawyers act upon the same principle in supporting the attempts of their private clients to secure or to oppose legislation, a very different condition is presented. In the first place, the counsel selected to represent important private interests possesses usually ability of a high order, while the public is often inadequately represented or wholly unrepresented. Great unfairness to the public is apt to result from this fact. Many bills pass in our legislatures which would not have become law, if the public interest had been fairly represented; and many good bills are defeated which if supported by able lawyers would have been enacted. Lawyers have, as a rule, failed to consider this distinction between practice in courts involving only private interests, and practice before the legislature or city council involving public interests. Some men of high professional standing have even endeavored to justify their course in advocating professionally legislation which in their character as citizens they would have voted against.

* * *

Here, consequently, is the great opportunity in the law. The next generation must witness a continuing and ever-increasing contest between those who have and those who have not. The industrial world is in a state of ferment. The ferment is in the main peaceful, and, to a considerable extent, silent; but there is felt to-day very widely the inconsistency in this condition of political democracy and industrial absolutism. The people are beginning to doubt whether in the long run democracy and absolutism can co-exist in the same community; beginning to doubt whether there is a justification for the great inequalities in the distribution of wealth, for the rapid creation of fortunes, more mysterious than the deeds of Aladdin's lamp. The people have begun to think; and they show evidences on all sides of a tendency to act. . . . The people's thought will take shape in action; and it lies with us, with you to whom in part the future belongs, to say on what lines the action is to be expressed; whether it is to be expressed wisely and temperately, or wildly and intemperately; whether it is to be expressed on lines of evolution or on lines of revolution. Nothing can better fit you for taking part in the solution of these problems, than the study and preëminently the practice of law. Those of you who feel drawn to that profession may rest assured that you will find in it an opportunity for usefulness which is probably unequalled. There is a call upon the legal profession to do a great work for this country.

Notes

1. Brandeis "practiced what he preached." Earnings from his corporate practice financed a substantial representation of public

interest causes. He "reimbursed" his law firm for the time that he spent in his *pro bono* practice. In one case, he paid his own firm $25,000 for his own time used on a public interest case.[1]

Brandeis was concerned with the public interest in his corporate practice, as well as his *pro bono* practice. At the contentious Senate hearings over Brandeis' nomination to the United States Supreme Court, he was criticized by some for taking a "judicial attitude toward his clients."

> "A banker testified that Brandeis, as a lawyer, had required satisfaction of the justness of the banker's cause before deciding to take it on. No other lawyer he had ever dealt with, the banker testified, raised that question."[2]

2. Should, as Brandeis suggests, lawyers appearing before legislative bodies have a different responsibility than those appearing in court? In a legislative setting, are adjustments in the adversary ethic in order? The comments to Model Rule 3.9 state "legislatures and administrative agencies have a right to expect lawyers to deal with them as they deal with courts."

3. In addition to the professional rules, lawyers appearing before legislative bodies may be subject to laws regulating lobbyists. These laws often require registration as a lobbyist, and compliance with other regulations governing contact with legislators. The Federal Regulation of Lobbying Act is found at 2 U.S.C. § 261-70. The relationship between legal ethics and the ethics governing lobbyists is explored in Thomas M. Susman, *The Lobbying Manual: A Compliance Guide for Lawyers and Lobbyists* (1993).

4. May a lawyer, as a private citizen, advocate changes in the law that are contrary to client interests? *See* Model Rules 1.2(b) and 6.4.

Imperial Discount Corp. v. Jake Aiken
38 Misc. 2d 187, 238 N.Y.S.2d 269 (N.Y. Civ. Ct. 1963)

FRANK COMPOSTO, Judge.

This is an action on a retail installment contract by Imperial Discount Corporation, an alleged purchaser for value of said contract.

---

[1] *See* Thomas L. Shaffer, *American Legal Ethics: Text, Readings, and Discussion Topics* 242 (1985) (citing Michael Schudson, "Public, Private and Professional Lives: The Correspondence of David Dudley Field and Samuel Bowles," 21 *Am. J. Legal Hist.* 191, 210-11 (1977)).

[2] *Id.* (quoting Schudson, *supra*, note 1 at 210). For further discussion of Brandeis and his law practice, *see id.* at 241-308.

After a hearing held on this inquest, the plaintiff's complaint is dismissed.

Despite the fact that there is no appearance on behalf of the defendant, the Court deems itself duty-bound to require of the plaintiff that minimum measure of proof to sustain its cause of action. While the Court will sustain a recovery to which a plaintiff is justly and fairly entitled, it will not grant judgment where, as here, plaintiff has failed to prove to the satisfaction of the Court that it met the statutory prerequisites.

The defendant, owner of a 1955 Oldsmobile, purchased a Delco battery on credit from a retail auto store for $29.30. In order to be permitted to pay by weekly installments, he agreed to a "credit service charge of $5.70." He thus started his journey into the cavernous depths of indebtedness with his 1955 Oldsmobile, a new Delco battery and a debt of $35.00, attested to by his signature on the aforesaid retail installment contract with its inevitable fine print and legalistic verbiage.

He failed to make due and timely weekly payments, and there came a time when a summons and verified complaint of eight paragraphs was served upon him in this case. All of the allegations or charges hereinafter mentioned are made, according to the verified complaint, "pursuant to the terms of the said chattel mortgage and retail installment contract."

Paragraph third of the complaint relates to the purchase by defendant "of certain goods, wares, and merchandise (the battery), at the agreed and stated price of $35.00, no part of which has been paid, excepting the sum of $23.25, leaving a balance due and owing of $11.75."

Paragraph fourth alleges the defendant owes late charges of twenty-five cents.

Paragraph fifth alleges defendant owes plaintiff's attorney fees of $16.80.

Paragraph sixth alleges the defendant owes plaintiff repossessing charges of $45.00. The retail installment contract had a provision that "The buyer hereby mortgages the motor vehicle hereinafter described as additional security for the payment of the time balance set forth above, together with any other motor vehicle hereinafter acquired in replacement thereof." Plaintiff caused the defendant's automobile to be repossessed, and as alleged in paragraph seventh, the repossessed automobile was sold at public auction, and the defendant owes auctioneer's fees of $35.00 and storage charges of $70.00, based on a charge of $2.50 per day for 28 days.

Paragraph eighth is the only paragraph in which the defendant may find a modicum of comfort. It does not allege he owes for any item of damage—in fact, he is given credit for $50, the amount for which his repossessed automobile was sold. Then follows the allegation "That pursuant to the said chattel mortgage and installment contract, there is presently due the total of $128.80."

When the defendant's journey, which started with an indebtedness of $35.00, of which $23.25 had been paid, leaving a balance of $11.75, reached its unsought destination in this court, the defendant was *sans* his battery, *sans* his automobile, and confronted with a demand for "judgment for $128.80, together with interest, costs, and disbursements of this action." The futility of trying to free himself of the engulfing accumulation of charges must have so overwhelmed the defendant, that he failed to answer the summons and complaint, and thus this inquest.

The defendant must now have realized the import of the despairing observation that "For want of a nail, a shoe was lost; for want of a shoe, a horse was lost; for want of a horse, a kingdom was lost." For want of $11.75, this defendant lost the battery, lost his 1955 Oldsmobile, and is subject to a judgment for $128.80.

The proof offered by plaintiff fails to satisfy the Court that it complied with all the prerequisites of the applicable law; but transcending questions of proof the conscience of the Court is shocked by the mountainous pyramiding of charges imposed on a defaulting installment buyer, which are seemingly sanctioned by the Retail Installment Sales Act [c]. Apparently this is not an isolated case. The Court is of the opinion that the Legislature never contemplated such oppressive, confiscatory, and unconscionable results. If this is an example of the practical working of the aforesaid law, then clearly the need for remedial legislation is manifest.

Judgment on inquest denied, complaint dismissed.

Note

Brandeis criticizes lawyers both for failing to represent public interests and for failing to take the public interest into consideration when representing corporations. Which is the problem in this case? Did the problem arise when litigation began or before? Did Aiken need legal representation or did Imperial Discount Corporation need a different sort of representation? If you think that Aiken needed legal representation, at what point did he need it? Should he have had a lawyer review the retail installment contract? Should Imperial's lawyer have drafted this contract? Imperial lost this case, but it may be that many consumers paid substantial amounts to Imperial under purchase agreements containing this language.

Read Model Rules 6.1 to 6.5[3]

The Legal Needs of the Poor

The *Aiken* case illustrates the large number of generally invisible unmet legal needs of the poor and middle class in the United States. Two studies in recent years demonstrate that ordinary people in the United States have substantial unmet legal needs. The American Bar Foundation study, conducted initially in 1974 and updated in 1989,[4] found, for example, that people in America take to a lawyer only one percent of job discrimination problems, 10 percent of tort problems, and 36 percent of real property problems.[5] Another study found that only 20 percent of the legal problems of those with income of 125 percent or less of the poverty level receive legal services.[6]

Concern with the unmet legal needs of the poor led the federal government in 1974 to establish the Legal Services Corporation. The number of attorneys employed by the Legal Services Corporation grew to 6,000 in 1980, but federal budget cuts reduced that number to 4,000 in 1995.

---

[3]   For MR 6.1 *cf.*, EC 2-25, 8-3; there is no Cal. Rules counterpart. For MR 6.2 *cf.*, EC 2-29 to -30; there is no Cal. Rules counterpart. For MR 6.3 *cf.* Cal. Rules 1-600; there is no Model Code counterpart. There is no comparable provision in either the Model Code or the Cal. Rules to MR 6.4 or 6.5.

[4]   Barbara A. Curran & Francis O. Spaulding, *The Legal Needs of the Public* (1974), and Barbara A. Curran, "Report on the 1989 Survey of the Public's Use of Legal Services," in ABA Consortium on Legal Services for the Public, *Two Nationwide Surveys: 1989 Public Assessment of the Poor & Public Generally* 55 (1989), *cited in* Roger C. Cramton, "Delivery of Legal Services to Ordinary Americans," 44 *Case W. Res. L. Rev.* 531, 541 (1994).

[5]   *Id.* at 542-43.

[6]   The Spangenberg Group, Inc., "National Survey of the Civil Legal Needs of the Poor," in ABA Consortium on Legal Services for the Public, *Two Nationwide Surveys: 1989 Pilot Assessment of the Poor & Public Generally* 37 (1989), *cited id.* at 543, n. 33.

An early Kutak Commission draft of MR 6.1 would have required lawyers to provide *pro bono* legal services.[7] The rule that eventually emerged is one of the only Model Rules that uses hortatory language: "A lawyer *should* render public interest legal service." In 1993, after attempts to require public service, the ABA amended the rule to suggest that lawyers provide 50 hours of *pro bono* service a year. The 2002 amendments added the following language: "Every lawyer has a professional responsibility to provide legal services to those unable to pay."

Several jurisdictions have debated proposals that would require public service representation. We will look at one such debate. In the late 1980s, Chief Judge Wachtler of the New York Court of Appeals appointed the Marrero Committee (named after its chairman) to consider the legal needs of the poor. In 1990, the Marrero Committee proposed that the professional rules require lawyers to provide legal services to the poor. Under the Marrero proposal, lawyers could meet the requirement in one of three methods. First, they could contribute 40 hours of legal services every two years. Within a law firm, the hours of one lawyer could be used to meet the requirements of other lawyers. Second, lawyers could hire another lawyer to provide their legal services. As a third alternative, lawyers in firms of ten or less could pay $1000 for the provision of legal services to the poor. We begin with portions of the Marrero Committee's report.

Committee to Improve the Availability of Legal Services, "Final Report to the Chief Judge of the State of New York"
19 *Hofstra L. Rev.* 755, 824-28 (1990)
* * *

F. Mandatory vs. Voluntary Plan

[I]n framing its response to the legal services crisis the Committee considered whether the problem could be adequately remedied by alternate plans that would rely primarily on voluntary rather than obligatory measures. After extensive debate of the merits of each approach the Committee rejected the voluntarism alternative as inappropriate and unresponsive to the need. A majority of the

---

[7]   Kutak Commission Discussion Draft, Proposed Rule 6.1 (Jan. 30, 1980).

organized Bar in the State, however, reached a contrary view. While acknowledging, at the Committee's public hearings and in written comments, that a significant unmet need exists for free civil legal services for the poor, almost uniformly bar associations across the State concluded that any contribution by lawyers to relieve the problem should be strictly voluntary. In fact, stimulated by the Committee's proposals, the State Bar Association and several county bar associations formulated their own alternative plans, all of which rely on raising lawyers' contribution of voluntary pro bono services to unprecedented heights.

[W]e believe that the voluntary/mandatory debate reflects a fundamental difference in professional outlook towards the lawyer's pro bono obligation. Some proponents of voluntarism seem to regard lawyers' public interest service as individual charity. In the context of the legal services crisis, we see it as a professional duty. As charity, a pro bono service contribution would take lesser rank among lawyers' other professional pressures and even personal commitments that are not obligatory. As a professional duty, rendering pro bono services rises to the standing of an unavoidable obligation. This distinction is not merely philosophical, but has a practical effect in public policy. Because as a public and professional duty the lawyers' pro bono obligation could not easily be avoided, its recognition as such is likely to result in the contribution of more legal services than a program understood and carried out as charity, under which every contribution is a purely discretionary act of kindness.

Second, the Committee expressed deep skepticism about the prospects for increasing volunteer legal services on a sustained basis to the optimistic levels the organized Bar hopes to attain. We voiced doubts not because we would discount the value of the legal services that volunteer lawyers provide to the poor, nor because of any a priori bias against alternatives to the Committee's plan. Rather, we were persuaded by substantial empirical evidence that volunteer efforts would not succeed in significantly closing the gap between legal services available to the poor and the critical need. The recent history of a number of campaigns in several jurisdictions to enlist significant numbers of volunteer lawyers for pro bono service proves the point.

* * *

* * * [A] fair estimate of the rate of pro bono participation in organized Bar programs [for the poor] by all admitted attorneys in the

State [of New York] would be roughly 10 percent, a number in line with estimates of the nation-wide proportion of lawyers performing pro bono services for the poor.

But even if the level of voluntary pro bono participation in any given period were to rise dramatically, it would not correct one basic flaw of voluntarism that affects not just legal services, but other activities deemed to be merely charity: participation is essentially uneven and sometimes unreliable. It takes extraordinary effort and resources, as well as extraordinary leadership, to appreciably boost voluntary contributions of services. And generally the intensity of effort is not sustained at its peak. Rather, it fluctuates from time to time, intensifying in direct proportion to the impact and proximity of significant events and applied pressure from the boosters of voluntarism, but ebbing as pressure lets up, as the initial volunteer campaign euphoria fades, as news coverage ends, as the leadership propelling the voluntary drives changes, as the interest and commitment of volunteers wane when other professional demands reclaim their higher priorities in sum, as life, like water, returns to its more natural level when the intensity of focus of voluntarism subsides. Then, foreseeably, charity's impulse slackens to its more customary pace and the booster's appeal begins to lose force.

Actual results of some recent efforts to boost volunteer legal services revealed the fundamental inadequacy of voluntarism and confirm our doubts about the reality of achieving better prospects. In New York, the Association of the Bar of the City of New York organized Volunteers of Legal Service, Inc. (VOLS) in 1984. Law firms in the City were asked to pledge a minimum of 30 hours of pro bono legal services per attorney. With the Association of the Bar strongly behind the campaign, 75 firms with approximately 9500 lawyers pledged. Although most of the largest firms were included, these represent a small percentage of New York City's more than 1850 law firms and about 16 percent of the approximately 57,000 lawyers practicing in the City. In a recent survey of the program, 43 of the 75 firms responded. Of these, 32 (with 5892 lawyers) reported that they had reached the goal for the year. Twenty-six of the responding firms said that they had met the standard during each of the five years since the program began. Fourteen indicated that they had not met the goal for the year, although they provided services at a lower per-lawyer standard. We cite this record to exemplify not a particular failure of voluntarism, but the reasonable limits of its success. The VOLS results may reflect the maximum achievement that voluntarism can reasonably be expected to yield over time under the most favorable circumstances. It sustains our view that even in a climate of urgency, backed by dynamic, respected and committed leadership, and directed at the segment of the profession best placed to contribute, charity can squeeze out volunteers only so far.

* * *

The validity of our skepticism was most recently confirmed by events prompted by the Committee's proposal. At all of our public hearings, local bar associations, one after another, spoke with pride of impressive programs and campaigns they had recently embarked upon to increase voluntarism among their members in projects designed to meet the legal services needs of the poor. These efforts were worthy, creative, did credit to their sponsors and were long overdue. But among the associations which had programs already underway, none reported volunteer lawyer participation in excess of 10 to 15 percent of their members and, of course, still smaller proportions of the lawyers practicing in their geographic areas. From one point of view, these results are impressive; but from the point of view of rallying all of the Bar to do its duty of meeting the need for legal services for the poor, the results are modest indeed. They are more disappointing given the undeniable spur provided by 'apprehension of mandatory pro bono. This experience underscores our basic point: Herculean efforts producing voluntary responses praiseworthy by historical standards simply do not produce a response acceptable by any other practical measure.

* * *

In short, then, the "voluntarism" so eloquently extolled and advocated by the organized Bar may well amount to little more than a rallying cry for the status quo. When all is said and done, only the same disappointingly small proportion of practicing attorneys who now contribute pro bono efforts to the poor would be counted upon to continue bearing the full load for the rest of the legal profession. To shunt the weight of this responsibility to a limited number of volunteers and permit as many as 85 to 90 percent of the other members of the Bar to escape their proper share of a professional duty in times of critical need, we believe, is unconscionable in principle and inherently unfair to those who do contribute. Perhaps even more important, it would inevitably shortchange the legal needs of the poor and fail to give the corresponding crisis in our legal system the serious consideration and response it requires. Given the magnitude of the problems and their deeper implications, it is a shirking of professional responsibility for every attorney capable of doing so not to make some reasonable contribution to relieve the unmet legal services need, and instead to let volunteers and the rest of society respond when and if they choose to do so.

[A]dherents of voluntarism also argue that the relative effectiveness of voluntary versus mandatory programs favors their approach. Volunteers, they say, would provide more effective service because they would contribute willingly, unhindered by the counterproductive resentment that lawyers would feel under a compulsory rule. We disagree. * * *

* * *

[In our view lawyers would accept and fulfill their pro bono services responsibilities professionally and effectively.] First, it is ingrained in lawyers' professional training to perform effectively and advocate zealously on behalf of their clients, consistent with the ethical canons that enjoin their utmost professional effort in providing legal representation. And second, we feel that lawyers would respond to compulsory service not only as lawyers but as citizens. We know from experience that most citizens, especially in times of crisis, generally respond to obligatory civic duties with appropriate public spirit and good faith. Jury duty, military service, and even paying taxes often cause inconvenience and are sometimes greeted with initial resentment. But, when called to serve, most people place personal attitudes aside, recognize the public purpose and higher duty involved in the call and comply uneventfully. No persuasive reason has been given for us to believe that lawyers would react differently to required pro bono service, especially if, as is the case with the Committee's proposal, the obligation is flexibly drawn and reasonably administered.

* * *

Roger C. Cramton, "Mandatory Pro Bono"
19 *Hofstra L. Rev.* 1113, 1132-33, 1135-36 (1991)

* * *

MORAL OBJECTIONS TO PRO BONO REQUIREMENT

The principal moral objections to mandatory pro bono are:

First, it is a violation of individual liberty to compel a lawyer to give her time to particular activities. * * *

* * * This is a normative question resting upon an assessment of competing moral claims and of prudential considerations such as the seriousness of the social need and the relative desirability of alternatives.

Second, opponents of mandatory pro bono argue that converting a gift of volunteered service into a compelled exaction spoils the moral significance of the basic choice we all should make. Such choices are the embodiment of what it means to be a good lawyer. In a sense, the concept of mandatory pro bono is an oxymoron, like military music. The pro bono concept has at its heart the idea of the committed citizen who chooses to further the public interest rather than exclusively his own. Is the moral significance of this choice decreased when the ideal of aspiration is replaced by the morality of duty? Will duty produce better results than the continued assertion of moral obligation? The better view embraces the preference of private choice over public mandate. There is some validity to George Bush's "thousand points of light." Requiring citizens to work on the roads or to staff soup lines as a civic obligation is at odds with present-day notions of liberty and moral choice. Arguably, taxing them to provide these services is less of an imposition.

Law, as well as moral thinking, distinguishes between the payment of money and compelled services. Just as specific performance is thought of as an exceptional remedy as distinct from an award of damages, ordering an individual to provide services is more intrusive upon the core of individuality than a general law requiring the same individual to pay money (e.g., a portion of income). Although taxation can be onerous, requirements that take the form of personal service are more likely to result in angry or principled opposition.

Finally, mandatory pro bono proposals tend to be regressive and inequitable, imposing a heavy burden on economically marginal lawyers and harried associates, while treating more gently those at the senior ranks of large law firms. The Marrero proposal does not avoid this unfairness. The senior partners of a large law firm can meet their pro bono obligation by assigning an associate to work six months in a legal services office or by pooling dollar contributions to hire a full-time poverty lawyer at the much lower paying poverty-law scale. These alternatives are either unavailable or impracticable for the solo practitioner or the small-firm lawyer. Moreover, the $1,000 tax is highly regressive when applied to lawyers who are earning, respectively, $30,000 and $300,000. A proposal framed in terms of a percentage of income or a percentage of legal fees would more fairly reflect economic reality. * * *

The underlying issue, of course, is whether lawyers should be singled out for this tax. We do not expect farmers or grocers to feed the poor, or doctors to devote a substantial portion of their income to subsidized health care. These occupational groups are not expected to undertake an obligation to meet these massive social problems. Instead, we look to the general taxpayer for support. Taking a different view with respect to lawyers must rest on arguments that lawyers are different because law is different. Law is the glue that holds the community together; lawyers are given exclusive privileges in maintaining and operating the legal infrastructure. Part of the quid pro quo for this professional monopoly is the obligation to insure that the less fortunate have access to the legal system.

A DUTY TO SERVE?

Some lawyers will resolve the issue on the basis of the practical and moral considerations just discussed. But others will be more influenced by fundamental ideas of what it means to be a lawyer. Is there a professional obligation to insure that the legal needs of everyone are met without regard to ability to pay? Legal practitioners for centuries have provided no-fee or reduced-fee services to causes they thought worthwhile and professional aspirations have included the moral assertion that the individual lawyer should participate in public interest endeavors. However, this moral claim has not hardened into a mandatory obligation. * * *

Does a mandatory obligation flow directly from ideas of "professionalism?" One argument of this character is based on the historical tradition, just discussed, of lawyers devoting substantial time to worthy causes and of responding to court appointments. No one disputes the tradition; the issue is whether it is confined to a moral obligation—a duty of aspiration—and whether putting it in mandatory form is inconsistent with that tradition. A second argument rests on the fact that the lawyer's license is an exclusive privilege—non-lawyers are prohibited from engaging in "the practice of law." The functionalist view of a profession often includes the assertion of a quid pro quo between society and the profession: the profession agrees to undertake public service obligations in return for privileges that protect it from internal and external competition, thus providing practitioners with the material security that makes possible uncompensated public service.

Although this approach may have had some validity in the smalltown America of the past, in which the fees of a secure and well-established lawyer would vary with the client's ability to pay, it is fanciful in today's world. Nearly 800,000 lawyers are engaged in an increasingly competitive search to find and retain paying clients. A small number of large law firms, who are in a special position to charge high fees for important transactions or litigations in which they are viewed as having superior qualifications, may still be partly shielded from market pressures. But, the mass of lawyers, both in the corporate-law firm sector and in the individual-client service sector, are operating in a competitive market place.

Further, it is no longer accurate to speak of a professional monopoly. Growth in the number of lawyers, the abandonment of restraints against internal competition (e.g., advertising and solicitation of clients, minimum fee schedules, and barriers to new forms of delivery such as closed plans in prepaid legal services), and changes in legal culture have reduced or eliminated opportunities for cross-subsidization. External competition from other service providers is also increasing, with the consequence that the prohibition of unauthorized practice of law is being narrowed to in-court representation.

Many policy arguments support a continued reliance on competition to protect consumers and to provide them with more options. Lawyers should operate in a much more open and competitive marketplace for services of all kinds. Lawyers do have special responsibilities for the maintenance of a just legal system, but each lawyer should not be viewed as a resource that can be tapped to meet general social needs. A more desirable alternative to mandatory pro bono, in my view, is an increase in public funding of civil legal assistance for the poor and a deregulation of the marketplace for services that would provide more low-cost alternatives.

* * *

Note

The arguments for deregulation of many aspects of the legal profession appear in the following section.

––––––––––

David Luban has developed a proposal for mandatory pro bono service that is similar in some respects to that of the Marrero Commission. We do not include the specifics of his proposal, but the following segment of his article addresses some of the issues raised by Roger Cramton.

David Luban, "Mandatory Pro Bono: A Workable (and Moral) Plan"
64 *Mich. B. J.* 280, 282-83 (1985)
* * *

[A mandatory pro bono plan would realize "positive human goods—for lawyers as well as their poverty-vexed clients."]

* * * Pro bono practitioners have a better chance to understand and represent the interests of members of an entirely different social class and background from most lawyers and their clients; to gain insight into the day-to-day problems of the poor (and of the lawyers who normally represent them!)—to "see around one's corner." Office lawyers can get the client contact they often miss. ("I don't want 'feedback,'" Murray Bookchin once said, "I want conversations with living human beings.")

At its best, the plan can be a community-building, cosmopolitan experience, for cosmopolitanism does not mean more ethnic restaurants, it means experience that cuts across lines of class, race, and background, experience that knits together the antipodes of the community in an alliance based on common humanity.

THE MORAL OBJECTIONS

No doubt it is morally worthy to engage *willingly* in pro bono work. But many lawyers argue that it is morally impermissible to *require* lawyers to engage in it. They do not deny that poor people need legal assistance they can't afford. Nor do they deny that the community has the obligation to offer all its citizens meaningful access to justice, and the right to obtain from its members the means to do so. But they argue that if the community wants to meet the legal needs of the poor, it should use tax money to fund legal aid or compensate private attorneys. That way the *entire* community bears the cost of meeting a community need.

A pro bono obligation, on the other hand, conscripts lawyers to work below their market rate, and is thus an unfair "conscription tax" to supply the poor with legal representation. "No representation without compensation—it's unjust taxation!" is the argument. (Opponents of the military draft argue that the draft is similarly an unfair conscription tax on 18-to-26-year-old men.)

This is a powerful argument, and the obvious reply, "The community can't afford the market rate," merely invites the obvious counter, "It has no right to demand services for free." Wouldn't it be wrong for the community to require grocers to feed the hungry "pro bono," if it is unwilling to tax itself to feed the hungry?

Nor will it suffice to argue (as some courts have) that the lawyer's license is a grant of the state, to which the state may attach a pro bono string (or any other string it desires). Grocers are also licensed, yet it would be morally pernicious to palm off an obligation of the whole community—to feed its hungry—onto grocers as a condition of licensure. Grocers run their businesses to make their livings, and it seems iniquitous to treat the license needed to make one's living as a mere perk granted by the state under whatever conditions it chooses to impose. At that point the grocer has become a predicate of the license, rather than the other way around.

Yet this argument from the grocer-analogy reveals the analogy's shortcomings. The grocery business could exist without state participation. That is why the state's licensing function is used to regulate the business only for consumer protection. Lawyers, by contrast, retail law—a commodity manufactured by the state. Moreover, they have been granted a monopoly on this commodity—a grant not only in the form of unauthorized practice regulations (which the bar zealously enforces despite the lack of support from the consumers they ostensibly protect), but in other forms that are vastly more pervasive.

Laws are written in such a way that they can be interpreted only by lawyers; judicial decisions are crafted to be intelligible to the legally-trained. Court regulations, even courthouse architecture, are designed around the needs of the law-retailers. The adversary system itself is predicated on the monopoly of lawyers.

This is the difference between the lawyer and the grocer: The lawyer's lucrative monopoly would not exist without the community and its state. The monopoly, and indeed the product it monopolizes, is an artifice of the community. The community has shaped the lawyer's retail product with him or her in mind; it has made the law to make the lawyer indispensable. The community, as a consequence, has the right to condition its handiwork on the fulfillment of the monopoly's legitimate purpose by its beneficiaries.

The system of law-retailing has a legitimate purpose, and indeed only one. It is expressed in the slogan "Equal Justice Under Law." Without equal justice under law, the system has no legitimacy, and the legal profession's lucrative monopoly on retailing law should be broken.

Law practice is not a victimless pastime. It is an adversarial profession, and those who can't afford it are often damaged by those who can. One day in housing court, watching lawyers winning default judgments or evictions against poor people who may have had a defense if only they had a lawyer, can convince any lawyer of that.

Even when the result is defensible, as it sometimes is, the mismatch is a scandal—an instance of what Philadelphia Common Pleas Judge Lois Forer has denounced as "apartheid justice."

Even an office practice that on the face of it has no poor people as adversaries may harm the poor. The law allows us to do many things we couldn't do otherwise—it extends our range of action to a tremendous extent. When lawyers secure these advantages for their clients, safeguarding their interests against a range of potential adversaries, they change the face of society. They set up a network of social practices from which the poor are excluded, and this exclusion itself underscores and intensifies the pariah status of the poor.

This is a second way in which the grocer-analogy breaks down. The grocer does not make the hungry worse off by selling to the cash customer; grocery retailing is not an adversarial profession. But law-retailing is.

These, then, are the moral sources of the lawyer's pro bono obligation, or more precisely, of the community's right to impose a pro bono obligation on lawyers when necessary. Not a conscription tax, it should instead be seen as a re-shaping of the lawyer's professional role: (1) to fulfill the very social purpose that gives that role its point, that makes it worth the community's while to create it, and (2) to guard against third-party harms created by the business-as-usual of that role—"externalities," an economist would call them—inflicted upon the unrepresented.

These two sources, it should be noted, correspond to the social-contract principle and the no-harm principle that even libertarian philosophers accept.

What of the second objection, that changing pro bono work from a gift to a duty destroys its moral significance? Frankly, I don't believe it. Those lawyers who perform pro bono work for the poor at present will continue to do so; they will rejoice because the Pro Bono Office is a much more efficient way for clients to find their way to the lawyers' offices. * * * And what [of the loss-of-moral-significance argument when made by] those lawyers who do no pro bono work and who would do none? One hesitates to state the obvious, but here it is: You can't appeal to the moral significance of a gift you have no intention of giving.

* * *

At present, the bar is not shouldering its burden. As the Legal Services Corporation has fallen on hard times, a few responsible law firms and many individual lawyers have stepped-up their pro bono efforts. But in conversations with bar association pro bono finders, I have learned that overall it is becoming more difficult, not less, to find attorneys willing to take on pro bono cases.

Why is this? Recently, newspaper columnist Ellen Goodman wrote that we now seem to think of poverty in a different way. In years past we sympathized with the poor as victims. Now we regard them merely as losers. "In our political dictionary," Goodman writes, "a victim is blameless while a loser can only blame himself. In our political landscape, we may ask the government to lend a hand to victims, but not to waste handouts on losers. The 'needy' may elicit guilt and help from more affluent neighbors. But losers get only scorn. . . We used to call this blaming the victim. Now we call it winning."

I would hate to think this is true, for if so it shows a meanness of spirit that is unworthy of a civilized nation. There is no better way for the bar to commit itself to equal justice under law *for all*, and thus to a concept of community richer and more generous than the Society of Winners and Losers, than to take upon itself an effective pro bono obligation.

Notes

1.   The authors of the Marrero Report characterize a lawyer's obligation to do pro bono work as a matter of "professional duty" rather than "individual charity." Does society have an obligation to provide legal services to the poor? Is the provision of legal services to those who cannot afford them a matter of justice (treating each person according to his due) or a matter of charity (unmerited generosity)? Or is provision of legal services a matter of political expediency?

2.   Who gets the better of the argument over the grocer analogy? Over whether law practice is a monopoly?

3.   Is Luban's argument convincing? At one point, Luban implies that all legal transactions have winners and losers, and that the unrepresented poor will always lose. The facts of the *Imperial Discount* case at the beginning of this section may provide support for his position (though the result does not). But some commercial transactions are mutually beneficial. For every unconscionable purchase agreement, such as the one that surfaced in the *Imperial Discount* case, there are many purchase agreements that enable both parties to benefit.

4.   William Simon shares David Luban's belief that the legal problems of the poor are the result of the self-serving decisions of wealthy clients and their lawyers. Simon argues, however, that making legal services available to the poor is an implausible means of overcoming the unfairness of the adversary system. "There is no practical way of equalizing access to legal services sufficiently to preclude oppression. The society is not prepared to make the enormous expenditures necessary to provide everyone with substantial access to

legal assistance." William H. Simon, "The Ideology of Advocacy: Procedural Justice and Professional Ethics," 1978 *Wis. L. Rev.* 30, 50. Simon cites a "conservative" estimate that "[i]t would require something on the order of a tenfold increase in the size of the *entire* bar to begin to provide the whole population with the legal services that the affluent presently enjoy." *Id.* at n.50, *citing* Bellow & Kettleson, *The Mirror of Public Interest Ethics: Problems and Paradoxes* 57 (1977) (unpublished manuscript on file with Simon). The *Imperial Discount v. Aiken* case may provide some support for Simon's argument. It is hard to imagine either the state or the bar providing lawyers to all of the Jake Aikens in the country for evaluation of all of their purchase contracts. Simon's proposals address those who take advantage of the poor. In 1978, Simon proposed that lawyers and clients (especially wealthy and corporate clients) treat decisions in the law office "as a matter of *personal* ethics." *Id.* at 131-32 (emphasis in original). More recently, Simon has advocated that lawyers (clients are no longer in Simon's decision-making process) take those actions that seem most likely to promote the concept of justice found in our "legal ideals." *See* William H. Simon, "Ethical Discretion in Lawyering," 101 *Harv. L. Rev.* 1083, 1083-84, 1090 (1988). For a discussion of Simon's positions, *see* Thomas L. Shaffer & Robert F. Cochran, Jr., *Lawyers, Clients, and Moral Responsibility* 32-34, 56-58 (1994).

5. Stephen Wexler has concluded that if all of the lawyers in the country worked for the poor, they would be unable to meet their legal needs. He suggests that "the object of practicing poverty law must be to organize poor people, rather than to solve their legal problems." Stephen Wexler, "Practicing Law for Poor People," 79 *Yale L.J.* 1049, 1053 (1970). Yet lawyers attempting to "organize poor people, rather than solve the legal problems" risk imposing the lawyers' political agenda on the poor rather than serving their needs. Professor Deborah Rhode has observed that difficult ethical issues emerge when class actions are used to make structural changes in public and private institutions. Who determines the objectives of representation? Who must be consulted as the representation progresses and settlement becomes an option? *See* Deborah Rhode, "Class Conflicts in Class Actions," 34 *Stan. L. Rev.* 1183 (1982).

6. The New York proposal for mandatory pro bono service divided the New York bar. Chief Judge Wachtler postponed action on

the proposal in the hope that the debate the proposal generated would stimulate sufficient voluntary service by attorneys for the poor.

7.   Under the Marrero proposal (and David Luban's proposal), lawyers would only get pro bono "credit" for legal services for the poor. Roger Cramton argues that giving credit only to service to the poor under a mandatory pro bono plan would lead lawyers to shift their pro bono work away from other charitable organizations.

8.   Courts have the power in individual criminal cases to compel attorneys to accept appointment. *Powell v. Alabama*, 287 U.S. 45, 73, 53 S. Ct. 55, 65, 77 L. Ed. 158, 172 (1932).

9.   The Ethics 2000 Commission considered, but rejected, proposals to make *pro bono* service mandatory. It added the first sentence of MR 6.1: "Every lawyer has a professional responsibility to provide legal services to those unable to pay."

B. The Profession's Monopoly on the Practice of Law

Read Model Rules 5.4 to 5.7[8]

Hackin v. Arizona
389 U.S. 143, 88 S.Ct. 325, 19 L. Ed. 2d 347 (1967)

[Appellant was convicted of unauthorized practice of law. His conviction was affirmed by the Supreme Court of Arizona (102 Ariz. 218, 427 P.2d 910), and he appealed to the United States Supreme Court. Additional facts appear in the dissenting opinion.]

PER CURIAM.

* * * The motion to dismiss is granted and the appeal is dismissed for want of a substantial federal question.

Mr. Justice DOUGLAS, dissenting.

Appellant, who is not a licensed attorney, appeared in a state court habeas corpus proceeding on behalf of an indigent prisoner. The indigent prisoner was being held for extradition to Oklahoma, where he had been convicted of murder and had escaped from custody. Appellant had previously attempted to secure for the prisoner appointed counsel to argue in court the prisoner's contention that his Oklahoma

---

[8]   For MR 5.4 *cf.*, DR 3-102(A), 3-103(A), 5-107(B)-(C); Cal. Rules 1-310 to -320. For MR 5.5 *cf.*, DR 3-101(A)-(B); Cal. Rules 1-300. For MR 5.6 *cf.*, DR 2-108; Cal Rules 1-500. There is no Model Code or Cal. Rules counterpart to MR 5.7.

conviction was invalid due to denial of certain constitutional rights. But in Arizona an indigent has no right to appointed counsel at habeas corpus proceedings [c] including habeas corpus proceedings that are part of the extradition process [c]. Unable to obtain counsel for the indigent, appellant chose to represent him himself and was convicted of a misdemeanor for violation of an Arizona statute providing that 'No person shall practice law in this state unless he is an active member of the state bar in good standing. * * *' [C].

Appellant contends that this statute suffers from overbreadth and vagueness and is unconstitutional on its face because it interferes with the rights of the destitute and ignorant—those who cannot acquire the services of counsel—to obtain redress under the law for wrongs done to them. He also alleges the statute is unconstitutional as applied here, where appellant acted on behalf of the indigent prisoner only after exhaustive efforts to obtain appointed counsel. Appellant is no stranger to the law. He graduated from an unaccredited law school but was refused admission to the Arizona Bar. [C].

The claim that the statute deters constitutionally protected activity is not frivolous. Whether a State, under guise of protecting its citizens from legal quacks and charlatans, can make criminals of those who, in good faith and for no personal profit, assist the indigent to assert their constitutional rights is a substantial question this Court should answer.

Rights protected by the First Amendment include advocacy and petition for redress of grievances (*NAACP* v. *Button*, 371 U.S. 415, 429; *Edwards* v. *South Carolina*, 372 U.S. 229, 235, 83 S.Ct. 680, 9 L.Ed.2d 697), and the Fourteenth Amendment ensures equal justice for the poor in both criminal and civil actions (see *Williams* v. *Shaffer*, 385 U.S. 1037 (dissenting opinion)). But to millions of Americans who are indigent and ignorant—and often members of minority groups—these rights are meaningless. They are helpless to assert their rights under the law without assistance. They suffer discrimination in housing and employment, are victimized by shady consumer sales practices, evicted from their homes at the whim of the landlord, denied welfare payments, and endure domestic strife without hope of the legal remedies of divorce, maintenance, or child custody decrees.

If true equal protection of the laws is to be realized, an indigent must be able to obtain assistance when he suffers a denial of his rights. Today, this goal is only a goal. Outside the area of criminal proceedings covered by our decisions [Cc], counsel is seldom available to the indigent. As this Court has recognized, there is a dearth of lawyers who are willing, voluntarily, to take on unprofitable and unpopular causes. [Cc].

Some States, aware of the acute shortage of lawyers to help the indigent, have utilized the abilities of qualified law students to advise indigents and even to represent them in court in limited circum-stances. But where this practice is not sanctioned by law, the student advocate for the poor may be subjected to criminal penalty under broadly drafted statutes prohibiting unauthorized practice of law.

There is emerging, particularly in the ghetto areas of our cities, a type of organization styled to bring a new brand of legal assistance to the indigent. These groups, funded in part by the Federal Office of Economic Opportunity, characteristically establish neighborhood offices where the poor can come for assistance. They attempt to dispense services on a comprehensive integrated scale, using lawyers, social workers, members of health professions, and other nonlawyer aides. These new and flexible approaches to giving legal aid to the poor recognize that the problems of indigents—although of the type for which an attorney has traditionally been consulted— are too immense to be solved solely by members of the bar. The supply of lawyer manpower is not nearly large enough. * * *

The so-called "legal" problem of the poor is often an unidentified strand in a complex of social, economic, psychological, and psychiatric problems. Identification of the "legal" problem at times is for the expert. But even a "lay" person can often perform that function and mark the path that leads to the school board, the school principal, the welfare agency, the Veterans Administration, the police review board, or the urban renewal agency. If he neither solicits nor obtains a fee for his services, why should he not be free to act? Full-fledged representation in a battle before a court or agency requires professional skills that laymen lack; and therefore the client suffers, perhaps grievously, if he is not represented by a lawyer. But in the intermediate zone where the local pastor, the social worker, or best friend commonly operates, is there not room for accommodation? Dean Charles E. Ares recently said:

> ". . . [T]he *structure* of the legal profession is middle class in its assumptions. We assume that the lawyer can sit quietly in his office awaiting the knock on the door by a client who has discovered that he has a legal problem and has found the way to the lawyer's office. . . . This assumption is not valid for the great mass of people who live in

poverty in the United States. . . . The ways in which this structure can be changed open exciting and interesting prospects." Poverty, Civil Liberties, and Civil Rights: A Symposium, 41 N.Y.U. L. Rev. 328, 346 (1966).

Moreover, what the poor need, as much as our corporate grants, is protection before they get into trouble and confront a crisis. This means "political leadership" for the "minority poor." *Id.*, at 351. Lawyers will play a role in that movement; but so will laymen. The line that marks the area into which the layman may not step except at his peril is not clear. I am by no means sure the line was properly drawn by the court below where no lawyer could be found and this layman apparently served without a fee.

* * *

Broadly phrased unauthorized-practice-of-law statutes such as that at issue here could make criminal many of the activities regularly done by social workers who assist the poor in obtaining welfare and attempt to help them solve domestic problems. Such statutes would also tend to deter programs in which experienced welfare recipients represent other, less articulate, recipients before local welfare departments.

As this Court's decision in *NAACP* v. *Button, supra* [NAACP entitled to seek plaintiffs and provide them with legal counsel], and *Railroad Trainmen* v. *Virginia Bar*, 377 U.S. 1, indicate, state provisions regulating the legal profession will not be permitted to act as obstacles to the rights of persons to petition the courts and other legal agencies for redress. Yet statutes with the broad sweep of the Arizona provision now before this Court would appear to have the potential to "freeze out" the imaginative new attempts to assist indigents realize equal justice, merely because lay persons participate. Cf. *NAACP* v. *Button*, 371 U.S., at 436. As we said in *Button*, the threat of sanctions may deter as forcefully as the imposition of the sanctions. *Id.*, at 433. In such circumstances, "the State may prevail only upon showing a subordinating interest which is compelling." [C]. Certainly the States have a strong interest in preventing legally untrained shysters who pose as attorneys from milking the public for pecuniary gain. *Cf. NAACP* v. *Button*, at 441. But it is arguable whether this policy should support a prohibition against charitable efforts of nonlawyers to help the poor. [C]. It may well be that until the goal of free *legal* assistance to the indigent in all areas of the law is achieved, the poor are not harmed by well-meaning, charitable assistance of laymen. On the contrary, for the majority of indigents, who are not so fortunate to be served by neighborhood legal offices, lay assistance may be the only hope for achieving equal justice at this time.

* * *

Notes

1.   Justice Douglas gives several examples of areas where the poor need legal assistance—housing, employment, sales contracts. Is there a greater obligation of the profession to ensure access to legal services where the poor are defendants, rather than plaintiffs? Does it matter that the poor person has not initiated the legal proceeding, but must respond effectively in order to preserve his or her legal rights?

2.   Every state has statutes that prohibit the "practice of law" by those who are not licensed lawyers. However, exactly what constitutes the "practice of law at a given time cannot be easily defined. Nor should it be subject to such rigid and traditional definition as to ignore the public interest." *Unauthorized Practice of Law Comm. v. Department of Workers' Compensation*, 543 A.2d 662, 665 (R.I. 1988) (holding that employees of the Department of Workers' Compensation did not engage in the unauthorized practice of law when assisting injured workers in informal hearings).

3.   Does assisting people to complete standardized forms for obtaining an uncontested divorce constitute the practice of law? *See The Florida Bar* v. *Brumbaugh*, 355 So.2d 1186 (Fla. 1978) (woman who advertised her services as secretarial and provided customers completed forms for dissolution of marriage engaged in the unauthorized practice of law).

Multi-Jurisdictional Practice

With the growth of national and inter-national corporate business has come the growth of national and inter-national law practice. This growth in the "multi-jurisdictional" practice of law has run into conflict with traditional state rules barring the unauthorized practice of law, as illustrated by the following case.

Birbrower, Montalbano, Condon & Frank
v. Superior Court
949 P.2d 1; 70 Cal. Rptr. 2d 304 (1998)

[Defendant law firm, Birbrower, Montalbano, Condon & Frank (Birbrower), a New York law firm with no attorneys licensed to practice in California, entered into a representation agreement with ESQ, a California corporation. Birbrower agreed to represent ESQ in a dispute with Tandem Computers that arose out of a software and marketing agreement between ESQ and Tandem. The software agreement stated that it was to be governed by the "internal laws of the State of California." It also stated that if disputes arose under it, they were to be resolved by arbitration under the rules of the American Arbitration Association.

[During the course of representing ESQ, Birbrower attorneys made several trips to California. Their work in California included numerous meetings with ESQ employees and accountants, negotiating with Tandem representatives, and interviewing potential arbitrators. ESQ settled the Tandem dispute and it never went to arbitration.

[ESQ sued Birbrower alleging malpractice; Birbrower counterclaimed seeking payment of $1million under its fixed fee agreement with ESQ. The trial court awarded summary judgement to ESQ on Birbower's counterclaim, based on its conclusion that Birbower had engaged in the unauthorized practice of law in California. The Court of Appeals affirmed its decision.]

CHIN, J.

Business and Professions Code section 6125 states:

"No person shall practice law in California unless the person is an active member of the State Bar."

* * *

* * * The prohibition against unauthorized law practice is within the state's police power and is designed to ensure that those performing legal services do so competently. [C].

A violation of section 6125 is a misdemeanor. (§ 6126.) Moreover, "No one may recover compensation for services as an attorney at law in this state unless [the person] was at the time the services were performed a member of The State Bar." [C]

Although the Act did not define the term "practice law," case law explained it as "'the doing and performing services in a court of justice in any matter depending therein throughout its various stages and in conformity with the adopted rules of procedure.'" (*People v. Merchants Protective Corp. (1922) 189 Cal. 531, 535, 209 P. 363 (Merchants*).) *Merchants* included in its definition legal advice and legal instrument and contract preparation, whether or not these subjects were rendered in the course of litigation. [Cc]. * * *

* * *

Section 6125 has generated numerous opinions on the meaning of "practice law" but none on the meaning of "in California." In our view, the practice of law "in California" entails sufficient contact with the California client to render the nature of the legal service a clear legal representation. In addition to a quantitative analysis, we must consider the nature of the unlicensed lawyer's activities in the state. Mere fortuitous or attenuated contacts will not sustain a finding that the unlicensed lawyer practiced law "in California." The primary inquiry is whether the unlicensed lawyer engaged in sufficient activities in the state, or created a continuing relationship with the California client that included legal duties and obligations.

Our definition does not necessarily depend on or require the unlicensed lawyer's physical presence in the state. Physical presence here is one factor we may consider in deciding whether the unlicensed lawyer has violated section 6125, but it is by no means exclusive. For example, one may practice law in the state in violation of section 6125 although not physically present here by advising a California client on California law in connection with a California legal dispute by telephone, fax, computer, or other modern technological means. Conversely, although we decline to provide a comprehensive list of what activities constitute sufficient contact with the state, we do reject the notion that a person *automatically* practices law "in California" whenever that person practices California law anywhere, or "virtually" enters the state by telephone, fax, e-mail, or satellite. (See e.g., *Baron v. City of Los Angeles (1970) 2 Cal. 3d 535, 543 86 Cal. Rptr. 673, 469 P.2d 353, [42 A.L.R.3d 1036] (Baron)* ["practice law" does not encompass all professional activities].) * * * We must decide each case on its individual facts.

* * *

If we were to carry the dissent's narrow interpretation of the term "practice law" to its logical conclusion, we would effectively limit section 6125's application to those cases in which nonlicensed out-of-state lawyers appeared in a California courtroom without permission. [C] * * * [T]he dissent's definition of "practice law" * * * substantially undermines the Legislature's intent to protect the public from those giving unauthorized legal advice and counsel.

* * *

[Birbrower argues] that we do not further the statute's intent and purpose--to protect California citizens from incompetent attorneys--by enforcing it against out-of-state attorneys. Birbrower argues that because out-of-state attorneys have been licensed to practice in other jurisdictions, they have already demonstrated sufficient competence to protect California clients. But Birbrower's argument overlooks the obvious fact that other states' laws may differ substantially from California law. Competence in one jurisdiction does not necessarily guarantee competence in another. By applying section 6125 to out-of-state attorneys who engage in the extensive practice of law in California without becoming licensed in our state, we serve the statute's goal of assuring the competence of all attorneys practicing law in this state. [C] .

* * *

Assuming that section 6125 does apply to out-of-state attorneys not licensed here, Birbrower alternatively asks us to create an exception to section 6125 for work incidental to private arbitration or other alternative dispute resolution proceedings. Birbrower points to fundamental differences between private arbitration and legal proceedings, including procedural differences relating to discovery, rules of evidence, compulsory process, cross-examination of witnesses, and other areas. [C]. As Birbrower observes, in light of these differences, at least one court has decided that an out-of-state attorney could recover fees for services rendered in an arbitration proceeding. (See *Williamson v. John D. Quinn Const. Corp. (S.D.N.Y. 1982) 537 F. Supp. 613, 616 (Williamson)*.)

* * *

We decline Birbrower's invitation to craft an arbitration exception to section 6125's prohibition of the unlicensed practice of law in this state. Any exception for arbitration is best left to the Legislature * * *.

* * *

Because Birbrower violated section 6125 when it engaged in the unlawful practice of law in California, the Court of Appeal found its fee agreement with ESQ unenforceable in its entirety. * * * We agree with the Court of Appeal to the extent it barred Birbrower from recovering fees generated under the fee agreement for the unauthorized legal services it performed in California. We disagree with the same court to the extent it implicitly barred Birbrower from recovering fees generated under the fee agreement for the limited legal services the firm performed in New York.

It is a general rule that an attorney is barred from recovering compensation for services rendered in another state where the attorney was not admitted to the bar. (Annot., Right of Attorney Admitted in One State to Recover Compensation for Services Rendered in Another State Where He Was Not Admitted to the Bar *(1967) 11 A.L.R.3d 907; Hardy, supra, 99 Cal. App. 2d at p. 576.)* * * *

* * *

We agree with Birbrower that it may be able to recover fees under the fee agreement for the limited legal services it performed for ESQ in New York to the extent they did not constitute practicing law in California, even though those services were performed for a California client. Because section 6125 applies to the practice of law in California, it does not, in general, regulate law practice in other states. [C]. Thus, although the general rule against compensation to out-of-state attorneys precludes Birbrower's recovery under the fee agreement for its actions in California, the severability doctrine may allow it to receive its New York fees generated under the fee agreement. * * *

* * *

KENNARD, J., Dissenting

* * *

The majority focuses its attention on the question of whether the New York lawyers had engaged in the practice of law *in California,* giving scant consideration to a decisive preliminary inquiry: whether, through their activities here, the New York lawyers had engaged in the practice of law *at all.* In my view, the record does not show that they did. In reaching a contrary conclusion, the majority relies on an overbroad definition of the term "practice of law." I would adhere to this court's decision in *Baron v. City of Los Angeles (1970) 2 Cal. 3d 535, 86 Cal. Rptr. 673, 469 P.2d 353, [42 A.L.R.3d 1036],* more narrowly defining the practice of law as the representation of another in a judicial proceeding or an activity requiring the application of that degree of legal knowledge and technique possessed only by a trained legal mind. Under this definition, this case presents a triable issue of material fact as to whether the New York lawyers' California activities constituted the practice of law.

* * *

[The majority] charges that the narrowing construction of the term "practice of law" that this court adopted in *Baron* "effectively limit[s] section 6125's application to those cases in which nonlicensed out-of-state lawyers appeared in a California courtroom without permission." [C]. Fiddlesticks. Because the *Baron* definition encompasses all activities that " 'reasonably demand application of a trained legal mind' "(*Baron, supra, 2 Cal. 3d at p. 543),* the majority's assertion would be true only if there were no activities, apart from court appearances, requiring application of a trained legal mind. Many attorneys would no doubt be surprised to learn that, for example, drafting testamentary documents for large estates, preparing merger agreements for multinational corporations, or researching complex legal issues are not activities that require a trained legal mind.

According to the majority, use of the *Baron* definition I have quoted would undermine protection of the public from incompetent legal practitioners. [C]. The *Baron* definition provides ample protection from incompetent legal practitioners without infringing upon the public's interest in obtaining advice and representation from other professionals, such as accountants and real estate brokers, whose skills in specialized areas may overlap with those of lawyers. This allows the public the freedom to choose professionals who may be able to provide the public with needed services at a more affordable cost. (See Wolfram, Modern Legal Ethics, *supra*, at p. 831; Rhode, *Policing the Professional Monopoly: A Constitutional and Empirical Analysis of Unauthorized Practice Prohibitions (1981) 34 Stan.L.Rev. 1, 97-98;* Weckstein, *Limitations on the Right to Counsel: The Unauthorized Practice of Law, 1978 Utah L.Rev. 649, 650.)* As this court has recognized, there are proceedings in which nonattorneys "are competent" to represent others without undermining the protection of the public interest. (*Consumers Lobby Against Monopolies v. Public Utilities Com. (1979) 25 Cal. 3d 891, 913-914 [160 Cal. Rptr. 124, 603 P.2d 41].)*

* * *

The majority's overbroad definition [of the practice of law] would affect a host of common commercial activities. On point here are comments that Professor Deborah Rhode made in a 1981 article published in the Stanford Law Review: "For many individuals, most obviously accountants, bankers, real estate brokers, and insurance agents, it would be impossible to give intelligent counsel without reference to legal concerns that such statutes reserve as the exclusive province of attorneys. As one [American Bar Association] official active in unauthorized practice areas recently acknowledged, there is growing recognition that ' "all kinds of other professional people are practicing law almost out of necessity." ' Moreover, since most legislation does not exempt gratuitous activity, much advice commonly imparted by friends, employers, political organizers, and newspaper commentators constitutes unauthorized practice. For example, although the organized bar has not yet evinced any inclination to drag [nationally syndicated advice columnist] Ann Landers through the courts, she is plainly fair game under extant statutes [proscribing the unauthorized practice of law]." (Rhode, [*supra*] *at p. 47,* fns. omitted.)

Unlike the majority, I would for the reasons given above adhere to the more narrowly drawn definition of the practice of law that this court articulated in *Baron, supra, 2 Cal. 3d 535, 543:* the representation of another in a judicial proceeding or an activity requiring the application of that degree of legal knowledge and technique possessed only by a trained legal mind. Applying that definition here, I conclude that the trial court should not have granted summary adjudication for plaintiffs based on the Birbrower lawyers' California activities. * * *

* * *

Representing another in an arbitration proceeding does not invariably present difficult or doubtful legal questions that require a trained legal mind for their resolution. Under California law, arbitrators are "not ordinarily constrained to decide according to the rule of law ...." [C]. Thus, arbitrators, " 'unless specifically required to act in conformity with rules of law, may base their decision upon broad principles of justice and equity, and in doing so may expressly or impliedly reject a claim that a party might successfully have asserted in a judicial action.' [C]. They " 'are not bound to award on principles of dry law, but may decide on principles of equity and good conscience, and make their award *ex aequo et bono* [according to what is just and good].' [C]. For this reason, "the existence of an *error of law* apparent on the face of the [arbitration] award *that causes substantial injustice* does not provide grounds for judicial review." [Cc].

* * *

Commonly used arbitration rules further demonstrate that legal training is not essential to represent another in an arbitration proceeding. Here, for example, Birbrower's clients agreed to resolve any dispute arising under their contract with Tandem using the American Arbitration Association's rules, which allow any party to be "represented by counsel *or other authorized representative*." (Am. Arbitration Assn., Com. Arbitration Rules (July 1, 1996) § 22, italics added.) Rules of other arbitration organizations also allow for representation by nonattorneys. * * *

The American Arbitration Association and other major arbitration associations thus recognize that nonattorneys are often better suited than attorneys to represent parties in arbitration. The history of arbitration also reflects this reality, for in its beginnings arbitration was a dispute-resolution mechanism principally used in a few specific trades (such as construction, textiles, ship chartering, and international sales of goods) to resolve disputes among businesses that turned on factual issues uniquely within the expertise of members of the trade. In fact, "rules of a few trade associations forbid representation by counsel in arbitration proceedings, because of their belief that it would complicate what might otherwise be simple proceedings." (Jay E. Grenig, Alternative Dispute Resolution (1997) § 5.2, p. 81.) The majority gives no adequate justification for its decision to deprive parties of their freedom of contract and to make it a crime for anyone but California lawyers to represent others in arbitrations in California.

* * *

Notes

1.   Under the majority opinion, could the Birbower firm recover all of its fees if all of its work had been done from New York through telephone, fax, and email?

2.   In 2002, the ABA adopted substantial amendments to MR 5.5 (b). Would Birbrower be subject to discipline under it?

3.   Arbitration is much like litigation, except that it is conducted before a private judge, generally selected by the parties, rather than a state-appointed judge. There is no jury. Generally, the decision of an arbitrator is not subject to appeal. As Justice Kennard notes in her

dissent, arbitrators are not required to follow the law, but may base their decisions on "broad principles of justice and equity." But arbitrators give great weight to the law, and party representatives argue the law before arbitrators. To the extent that they argue the law, is representing a client in arbitration "the practice of law." Is arguing "broad principles of justice and equity" to a legal decision-maker "the practice of law"? Justice Kennard says that, "Representing another in an arbitration proceeding does not invariably present difficult or doubtful legal questions that require a trained legal mind for their resolution." But the same could be said for much litigation.

4.   Increasingly, parties are resolving cases through arbitration, mediation, and other forms of alternative dispute resolution. Is allowing out-of-state lawyers or non-lawyers to represent clients in these processes likely to reduce the amount of work that is reserved for in-state lawyers?

5.   *In-House Counsel to an Organization* - Several states have adopted rules permitting in-house legal counsel to practice within the jurisdiction, even if the lawyer is not admitted within it. *See* jurisdictions cited at Restatement (Third) of the Law Governing Lawyers § 3, Reporter's Note to Comment f. The Comment to the Restatement says, "Leniency is appropriate because the only concern is with the client-employer, who is presumably in a good position to assess the quality and fitness of the lawyer's work." Id., Comment f. If the Comment is correct, should a state allow organizations and other sophisticated clients to have outside counsel (counsel who practice with law firms) from other jurisdictions do work for them within the state? Should organizations and other sophisticated clients be able to have non-lawyers represent them?

6.   Note that the *Birbrower* trial court and the California Court of Appeals denied all fees to the Birbrower law firm. This was an example of the denial of fees as a sanction, as we mentioned in Chapter One. Here the state supreme court allowed those fees earned out of state, but other courts have denied any fees for out-of-state lawyers. *See Chandris v. Yanakakis*, 668 So.2d 180 (Fla. 1995). For an extensive discussion of the problems unauthorized practice of law statutes pose for lawyers with multi-jurisdictional practices, *see* Charles W. Wolfram, "Sneaking Around in the Legal Profession: Interjurisdictional Unauthorized Practice by Transactional Lawyers," 36 *S. Tex. L. Rev.* 665 (1995).

In the prior section, one of David Luban's justifications for mandatory pro bono representation was the lawyer's monopoly on the right to practice law. Roger Cramton criticized proposals for mandatory pro bono legal service. Cramton argued for broadening access to legal services through increased public funding of legal services for the poor and deregulation of the legal profession. The following excerpt presents his discussion of deregulation of form-of-practice restrictions. It also (in text and footnotes) summarizes some important cases in which the Supreme Court has outlawed aspects of deregulation under First Amendment provisions.

Roger C. Cramton, "Delivery of Legal Services to Ordinary Americans"

44 *Case W. Res. L. Rev.* 531, 564-65, 574-78, 616 (1994)

* * *

[One] way to reduce the cost of legal services, favored by a number of commentators, involves deregulation of the practice of law.[9] Increased competition within the legal profession and with nonlawyer service providers, it is argued, would lower the cost of routine legal services and make them more available to the public at acceptable levels of quality. This approach would eliminate the professional monopoly and the remaining restrictions on form of practice. Nonlawyers would be able to compete with lawyers in the provision of legal services by delivering services directly to clients (with a possible exception for representation of criminal defendants) or by employing various combinations of lawyers and paralegals to perform legal tasks on a high-volume, low-cost basis. * * *

* * *

---

[9]   [Law review article footnote 88] *See* W. Clark Durant, *Maximizing Access to Justice: A Challenge to the Legal Profession, in* LEGAL ETHICS 832-40 (Deborah L. Rhode & David Luban eds., 1992). Durant, then chairman of the board of the Legal Services Corporation, called for replacement of the Corporation by deregulation of the legal profession:

> The overall effect of this system created and operated by lawyers is to limit entry into the profession, to discourage competition, to increase prices, delays and costs and ultimately to deny access to justice for the poor, for all of us. The legal cartel's heaviest burden falls on the poor. They are denied choices and access. They are denied advocates and opportunities.

Id. at 838.

3. Form-of-Practice Restrictions

Model Rule 5.4 forbids a lawyer to "form a partnership with a nonlawyer if any of the activities of the partnership consist of the practice of law," forbids a lawyer to "share legal fees with a nonlawyer," and states that a "lawyer shall not practice with or in the form of a professional corporation or association . . . if . . . a nonlawyer owns any interest therein . . . ; a nonlawyer is a corporate director or officer thereof; or . . . a nonlawyer has the right to direct or control the professional judgment of a lawyer." The Comment states that "[t]hese limitations are to protect the lawyer's professional independence of judgment."

Should nonlawyers be prohibited from investing in, managing, and profiting from companies that provide legal services? Critics of form-of-practice restrictions argue that the legal services market would benefit from enlarged competition and increased investment.[10] Allowing accounting firms, banks, insurance companies, or retailers to diversify into legal services would serve that purpose. On the other hand, especially when legal services are combined with another business activity, such as the provision of banking or insurance services, legal advice may be distorted by the desire to sell these other services. The policy question is whether professional discipline or malpractice exposure of lawyer and non-lawyer participants who violated professional standards (e.g., breach of confidentiality or conflict of interest) would provide sufficient protection to consumers of service providers owned or managed by non-lawyers.

Restrictions on the ownership and management of organizations providing legal services to the public have important implications for the cost, variety, and availability of legal services to middle-class Americans. For a time, the organized bar strongly opposed any group legal service arrangements on the grounds that impermissible solicitation was involved. * * * [C]ourt decisions required

---

[10]   [Law review article footnote 116] For criticism of M.R. 5.4, see Stephen Gillers, *What We Talked About When We Talked About Ethics: A Critical View of the Model Rules*, 46 OHIO ST.L.J. 243, 266-69 (1985). Gillers argues that M.R. 5.4 serves the interests of established firms, with accumulated capital and clientele, rather than the interests of lawyers generally, especially younger lawyers who would benefit from increased opportunities in salaried employment; it also harms consumers by suppressing competition in the supply of services.

abandonment of this position[11] * * * [The profession has] steadfastly opposed relaxation of requirements that organizations delivering legal services be limited in ownership and control to members of the bar. The specter of national retailers, insurance companies and major banks, among others, offering legal services generally, or to their customers through multiple offices, continues to alarm the profession. Form-of-practice restrictions, such as those embodied in Model Rule 5.4, are the profession's barrier to these forms of competition.

Provision of legal services by organizations owned or managed by non-lawyers presents a variety of standard professional responsibility problems. The lawyers who actually perform the legal work generally are selected or employed by the organizers of the plan. Will the independent judgment of the lawyer in serving a client through the plan be distorted or controlled by the interests of the operator of the plan? The same possibilities are present whenever a third person selects and pays a client's lawyer (e.g., a liability insurer providing a defense to an insured) or whenever an organization hires staff lawyers (e.g., corporate legal staff). Second, group legal services plans often rely on advertising, raising the same issues involved in other advertising of legal services. Should an insurance company be permitted to call or solicit members of the public to enroll in a prepaid legal services plan in the same manner in which those companies merchandise life and health insurance to the public? Third, many plans employ nonlawyers to administer plans and to perform paralegal functions. Use of non-lawyer staff may constitute the unauthorized practice of law.

Underlying all of these issues is one of competition with general practitioners in the provision of legal services to ordinary Americans. Hostility to group legal services comes primarily from bar leaders

---

[11] [Law review article footnote 117] *See* United Transp. Union v. State Bar of Mich., 401 U.S. 576, 585 (1971) ("The common thread running through our decisions in *NAACP v. Button, Trainmen, and United Mine Workers* is that collective activity undertaken to obtain meaningful access to the courts is a fundamental right within the protection of the First Amendment."); Brotherhood of R.R. Trainmen v. Virginia *ex rel.* Va. State Bar, 377 U.S. 1, 8 (1964) ("The First and Fourteenth Amendments protect the right of the members through their Brotherhood to maintain and carry out their plan for advising workers who are injured to obtain legal advice and for recommending specific lawyers . . . . And, of course, lawyers accepting employment under this constitutionally protected plan have a like protection which the State cannot abridge."); NAACP v. Button, 371 U.S. 415, 444-45 (1963) (holding that the First Amendment protects the NAACP's right to seek plaintiffs and provide them with counsel; state's interest in preventing barratry, maintenance and champerty is not a compelling state interest justifying limiting First Amendment freedoms).

representing the interests of general practitioners who are the lawyers primarily threatened by competition from group legal services plans (e.g., the loss of work-injury cases handled by a union plan).

The Kutak Commission's draft of what became Model Rule 5.4 eliminated the form-of-practice requirements restricting group legal services. Under the proposal, a lawyer could be employed by any organization engaged in the delivery of legal services as long as the organization respected a lawyer's professional judgment, protected client confidential information, avoided impermissible advertising or solicitation, and charged only fees reasonable in amount. The Commission's proposal, however, was dropped from the Model Rules by the ABA House of Delegates at the last minute. Professor Geoffrey Hazard, the reporter for the Kutak Commission, reports: "During the debate . . . someone asked if [the Kutak] proposal would allow Sears Roebuck to open a law office. When they found out it would, that was the end of the debate."

Model Rule 5.4 (and its Model Code antecedents) assumes that lay managers of a legal services organization will be tempted, more than are lawyer managers, to interfere with the professional relationships of employed lawyers when it is profitable to do so and that the problem is so serious that a prophylactic rule prohibiting lay management is necessary. These assumptions are questionable at best. After-the-fact remedies for violation of professional standards (e.g., discipline, malpractice liability, and court sanctions) will provide sufficient protection to consumers.

* * *

The current restrictions on ownership and control of organizations engaged in the practice of law (e.g., Model Rule 5.4) curtail investment and restrict competition in legal services markets to the detriment of consumers. The amended rule should be substantially the same as that proposed by the Kutak Commission's 1981 draft. * * *

* * *

Notes

1. Should Sears Roebuck be allowed to open a law office?

2. Recently, it was estimated that about seventeen million Americans now are covered by some sort of prepaid legal service plan. This has become possible largely as a result of the Supreme Court's decisions upholding the right of nonprofit groups, such as unions and political

organizations, to provide legal services to their members. Consequently, most of the plans are operated by or on behalf of these organizations.

The developments in the area of for-profit plans are even more significant. Typically the participants in such plans pay a small monthly premium in return for the provider's guarantee of certain minimum legal services from a lawyer who has contracted with the plan providers. In the last several years, a number of for-profit plans have been initiated, and they are being marketed widely throughout the country. Montgomery Ward, for example, offers 3 separate legal services plans that now cover 500,000 persons in 41 states. Prepaid Legal Services Inc., a publicly traded company based in Oklahoma, covers about 150,000 persons in 22 states. Amway Corporation also is marketing plans, as are a number of insurance companies.

Although there are no special ethical restrictions on such plans when marketed exclusively by lawyers, there is continuing uncertainty under the lawyer codes and the unauthorized practice rules as to the permissibility of for-profit prepaid legal services plans marketed by non-lawyers.

Thomas R. Andrews, "Nonlawyers in the Business of Law: Does the One Who Has the Gold Really Make the Rules?" 40 *Hastings L.J.* 577, 636-7 (1989). What provisions of the Model Rules create this "continuing uncertainty . . . as to the permissibility of for-profit prepaid legal services plans marketed by nonlawyers"? Should the Rules be amended to clearly permit or prohibit such plans?

C. Advertising and Solicitation

Read Model Rules 7.1 to 7.2 and 7.4 to 7.5[12]

Bates v. State Bar of Arizona
433 U.S. 350 97 S. Ct. 2691, 53 L. Ed. 2d 810 (1977)

MR. JUSTICE BLACKMUN delivered the opinion of the Court.

As part of its regulation of the Arizona Bar, the Supreme Court of that State has imposed and enforces a disciplinary rule that restricts advertising by attorneys. * * *

* * *

---

[12]   For MR 7.1 *cf.*, DR 2-101; Cal. Rules 1-400. For MR 7.2 *cf.*, DR 2-101, 2-103; Cal. Rules 1-400. For MR 7.4 *cf.*, DR 2-105 (A); EC 2-14; Cal. Rules 1-400 (D)(6). For MR 7.5 *cf.*, DR 2-102; Cal. Rules 1-400 (E), Standards (6)-(9).

Appellants John R. Bates and Van O'Steen are attorneys licensed to practice law in the State of Arizona. As such, they are members of the appellee, the State Bar of Arizona. After admission to the bar in 1972, appellants worked as attorneys with the Maricopa County Legal Aid Society. [C].

In March 1974, appellants left the Society and opened a law office, which they call a "legal clinic," in Phoenix. Their aim was to provide legal services at modest fees to persons of moderate income who did not qualify for governmental legal aid. [C]. In order to achieve this end, they would accept only routine matters, such as uncontested divorces, uncontested adoptions, simple personal bankruptcies, and changes of name, for which costs could be kept down by extensive use of paralegals, automatic typewriting equipment, and standardized forms and office procedures. More complicated cases, such as contested divorces, would not be accepted. [C]. Because appellants set their prices so as to have a relatively low return on each case they handled, they depended on substantial volume. [C].

After conducting their practice in this manner for two years, appellants concluded that their practice and clinical concept could not survive unless the availability of legal services at low cost was advertised and, in particular, fees were advertised. [C]. Consequently, in order to generate the necessary flow of business, that is, "to attract clients," [c], appellants on February 22, 1976, placed an advertisement [c] in the Arizona Republic, a daily newspaper of general circulation in the Phoenix metropolitan area. As may be seen, the advertisement stated that appellants were offering "legal services at very reasonable fees," and listed their fees for certain services.

Appellants concede that the advertisement constituted a clear violation of Disciplinary Rule 2-101 (B), [c]. The disciplinary rule provides in part:

> "(B) A lawyer shall not publicize himself, or his partner, or associate, or any other lawyer affiliated with him or his firm, as a lawyer through newspaper or magazine advertisements, radio or television announcements, display advertisements in the city or telephone directories or other means of commercial publicity, nor shall he authorize or permit others to do so in his behalf."

* * *

* * * [Because the Arizona Supreme Court] felt that appellants' advertising "was done in good faith to test the constitutionality of DR 2-101 (B)," it [imposed a sanction of] censure only. [C].

* * *

Last Term, in *Virginia Pharmacy Board* v. *Virginia Consumer Council*, 425 U.S. 748 (1976), the Court considered the validity under the First Amendment of a Virginia statute declaring that a pharmacist was guilty of "unprofessional conduct" if he advertised prescription drug prices. We recognized that the pharmacist who desired to advertise did not wish to report any particularly newsworthy fact or to comment on any cultural, philosophical, or political subject; his desired communication was characterized simply: "'I will sell you the X prescription drug at the Y price.'" *Id.*, at 761. Nonetheless, we held that commercial speech of that kind was entitled to the protection of the First Amendment.

* * * The listener's interest is substantial: the consumer's concern for the free flow of commercial speech often may be far keener than his concern for urgent political dialogue. Moreover, significant societal interests are served by such speech. Advertising, though entirely commercial, may often carry information of import to significant issues of the day. [C]. And commercial speech serves to inform the public of the availability, nature, and prices of products and services, and thus performs an indispensable role in the allocation of resources in a free enterprise system. [C]. In short, such speech serves individual and societal interests in assuring informed and reliable decisionmaking. [C].

* * *

The heart of the dispute before us today is whether lawyers also may constitutionally advertise the *prices* at which certain routine services will be performed. Numerous justifications are proffered for the restriction of such price advertising. We consider each in turn:

1. *The Adverse Effect on Professionalism.* Appellee places particular emphasis on the adverse effects that it feels price advertising will have on the legal profession. The key to professionalism, it is argued, is the sense of pride that involvement in the discipline generates. It is claimed that price advertising will bring about commercialization, which will undermine the attorney's sense of dignity and self-worth. The hustle of the marketplace will adversely affect the profession's service orientation, and irreparably damage the delicate

balance between the lawyer's need to earn and his obligation selflessly to serve. * * *

* * * [W]e find the postulated connection between advertising and the erosion of true professionalism to be severely strained. At its core, the argument presumes that attorneys must conceal from themselves and from their clients the real-life fact that lawyers earn their livelihood at the bar. We suspect that few attorneys engage in such self-deception. And rare is the client, moreover, even one of modest means, who enlists the aid of an attorney with the expectation that his services will be rendered free of charge. * * *

2. *The Inherently Misleading Nature of Attorney Advertising.* It is argued that advertising of legal services inevitably will be misleading (a) because such services are so individualized with regard to content and quality as to prevent informed comparison on the basis of an advertisement, (b) because the consumer of legal services is unable to determine in advance just what services he needs, and (c) because advertising by attorneys will highlight irrelevant factors and fail to show the relevant factor of skill.

We are not persuaded that restrained professional advertising by lawyers inevitably will be misleading. Although many services performed by attorneys are indeed unique, it is doubtful that any attorney would or could advertise fixed prices for services of that type. The only services that lend themselves to advertising are the routine ones: the uncontested divorce, the simple adoption, the uncontested personal bankruptcy, the change of name, and the like—the very services advertised by appellants. * * *

3. *The Adverse Effect on the Administration of Justice.* Advertising is said to have the undesirable effect of stirring up litigation. The judicial machinery is designed to serve those who feel sufficiently aggrieved to bring forward their claims. Advertising, it is argued, serves to encourage the assertion of legal rights in the courts, thereby undesirably unsettling societal repose. There is even a suggestion of barratry. [C].

But advertising by attorneys is not an unmitigated source of harm to the administration of justice. It may offer great benefits. Although advertising might increase the use of the judicial machinery, we cannot accept the notion that it is always better for a person to suffer a wrong silently than to redress it by legal action. As the bar acknowledges, "the middle 70% of our population is not being reached or served adequately by the legal profession." ABA, Revised Handbook on Prepaid Legal Services 2 (1972). Among the reasons for this underutilization is fear of the cost, and an inability to locate a suitable lawyer. * * *

* * *

In holding that advertising by attorneys may not be subjected to blanket suppression, and that the advertisement at issue is protected, we, of course, do not hold that advertising by attorneys may not be regulated in any way. We mention some of the clearly permissible limitations on advertising not foreclosed by our holding.

Advertising that is false, deceptive, or misleading of course is subject to restraint. * * *   In fact, because the public lacks sophistication concerning legal services, misstatements that might be overlooked or deemed unimportant in other advertising may be found quite inappropriate in legal advertising. For example, advertising claims as to the quality of services—a matter we do not address today—are not susceptible of measurement or verification; accordingly, such claims may be so likely to be misleading as to warrant restriction. Similar objections might justify restraints on in-person solicitation. * * *

* * *

The constitutional issue in this case is only whether the State may prevent the publication in a newspaper of appellants' truthful advertisement concerning the availability and terms of routine legal services. We rule simply that the flow of such information may not be restrained, and we therefore hold the present application of the disciplinary rule against appellants to be violative of the First Amendment.

The judgment of the Supreme Court of Arizona is therefore affirmed in part and reversed in part.

It is so ordered.

Notes

1.   In *Bates* the ABA argued that lawyer advertising would have a detrimental effect on "professionalism." What did the ABA mean by the term "professionalism"? *Cf.* our discussion of professionalism *supra* page 1. Has advertising had a detrimental effect?

2.   Subsequent Supreme Court cases discussed in *Bates* generally have resolved issues based on the same principles. Lawyers who convey truthful information are protected. *In re R. M. J.*, 455 U. S. 191,

102 S. Ct. 929, 71 L. Ed. 2d 64 (1982) (Missouri rule limiting designation of areas of practice to certain wording and prohibiting the designation of jurisdictions in which licensed to practice struck down); *Zauderer* v. *Office of Disciplinary Counsel of the Supreme Ct. of Ohio*, 471 U.S. 626, 105 S. Ct. 2265, 85 L. Ed. 2d 652 (1985) (lawyer entitled to run advertisement containing an illustration of a Dalkon Shield and advice that the statute of limitations had not run on Dalkon Shield claims); *Shapero* v. *Kentucky Bar Ass'n*, 486 U.S. 466, 108 S. Ct. 1916, 100 L. Ed. 2d 475 (1988) (ban on direct mail advertising prohibited); *Peel* v. *Attorney Registration and Disciplinary Comm's of Ill.*, 496 U.S. 91, 110 S. Ct. 2281, 110 L. Ed. 2d 83 (1990) (plurality opinion; lawyer entitled to identify himself as certified as a civil trial specialist by a bona fide private organization). States can prohibit lawyers from conveying misleading information. *Zauderer, supra.* (state can require lawyer advertising contingent fee to state that client must pay litigation costs).

3.   Are any of the limitations on advertising under the current Model Rules likely to be held unconstitutional?

Read Model Rule 7.3[13]

At the time that the following two cases were decided, the Model Code's Disciplinary Rules 103 and 104 prohibited lawyers from recommending themselves to prospective clients.

In re Primus
436 U.S. 412, 98 S. Ct. 1893, 56 L. Ed. 2d 417 (1978)

[Appellant, Edna Smith Primus, was a volunteer lawyer for the American Civil Liberties Union (ACLU). In 1973, newspapers reported that pregnant mothers on public assistance in Aiken County, S. C., were being sterilized as a condition of the continued receipt of Medicaid benefits. Appellant met with a group of women who had been sterilized. She advised them of their legal rights and suggested the possibility of a lawsuit. She wrote a letter to one of them, informing her of the ACLU's offer of free legal representation. The Supreme Court of South Carolina gave appellant a public reprimand.]

---

[13]   *Cf.*, DR 2-103-104; Cal. Rules 1-400; CAL. BUS. & PROF. CODE § 6152 (West 1995).

Mr. Justice Powell delivered the opinion of the Court.

We consider on this appeal whether a State may punish a member of its Bar who, seeking to further political and ideological goals through associational activity, including litigation, advises a lay person of her legal rights and discloses in a subsequent letter that free legal assistance is available from a nonprofit organization with which the lawyer and her associates are affiliated.

* * *

* * * [W]e decide today in *Ohralik* v. *Ohio State Bar Assn.* [which appears following this opinion] that the States may vindicate legitimate regulatory interests through proscription, in certain circumstances, of in-person solicitation by lawyers who seek to communicate purely commercial offers of legal assistance to lay persons.

Unlike the situation in *Ohralik*, however, appellant's act of solicitation took the form of a letter to a woman with whom appellant had discussed the possibility of seeking redress for an allegedly unconstitutional sterilization. This was not in-person solicitation for pecuniary gain. Appellant was communicating an offer of free assistance by attorneys associated with the ACLU, not an offer predicated on entitlement to a share of any monetary recovery. And her actions were undertaken to express personal political beliefs and to advance the civil-liberties objectives of the ACLU, rather than to derive financial gain. The question presented in this case is whether, in light of the values protected by the First and Fourteenth Amendments, these differences materially affect the scope of state regulation of the conduct of lawyers.

* * *

* * * [The ACLU] has represented individuals in litigation that has defined the scope of constitutional protection in areas such as political dissent, juvenile rights, prisoners' rights, military law, amnesty, and privacy. [C]. For the ACLU, as for the NAACP, "litigation is not a technique of resolving private differences"; it is "a form of political expression" and "political association." 371 U. S., at 429, 431.

* * *

Appellant's letter of August 30, 1973, to Mrs. Williams thus comes within the generous zone of First Amendment protection reserved for associational freedoms. The ACLU engages in litigation as a vehicle for effective political expression and association, as well as a means of communicating useful information to the public. [Cc]. As *Button*

[*NAACP* v. *Button*, 317 U. S. 415 (1963)] indicates, and as appellant offered to prove at the disciplinary hearing, [c], the efficacy of litigation as a means of advancing the cause of civil liberties often depends on the ability to make legal assistance available to suitable litigants. * * *

* * *

The Disciplinary Rules in question sweep broadly. Under DR 2-103 (D)(5), a lawyer employed by the ACLU or a similar organization may never give unsolicited advice to a lay person that he retain the organization's free services * * *. [T]he Rules in their present form have a distinct potential for dampening the kind of "cooperative activity that would make advocacy of litigation meaningful," *Button*, *supra*, at 438, as well as for permitting discretionary enforcement against unpopular causes.

* * *

Where political expression or association is at issue, this Court has not tolerated the degree of imprecision that often characterizes government regulation of the conduct of commercial affairs. The approach we adopt today in *Ohralik*, [*see infra*.] that the State may proscribe in-person solicitation for pecuniary gain under circumstances likely to result in adverse consequences, cannot be applied to appellant's activity on behalf of the ACLU. Although a showing of potential danger may suffice in the former context, appellant may not be disciplined unless her activity in fact involved the type of misconduct at which South Carolina's broad prohibition is said to be directed.

* * *

* * * The judgment of the Supreme Court of South Carolina is

Reversed.

* * *

MR. JUSTICE REHNQUIST, dissenting.

* * *

* * * A State may rightly fear that members of its Bar have powers of persuasion not possessed by laymen, [c], and it may also fear that such persuasion may be as potent in writing as it is in person. Such persuasion may draw an unsophisticated layman into litigation contrary to his own best interests, [c], and it may force other citizens of South Carolina to defend against baseless litigation which would not

otherwise have been brought. I cannot agree that a State must prove such harmful consequences in each case simply because an organization such as the ACLU or the NAACP is involved.

I cannot share the Court's confidence that the danger of such consequences is minimized simply because a lawyer proceeds from political conviction rather than for pecuniary gain. A State may reasonably fear that a lawyer's desire to resolve "substantial civil liberties questions," 268 S. C. 259, 263, 233 S. E. 2d 301, 303 (1977), may occasionally take precedence over his duty to advance the interests of his client. It is even more reasonable to fear that a lawyer in such circumstances will be inclined to pursue both culpable and blameless defendants to the last ditch in order to achieve his ideological goals. Although individual litigants, including the ACLU, may be free to use the courts for such purposes, South Carolina is likewise free to restrict the activities of the members of its Bar who attempt to persuade them to do so.

I can only conclude that the discipline imposed upon Primus does not violate the Constitution, and I would affirm the judgment of the Supreme Court of South Carolina.

Ohralik v. Ohio State Bar Ass'n
436 U.S. 447 98 S. Ct. 1912, 56 L. Ed. 2d 444 (1978)

MR. JUSTICE POWELL delivered the opinion of the Court.
* * *

Appellant, a member of the Ohio Bar, lives in Montville, Ohio. Until recently he practiced law in Montville and Cleveland. On February 13, 1974, while picking up his mail at the Montville Post Office, appellant learned from the postmaster's brother about an automobile accident that had taken place on February 2 in which Carol McClintock, a young woman with whom appellant was casually acquainted, had been injured. [Another young woman, Wanda Lou Holbert, had also been injured in the accident.] Appellant made a telephone call to Ms. McClintock's parents, who informed him that their daughter was in the hospital. Appellant suggested that he might visit Carol in the hospital. Mrs. McClintock assented to the idea, but requested that appellant first stop by at her home.
* * *

Appellant proceeded to the hospital, where he found Carol lying in traction in her room. After a brief conversation about her condition, appellant told Carol he would represent her and asked her to sign an agreement. Carol said she would have to discuss the matter with her parents. She did not sign the agreement, but asked appellant to have her parents come to see her. Appellant also attempted to see Wanda Lou Holbert, but learned that she had just been released from the hospital. [C]. He then departed for another visit with the McClintocks.

On his way appellant detoured to the scene of the accident, where he took a set of photographs. He also picked up a tape recorder, which he concealed under his raincoat before arriving at the McClintocks' residence. Once there, he re-examined their automobile insurance policy, discussed with them the law applicable to passengers, and explained the consequences of the fact that the driver who struck Carol's car was an uninsured motorist. Appellant discovered that the McClintocks' insurance policy would provide benefits of up to $12,500 each for Carol and Wanda Lou under an uninsured-motorist clause. Mrs. McClintock acknowledged that both Carol and Wanda Lou could sue for their injuries, but recounted to appellant that "Wanda swore up and down she would not do it." [C]. The McClintocks also told appellant that Carol had phoned to say that appellant could "go ahead" with her representation. Two days later appellant returned to Carol's hospital room to have her sign a contract, which provided that he would receive one-third of her recovery.

In the meantime, appellant obtained Wanda Lou's name and address from the McClintocks after telling them he wanted to ask her some questions about the accident. He then visited Wanda Lou at her home, without having been invited. He again concealed his tape recorder and recorded most of the conversation with Wanda Lou. After a brief, unproductive inquiry about the facts of the accident, appellant told Wanda Lou that he was representing Carol and that he had a "little tip" for Wanda Lou: the McClintocks' insurance policy contained an uninsured-motorist clause which might provide her with a recovery of up to $12,500. The young woman, who was 18 years of age and not a high school graduate at the time, replied to appellant's query about whether she was going to file a claim by stating that she really did not understand what was going on. Appellant offered to represent her, also, for a contingent fee of one-third of any recovery, and Wanda Lou stated "O. K."

Wanda's mother attempted to repudiate her daughter's oral assent the following day, when appellant called on the telephone to speak to

Wanda. Mrs. Holbert informed appellant that she and her daughter did not want to sue anyone or to have appellant represent them, and that if they decided to sue they would consult their own lawyer. Appellant insisted that Wanda had entered into a binding agreement. * * * Carol also eventually discharged appellant. Although another lawyer represented her in concluding a settlement with the insurance company, she paid appellant one-third of her recovery in settlement of his lawsuit against her for breach of contract.

Both Carol McClintock and Wanda Lou Holbert filed complaints against appellant with the Grievance Committee of the Geauga County Bar Association. The County Bar Association referred the grievance to appellee, which filed a formal complaint with the Board of Commissioners on Grievances and Discipline of the Supreme Court of Ohio. After a hearing, the Board found that appellant had violated Disciplinary Rules (DR) 2-103 (A) and 2-104 (A) of the Ohio Code of Professional Responsibility. [Cf. MR 7.3]. The Board rejected appellant's defense that his conduct was protected under the First and Fourteenth Amendments. The Supreme Court of Ohio adopted the findings of the Board, reiterated that appellant's conduct was not constitutionally protected, and increased the sanction of a public reprimand recommended by the Board to indefinite suspension.

* * *

Appellant contends that his solicitation of the two young women as clients is indistinguishable, for purposes of constitutional analysis, from the advertisement in *Bates*. Like that advertisement, his meetings with the prospective clients apprized them of their legal rights and of the availability of a lawyer to pursue their claims. According to appellant, such conduct is "presumptively an exercise of his free speech rights" which cannot be curtailed in the absence of proof that it actually caused a specific harm that the State has a compelling interest in preventing. [C]. But in-person solicitation of professional employment by a lawyer does not stand on a par with truthful advertising about the availability and terms of routine legal services, let alone with forms of speech more traditionally within the concern of the First Amendment.

Expression concerning purely commercial transactions has come within the ambit of the Amendment's protection only recently. In rejecting the notion that such speech "is wholly outside the protection of the First Amendment," *Virginia Pharmacy* [*Board* v. *Virginia Citizens Consumer Council*, 425 U. S. 748, 761 (1976)], we were careful not to hold "that it is wholly undifferentiable from other forms" of speech. 425 U. S., at 771 n. 24. We have not discarded the "common-sense" distinction between speech proposing a commercial transaction, which occurs in an area traditionally subject to government regulation, and other varieties of speech. *Ibid.* To require a parity of constitutional protection for commercial and noncommercial speech alike could invite dilution, simply by a leveling process, of the force of the Amendment's guarantee with respect to the latter kind of speech. Rather than subject the First Amendment to such a devitalization, we instead have afforded commercial speech a limited measure of protection, commensurate with its subordinate position in the scale of First Amendment values. * * *

* * *

* * * Unlike a public advertisement, which simply provides information and leaves the recipient free to act upon it or not, in-person solicitation may exert pressure and often demands an immediate response, without providing an opportunity for comparison or reflection. The aim and effect of in-person solicitation may be to provide a one-sided presentation and to encourage speedy and perhaps uninformed decisionmaking; there is no opportunity for intervention or counter-education by agencies of the Bar, supervisory authorities, or persons close to the solicited individual. * * *

* * *

* * * The American Bar Association, as *amicus curiae*, defends the rule against solicitation primarily on three broad grounds: It is said that the prohibitions embodied in DR 2-103 (A) and 2-104 (A) serve to reduce the likelihood of overreaching and the exertion of undue influence on lay persons, to protect the privacy of individuals, and to avoid situations where the lawyer's exercise of judgment on behalf of the client will be clouded by his own pecuniary self-interest.

* * *

* * * [A]ppellant errs in assuming that the constitutional validity of the judgment below depends on proof that his conduct constituted actual overreaching or inflicted some specific injury on Wanda Holbert or Carol McClintock. His assumption flows from the premise that nothing less than actual proved harm to the solicited individual would be a sufficiently important state interest to justify disciplining the attorney who solicits employment in person for pecuniary gain.

Appellant's argument misconceives the nature of the State's interest. The Rules prohibiting solicitation are prophylactic measures whose objective is the prevention of harm before it occurs. The Rules were applied in this case to discipline a lawyer for soliciting employment for pecuniary gain under circumstances likely to result in the adverse consequences the State seeks to avert. In such a situation, which is inherently conducive to overreaching and other forms of misconduct, the State has a strong interest in adopting and enforcing rules of conduct designed to protect the public from harmful solicitation by lawyers whom it has licensed.

The State's perception of the potential for harm in circum-stances such as those presented in this case is well founded. The detrimental aspects of face-to-face selling even of ordinary consumer products have been recognized and addressed by the Federal Trade Commission, and it hardly need be said that the potential for overreaching is significantly greater when a lawyer, a professional trained in the art of persuasion, personally solicits an unsophisticated, injured, or distressed lay person. Such an individual may place his trust in a lawyer, regardless of the latter's qualifications or the individual's actual need for legal representation, simply in response to persuasion under circumstances conducive to uninformed acquiescence. * * *

The efficacy of the State's effort to prevent such harm to prospective clients would be substantially diminished if, having proved a solicitation in circumstances like those of this case, the State were required in addition to prove actual injury. Unlike the advertising in *Bates*, in-person solicitation is not visible or otherwise open to public scrutiny. Often there is no witness other than the lawyer and the lay person whom he has solicited, rendering it difficult or impossible to obtain reliable proof of what actually took place. This would be especially true if the lay person were so distressed at the time of the solicitation that he could not recall specific details at a later date. * * *

On the basis of the undisputed facts of record, we conclude that the Disciplinary Rules constitutionally could be applied to appellant. He approached two young accident victims at a time when they were especially incapable of making informed judgments or of assessing and protecting their own interests. He solicited Carol McClintock in a hospital room where she lay in traction and sought out Wanda Lou Holbert on the day she came home from the hospital, knowing from his prior inquiries that she had just been released. * * *

* * * The facts in this case present a striking example of the potential for overreaching that is inherent in a lawyer's in-person solicitation of

professional employment. They also demonstrate the need for prophylactic regulation in furtherance of the State's interest in protecting the lay public. We hold that the application of DR 2-103 (A) and 2-104 (A) to appellant does not offend the Constitution.

Accordingly, the judgment of the Supreme Court of Ohio is

Affirmed.

Notes

1. The *Primus/Ohralik* line between pecuniary solicitation and political association may not be as clear as it initially appears. In his dissent in *Primus*, Justice Rehnquist said that the distinction between commercial speech and political speech

> is subject to manipulation by clever practitioners. If Albert Ohralik, like Edna Primus, viewed litigation "'not [as] a technique of resolving private differences,'" but as "'a form of political expression' and 'political association,'" [c], for all that appears he would be restored to his right to practice. And we may be sure that the next lawyer in Ohralik's shoes who is disciplined for similar conduct will come here cloaked in the prescribed mantle of "political association" to assure that insurance companies do not take unfair advantage of policyholders.

Would the solicitation in *Primus* be protected if the ACLU was entitled to a contingent fee? If the ACLU would be awarded legal fees under a civil rights statute?

2. What result if following a railroad disaster, the minister in a poor community contacts a lawyer and helps him meet with and obtain clients from among the injured members of his congregation. Is this political association?

3. Does the Supreme Court assume that a lawyer who is motivated by financial gain is more likely to overreach a client than one who is motivated by political and social concerns? Ironically, the very problem that the ACLU lawyer wanted to litigate in *Primus* was the allegation that doctors overreached patients because of political and social concerns.

4. David Luban considers the possibility that lawyers motivated by political concerns will overreach their clients in his book *Lawyers and Justice,* 317-391 (1988):

> I concede the truth of four charges: that public interest lawyers bent on law reform recruit clients as plaintiffs; that they sometimes manipulate their clients and put the interests of the cause above those of the clients;

that they occasionally file class actions, even though a large part of the class invoked, sometimes a majority, opposes them; and that there will be times when "their handling of the test cases serves, not the enlightened self-interest of the poor, but the political theories of the lawyers themselves."

Quoting Charles W. Wolfram, *Modern Legal Ethics* at 940 (1986). In light of these charges, should the profession be as concerned, more concerned, or less concerned about the lawyer who is representing a client for political reasons as the lawyer who is representing a client for financial gain?

Monroe H. Freedman and Abbe Smith,
Understanding Lawyers' Ethics
329, 331-32, 350-51 (2d. ed., 2002)

Solicitation of Clients: The Professional Responsibility to Chase Ambulances

A five-year-old boy named Ernest Gene Gunn was seriously injured when he was hit by a car driven by John J. Washek. Shortly after the accident, the boy's mother was visited at home by an adjuster from Mr. Washek's insurance company. The adjuster told Ms. Gunn that there was no need for her to hire a lawyer, because the company would make a settlement as soon as Ernest was out of his doctor's care. If Ms. Gunn was not satisfied at that time, he explained, she could get a lawyer and file suit.

Ernest's injuries were sufficiently severe to require a doctor's care for twenty-three months. During that time, the adjuster was regularly in touch with Ms. Gunn. At the end of Ernest's medical treatment, however, despite several efforts on her part to reach him, the adjuster was unavailable. Finally, she retained a lawyer, who promptly filed suit for her. Ernest Gunn never did have his day in court, however, because the insurance company successfully pleaded a two-year statute of limitations.

* * *

The legal profession failed in its responsibilities when a plaintiff's lawyer was not at Ms. Gunn's doorstep at least as soon as the insurance adjuster. As Justice Musmanno noted in dissent in a case similar to *Gunn*:

> [The plaintiff] knew nothing about the statute of limitations. He had an eighth grade education. He had five small children [one of whom lost

all power of speech and locomotion in the accident at issue]; he lived in a renovated garage. Neither his sociological status nor his limited studies would acquaint him with a statute of limitations.

Referring to just such a person, former Attorney General Ramsey Clark has remarked, "A citizen who is unaware of his rights is hard to distinguish from a subject who has none."

Nor is Ms. Gunn's problem a unique one. More than thirty years ago, Illinois Supreme Court Judge Bristow observed that "insurance companies, railroads, airlines and other industries in whose operation some people are certain to be maimed or killed have highly organized mechanisms of defense." Unfair tactics of claim agents for these corporations range from "excessive zeal to . . . shocking fraud." Obviously, "[e]ven the most scrupulous claim agent cannot fairly represent both claimant and defendant." Thus, only through "timely arrival of the solicitor" can a claimant hope to receive "an amount that a court and jury deem adequate and just."

* * *

Consider, for example, a story in *The New York Times* relating to an accident in which twenty-one children drowned and sixty others were injured when a school bus plunged into a water-filled gravel pit in Alton, Texas. Fully four months after the accident, the *Times* ran a front-page story with a three-column headline: "Where 21 Youths Died, Lawyers Wage a War." The story tells of a "parade of lawyers" that began almost immediately after the accident, and of "fierce competition" among the lawyers to represent the families. On page one, the *Times* identifies "one benefit, if that is what it is: a poor and undereducated community, made up largely of Hispanic field laborers, has acquired a new kind of sophistication." This questionable benefit, according to the *Times*, is that people who wanted to grieve without the intrusion of lawyers are now saying, "When this happens to you, you hire a lawyer and you get money."

The important part of the story is on an inside page, at the very end, and is written in a way that makes it appear to be unrelated to the main story that preceded it. There we learn that the 3,000 people who live in Alton have returned to "the anonymous, poverty-stricken lives they led before the bus crashed into the water." Because the students who died were among the poorest in the high school, the response among the other students was "much less than if it was the star quarterback."

With the filing of that story, the last of the reporters also left Alton. Although the *Times'* prominent and lengthy critique of the "parade of lawyers" did not mention the fact, only the lawyers remained to serve the members of this "poor, undereducated community, made up largely of Hispanic field laborers." Subsequently, in a brief item buried on an inside page, the *Times* reported that the lawyers for 16 of the families whose children had been killed had obtained a settlement of $67.5 million for their clients.

In short, the legal system succeeded in providing equal protection and due process of law to poverty-stricken people whom all others were content to abandon. That is the story that deserved, but never received, a front-page headline.

* * *

Notes

1. Should the professional rules discourage or encourage solicitation for financial gain? Might a rule which merely prohibited overreaching be preferable? Did Ohralik provide a public service when he alerted Carol McClintock and Wanda Lou Holbert that the insurance policy covered injuries caused by an uninsured driver?

2. In 1990, the state of Florida amended its solicitation rule to forbid written or oral communication with a prospective client if the communication "concerns an action for personal injury or wrongful death or otherwise relates to an accident or disaster . . . unless the accident or disaster occurred more than thirty days prior to the mailing of the communication." This provision was challenged as violating the commercial free speech rights of attorneys. In *Florida Bar v. Went For It, Inc.*, 115 S. Ct. 2371, 132 L. Ed. 2d 541 (1995), the Supreme Court upheld the rule as a reasonable regulation of speech which serves the substantial state interest of "protecting injured Floridians from invasive conduct by lawyers and in preventing the erosion of confidence in the profession that such repeated invasions have engendered." *Id.* at 2381.

3. If lawyers can be forbidden from communicating with injured parties for thirty days after the event causing the injury, should insurance companies be forbidden from obtaining settlement agreements during the same period? Should such agreements be voidable, at least, if obtained from an injured party that was not represented while entering into the agreement?

Chapter Eight

JUDGES

A. Introduction to Judicial Discipline

Read the Preamble to the ABA Model Code of Judicial Conduct (MCJC) and Model Rule 8.3(b)[1]

As with lawyer codes, the ABA has adopted three sets of judicial codes in its history. The House of Delegates adopted the Canons of Judicial Ethics in 1924. Many states adopted the Judicial Canons, but many did not. In 1972, the ABA adopted the Code of Judicial Conduct (CJC). It was succeeded in 1990 by the Model Code of Judicial Conduct (MCJC). The 1972 and 1990 Codes are quite similar in substance and form. Both are composed of canons (broad statements of principle), rules, and commentary, but the numbering of the canons and rules differs. The 1990 MCJC is gender neutral, the 1972 CJC is not. Both the CJC and the MCJC were widely adopted by the states.[2]

Procedures for judicial discipline vary from state to state. Typically, complaints are made to a judicial commission, which investigates and makes recommendations to the state supreme court. Often initial investigations of judicial commissions are confidential. Should they be? See *Kamasinski v. Judicial Review Council,* 44 F.3d 106 (2d Cir. 1994). Judicial discipline can range from reprimand to removal from office.

Federal judges appointed under the provisions of Article III of the Constitution may be removed only by impeachment. Judges appointed under the terms of Article I of the Constitution can be disciplined in any manner consistent with the terms of the statute that establishes the court in which the judge sits. In 1973, the Judicial Conference of the United States adopted the Code of

---

[1]   For MR 8.3(b), *cf.* DR 1-103(A); EC 1-4; there is no Cal. Rules counterpart to MR 8.3(b).

[2]   This book will focus on the MCJC. Following citations in cases to other judicial codes, we will cite in brackets to the comparable MCJC provision. Notes following the cases will identify some of the significant differences between the CJC and the MCJC.

Conduct for United States Judges. It is similar in many respects to the ABA's Code of Judicial Conduct. In 1980 Congress passed 28 U.S.C. § 372(c) which establishes procedures for a panel of federal judges to impose discipline short of impeachment. Initially subjected to attacks as creating unconstitutional limitations on the independence of the judiciary and failing to provide constitutionally-required protections of due process, the statute has been upheld. *See Hastings* v. *Judicial Conference of U.S.*, 829 F.2d 91 (D.C.Cir., 1987) cert. denied 485 U.S. 1014 (1988).

B. Integrity, Independence, and Propriety

Read MCJC Canons 1 and 2

In re Inquiry of Lee
336 So.2d 1175 (Fla. 1976)

PER CURIAM.

We have before us a recommendation of the Judicial Qualifications Commission for a public reprimand of Judge J. Cail Lee of the Seventeenth Judicial Circuit, for conduct unbecoming a member of the judiciary. * * *

* * *

The Commission's finding that Judge Lee engaged in sexual activities with a member of the opposite sex not his wife in a parked automobile is adequately supported by evidence in the record before us. Judge Lee has clearly engaged in conduct unbecoming a member of the judiciary.

The Commission has recommended as the only discipline for Judge Lee that we issue a public reprimand. Although there is no express finding or statement by the Commission as to why this discipline was preferred over others that are available, such as removal from office, we assume from our independent review of the record that the Commission was influenced by:

(1) undisputed testimony and other supportive evidence to the effect that Judge Lee is an able jurist who is well-regarded by the bench and bar in Broward County, and that this extra-judicial incident will not impair his ability to function as a judge in that community; and

(2) Judge Lee's uncontradicted, sworn statement to the Commission stating that:

> "my presence and the time and place of the incident resulted from my having had too much to drink, occurred during an early Sunday morning on a holiday weekend, and did not in any way involve my judicial office. Neither the other party alleged to be involved in this incident nor any member of her family has ever appeared before me, or on behalf of, a party or witness, corporate or individual at any time, ever. Furthermore, during the almost three months since this incident occurred, I have not taken a single drink of any alcoholic beverage of any kind, in any place, in any amount, nor do I intend to do so in the future."

Under the totality of circumstances in this case, we accept the recommendation of the Commission and hereby reprimand Judge Lee for his conduct in this matter. * * *

Judge Lee is immediately reinstated to his duties as a circuit judge of the Seventeenth Judicial Circuit of Florida. This Court, however, under its administrative authority, directs that he shall not exercise jurisdiction in any criminal case without the express approval of the Chief Justice of this Court. It appearing that Judge Lee's right of rehearing has been waived, this Court dispenses with rehearing.

It is so ordered.

Notes

1.   Do you agree that "this extra-judicial incident will not impair his ability to function as a judge"? If so, why is this a concern of the Supreme Court? Why is he reprimanded? To what degree did the judge's excuse of drunkenness influence the court?

2.   Canon 9 of the 1969 ABA Model Code of Professional Responsibility provided that, "A Lawyer Should Avoid Even the Appearance of Impropriety." The 1983 ABA Model Rules dropped the provision for lawyers concerning the appearance of impropriety, noting that such a standard is too vague to be a useful test. *See* Comment to MR 1.5. The 1990 ABA Model Code of Judicial Conduct retained the 1972 Code's Canon requirement that a judge avoid "the Appearance of Impropriety in All of the Judge's Activities." MCJC 2. Is there reason to require judges, and not lawyers, to avoid the appearance of impropriety?

C. Impartiality, Diligence, and Dignity

Read MCJC 3A-D

In the Matter of Hague
315 N.W.2d 524 (Mich. 1982)

Justice RYAN

This is a judicial discipline proceeding in which Judge William C. Hague of the Recorder's Court, Traffic and Ordinance Division, is charged with four general categories of misconduct:

I.   Disobedience of valid orders entered by superior courts,

II.   Refusal to follow the decisions of higher courts,

III.   Abuse of the contempt power, and

IV.   Improperly excluding attorneys from his courtroom.

* * *

Refusal To Follow

The Decisions Of Higher Courts

Several years prior to the events here involved, Detroit adopted its gun-control ordinance which provided for a mandatory minimum penalty upon conviction of a $400 fine and "a term of imprisonment" if, at the time of the violation, the firearm is loaded.

Shortly thereafter, Judge Hague held this ordinance to be unconstitutional for the reasons, *inter alia*, that the state had preempted the firearm-control field.

The City of Detroit sought and obtained a writ of superintending control in the circuit court. The circuit judge ruled in a written opinion that the state had not preempted the gun-control field and that the ordinance was valid. Judge Hague appealed to the Court of Appeals which affirmed the circuit court, declaring:

> "We therefore conclude that the State of Michigan has not preempted firearms control. The circuit court order of superintending control is affirmed." *Detroit v. Recorder's Court Judge, Traffic & Ordinance Division*, 56 Mich.App. 224, 223 N.W.2d 722 (1974).

Judge Hague continued to dismiss gun-control cases at the arraignment or, upon trial, finding defendants not guilty for the announced reason that the ordinance violates the constitutional right to bear arms and that the city is without authority to legislate a mandatory minimum sentence.

Once again the city sought and obtained a writ of superintending control from the circuit court. The circuit judge held the ordinance to be valid and declared Judge Hague to be in error with respect to both of the grounds upon which he was holding the ordinance to be unconstitutional. Again, Judge Hague appealed to the Court of Appeals, which affirmed the circuit court and specifically held that the ordinance did not violate the constitutional right to bear arms and that the mandatory minimum sentence provision was valid, concluding with the statement:

> "The ordinance is constitutionally sound." *Detroit v. Recorder's Court Judge, Traffic & Ordinance Division*, 71 Mich.App. 414, 248 N.W.2d 566 (1976).

Notwithstanding the foregoing decisions of the Court of Appeals in 1974 and 1976 which affirmed issuance of writs of superintending control, Judge Hague continued, on at least eight occasions, from September, 1977 through October, 1978, to dismiss gun-control cases at the arraignment stage or found defendants not guilty after trial, or partial trial, citing precisely the same theories of unconstitutionality the Court of Appeals had rejected.

*   *   *

* * * Where, as here, a judge's decision striking down a law as unconstitutional is directly contrary to appellate precedent of which he is aware and obviously based upon his widely publicized personal belief about what the law should be rather than what it is, the public perception of impartiality of the justice system is seriously harmed. Code of Judicial Conduct, Canon 2(B) [*Cf.* MCJC 2(A)]. * * *

When a panel of the Court of Appeals, having jurisdiction of a matter as it did in this case, declares a law to be valid and enforceable, a trial judge is bound by that decision until another panel of the Court of Appeals or this Court rules otherwise, whether he agrees with the decision or not. * * *

Judge Hague not only disregarded the binding precedent announced by the Court of Appeals with respect to the constitutionality of the gun-control ordinance, he publicly declared his refusal to follow it, saying, as the record discloses:

* * *

"That decision I'm telling you-and you can communicate it to the judge who made it-is not binding on me. I don't have to follow that decision. The Court of Appeals doesn't make the law in this State.["]

* * *

We agree with the commission that in this case respondent's dismissal of gun-control cases was not the result of reasoned judgment but the product of his personal prejudices. By his lack of reasoned enforcement of the ordinance in question and willful disregard of the law as enunciated by the Court of Appeals, Judge Hague violated his oath of office, engendered disrespect for the law and improperly interfered with the proper administration of justice. [Cc].

[The Michigan Supreme Court also found that in a similar manner, Judge Hague had refused to enforce a Detroit ordinance which mandated a 20 day jail sentence for solicitation of prostitution. Judge Hague dismissed hundreds of prostitution cases for reasons having no basis in law, such as that the citation was issued on improper forms. On four occasions, the Chief Judge of Judge Hague's circuit ordered him to stop dismissing cases on an improper basis claimed by Judge Hague. On each occasion, Judge Hague began dismissing cases on another ground having no basis in law.]

CONCLUSION

The tale which unfolds upon a reading of the hundreds of pages of testimony, exhibits, briefs, and findings of fact and conclusions of law, is of a trial judge at ideological war with local prosecuting authorities over enforcement of non-traffic ordinances with the substance of which he does not agree. His longstanding and outspoken public opposition to the mandatory minimum penalties of the City of Detroit prostitution and gun-control ordinances led him to frustrate enforcement of this ordinance with every means at his disposal during his periodic two-week term as presiding judge. His depth of conviction that the ordinance penalties are unjust blinded him to an appreciation of the limits of his adjudicative role in the criminal justice process, and moved him to deny the authority of higher courts who declared he was in error and ultimately led him to disobey those orders because he did not agree with them. In the process he abused the contempt power of his office by threatening punishment to those who, in accordance with their own oath of office, attempted to follow and enforce the law he opposed. When that failed he attempted to usurp the authority of the Supreme Court by improperly denying three attorneys their right to practice law in the courtroom in which they, like he, were assigned to serve.

It was in his inability to separate the authority of the judicial office he holds from his personal convictions that Judge Hague lost his way. In the particulars described, unable to see that he was the servant of the law and not its embodiment, he set himself above it.

As a sister court declared recently:

"An intoxication with judicial power which would ignore basic constitutional precepts is a wholly unacceptable syndrome that cannot be tolerated * * *. To brook it in a single courtroom would not only degrade the courts in general, but would affront the vast majority of * * * judges who perceive their courtrooms as 'place[s] of justice,' rather than arenas for exhibitionism by display, before an intimidated audience, of naked and illegal judicial power." In the Matter of Yengo, 72 N.J. 425, 450, 371 A.2d 41, 57 (1977).

Judge Hague's disobedience of superior court orders, refusal to follow settled and binding case precedent, abuse of the contempt powers and unjustified exclusion of attorneys from the courtroom is a mosaic of willful misconduct designed solely to frustrate enforcement of laws he was oath-bound to uphold. It was repeated and defiant and, because of the widespread publicity given it within the courtroom and in the community at large, can only have seriously damaged public esteem for the judiciary in general, engendered disrespect for the law, exposed the courts to obloquy, contempt, censure and reproach and brought ridicule upon Judge Hague as a judicial officer.

We conclude that in all four types of misconduct detailed hereinbefore, the respondent failed to uphold his oath to faithfully discharge the duties of his office, Const.1963, art. 11, § 1; undermined the "integrity and independence of the judiciary," Code of Judicial Conduct, Canon 1; created "impropriety and the appearance of impropriety", Id., Canon 2; failed to maintain the integrity of the legal profession, Code of Professional Responsibility and Canons, Canon 1; engaged in conduct prejudicial to the proper administration of justice, Code of Professional Responsibility and Canons, DR 1-102(A)(5), GCR 1963, 953(1) and 932.4(b)(iv); exposed the courts to "obloquy, contempt, censure and reproach", GCR 1963, 953(2); and therefore failed to conform his behavior to the applicable standards of conduct, GCR 1963, 952.1 and 953(4).

We adopt the recommendation of the Judicial Tenure Commission and order Judge William C. Hague be suspended without pay from the discharge of all his judicial duties or administrative responsibility for a period of 60 days. Final process to effectuate this order of suspension shall issue immediately upon release of this opinion.

Notes

1. Can you distinguish Judge Hague's actions in the gun control cases from the actions of judges who based on questionable legal authority are quick to stop the implementation of the death penalty? In what Robert Bork denounced as "An Outbreak of Judicial Civil Disobedience," Ninth Circuit judges in 1992 issued several last minute stays of the execution of Robert Alton Harris. Harris was convicted of the 1978 murder of two teenage boys and sentenced to death. Following a decade of unsuccessful habeas corpus petitions and appeals, Harris was scheduled to be executed in the early morning hours of April 21, 1992. On the evening of April 20, ten Ninth Circuit judges issued a stay of execution. Later that night, the stay was vacated by the U.S. Supreme Court, which stated:

> This claim could have been brought more than a decade ago. There is no good reason for this abusive delay, which has been compounded by last-minute attempts to manipulate the judicial process.

Gomez v. U.S. District Court, 503 U.S. 653, 654 (1992). At 3:49 a.m. on April 21, Harris was strapped in for execution, but seconds before he was to be executed, Ninth Circuit Court Judge Harry Pregerson issued another stay of execution. Within two hours, the U.S. Supreme Court vacated the stay of execution and issued an unprecedented order that "[n]o further stays of Robert Alton Harris' execution shall be entered by the federal courts except upon order of this Court." *Vasquez v. Harris*, 503 U.S. 1000 (1992). Harris was executed that day at 6:00 a.m. For a more developed account of the facts and a criticism of the Supreme Court's actions, *see* Evan Caminker and Erwin Chemerinsky, "The Lawless Execution of Robert Alton Harris," 102 *Yale L.J.* 225 (1992). For a criticism of the judges who granted the last minute stays, *see* Robert H. Bork, "An Outbreak of Judicial Civil Disobedience," *The Wall Street Journal* A19 (April 29, 1992).

2. MRJC 3B(7) prohibits judges from initiating, permitting, or considering a case *ex parte*. The prohibition has been extended to judge's law clerks. In *Kennedy v. Great Atlantic & Pacific Tea Co.*, 551 F.2d 593 (5th Cir. 1977), the plaintiff alleged that he slipped on defendant's floor after a rainstorm. Defendant denied that it was wet. Following a rainstorm that occurred pending trial, the trial judge's law clerk went to the store to see if the spot was wet. It was. The plaintiff's attorney called the law clerk as a witness at trial and the jury rendered a verdict for the plaintiff. The appellate court vacated the judgment on the grounds that the clerk's visit to the store was an *ex parte* communication.

3. MRJC 3B(4) requires a judge to "be patient, dignified and courteous to litigants." In *Spruance v. Commission on Judicial Qualifications*, 13 Cal. 3d 778, 788-89, 532 P.2d 1209, 1216, 119 Cal. Rptr. 841, 848 (1975), in addition to other indiscretions, a judge was found to have treated

> litigants in a cavalier, rude and improper manner. Thus, in count I-A, petitioner was alleged to have expressed his disbelief in the testimony of a defendant by having created a sound commonly referred to as a "raspberry" and in count I-B, petitioner was charged with having made a vulgar gesture (giving the "finger" or *digitus impudicus*) in reprimanding a defendant for coming in late in a traffic matter.

The Court found that:

> The petitioner used the gesture to indicate that the tardiness of the defendant demonstrated the latter's lack of respect for the court and not to demean the defendant nor to suggest the attitude of the court toward the defendant.

Id. at 789, 532 P.2d at 1216, 119 Cal. Rptr. at 848 n.9. The court also found the judge guilty of giving special treatment to his friends and political supporters and altering the reported disposition of his own traffic case so as to convey the false impression that he had completed traffic school. The Court removed the judge from office.

United States v. Microsoft

253 F.3d 34 (D.C. Cir. 2001)

[The United States alleged that Microsoft committed anti-trust violations. After a bench trial, District Judge Robert Penfield Jackson found the company guilty and ordered various remedies, including divestiture. The Court of Appeals affirmed the finding of monopoly power. It held that exclusion of Microsoft's internet browser from a program removal utility was exclusionary conduct.]

* * *

A. The District Judge's Communications with the Press

Immediately after the District Judge entered final judgment on June 7, 2000, accounts of interviews with him began appearing in the press. Some of the interviews were held after he entered final judgment. *See* Peter Spiegel, *Microsoft Judge Defends Post-trial Comments*, FIN. TIMES (London), Oct. 7, 2000, at 4; John R. Wilke, *For Antitrust Judge, Trust, or Lack of It, Really Was the Issue--In an Interview, Jackson Says Microsoft Did the Damage to Its Credibility in Court*, WALL ST. J., June 8, 2000, at A1. The District Judge also aired his views about the case to larger audiences, giving speeches at a college and at an antitrust seminar. [Cc].

From the published accounts, it is apparent that the Judge also had been giving secret interviews to select reporters before entering final judgment--in some instances long before. The earliest interviews we know of began in September 1999, shortly after the parties finished presenting evidence but two months before the court issued its Findings of Fact. [Cc]. * * * The Judge "embargoed" these interviews; that is, he insisted that the fact and content of the interviews remain secret until he issued the Final Judgment.

* * *

The published accounts indicate that the District Judge discussed numerous topics relating to the case. Among them was his distaste for the defense of technological integration-one of the central issues in the lawsuit. * * * "It was quite clear to me that the motive of Microsoft in bundling the Internet browser was not one of consumer convenience.

The evidence that this was done for the consumer was not credible. ...
The evidence was so compelling that there was an ulterior motive."
Wilke, WALL ST. J.) * * *

Reports of the interviews have the District Judge describing
Microsoft's conduct, with particular emphasis on what he regarded as
the company's prevarication, hubris, and impenitence. * * * He told
reporters that Bill Gates' "testimony is inherently without credibility"
and "if you can't believe this guy, who else can you believe?" [Joel
Brinkley & Steve Lohr, *U.S. V. Microsoft* 278 (2001)]; Brinkley &
Lohr, N.Y. TIMES * * *

* * * The Judge told a college audience that "Bill Gates is an
ingenious engineer, but I don't think he is that adept at business ethics.
He has not yet come to realise [sic] things he did (when Microsoft was
smaller) he should not have done when he became a monopoly."
Spiegel, FIN. TIMES. Characterizing Gates' and his company's "crime"
as hubris, the Judge stated that "if I were able to propose a remedy of
my devising, I'd require Mr. Gates to write a book report" on Napoleon
Bonaparte, "because I think [Gates] has a Napoleonic concept of
himself and his company, an arrogance that derives from power and
unalloyed success, with no leavening hard experience, no reverses."
Auletta, THE NEW YORKER , at 41; *see also* AULETTA, WORLD WAR
3.0, at 397.* * *

* * *

The District Judge also secretly divulged to reporters his views on
the remedy for Microsoft's antitrust violations. * * * [One] reporter has
the Judge asking "were the Japanese allowed to propose terms of their
surrender?" Spiegel, FIN. TIMES. [He] told reporters the month before
he issued his break-up order that "assuming, as I think they are, [ ] the
Justice Department and the states are genuinely concerned about the
public interest," "I know they have carefully studied all the possible
options. This isn't a bunch of amateurs. They have consulted with
some of the best minds in America over a long period of time." "I am
not in a position to duplicate that and re-engineer their work. There's
no way I can equip myself to do a better job than they have done."
Brinkley & Lohr, N.Y. TIMES ; *cf. Final Judgment*, at 62-63.

* * * [Two months before his decision to break up the company,
the Judge told a reporter the following story: A "North Carolina mule
trainer"] had a trained mule who could do all kinds of wonderful tricks.

One day somebody asked him: "How do you do it? How do you train the mule to do all these amazing things?" "Well," he answered, "I'll show you." He took a 2-by-4 and whopped him upside the head. The mule was reeling and fell to his knees, and the trainer said: "You just have to get his attention." Brinkley & Lohr, U.S. v. MICROSOFT 278. The Judge added: "I hope I've got Microsoft's attention." [Cc].

B. Violations of the Code of Conduct for United States Judges

The Code of Conduct for United States Judges was adopted by the Judicial Conference of the United States in 1973. It prescribes ethical norms for federal judges as a means to preserve the actual and apparent integrity of the federal judiciary. Every federal judge receives a copy of the Code, the Commentary to the Code, the Advisory Opinions of the Judicial Conference's Committee on Codes of Conduct * * *.

* * * [Canon 3A(6) forbids] federal judges to comment publicly "on the merits of a pending or impending action[.]" [Contrast MCJC 3B(9), *see* note 1 following this case] * * *

The Microsoft case was "pending" during every one of the District Judge's meetings with reporters; the case is "pending" now; and even after our decision issues, it will remain pending for some time. The District Judge breached his ethical duty under Canon 3A(6) each time he spoke to a reporter about the merits of the case. * * * And these were not just any members of the public. Because he was talking to reporters, the Judge knew his comments would eventually receive widespread dissemination.

*   *   *

Far from mitigating his conduct, the District Judge's insistence on secrecy--his embargo--made matters worse. Concealment of the interviews suggests knowledge of their impropriety. Concealment also prevented the parties from nipping his improprieties in the bud. Without any knowledge of the interviews, neither the plaintiffs nor the defendant had a chance to object or to seek the Judge's removal before he issued his Final Judgment.

*   *   *

In addition to violating the rule prohibiting public comment, the District Judge's reported conduct raises serious questions under Canon 3A(4). That Canon states that a "judge should accord to every person who is legally interested in a proceeding, or the person's lawyer, full right to be heard according to law, and, except as authorized by law, neither initiate nor consider *ex parte* communications on the merits, or procedures affecting the merits, of a pending or impending proceeding." CODE OF CONDUCT Canon 3A(4). [Cf. MCJC 3B(7) ("shall")].

What did the reporters convey to the District Judge during their secret sessions? * * * [We] think it safe to assume that these interviews were not monologues. Interviews often become conversations. When reporters pose questions or make assertions, they may be furnishing information, information that may reflect their personal views of the case. The published accounts indicate this happened on at least one occasion. Ken Auletta reported, for example, that he told the Judge "that Microsoft employees professed shock that he thought they had violated the law and behaved unethically," at which time the Judge became "agitated" by "Microsoft's 'obstinacy'." *Id.* at 369. It is clear that Auletta had views of the case. As he wrote in a *Washington Post* editorial, "Anyone who sat in [the District Judge's] courtroom during the trial had seen ample evidence of Microsoft's sometimes thuggish tactics." Ken Auletta, *Maligning the Microsoft Judge*, WASH. POST, Mar. 7, 2001, at A23.

* * *

Another point needs to be stressed. Rulings in this case have potentially huge financial consequences for one of the nation's largest publicly-traded companies and its investors. The District Judge's secret interviews during the trial provided a select few with inside information about the case, information that enabled them and anyone they shared it with to anticipate rulings before the Judge announced them to the world. Although he "embargoed" his comments, the Judge had no way of policing the reporters. For all he knew there may have been trading on the basis of the information he secretly conveyed. The public cannot be expected to maintain confidence in the integrity and impartiality of the federal judiciary in the face of such conduct.

C. Appearance of Partiality

* * * Microsoft urges the District Judge's disqualification under § 455(a): a judge "shall disqualify himself in any proceeding in which his impartiality might reasonably be questioned." 28 U.S.C. § 455(a). [Cf. MCJC 3E]. The standard for disqualification under § 455(a) is an

objective one. The question is whether a reasonable and informed observer would question the judge's impartiality. [Cc].

"The very purpose of § 455(a) is to promote confidence in the judiciary by avoiding even the appearance of impropriety whenever possible." [C]. As such, violations of the Code of Conduct may give rise to a violation of §455(a) if doubt is cast on the integrity of the judicial process. It has been argued that any "public comment by a judge concerning the facts, applicable law, or merits of a case that is *sub judice* in his court or any comment concerning the parties or their attorneys would raise grave doubts about the judge's objectivity and his willingness to reserve judgment until the close of the proceeding." William G. Ross, *Extrajudicial Speech: Charting the Boundaries of Propriety*, 2 GEO. J. LEGAL ETHICS 589, 598 (1989). * * *

* * *

In this case * * * [t]he public comments were not only improper, but also would lead a reasonable, informed observer to question the District Judge's impartiality. Public confidence in the integrity and impartiality of the judiciary is seriously jeopardized when judges secretly share their thoughts about the merits of pending cases with the press. Judges who covet publicity, or convey the appearance that they do, lead any objective observer to wonder whether their judgments are being influenced by the prospect of favorable coverage in the media. Discreet and limited public comments may not compromise a judge's apparent impartiality, but we have little doubt that the District Judge's conduct had that effect. Appearance may be all there is, but that is enough to invoke the Canons and §455(a).

Judge Learned Hand spoke of "this America of ours where the passion for publicity is a disease, and where swarms of foolish, tawdry moths dash with rapture into its consuming fire. . . ." LEARNED HAND, THE SPIRIT OF LIBERTY 132-33 (2d ed. 1953). Judges are obligated to resist this passion. Indulging it compromises what Edmund Burke justly regarded as the "cold neutrality of an impartial judge." Cold or not, federal judges must maintain the appearance of impartiality. What was true two centuries ago is true today: "Deference to the judgments and rulings of courts depends upon public confidence in the integrity and independence of judges." CODE OF CONDUCT Canon 1 cmt. Public confidence in judicial impartiality cannot survive if judges, in disregard of their ethical obligations, pander to the press.

* * * Rather than manifesting neutrality and impartiality, the reports of the interviews with the District Judge convey the impression of a judge posturing for posterity, trying to please the reporters with colorful analogies and observations bound to wind up in the stories they write. Members of the public may reasonably question whether the District Judge's desire for press coverage influenced his judgments, indeed whether a publicity-seeking judge might consciously or subconsciously seek the publicity-maximizing outcome. We believe, therefore, that the District Judge's interviews with reporters created an appearance that he was not acting impartially, as the Code of Conduct and §455(a) require.

D. Remedies for Judicial Misconduct and Appearance of Partiality

1. Disqualification

Disqualification is mandatory for conduct that calls a judge's impartiality into question. [C]. Section 455 does not prescribe the scope of disqualification. Rather, Congress "delegated to the judiciary the task of fashioning the remedies that will best serve the purpose" of the disqualification statute. [C].

At a minimum, § 455(a) requires prospective disqualification of the offending judge, that is, disqualification from the judge's hearing any further proceedings in the case. [C]. Microsoft urges retroactive disqualification of the District Judge, which would entail disqualification antedated to an earlier part of the proceedings and vacatur of all subsequent acts. [C].

* * *

[We] conclude that the appropriate remedy for the violations of § 455(a) is disqualification of the District Judge retroactive only to the date he entered the order breaking up Microsoft. We therefore will vacate that order in its entirety and remand this case to a different District Judge, but will not set aside the existing Findings of Fact or Conclusions of Law (except insofar as specific findings are clearly erroneous or legal conclusions are incorrect).

This partially retroactive disqualification minimizes the risk of injustice to the parties and the damage to public confidence in the judicial process. Although the violations of the Code of Conduct and § 455(a) were serious, full retroactive disqualification is unnecessary.

It would unduly penalize plaintiffs, who were innocent and unaware of the misconduct, and would have only slight marginal deterrent effect.

Most important, full retroactive disqualification is unnecessary to protect Microsoft's right to an impartial adjudication. The District Judge's conduct destroyed the appearance of impartiality. Microsoft neither alleged nor demonstrated that it rose to the level of actual bias or prejudice. There is no reason to presume that everything the District Judge did is suspect. [Cc]. Although Microsoft challenged very few of the findings as clearly erroneous, we have carefully reviewed the entire record and discern no basis to suppose that actual bias infected his factual findings.

The most serious judicial misconduct occurred near or during the remedial stage. It is therefore commensurate that our remedy focus on that stage of the case. The District Judge's impatience with what he viewed as intransigence on the part of the company; his refusal to allow an evidentiary hearing; his analogizing Microsoft to Japan at the end of World War II; his story about the mule--all of these out-of-court remarks and others, plus the Judge's evident efforts to please the press, would give a reasonable, informed observer cause to question his impartiality in ordering the company split in two.

* * *

Notes

1.   The Circuit Court found Judge Jackson to have violated Canon 3A(6) of the Code of Conduct for United States Judges, which requires federal judges to "avoid public comment on the merits []of pending or impending" cases. The analogous provision of the ABA's Code of Judicial Conduct, MCJC 3B(9), provides:

> A judge shall not, while a proceeding is pending or impending in any court, make any public comment that might reasonably be expected to affect its outcome or impair its fairness or make any nonpublic comment that might substantially interfere with a fair trial or hearing. * * *

Would Judge Jackson have been in violation of the MCJC provision? Which judicial code provision is better?

2.   Press reports appeared *after* judgment was entered. Since they appeared after judgment, did they cause any harm?

3.   This was a bench trial--there was no jury to influence. In light of this fact, did the judge's disclosures cause any harm?

4.   If the judge's remarks had been made public before he rendered his decision would they have been cause for disqualification from the entire case? (28 U.S.C.A. § 455(a) requires a judge "disqualify himself in any proceeding in which his impartiality might reasonably be questioned.") Do you find the Circuit Court's argument for its "bifurcated" decision on disqualification convincing?

5.   If Judge Jackson had been a lawyer representing a client in the case, rather than the judge, could he be disciplined for his comments to the press under MR 3.6? Should lawyers and judges be under the same limitations in their comments to the press regarding pending cases? The California Supreme Court has held that comments by judges pose different, and more serious, dangers to the public's confidence in the judiciary.

> Because judges and attorneys play different roles in the judicial process, their public comments on pending judicial proceedings threaten the fairness of those proceedings in different ways and to different degrees. The public understands that in judicial proceedings lawyers, although also officers of the court, are advocates for the interests of their clients [cc]; therefore, the public does not expect a high degree of neutrality or objectivity when lawyers comment on pending cases, nor does the public expect all attorneys to assess the merits of pending cases in the same way. Judges, by contrast, cannot be advocates for the interests of any parties; they must be, and be perceived to be, neutral arbiters of both fact and law who apply the law uniformly and consistently. Because judges are both [cc] "highly visible member[s] of government" [cc] and neutral decision makers in all court proceedings, their public comments will be received by the public as more authoritative than those of lawyers. And because judges have this greater influence over public opinion, inappropriate public comment by judges poses a much greater threat to the fairness of judicial proceedings than improper public comment by lawyers.

> A judge's public comment on a pending case threatens the state's interest in maintaining public confidence in the judiciary whether or not the case to which the comment is directed is pending before the commenting judge. When the case is pending before the commenting judge, the public may perceive the comment as indicating that the judge has prejudged the merits of the controversy or is biased against or in favor of one of the parties. [Cc]. When the case is pending before a judge

other than the commenting judge, the public may perceive the comment as an attempt to influence the judge who is charged with deciding the case. [Cc] Such comments may also create the public impression that the judge has abandoned the judicial role to become an advocate for the judge's own ruling or for the position advanced by one of the parties.

Broadman v. Commission on Judicial Performance, 959 P.2d 715, 727 (Cal. 1999).

D. Disqualification

Read MCJC 3E-F

MCJC 3B(1) states, "A judge shall hear and decide matters assigned to the judge except those in which disqualification is required." Disqualification can work a substantial hardship on the parties, other judges, and the judicial system. In addition, if judges are too quick to disqualify themselves, parties can shop for judges. Chief Justice Rehnquist once said:

> During my sixteen years of the private practice of law, the judge who was the most "sensitive" to the "appearance of impropriety" of any I knew sat in a court of general jurisdiction in the state where I practiced. He was so "sensitive" to the appearance of impropriety that if he had so much as shaken hands at a large political gathering with one of the litigants who appeared before him, he would summarily disqualify himself. The principal result of this "sensitivity" on his part, so far as I could see, was that at least one working day a week he was able to reach the first tee of the golf course before eleven o'clock in the morning, or else get home and do some of those odd jobs which escape the attention of all of us on the weekends.[3]

The rules give judges little room for error. On one hand, they must disqualify themselves if "the judge's impartiality might reasonably be questioned." MCJC 3E(1). On the other, they must not disqualify themselves unless "disqualification is required." MCJC 3B(1). Consider the limits on the judge's discretion as you read the next cases.

---

[3]   William H. Rehnquist, "Sense and Nonsense About Judicial Ethics," 28 Record of the Association of the Bar of the City of New York 694, 712-713 (1973).

State v. Ahearn

137 Vt. 253, 403 A.2d 696 (1979)

Justice DALY

In a trial by jury the defendant was found guilty upon two informations, charging assault and robbery while armed with a dangerous weapon * * *

The defendant conducted his own defense. However stand-by counsel, appointed by the trial court, was available to assist if he so requested. The defendant did not, at any time, deny that he committed the crimes. Indeed, in his opening statement and in his own testimony, he admitted the commission of the crimes. Rather, he relied on a unique defense of temporary insanity. The defense arises out of a long imprisonment, including seven years of solitary confinement. The defendant contended that extended incarceration made him subject to sudden, uncontrollable urges that resulted in violence and theft. The jury rejected his defense, finding him guilty upon each charge.

[At trial, defendant requested the opportunity to confer with each witness for five minutes immediately before placing the witness on the stand. This request was denied. The Supreme Court held that the trial judge acted properly.]

* * *

The next claim of error derives from the defendant's own outbursts. After the testimony of his first witness, the defendant asked for a five-minute recess before he called his next witness. As indicated above his request was denied. A bench conference ensued. When the defendant became emotionally excited, the jury was excused. He became increasingly indignant, abusive, and obscene, insisting that he would not continue until he had had a conference with the next witness. Faced with the defendant's intransigence, the judge called the public defender to the bench, saying that the defendant was to be excluded from the courtroom. At that point, the defendant picked up a loudspeaker and hurled it at the judge. It struck him in the face. Court officers tackled the defendant and carried him out.

Following a recess, the defendant was given the alternative of appearing in restraints or of being excluded from the courtroom. He chose the former and again rejected the public defender. Asked how the handcuffs would be explained to the jury, the court replied that they would not be. When the trial resumed, the defendant questioned witnesses and made oral argument, while seated at counsel table with his handcuffs shackled to a restraining belt.

* * *

The defendant now avers that the judge should have disqualified himself at trial and at sentencing, although disqualification was only hinted at at trial and was never raised at sentencing. He relies on Canon 3(C)(1) of the Code of Judicial Conduct [*Cf.* MCJC 3E(1)(a)]: "A judge should disqualify himself in a proceeding in which his impartiality might reasonably be questioned, including but not limited to instances where: (a) he has a personal bias or prejudice concerning a party. . . ." [C]. Where a judge has been struck in the face by a defendant, he argues, the judge's subsequent impartiality might reasonably be questioned.

"In order to maintain a colorable claim of judicial disqualification against the presiding judge, defendant must affirmatively show bias or prejudice directed against him." [C]. No such showing has been made. The mere fact that the defendant attacked the judge does not alone support a claim of disqualification. Indeed, a defendant's misconduct will not lightly be allowed to disrupt a trial. "Schemes to drive a judge out of the case . . . should not be allowed to succeed." A.B.A. Standards Relating to the Judge's Role in Dealing With Trial Disruptions, § F.5, at 21 (1971).

The defendant's contention that a different judge should have been appointed for sentencing is more cogent, but he does not satisfy his burden on review. "It is the existence of bias or prejudice in [the trial judge's] mind against the respondent which must be clearly shown." [Cc]. In support of his claim, he argues solely that the sentence is harsh.

In view of Canon 3(C)(1) [MCJC 3E (1)(a)], wherein a judge should disqualify himself if his impartiality might reasonably be questioned, we feel that it would have been better for the judge to have stepped aside. [C]. However, we cannot agree that the sentence itself clearly establishes the existence of bias or prejudice against the defendant. While the sentence is certainly severe, it is not, in view of the crimes for which the defendant was convicted and in light of his twelve previous felony convictions, inappropriate. No bias or prejudice having been shown, reversible error does not appear.

Judgment affirmed.

Notes

1.   Should the judge have stepped aside for the sentencing hearing as suggested by the Vermont Supreme Court? Could his impartiality "reasonably be questioned" under MCJC? If he stepped aside, what policy implications would arise?

2.   Might a judge's impartiality "reasonably be questioned" if one of the parties is represented by:

   a.   the judge's former partner;

   b.   the judge's former law clerk;

   c.   the ex-governor who appointed the judge to the bench;[4]

   d.   the spouse of the governor when the judge is subject to reappointment by the governor.[5]

Both in his writings and in his decisions, Judge John Noonan of the Ninth Circuit Court of Appeals has been consistently pro-life, opposing abortion, capital punishment, and euthanasia. For example, prior to coming on the bench, he published articles opposing abortion;[6] as a judge he issued or joined in issuing stays of the execution of Robert Alton Harris (discussed *infra* this chapter,

---

[4]   Maura Dolan, "4 Justices to Withdraw From Case; Insurance: Group Alleges the Appearance of Impropriety in Matter Involving Former Gov. Deukmejian, Who Appointed The Judges. Such Charges Are Insulting, Jurist Says," *Los Angeles Times*, at A25 (March 25, 1994).

[5]   *Cf.* Owen Ullmann & Mike McNamee, "Married With Conflicts; Bill & Hill & Rod & Carla & the Problem of Capital Power Couples," *The Washington Post*, at C1 (April 10, 1994).

[6]   John T. Noonan, Jr., "An Almost Absolute Value in History," *in The Morality of Abortion: Legal and Historical Approaches* (John T. Noonan, Jr., ed. 1970); John T. Noonan, Jr., *A Private Choice: Abortion in America in the Seventies* (1979); John T. Noonan, Jr., "Liberal Laxists," 6 *The Human Life Review* 32 (1980); and John T. Noonan, Jr., "The Root and Branch of *Roe v. Wade*," 63 *Neb. L. Rev.* 668 (1984).

Section C);[7] and wrote the decision in which the Ninth Circuit held that there is no constitutional right to assisted suicide.[8]   Judge Noonan is Roman Catholic. In the following case, an abortion clinic filed a civil action against protestors, seeking treble damages under the Racketeer Influenced and Corrupt Organizations Act (RICO). The Ninth Circuit, in an opinion joined by Judge John Noonan, reversed a judgment entered in favor of the clinic, 63 F.3d 863. The abortion clinic filed a petition for rehearing and a motion that Judge Noonan recuse himself. The following is Judge Noonan's opinion on the motion for recusal.

Feminist Women's Health Center v. Codispoti
69 F.3d 399 (9th Cir. 1995)

ORDER

NOONAN, Circuit Judge

The Constitution of the United States, Article VI, provides: "no religious Test shall ever be required as a Qualification to any Office or public Trust under the United States." The plaintiffs in this petition for rehearing renew their motion that I recuse myself because my "fervently-held religious beliefs would compromise [my] ability to apply the law." This contention stands in conflict with the principle embedded in Article VI.

It is a matter of public knowledge that the Catholic Church, of which I am a member, holds that the deliberate termination of a normal pregnancy is a sin, that is, an offense against God and against neighbor. Orthodox Judaism also holds that in most instances abortion is a grave offense against God. The Church of Jesus Christ of Latter-Day Saints proscribes abortion as normally sinful. These are only three of many religious bodies whose teaching on the usual incompatibility of abortion with the requirements of religious morality would imply that the plaintiffs' business

---

[7]   See Harris v. Vasquez, 901 F.2d 724 (9th Cir. 1990) (issuing stay of execution) and Gomez v. U.S. District Court, No. 9270237 (9th Cir. April 20, 1992) (joining nine other judges in issuing stay on the eve of execution) *vacated*, 503 U.S. 653.

[8]   Compassion in Dying v. Washington, 49 F.3d 586 (9th Cir. 1995) (2-1 decision rejecting challenge to Washington's law prohibiting suicide), *overruled by* 1996 WL 94848 (9th Cir. 1996) (en banc).

is disfavored by their adherents. *See* Theresa V. Gorski, *Kendrick and Beyond: Re-establishing Establishment Clause Limits on Government Aid to Religious Social Welfare Organizations*, 23 Colum.J.L. & Soc.Probs. 171 (1990). If religious beliefs are the criterion of judicial capacity in abortion-related cases, many persons with religious convictions must be disqualified from hearing them. In particular, I should have disqualified myself from hearing or writing *Johnston v. Koppes*, 850 F.2d 594 (9th Cir.1988), upholding the constitutional rights of an advocate of abortion.[9]

True, the plaintiffs qualify my beliefs as "fervently-held" as if to distinguish my beliefs from those that might be lukewarmly maintained. A moment's consideration shows that the distinction is not workable. The question is whether incapacitating prejudice flows from religious belief. The question is to be judged objectively as a reasonable person with knowledge of all the facts would judge. *Moideen v. Gillespie*, 55 F.3d 1478, 1482 (9th Cir.1995). As long as a person holds the creed of one of the religious bodies condemning abortion as sinful he must be accounted unfit to judge a case involving abortion; the application of an objective, reasonable-person standard leads inexorably to this conclusion if the plaintiffs' contention is supportable. No thermometer exists for measuring the heatedness of a religious belief objectively. Either religious belief disqualifies or it does not. Under Article VI it does not.

The plaintiffs may object that the disqualification applies only to cases involving abortion; they are not disqualifying Catholics, Jews, Mormons and others from all judicial office. This distinction, too, is unworkable. The plaintiffs are contending that judges of these denominations cannot function in a broad class of cases that have arisen frequently in the last quarter of a century. The plaintiffs seek to qualify the office of federal judge with a proviso: no judge with religious beliefs condemning abortion may function in abortion cases. The sphere of action of these judges is limited and reduced.

---

[9] In *Johnston* the Ninth Circuit, in an opinion written by Judge Noonan, held that a California state employee had established triable issues of fact bearing on whether she had been reassigned because she attended a legislative hearing on the use of state funds for abortions.

The proviso effectively imposes a religious test on the federal judiciary.

The plaintiffs' motion of recusal is denied.

Notes

1.   [The lawyer who brought the recusal motion in this case, Kristin Houser] said it was based not on Noonan's Catholicism but on articles he published roughly 15 years ago in a periodical called Human Life Review. According to the recusal motion, Noonan's 1980 article cited "atrocities committed on . . . female patients" as "testimony to the kind of person often attracted to the abortion business."[10]

2.   Are the religious views of a judge likely to influence his or her decisions? Should they?

3.   Should Judge Noonan have been disqualified from deciding this case because his church opposes abortion? Should he have been disqualified if his church supported abortion? Should a judge have been disqualified if she was a member of a secular organization, such as the National Organization for Women or the Republican Party, which has taken a stand on abortion?

4.   MCJC 3E(c) requires a judge to disqualify herself if she has "an economic interest" in the subject matter in controversy. In the terminology section of the MCJC, "economic interest" is defined as "more than a de minimis legal or equitable interest." The 1972 CJC had a similar provision, but it defined "financial interest" to mean an interest "however small." CJC 3C(3)(b). In *In re Cement Antitrust Litigation*, 688 F.2d 1297 (9th Cir. 1982), a judge's wife owned stock in several of the plaintiff class members. The Ninth Circuit upheld the judge's decision to recuse himself under the U.S. Code's comparable "however small" requirement, noting:

> after five years of litigation, a multi-million dollar lawsuit of major national importance, with over 200,000 class plaintiffs, grinds to a halt over Mrs. Muecke's $29.70.

Id. at 1313.

---

[10]   Keith Donoghue, "Noonan Rejects Recusal Motion in Abortion Case; Catholic Judge Says Religious Litmus Test Would Be Unlawful", *The Recorder* 1 (November 8, 1995).

E. Extra-Judicial and Political Activities

Read MCJC 4-5 and Model Rule 8.2(b)[11]

In re Bonin
375 Mass. 680, 378 N.E.2d 669 (1978)

In disciplinary proceeding involving Chief Justice of the Superior Court, the Supreme Judicial Court, Suffolk County, held that his giving of employment to individuals connected with client which has given him gifts and attendance at meeting under circumstances in which he has good reason to infer that meeting involves matters which might come before superior court warrants public censure and suspension for reasonable period of time.

* * *

Findings of Fact

1.   In December, 1977, the Boston/Boise Committee (committee) was organized as "a committee of outrage at the recent handling of 24 indictments for alleged sex acts between men and boys in the Boston area." The committee sponsored a fundraising event at the Arlington Street Church on Wednesday, April 5, 1978, with Gore Vidal, a noted author, as the featured speaker. * * *

2.   On Sunday, April 2, 1978, the Boston Globe printed a brief announcement: "Author Gore Vidal will discuss 'Sex and Politics in Massachusetts' Wednesday evening at the Arlington Street Church. Admission is $5 and the funds will be used to benefit the Boston/Boise Committee." The Chief Justice saw the announcement and after lunch on Monday, April 3, went with a friend to the church, where they purchased four tickets. He asked the woman who sold the tickets what Boston/Boise was all about, and she answered, "It was a committee that was formed to counteract the negative publicity that had resulted from the indictments in Revere in December, ..."

* * * Later that day the Chief Justice had a conversation with people in his office about his attending a lecture to be given by Gore Vidal at the Arlington Street Church. There was reference to the church as a controversial church, of activities there including draft card burnings,

---

[11]   For MR 8.2(b), *cf.* DR 8-103; there is no Cal. counterpart to MR 8.2(b).

and of the possibility that some motorcycle riders might be there. In that conversation the Chief Justice referred to Gore Vidal as a "gay," apparently meaning an avowed homosexual.

3.   On April 4, 1978, William P. Homans, counsel for one of the defendants in the Revere cases, received a telephone message from the Boston/Boise Committee informing him that the Chief Justice would be at the Gore Vidal lecture on April 5, 1978. After receiving that message, Mr. Homans called Brian McMenimen, counsel for another of the defendants in the Revere cases, informed him of the message and said that they owed it to the Chief Justice to advise him that this was a fund raiser, the proceeds of which would be used to benefit the defendants in the Revere cases. They then agreed that Mr. McMenimen would call either the Chief Justice or Mr. Orfanello to give them that information.

4.   On April 5, 1978, Mr. McMenimen called Francis X. Orfanello, the administrative assistant to the Chief Justice. Mr. McMenimen told Mr. Orfanello that he understood the Chief Justice was planning to attend a lecture that night by Gore Vidal, sponsored by the Boston/Boise Committee. He referred to the Revere cases and said that the committee was formed for the benefit of those defendants, that the proceeds of the lecture were going to be used to defray some of the legal costs associated with the defense of those cases. He said "that the Chief Justice couldn't possibly know that this is, in essence, a defense fund raiser or else he'd never in a million years go to it." There was discussion of the committee and its connection with the "gay rights movement." Mr. Orfanello said he would give the Chief Justice the message.

* * * Mr. Orfanello testified that he told the Chief Justice the meeting was for the defense of the criminal defendants. The Chief Justice denied that anything was said about a fund raiser or use of the funds for the benefit of any particular defendants.

* * *

5.   At this time the Chief Justice knew from news media reports that the Revere cases were pending in the Superior Court. He also knew that homosexual cases arising out of arrests at the Boston Public Library were pending in the Boston Municipal Court and might eventually be tried in the Superior Court. He was not scheduled to sit as a judge in any of these cases, and would not in regular course be

called on to assign a judge to them unless there was a request or a special reason.

The Chief Justice should have known that the meeting at the Arlington Street Church would at least in part be a partisan rally in the interest of criminal defendants in cases pending in the Superior Court, that the Revere cases were likely to be discussed, and that the proceeds of ticket sales might be used in part for the benefit of the defendants in those cases. The Chief Justice should also have known that his attendance would not promote public confidence in the judiciary, and that it might reflect adversely on is [sic] impartiality, interfere with the performance of his judicial duties, and bring the judicial office into disrepute.

6.   On the evening of April 5, the Chief Justice, his wife and another couple attended the Gore Vidal lecture, arriving about 7:45 P.M. They were ushered to reserved seats in the second or third row, and remained throughout the program. * * *

Before Gore Vidal spoke there were several other speakers. There was discussion of the Revere cases and the Boston Public Library cases, of harassment of "gays" by the district attorney and the police, and of the current "witchhunt" and "show trials." * * *

Before Gore Vidal spoke there was a high degree of distraction and confusion, and the Chief Justice engaged in conversations with the others in his party. He and others testified that the proceedings were boring and that they heard only portions of the proceedings, although they could hear what was said from the pulpit when they listened. But he admitted hearing references to police arrests at the Boston Public Library, to the ages of the alleged victims in the Revere cases, and to police harassment, and we infer that he heard other statements about the Revere cases. He did hear what Gore Vidal said, and Gore Vidal discussed "very sinister" happenings in Boston attributable to the fact that 1978 is an election year, "the Revere Beach capers," a "witchhunt," and "entrapment" in the Boston Public Library arrests.

7.   After the lecture the Chief Justice was taken into an anteroom and introduced to Gore Vidal. He told Gore Vidal that he enjoyed the speech, and said it was "wrong to assume judges are troglodytes" (cave dwellers). The Chief Justice knew that his picture was being taken during the evening, but did not realize that a picture was being taken when he was talking to Gore Vidal. Either just before or just after he

spoke to Gore Vidal, the Chief Justice met Mr. McMenimen, who introduced himself. The Chief Justice asked whether he was the man who called Mr. Orfanello, and Mr. McMenimen answered, "Yes."

8.   On the morning of Thursday, April 6, a Boston newspaper carried a picture of the Chief Justice on the front page and a news story with the headline, "Bonin at benefit for sex defendants." On page three of the same newspaper was additional material and a picture of the Chief Justice chatting with Gore Vidal. * * *

* * *

It appears from the findings that the Chief Justice was negligent almost to the point of wilfulness in ignoring or brusquely dismissing information brought to his attention as to the character of the meeting—that the Revere cases would likely come in for partisan discussion, and that part of the proceeds of the meeting would likely be destined for the benefit of the defendants in those cases. Although the Chief Justice is not shown to have known these things as he entered the meeting, he had earlier been put on sufficient inquiry to try to find out. * * *

* * *

What was put in jeopardy by this neglect was the impartiality demanded of judges, as well as the appearance of impartiality, also demanded of them. A judge must distance himself from pending and impending cases by taking reasonable precautions to avoid extrajudicial contact with them. That duty is at the heart of the Code of Judicial Conduct. * * *

Certain of the evils flowing from disregard of the obligation of impartiality were realized conspicuously in the situation at bar. By his attendance at the meeting the Chief Justice not only exposed himself to ex parte or one-sided statements and argumentation on matters before his court, but further compromised his position by seeming to favor or to have particular sympathy with the views of the partisan group which sponsored the affair. . . . There can be little doubt that the episode had—and, we think, could have been expected to have—a negative effect on the confidence of the thinking public in the administration of justice in the Commonwealth.

It was suggested during the proceedings that judges should not be deterred from informing themselves about contentious issues of social importance, and that judges are helped in their professional thought and judgment by acquainting themselves with ideas and feelings current in their communities. Hence, it was argued, the Chief Justice's attendance at the meeting of April 5, which included the announced lecture by Gore Vidal, was not only not exceptionable but was commendable. The argument went so far as to intimate that to discipline the Chief Justice in these circumstances would invade his constitutional rights as a citizen—which he did not renounce or forgo by becoming a judge—to enjoy the benefits of free speech and of association with his fellow citizens.

We agree emphatically that "[c]omplete separation of a judge from extrajudicial activities is neither possible nor wise; he should not become isolated from the society in which he lives." ABA commentary on Canon 5(A) [*Cf.* Commentary to MCJC 4A]. We agree that it is well for a judge's intellectual interests to extend to a comprehension of the attitudes and beliefs of minority groups, not excepting minorities which are defined by their sexual views or preferences or behavior. In ordinary circumstances the Chief Justice or any judge would be entirely free to attend a public lecture about sex and politics whether or not sponsored by a "gay" group. Nor is a judge under any duty in ordinary situations to inquire minutely into the sponsorship of public meetings before undertaking to attend them. Excessive caution, self-consciousness, or self-abnegation of this kind is neither required nor desirable.

The special factor or difficulty in the present case—the stone of stumbling—which did call for caution was that the Chief Justice had good reason to infer that the particular meeting would trench on matters pending in his court; and so it did in fact. That called for a measure of abstention on his part. "A judge may participate in civic . . . activities," but on condition that they "do not reflect upon his impartiality." Canon 5(B) [*Cf.* MCJC 4B]. Toward preserving evenhandedness, and the outward signs of that quality, a judge "must . . accept restrictions on his conduct that might be viewed as burdensome by the ordinary citizen and should do so freely and willingly." ABA commentary on Canon 2(B) * * *. [*Cf.* Commentary on MCJC 2A]. * * *

* * * As the Chief Justice "should have known" the character of the meeting and its bearing on cases pending in his court, but nevertheless attended it, he violated Canons 2(A) and 5(B), in that he failed to conduct himself in a manner that promoted public confidence in the

integrity and impartiality of the judiciary and engaged in extra-judicial activities which reflected adversely on his impartiality and interfered with the performance of his judicial duties * * *

* * *

Disposition

We conclude that the facts proved concerning the events surrounding the Chief Justice's attendance at the meeting at the Arlington Street Church and the facts established with respect to the eighth and ninth charges warrant a public censure of Chief Justice Bonin. The Chief Justice's conduct was improper and created the appearance of impropriety, bias, and special influence. A judge, particularly a chief justice, must be sensitive to the impression which his conduct creates in the minds of the public. The Chief Justice has manifested an unacceptable degree of insensitivity to those special obligations which are imposed on a person in his position. He has failed to perceive that the public often does not distinguish between a chief justice as a judge and a chief justice as a person. * * *

Notes

1.   Is the Court more concerned that Judge Bonin heard the speech or that he did so publicly?

2.   MCJC 4C(2) prohibits judges from serving on governmental committees that are "concerned with issues of fact or policy on matters other than the improvement of the law, the legal system or the administration of justice." In 1963, President Lyndon Johnson asked Chief Justice Earl Warren to chair the commission investigating the assassination of President Kennedy. Johnson gave the following account of his conversation with the Chief Justice:

> "Warren told me he wouldn't do it under any circumstances . . . didn't think the Supreme Court justice ought to * * * [I expressed fears that a post-assassination panic could trigger a nuclear confrontation with the Soviet Union. Conspiracy theorists were blaming Soviet leader Nikita Khrushchev and Cuban dictator Fidel Castro.] All I want you to do is look at the facts . . . and determine who killed the president. And I think you can put on your uniform of World War I, fat as you are . . . and do anything you could to save one American life . . . and I'm surprised that you, the Chief Justice of the U.S., would turn me down

... And [Warren] started crying and said, 'Well, I won't turn you down ... I'll do just whatever you say.'"

Aaron Epstein & Christopher Scanlan, "LBJ Got Reluctant Warren To Lead Assassination Panel," *Los Angeles Daily News*, U1 (September 26, 1993) (quoting tapes of President Johnson's telephone conversations). The Warren Commission concluded that Lee Harvey Oswald killed President Kennedy, acting alone. Did Chief Justice Warren do the right thing?

Republican Party of Minnesota v. White

122 S.Ct. 2528, 153 L.Ed.2d 694 (2002)

Justice SCALIA delivered the opinion of the Court.

The question presented in this case is whether the First Amendment permits the Minnesota Supreme Court to prohibit candidates for judicial election in that State from announcing their views on disputed legal and political issues.

I

Since Minnesota's admission to the Union in 1858, the State's Constitution has provided for the selection of all state judges by popular election. [Cc]. Since 1912, those elections have been nonpartisan. [C]. Since 1974, they have been subject to a legal restriction which states that a "candidate for a judicial office, including an incumbent judge," shall not "announce his or her views on disputed legal or political issues." Minn.Code of Judicial Conduct, Canon 5(A)(3)(d)(i) (2000). [Contrast MCJC 5A(3)(d).] This prohibition, promulgated by the Minnesota Supreme Court and based on Canon 7(B) of the 1972 American Bar Association (ABA) Model Code of Judicial Conduct, is known as the "announce clause." Incumbent judges who violate it are subject to discipline, including removal, censure, civil penalties, and suspension without pay. [C]. Lawyers who run for judicial office also must comply with the announce clause. Minn. Rule of Professional Conduct 8.2(b) (2002) ("A lawyer who is a candidate for judicial office shall comply with the applicable provisions of the Code of Judicial Conduct"). Those who violate it are subject to, *inter alia,* disbarment, suspension, and probation. Rule 8.4(a); Minn. Rules on Lawyers Professional Responsibility 8-14, 15(a) (2002).

In 1996, one of the petitioners, Gregory Wersal, ran for associate justice of the Minnesota Supreme Court. In the course of the campaign, he distributed literature criticizing several Minnesota Supreme Court decisions on issues such as crime, welfare, and abortion. A complaint against Wersal challenging, among other things, the propriety of this literature was filed with the Office of Lawyers Professional Responsibility, the agency which, under the direction of the Minnesota Lawyers Professional Responsibility Board, investigates and prosecutes ethical violations of lawyer candidates for judicial office. The Lawyers Board dismissed the complaint; with regard to the charges that his campaign materials violated the announce clause, it expressed doubt whether the clause could constitutionally be enforced. Nonetheless, fearing that further ethical complaints would jeopardize his ability to practice law, Wersal withdrew from the election. In 1998, Wersal ran again for the same office. Early in that race, he sought an advisory opinion from the Lawyers Board with regard to whether it planned to enforce the announce clause. The Lawyers Board responded equivocally, stating that, although it had significant doubts about the constitutionality of the provision, it was unable to answer his question because he had not submitted a list of the announcements he wished to make.

Shortly thereafter, Wersal filed this lawsuit in Federal District Court against respondents, seeking, *inter alia,* a declaration that the announce clause violates the First Amendment and an injunction against its enforcement. * * *

II

Before considering the constitutionality of the announce clause, we must be clear about its meaning. Its text says that a candidate for judicial office shall not "announce his or her views on disputed legal or political issues." Minn.Code of Judicial Conduct, Canon 5(A)(3)(d)(i)(2002).

We know that "announc[ing] ... views" on an issue covers much more than *promising* to decide an issue a particular way. The prohibition extends to the candidate's mere statement of his current position, even if he does not bind himself to maintain that position after election. All the parties agree this is the case, because the Minnesota Code contains a so-called "pledges or promises" clause, which *separately* prohibits judicial candidates from making "pledges or promises of conduct in office other than the faithful and impartial performance of the duties of the office," *ibid.*--a prohibition that is not challenged here and on which we express no view.

* * *

Respondents contend that this still leaves plenty of topics for discussion on the campaign trail. These include a candidate's "character," "education," "work habits," and "how [he] would handle administrative duties if elected." [C]. Indeed, the Judicial Board has printed a list of preapproved questions which judicial candidates are allowed to answer. These include how the candidate feels about cameras in the courtroom, how he would go about reducing the caseload, how the costs of judicial administration can be reduced, and how he proposes to ensure that minorities and women are treated more fairly by the court system. [C]. Whether this list of preapproved subjects, and other topics not prohibited by the announce clause, adequately fulfill the First Amendment's guarantee of freedom of speech is the question to which we now turn.

III

As the Court of Appeals recognized, the announce clause both prohibits speech on the basis of its content and burdens a category of speech that is "at the core of our First Amendment freedoms"--speech about the qualifications of candidates for public office. [C]. The Court of Appeals concluded that the proper test to be applied to determine the constitutionality of such a restriction is what our cases have called strict scrutiny, the parties do not dispute that this is correct. Under the strict-scrutiny test, [C]. respondents have the burden to prove that the announce clause is (1) narrowly tailored, to serve (2) a compelling state interest. [C] In order for respondents to show that the announce clause is narrowly tailored, they must demonstrate that it does not "unnecessarily circumscrib[e] protected expression." [C].

The Court of Appeals concluded that respondents had established two interests as sufficiently compelling to justify the announce clause: preserving the impartiality of the state judiciary and preserving the appearance of the impartiality of the state judiciary.* * *

A

One meaning of "impartiality" in the judicial context--and of course its root meaning--is the lack of bias for or against either *party* to the proceeding. Impartiality in this sense assures equal application of the law. That is, it guarantees a party that the judge who hears his case will apply the law to him in the same way he applies it to any other party. This is the traditional sense in which the term is used. See Webster's New International Dictionary 1247 (2d ed.1950) (defining "impartial" as "[n]ot partial; esp., not favoring one more than another; treating all alike; unbiased; equitable; fair; just"). It is also the sense in which it is used in the cases cited by respondents and *amici* for the proposition that an impartial judge is essential to due process. [Cc].

We think it plain that the announce clause is not narrowly tailored to serve impartiality (or the appearance of impartiality) in this sense. Indeed, the clause is barely tailored to serve that interest *at all,* inasmuch as it does not restrict speech for or against particular *parties,* but rather speech for or against particular *issues.* To be sure, when a case arises that turns on a legal issue on which the judge (as a candidate) had taken a particular stand, the party taking the opposite stand is likely to lose. But not because of any bias against that party, or favoritism toward the other party. *Any* party taking that position is just as likely to lose. The judge is applying the law (as he sees it) evenhandedly.

B

It is perhaps possible to use the term "impartiality" in the judicial context (though this is certainly not a common usage) to mean lack of preconception in favor of or against a particular *legal view.* This sort of impartiality would be concerned, not with guaranteeing litigants equal application of the law, but rather with guaranteeing them an equal chance to persuade the court on the legal points in their case. Impartiality in this sense may well be an interest served by the announce clause, but it is not a *compelling* state interest, as strict scrutiny requires. A judge's lack of predisposition regarding the relevant legal issues in a case has never been thought a necessary component of equal justice, and with good reason. For one thing, it is virtually impossible to find a judge who does not have preconceptions about the law. As then-Justice REHNQUIST observed of our own Court: "Since most Justices come to this bench no earlier than their middle years, it would be unusual if they had not by that time formulated at least some tentative notions that would influence them in their interpretation of the sweeping clauses of the Constitution and their interaction with one another. It would be not merely unusual, but extraordinary, if they had not at least given opinions as to constitutional issues in their previous legal careers." [Cc]. Indeed, even if it were possible to select judges who did not have precon- ceived views on legal issues, it would hardly be desirable to do so. "Proof that a Justice's mind at the time he joined the Court was a complete *tabula rasa* in the area of constitutional adjudication would be evidence of lack of qualification, not lack of bias." [C]. The Minnesota Constitution positively forbids the selection to courts of general jurisdiction of judges who are impartial in the sense of having no views on the law. Minn. Const., Art. VI, § 5 ("Judges of the supreme court, the court of appeals and the district court shall be learned in the law"). And since avoiding judicial preconceptions on legal issues is neither possible nor desirable, pretending otherwise by attempting to preserve the "appearance" of that type of impartiality can hardly be a compelling state interest either.

C

A third possible meaning of "impartiality" (again not a common one) might be described as open-mindedness. This quality in a judge demands, not that he have no preconceptions on legal issues, but that he be willing to consider views that oppose his preconceptions, and remain open to persuasion, when the issues arise in a pending case. This sort of impartiality seeks to guarantee each litigant, not an *equal* chance to win the legal points in the case, but at least *some* chance of doing so. It may well be that impartiality in this sense, and the appearance of it, are desirable in the judiciary, but we need not pursue that inquiry, since we do not believe the Minnesota Supreme Court adopted the announce clause for that purpose.

Respondents argue that the announce clause serves the interest in open-mindedness, or at least in the appearance of open-mindedness, because it relieves a judge from pressure to rule a certain way in order to maintain consistency with statements the judge has previously made. The problem is, however, that statements in election campaigns are such an infinitesimal portion of the public commitments to legal positions that judges (or judges-to-be) undertake, that this object of the prohibition is implausible.   Before they arrive on the bench (whether by election or otherwise) judges have often committed themselves on legal issues that they must later rule upon. See, *e.g.*, *Laird* [*v. Tatum*, 409 U.S. 824, 831-33, 34 L.Ed.2d 50, 93 S.Ct. 7 (1972)] (describing Justice Black's participation in several cases construing and deciding the constitutionality of the Fair Labor Standards Act, even though as a Senator he had been one of its principal authors; and Chief Justice Hughes's authorship of the opinion overruling *Adkins v. Children's Hospital of D. C.,* 261 U.S. 525, 43 S.Ct. 394, 67 L.Ed. 785 (1923), a case he had criticized in a book written before his appointment to the Court).   More common still is a judge's confronting a legal issue on which he has expressed an opinion while on the bench. Most frequently, of course, that prior expression will have occurred in ruling on an earlier case. But judges often state their views on disputed legal issues outside the context of adjudication--in classes that they conduct, and in books and speeches. Like the ABA Codes of Judicial Conduct, the Minnesota Code not only permits but encourages this.   See Minn. Code of Judicial Conduct, Canon 4(B) (2002) ("A judge may write, lecture, teach, speak and participate in other extra-judicial activities concerning the law ..."); Minn.Code of Judicial Conduct, Canon 4(B), Comment. (2002) ("To the extent that time permits, a judge is encouraged to do so ...").   That is quite incompatible with the notion that the need for open-mindedness (or for the appearance of open-mindedness) lies behind the prohibition at issue here.

The short of the matter is this: In Minnesota, a candidate for judicial office may not say "I think it is constitutional for the legislature to prohibit same-sex marriages."   He may say the very same thing, however, up until the very day before he declares himself a candidate, and may say it repeatedly (until litigation is pending) after he is elected. As a means of pursuing the objective of open-mindedness that respondents now articulate, the announce clause is so woefully underinclusive as to render belief in that purpose a challenge to the credulous. [Cc]. * * *

* * *

IV

To sustain the announce clause, the Eighth Circuit relied heavily on the fact that a pervasive practice of prohibiting judicial candidates from discussing disputed legal and political issues developed during the last half of the 20th century. * * * The practice of prohibiting speech by judicial candidates on disputed issues, however, is neither long nor universal.

At the time of the founding, only Vermont (before it became a State) selected any of its judges by election. Starting with Georgia in 1812, States began to provide for judicial election, a development rapidly accelerated by Jacksonian democracy. By the time of the Civil War, the great majority of States elected their judges. [Cc]. We know of no restrictions upon statements that could be made by judicial candidates (including judges) throughout the 19th and the first quarter of the 20th century. Indeed, judicial elections were generally partisan during this period, the movement toward nonpartisan judicial elections not even beginning until the 1870's. [Cc]. Thus, not only were judicial candidates (including judges) discussing disputed legal and political issues on the campaign trail, but they were touting party affiliations and angling for party nominations all the while.

* * *

The Minnesota Supreme Court's canon of judicial conduct prohibiting candidates for judicial election from announcing their views on disputed legal and political issues violates the First Amendment. Accordingly, we reverse the grant of summary judgment to respondents and remand the case for proceedings consistent with this opinion.

It is so ordered.

Justice O'CONNOR, concurring.

I join the opinion of the Court but write separately to express my concerns about judicial elections generally. * * *

We of course want judges to be impartial, in the sense of being free from any personal stake in the outcome of the cases to which they are assigned. But if judges are subject to regular elections they are likely to feel that they have at least some personal stake in the outcome of every publicized case. Elected judges cannot help being aware that if the public is not satisfied with the outcome of a particular case, it could hurt their reelection prospects. [Cc]. Even if judges were able to suppress their awareness of the potential electoral consequences of their decisions and refrain from acting on it, the public's confidence in the judiciary could be undermined simply by the possibility that judges would be unable to do so.

Moreover, contested elections generally entail campaigning. And campaigning for a judicial post today can require substantial funds. [Cc]. Unless the pool of judicial candidates is limited to those wealthy enough to independently fund their campaigns, a limitation unrelated to judicial skill, the cost of campaigning requires judicial candidates to engage in fundraising. Yet relying on campaign donations may leave judges feeling indebted to certain parties or interest groups. [Cc]. Even if judges were able to refrain from favoring donors, the mere possibility that judges' decisions may be motivated by the desire to repay campaign contributors is likely to undermine the public's confidence in the judiciary. [Cc].

* * *

Minnesota has chosen to select its judges through contested popular elections instead of through an appointment system or a combined appointment and retention election system along the lines of the Missouri Plan. In doing so the State has voluntarily taken on the risks to judicial bias described above. As a result, the State's claim that it needs to significantly restrict judges' speech in order to protect judicial impartiality is particularly troubling. If the State has a problem with judicial impartiality, it is largely one the State brought upon itself by continuing the practice of popularly electing judges.

* * *

Justice GINSBURG, with whom Justice STEVENS, Justice SOUTER, and Justice BREYER join, dissenting.

* * *

Legislative and executive officials serve in representative capacities. They are agents of the people; their primary function is to advance the interests of their constituencies. Candidates for political offices, in keeping with their representative role, must be left free to inform the electorate of their positions on specific issues. Armed with such information, the individual voter will be equipped to cast her ballot intelligently, to vote for the candidate committed to positions the voter approves. Campaign statements committing the candidate to take sides on contentious issues are therefore not only appropriate in political elections, they are "at the core of our electoral process," [C] for they "enhance the accountability of government officials to the people whom they represent," [C].

Judges, however, are not political actors. They do not sit as representatives of particular persons, communities, or parties; they serve no faction or constituency. "[I]t is the business of judges to be indifferent to popularity." [Cc]. They must strive to do what is legally right, all the more so when the result is not the one "the home crowd" wants. [C]. Even when they develop common law or give concrete meaning to constitutional text, judges act only in the context of individual cases, the outcome of which cannot depend on the will of the public. [C].

* * *

The Court sees in this conclusion, and in the Announce Clause that embraces it, "an obvious tension,": The Minnesota electorate is permitted to select its judges by popular vote, but is not provided information on "subjects of interest to the voters,"--in particular, the voters are not told how the candidate would decide controversial cases or issues if elected. This supposed tension, however, rests on the false premise that by departing from the federal model with respect to who *chooses* judges, Minnesota necessarily departed from the federal position on the *criteria* relevant to the exercise of that choice.[12]

* * *

* * * Pledges or promises of conduct in office, however commonplace in races for the political branches, are inconsistent "with the judge's obligation to decide cases in accordance with his or her role."

---

[12]   [Dissenter's note 1] In the context of the federal system, how a prospective nominee for the bench would resolve particular contentious issues would certainly be "of interest" to the President and the Senate in the exercise of their respective nomination and confirmation powers, just as information of that type would "interest" a Minnesota voter. But in accord with a longstanding norm, every Member of this Court declined to furnish such information to the Senate, and presumably to the President as well. [C]. Surely the Court perceives no tension here; the line each of us drew in response to preconfirmation questioning, the Court would no doubt agree, is crucial to the health of the Federal Judiciary. * * * [C]ontrary to the Court's suggestion, there is nothing inherently incongruous in depriving those charged with choosing judges of certain information they might desire during the selection process.

[Cc]. This judicial obligation to avoid prejudgment corresponds to the litigant's right, protected by the Due Process Clause of the Fourteenth Amendment, to "an impartial and disinterested tribunal in both civil and criminal cases." [C]. The proscription against pledges or promises thus represents an accommodation of "constitutionally protected interests [that] lie on both sides of the legal equation." [Cc]. Balanced against the candidate's interest in free expression is the litigant's "powerful and independent constitutional interest in fair adjudicative procedure." [Cc].

* * *

In addition to protecting litigants' due process rights, the parties in this case further agree, the pledges or promises clause advances another compelling state interest: preserving the public's confidence in the integrity and impartiality of its judiciary. * * * As the Minnesota Supreme Court has recognized, all legal systems--regardless of their method of judicial selection--"can function only so long as the public, having confidence in the integrity of its judges, accepts and abides by judicial decisions." [C].

Prohibiting a judicial candidate from pledging or promising certain results if elected directly promotes the State's interest in preserving public faith in the bench. When a candidate makes such a promise during a campaign, the public will no doubt perceive that she is doing so in the hope of garnering votes. And the public will in turn likely conclude that when the candidate decides an issue in accord with that promise, she does so at least in part to discharge her undertaking to the voters in the previous election and to prevent voter abandonment in the next. The perception of that unseemly *quid pro quo*--a judicial candidate's promises on issues in return for the electorate's votes at the polls--inevitably diminishes the public's faith in the ability of judges to administer the law without regard to personal or political self-interest.* * *

* * *

Notes

1.   Does MCJC 5A(3)(d) violate the First Amendment? Which of the three meanings of impartiality identified by Justice Scalia applies to MCJC 3(E)?

2.   Justice O'Connor was elected to her first judicial position in Arizona. She is the only current United States Supreme Court justice to have run for judicial office. How do you think this experience influenced her views in this case?

3.   Judges who are elected often are perceived to be subject to more political pressure than those who are appointed. Some elected judges do not dispute this perception.

> In West Virginia, we have a system in which judges are elected, not appointed. If the citizens wanted appointed judges, they could have opted for appointed judges in the Judicial Reorganization Amendment of 1974. Accordingly, I disapprove of the efforts in the Judicial Code of Ethics and the new Code of Judicial Conduct to imply that judges are not political animals. In this State at least, we are. In order to be elected, we must run on party slates and we must win elections, primary and general.

> To accuse Judge Hill of engaging in improper activity [by endorsing another candidate] and to imply that his behavior is reprehensible is thus tantamount to buying a junkyard dog to guard your junkyard and then complaining that the creature is not an ideal companion for your minor children.

In re Hill, 190 W.Va. 165, 169, 437 S.E.2d 738, 742 (1993) (Neely, J., concurring).

4.   Appointed judges are also subject to political pressure. It is becoming increasingly common for members of the United States Senate Judiciary Committee to ask nominees to the federal bench specific questions regarding abortion and other controversial issues. In a footnote to her dissenting opinion, Justice Ginsburg praises the practice of nominees who refuse to answer such questions. How will the holding of the case affect nominees' ability to demur to questions regarding issues likely to come before their courts? Should nominees answer such questions? *See* MCJC 5A(3)(d). For an interesting discussion of the factors that are and should be a part of the judicial nomination process, *see* Laura E. Little, "Loyalty, Gratitude, and the Federal Judiciary," 44 *Am. U.L. Rev.* 699 (1995).

5.   The American Bar Association supports merit selection rather than election of judges. Is one method of selecting judges less political than the other, or are we simply substituting the "politics of the

backroom" for the "politics of the ballot box"? *See* Judith L. Maute, "Selecting Justice in State Courts: the Ballot Box or the Backroom?" 41 *S. Tex. L. Rev.* 1197 (2000).

6. MCJC 5C(2) specifically allows judicial campaign committees to solicit and accept "reasonable campaign contributions and public support from lawyers." Is this appropriate?

7. In *In re Kaiser*, 111 Wash.2d 275, 759 P.2d 392 (1988), Judge Kaiser ran for reelection. Will Roarty, his opponent, was endorsed by a group of lawyers that included lawyers who handled drunk driving cases. Judge Kaiser made the following campaign statements (among others): "Kaiser is Toughest On Drunk Driving. . . ." "Judge Kaiser's opponent, Will Roarty, receives the majority of his financial contributions from drunk driving defense attorneys. These lawyers do not want a tough, no-nonsense judge like Judge Kaiser." "[Their] primary interests are getting their clients off."

> The statement made by Judge Kaiser that DWI defense attorneys supported Will Roarty because their "primary interests are getting their clients off," and other statements with a similar import violate Canons [1 and 2(A)] of the CJC. The statements suggest, among other things, that justice is for sale and that certain defendants are not entitled to a fair trial. Such statements are improper in a judicial campaign.
>
> * * *
>
> Judge Kaiser's statements regarding contributions made by DWI defense attorneys violate these canons by calling into question the integrity and impartiality of the judiciary. Judge Kaiser suggested that, if elected, Roarty would not fairly and impartially apply the law to DWI defendants. He suggested that certain attorneys could and did buy favorable treatment for their clients, a class of defendants for whom there is little public sympathy. He suggested that there is something improper about attorneys contributing to a judicial campaign, when, of course, such contributions are entirely proper.

In re Kaiser, 111 Wash.2d 275, 281-82, 759 P.2d 392, 396 (1988). Judge Kaiser was censured.

INDEX

References are to pages

INDEX

DISCIPLINE OF LAWYERS
Duty to report lawyer misconduct, 17-20, 219-27
Procedure, 14-17
Sanctions, 16

DISCOVERY ABUSES
Informal sanctions, 172-73
Statutory sanctions, 165-72

ETHICS COMMISSION, 5

FEES
Abuses, 240-48
Contingent fees, 248-52
Denied due to lawyer misconduct, 24, 279-86
Double billing, 242-43, 246-47

FIRST AMENDMENT
Advertising, 291-96
Group legal services, 277, 289 n.11
Judicial elections, 339-50
Solicitation, 296-307
Trial publicity, 183-95
Unauthorized practice of law, 274-78

FORMER CLIENTS, 125-29

FORM-OF-PRACTICE RESTRIC-TIONS, 287-91

FRAUD
Attorney liability to third parties, 22, 203-07
Client fraud, Disclosure of, 72-80, 208-10
Malpractice liability insurance, 207

IN HOUSE CORPORATE COUNSEL
Duty to disclose misconduct, 227-36
Sex-based discrimination, 237-40

JUDGES
Code of Judicial Conduct, ABA Model, see this index
Courtesy, 317-18
Cultural activities, 333-38
Discipline of, 309-10
Disqualification, 323-32
Ex parte communications, 317
Following the law, 312-17
Impartiality, 318-26
Judicial elections, 339-50
Moral propriety, 310-11
Public comments, 318-26
Religion, 330-32

LAW FIRMS
Form-of-practice restrictions, 287-91
Responsibilities within law firms, 224-27

MALPRACTICE
Duty, 20, 21, 39-43, 210-17
Causation, 21-22
Codes of professional ethics as standard, 23
Standard of care, 21, 23
Third party claims, 22-23, 210-17

MODEL CODE OF PROFESSIONAL RESPONSIBILITY, ABA, 5, 7;
For citations to specific rules, see Table of Rules, Statutes and ABA Opinions, xiii

MODEL RULES OF PROFESSIONAL CONDUCT, ABA, 5-7
For citations to specific rules, see Table of Rules, Statutes and Opinions, xiii

MORAL RESPONSIBILITY
Advocacy, and, 147-65
Applicants to the bar, 9-13
Choice of clients, 25-39
Confidentiality and, 61-80
Moral risks to the professional, 2, 152-54
Reputation of lawyers for, 6

MULTI-JURISDICTIONAL PRACTICE, 278-86

NON-CLIENTS, 22-23, 210-17

OPINIONS, ABA, 8;
For citations to specific ABA Opinions, see Table of Rules, Statutes, and ABA Opinions, xiii

PATERNALISM, 44-59

PERJURY
Criminal client, by, 179-83

POOR, LEGAL REPRESENTATION FOR THE
Court appointed counsel, 274
Legal Services Corporation, 259
Mandatory pro bono proposals, 260-74
Need for legal services, 256-60

PROFESSION
Defined, 1
History of regulation, 3-6
Moral risks, 1-2, 152-54
Paternalism, 2, 44-59
Regulation of, 3-9
Self-protection, 1-2, 274-91

PROPERTY, CLIENT
Trust accounts, 252

INDEX

PROSECUTORS
Assertion of defendant attorney's conflict of
    interest, 118
Disclosure obligations, 195-202
Duty to seek justice, 202
Indictments, 202
Subpoenaing defense attorneys, 202-03
Trial publicity, 194

PUBLICITY, TRIAL, 183-95

PUBLIC SERVICE, 253-74; See also, this
    index, Poor, Legal Representation for the

**RESTATEMENT (THIRD) OF THE
LAW GOVERNING LAWYERS**, 8-9;
For citations to drafts of specific sections of
    the Restatement, see Table to Rules,
    Statutes, and ABA Opinions, xiii

SOLICITATION
Benefits of, 305-07
Commercial solicitation, 299-305
Criticism of, 298-304
Mailings, 296, 307
Political solicitation, 296-99

THIRD PARTIES, 22-23, 210-17

UNAUTHORIZED PRACTICE OF LAW
Criticism of limits on, 274-78
Out-of-state attorneys guilty of, 278-86

WORK PRODUCT DOCTRINE, 94-95